广东省高水平大学重点建设学科项目成果

系统功能语言学文献丛书

丛书主编：彭宣维 黄国文

从系统到实例
——理论与应用探索前沿

From System to Instance:
Frontiers of Theory and Application

彭宣维 ◉ 著

上海外语教育出版社
外教社 SHANGHAI FOREIGN LANGUAGE EDUCATION PRESS
www.sflep.com

图书在版编目（CIP）数据

从系统到实例：理论与应用探索前沿／彭宣维著.
—上海：上海外语教育出版社,2019
（系统功能语言学文献丛书）
ISBN 978－7－5446－5990－1

Ⅰ.①从… Ⅱ.①彭… Ⅲ.①功能(语言学)－研究 Ⅳ.①H0

中国版本图书馆 CIP 数据核字(2019)第 164951 号

出版发行：**上海外语教育出版社**
　　　　　（上海外国语大学内）　邮编：200083
电　　话：021-65425300（总机）
电子邮箱：bookinfo@sflep.com.cn
网　　址：http://www.sflep.com
责任编辑：蔡一鸣

印　　刷：启东市人民印刷有限公司
开　　本：635×965　1/16　印张 19.75　字数 313千字
版　　次：2019 年 10月第 1版　　2019 年 10月第 1次印刷
印　　数：1 100 册

书　　号：ISBN 978-7-5446-5990-1
定　　价：62.00 元

本版图书如有印装质量问题,可向本社调换
质量服务热线：4008-213-263　电子邮箱：editorial@sflep.com

谨此致谢

改变我人生轨迹的英语老师张久光老人

总　序

彭宣维　黄国文

　　初学者对文献的重要性往往缺乏足够的认识,想写文章的时候绞尽脑汁却一筹莫展,勉强凑一个东西出来却不入流:缺乏研究背景、缺乏研究问题、缺乏研究方法、缺乏创新观点、缺乏学科用语、缺乏组织策略、缺乏格式规范。

　　确定一个研究方向,可先从汉语文献中选择自己感兴趣的章节入手,再及英文著述,半年一年,便会有所心得;三年五载,自当独树一帜。实践表明,知识来源于文献,己见发端于文献,学科推进更是少不了文献。文献的重要性由此可见一斑。

　　为此,我们组织汇编了这套"系统功能语言学文献丛书",方便后学查阅细读,揣摩审视。丛书中既有综述介绍,也有前沿研究;有独著,也有合作;作者之中,有德高望重的耄耋长者,有硕果累累的学派中坚,也有勤奋精进的青年才俊。我们想借此机会感谢各位师友积极配合。

　　本丛书的内容涉及系统功能语言学理论与应用的各个方面,既体现了各位学者在学术领域孜孜不倦的研究历程,也凝结了中国系统功能语言学团队的集体智慧,代表了中国学人在这一领域的研究水平。读者可以看到,其中有不少高水平的成果发表于国外知名期刊,走向了国际学科前沿;有理论开拓,也有应用尝试。

　　今后,除了国际化和理论探索,本土化与应用研究仍将是一个需要集体努力的基本方向。从理论上看,除了语篇语境、词汇研究和语音书写,研究者还需放眼其他学派和其他学科领域,协同求进,积极从议题上做超学科思考。我们希望,应用研究能够成为各位同仁的责任意识,在诸如翻译理论与操作框架、语言生态视角、外语教育学、汉语系统描写、辞书多元义项梳理、语言过程的计算表征、语言的生理神经机制、语言的脑成像实证研究、语言病理、国家话语等等领域,打开全新的研究局面,取得丰硕的研究成果。

　　我们衷心感谢上海外语教育出版社对本丛书出版的鼎力支持,感谢各位责编的精心付出。

目　录

第一部分　理论范式探新

第二部分 及物性模式重构

第三部分　应 用 研 究

CONTENTS

图表目录

前　言

　　本书由三个部分构成：理论范式探新、及物性模式重构与应用研究，共十章。

　　在第一部分"理论范式探新"中，作者首先从总体上概述了系统功能语言学的基本学理及其研究走向，然后通过实例分析和理论阐述论证了作为词汇语法的上限级阶——语篇的形式特征，进而陈述了语言过程涉及的四个维度，以及在社交环境下工作记忆对语言过程加工的模型。本部分一共有三章：第一、二、三章。

　　第一章对系统功能语言学的学理及该学派的发展走向进行了概要性介绍。学理指科学研究的原理或法则。系统功能语言学的学理，集中体现在韩礼德及其同道构拟的一系列范式要素上，包括语言模型设计的适用性、泛时语言观、基于实例的系统先导性、人文性与科学性的有机统一、功能多元性、语言使用与模型设计的生态性、词汇语法的互补性等。它们彼此关联，协同构成系统功能语言学的学科范式。

　　第二章从系统和实例两个维度，阐述词汇语法的上限级阶是语篇，而非先前广为接受的小句（复句）。阐述从系统角度入手，着眼点是语素和词分别在更大级阶单位中的功能，包括词、词组/短语、小句、复句、篇章；从实例角度的论证则是个案性的，分别涉及时态语素、评价词语、信息词组与短语、及物性小句的形式化组织，途径是相关范畴成分的次第走向以及由此生成的二维平面模式；最后从理论上扼要阐述语篇组织的形式特征，纠正了先前的感性误识。据此，我们得到词类、句型、篇类三个典型的系统类别，既为第三章的立体语言模型，尤其是词汇语法的上限级阶——语篇，提供了应有的论证支持，也有助于进一步的相关理论考察，包括与形式层连成一体的语义层的模型建构。

　　第三章在系统功能语言学的经典和扩展模式的基础上介绍语言过程

涉及的四个维度及其工作记忆加工模型。语言的四个维度是：三个隐喻性的空间维度和一个隐喻性的时间维度。三个隐喻性的空间是：（一）横向层次维度——语义→词汇语法→语音书写；（二）纵深相位维度——概念、人际、个体的语义、词汇语法和语音书写范畴；（三）竖向级阶维度——词-篇连续体。语言过程是在经典系统功能语言学的前提下，以语言"实例化"为着眼点，采用工作记忆原理加以阐述的一个加工模型，意在为系统功能语言学关于语言的社会属性及基本范畴补足应有的认知加工环境；并以现在主义认识论为出发点，将关注重点从系统转到语言使用的过程上来，凸显语言使用的本来面目。

第二部分是"及物性模式重构"。作者阐述了作为经验模式的及物性应该具有的三种结构关系：过程模式、作格模式与主语模式，三者的抽象程度逐层递增；作者同时讨论了作格关系与消息推进的关系以及跟主语模式具有同等抽象程度的语态模式。因此，及物性模式的构成应该是：小句概念元功能→过程模式→作格模式→主语+语态模式。本部分也包括三章：第四、五、六章。

第四章对经典系统功能语法中体现概念元功能的小句——及物性过程模式进行了重构。这包括两层含义：由识解过程确立的及物性的性质以及由此决定的新的过程分类模式。具体而言，这一新的分类模式涉及两个维度：第一个维度是物质和心理两种基本经验类别；第二个维度涉及关系与作为两种识解方式。两个维度可以生成四个具有复合特征的新过程：物质-作为、物质-关系、心理-作为和心理-关系；经典理论中的言语和行为被归入物质-作为类，所谓的存在过程则分布于四个新的过程类别中。

第五章在韩礼德提出的作格分析模式的基础上，重新阐述作格分析在及物性中的地位、它和语态的关系、作格参与者之间的关系，进而分别从作格关系和语态类别的角度，考察消息推进的机制，建立新的作格语法系统。结论是：（一）作格分析中的参与者比过程类别中的参与者具有更多的概括性，它们是主语及主语结构的直接基础；（二）作格关系类别应和语态类别分开：作格关系和语态是两种不同抽象程度的语法关系；（三）作格关系类别和作格参与者是合取关系；（四）作格关系、语态类别与消息推进有内在关联。

第六章旨在说明：主语及主语结构在系统功能语法中，应该是在过程模式与作格模式基础上的进一步概括与抽象，它与语态地位是一样的，并与过程与作格模式一起，构成及物性的三个典型经验组织方式。经典系统功能语法将主语看作一个人际性的语法范畴；但我们认为，主语（以及主语结构）不是人际性的，而是体现小句概念意义的一个语法形式范畴；原语气成分中叫做主语的成分，在这里姑且叫做"互动语"，用于填充原先的语气成分结构。定式成分具有双重功能：同时协作体现概念性的时间意义"时间性"和人际性的社交意义"社交性"，其自身的语法功能则分别是时态操作特征和语气操作特征。因而，社交性→语气［语气成分（互动语+语气操作语）+剩余部分］；在概念相度上则有：（一）及物模式→（二）作格模式（作格关系→语态关系）→（三）主语结构等三个词汇语法次层次。

在本书最后的"应用研究"部分，作者首先运用信息理论对比分析了英汉语中原因连接成分的信息导入功能，然后进行语篇元功能维度的功能文体学研究、评价文体效应与解读模型，最后概述学科英语研究的必要性、可行性与具体操作方法。本部分一共分四章：第七、八、九、十章。

第七章试图说明，英汉语中表原因的连接成分具有引入已知信息与新信息的作用。为此，作者以语料库为基础，首先采用实例引证的方法说明上述假设，然后通过从语料库中得到的有关原因连接成分的使用频率来加以论证。结论是：这些表原因的连接成分，确有导入已知信息和新信息的系统特征。作者还通过个案分析，说明英汉语在原因连接成分对应上的常规及变化情况。本项研究不仅对理解英汉语有关现象有所补益，对原因连接成分的英汉互译和写作教学也具有指导意义。

第八章旨在从语篇功能的角度阐述文学语篇中的消息组织模式，这是之前功能文体学研究的薄弱环节。议题涉及主位和信息组织；所用实例主要是科幻短篇小说《地狱》，旁及其他必要材料。本章虽然是在先前的功能文体学的框架内写成的，但能说明文学语篇的评价主旨。

第九章通过实例分析介绍评价文体学的基本研究思路。文学文本的话语组织涉及经典文体学关注的相关前景化成分，但更有评价主旨引导下的文本整体评价意义建构：前者是网状关系，属于词汇语法范畴；后者是纺锤型模式，由不同评价范畴的累积与终极评价指向两个方向相反的圆锥型意义要素构成。这一过程涉及从评价主旨到文本组织的三种基本话语策略：谋篇视角、人际性语境对比与概念意义投射。为此，作者以当下流行的一首小诗为例,以"作者—文本—读者"为一体化解读机制作为出发点,演示了评价意义范畴应用于文学文本分析的一种解读效应模式,说明文学文本分析的多层次性,以此揭示文学是以评价为特点、手段和目的的互动性艺术话语行为,文学性就是评价性,超常规经验表述的是心理实在性。这一尝试是个案性质的,却对文体分析甚至对语篇语言学理论模型的建构具有启示意义。

第十章从我国英语教育改革面临的问题及其成因出发,指出学科英语研究对于英语教改的必要性与可行性,说明学科英语研究的范围及其语料库途径,以便进行系统而深入的差异对比与共同点概括。随后,作者在前人研究成果的基础上概述了学科英语的一些共同要素,包括连锁定义、专门分类、特殊表达、词汇密度、句法模糊性、语义非连续性和语法隐喻,介绍了跟语法隐喻有关的三个基本特点:内容表述的平稳感、意义抽象性与潜在的英汉语思维方式等。这些要素都是中国学生学习高层次英语的重点和难点。这一基础工作不仅有助于我们全面认识英语语言本身,而且能为我国的英语甚至外语教改提供内容参照依据。

这些篇章最初以不同方式发表在刊物或文集中,得到了各位主编和编辑的邀约与帮助,特别是黄国文、Jonathan Webster、蒋重跃、王和平、张辉、张后尘、徐珺、王克非、李鸿儒等诸位教授,作者谨此一并致谢。

彭宣维

第一部分

理论范式探新

系统功能语言学的学理及发展走向[①]

学界已有的对系统功能语言学的介绍,既有论文,也有专著,本章基于这些论述,尤其是韩礼德本人的有关认识,对系统功能语言学的学理及发展走向做一概述,主要涉及八个方面。

1.1 语言模型设计的适用性

适用性是系统功能语言学得以立足的根本。它以总体性、综合性与多维性为着眼点,描述与解释语言现象,关注语言使用的各种特定任务(Halliday 2008:204)。这种范式以语言行为及其使用环境为着眼点,有两个鲜明特点。

第一,它的研究方法具有综合性。简言之,它兼顾自下而上的归纳法与自上而下的理论引导,所以主张"语言事实源于理论的创造"这一基本

---

① 本章原载于《中国外语》2017年第1期,第13—17页。

观点（Halliday 1994：F38；另见古德曼 2008）。一方面，它细心梳理中西方语言学史上的相关论述，包括基于古希腊语和古拉丁语的研究成果（见 Halliday 2003 各处），并注重对语言使用现象的理论归纳（彭宣维 2009，2016；Peng 2015a）①。如今，学界通行的语料库研究方法就是上述基本思想的操作体现（伯明翰学派；也见 Halliday 1992b），但韩礼德同时有自己更为深刻的认识："语料库语言学家要求我们建立'基于语料库的语法'；为此我则不得不要求他们建立'基于语法的语料库'"（Halliday 2008：76）；事实上，"汉英对应评价意义语料库"（CEPCAM）就是以系统功能语法中的评价范畴为依据研制而成的（见彭宣维等 2012；彭宣维等 2015）。另一方面，它以系统与功能两个核心概念为基础，全方位构拟语言模型（Halliday 1961，1995；Martin 1992），既涉及语言本体的三个维度：层次（语义、语法、语音）、功能（概念、人际、语篇）和级阶（语素、词、词组/短语、小句、复句等），又包含语言事件的时间因素及其运作环境"社会文化语境"（彭宣维 2011，2013，2015b）。其中，意义是核心：它是确立语境的基础——通过功能性的语域变元构拟和连接语境（语场、语旨、语式；Hasan 1995），也是生成形式范畴的促动因素，并将自己构拟其中，所以它是形式的意义，是一个高度抽象的语篇单位；而形式是意义的形式，一种结构化和组织化了的过程；其底层是选择陈述（即在系统网络中对选择路径的表达，如在 a 和 b 两个选项中，选 a 还是选 b，或者同时选取。这样的过程描述就是选择陈述；Halliday 1967，1978a，1980，1995，2013）。可见，系统功能语言学的适用性源自以问题为导向的理论思考，旨在解决语言应用中面临的各种实际问题，诸如对一种语言本身的全面描写、语言/外语教育与教学、计算与翻译、社会-政治话语、语言发展与语言病理、语言的社会属性、语言的生理机制、语言的艺术功能、多模态等议题。

第二，这种范式的另一个突出特点是整体模型的开放性。换言之，鉴于目标的综合性，任何归纳获得的结果，如果既有范畴无法合理解释，均可确立新的范畴，并纳入其整体模型中。例如，在韩礼德模式中，情态一向附属于语气；马丁等人则把与情态有关的一系列现象独立开来，同其他

---

① 为便于查对，同一作者的同一中文文献，因体例原因，会在中英文行文中分别用中英文列出；书末参考文献也分中英文单列，但英文部分会提供相应的中文信息；同年发表的中英文文献 a,b,c 会因此分散到各自的中英文条目中。

相关现象一起,称为评价功能;出于同一原因,本书作者针对语言的权势功能试图构拟第三个人际意义次范畴(彭宣维 2011, 2015b)。

1.2　泛时语言观

　　系统功能语言学持一种泛时语言观。它认为,语言系统,即功能性的语言成分聚合群,是由两个历时维度的语言使用积累而成的。这两个维度是:(一)人类演化过程的种系发生(Phylogenesis);(二)社会个体成长历程的个体发生(Ontogenesis)。它们支配着共时维度的实例性话语发生(Logogenesis),后者也称语篇过程(Text Process)。例如,韩礼德认为,语篇中的任何一个句子均有四个维度的历史:种系发生意义上的语篇间性(Intertextuality;也译互文性或文本间性)、个体发生意义上的语言发展、当前待用的语言系统历史、话语发生过程意义上的语篇内历史(Halliday 1992a)。鉴于"过去总是处于现在状态"(Halliday 1999),过去的语言使用经验与当下的任务共现于长时工作记忆平台:由于任务关系,长时记忆中的相关信息因为熟悉度高,所以总是处于活跃的待用状态(见Ericsson & Kintsch 1995;Kintsch et al. 1999;Pearson 2001;Ward 2001;Halliday 2003: 7, 171, 280; 2008: 15, 189)。因此,语言事件是一个无时间特征(timeless)的概念(Halliday 1992a;Hasan 2016)。事实上,过去积累的任何语言成分及其使用经验,只有进入当下的关注范围,才可能被调用。索绪尔认为,语言泛时观(Panchrony)不具有现实性,从而严格区分语言研究的历时维度与共时维度(Diachrony and Synchrony)。但在实际操作中,历史语言学家发现索绪尔这一划分太过武断,一些认知语言学家也试图给予相应阐述,但大都是分析性的(构式语法有一个概念Inheritance,只是针对句子构式的描述性范畴);这一问题在系统功能语言学的泛时框架内得以消解。整体范式语言观有一个重要的应用价值,可以将作者/说话人、语篇/话语、读者/听者/译者关联为一个整体:与种系发生过程相关而累积的文化背景,会影响相关社团的个体发生过程及其意识形成,所以作者会通过语篇或话语中介,间接介入读者的阅读体验,三者是一体的(彭宣维 2015b)。这一点从社会文化传承(或称模因复制)和心理现实的角度,为伽德默尔的视域融合认识提供了社会心理工作机制,从而为语言教育的累增效应、语文辞书的义项辐射及其编纂、语内和语际翻译等学科的模型建构提供了理论支持。

1.3 基于实例的系统先导性

基于实例的系统先导性是以整体范式语言观为基础的,两者都顺应了现代认识论的发展。简言之,始于尼采的现代哲学,摈弃了西方传统哲学形而上的认识论和方法论,反对一切先验认识,主张从人自身的感知出发观察人和世界。这一思想竟在一些现代和后现代学者那里走向极端:他们否定历史,割裂传统,甚至否定现有的一切;与这种历史虚无主义和存在虚无主义的观点相对,另一些当代学者,尤其是海德格尔、伽德默尔、利科及其以后的阐释学家,虽然强调解读者的积极作用,但并不像巴尔特、德里达、福柯等解构主义者那样否认作者和语篇/话语的应有地位、否认历史、偏执于读者解读。阐释学家认可历史,只是这个意义上的历史不再是一种客观自在之物,而是解读者根据外化记忆(如书籍、录音、文物等)在当前视域下重构的认识现象(对比伽德默尔 2007)。在这一大的学术背景下,系统功能语言学的系统概念指以往话语过程累积形成的成分聚合体,它们以典型类别、次类和准类的方式储存在长时记忆中。这些成分不是个别现象,而是通过人类种系发生和社会个体发生过程形成的集体符号。事实上,语言实例是累积语言系统的前提,语言系统成分存在于语言实例中;而在一定共时层面上,已经形成的语言系统又反过来支配语言实例的运作方式,"因此,实例构成系统,系统又为每一实例决定其潜势"(Halliday 1990)。这一点同海德格尔(2006)关于"此在"与"存在"的相互关系相似。概言之,系统先导性是一种共时认识,但它有种系发生和个体发生两个历时维度做基础,更有话语发生做实例演示,所以能从理论上消解历时与共时的僵硬对立(见前文)。

1.4　人文性与科学性的有机统一

在系统功能语言学中,人文性与科学性的统一可以从两个方面得到说明。一方面,系统功能语言学的人文性体现在归纳与类推思辨上。例如,韩礼德早在 1966 年讨论语法、社会与名词的关系时就指出,名词化是人类对认识进行分类的必然结果,它在语法环境中生成,由一切技术进步可能面临的称名要求促成(Halliday 1966a)。这一点在他后来的论述中得到系统阐述:语法隐喻中的名词化,让变动的世界驻足静止,从而"给予它稳定性和永久性,你可以观察它,度量它,用它做实验。日常话语的语法能容忍甚至主张非确定性、变化与流动;科学语篇那种精致的名词化语法却强加了确定性、不变性和静态性。它识解的世界最终由事物构成"(Halliday 1999)。另一方面,系统语法是在计算机程序设计原理的基础上发展起来的,通过二分、三分甚至多分方法构建系统选择网络(对比刘海涛 2009),而这正是 20 世纪 70 年代初计算语言学取得突破性进展的一个重要基础。明确的选择路径决定了严格的分类原则,确定了语言现象的可计算性(见 Halliday 2005a)。按照常理,归纳和类推思辨可能与计算表征是对立甚至冲突的。不过,韩礼德在这里找到了一条合理的折中途径,这就是概率的概念。概率的思想源自模糊数学,自 20 世纪 60 年代以来,它在社会语言学的实地调查中得到广泛应用。系统功能语言学在此基础上采用概率方法解决系统描写问题,以此确立范畴分类和分布的依据及其强弱程度,从而将语言研究的人文性和科学性有机统一起来。

1.5　功能多元性

关于系统功能语言学的功能多元性,可参见胡壮麟等(2005)系统而明晰的阐述,这里做一点背景关联介绍。功能多元性源自哲学上的多元世界观。尼采隐喻性地宣称"上帝死了",也就宣告了人类关注自身感受与体验的权利的开始。这种自下而上的途径,可能因为人类各自不同的经历和经验而获得不同的看待世界的方式,彼此相同、相似、相反、相对,于是互结同盟,对抗异己,合作与冲突由此而生。这种多元并生认识,直接影响了尼采之后的所有思想领域,尤其是哲学、文学和艺术。语言研究的多元观始自布勒,由布拉格学派的代表人物马泰休斯加以发展,再由布拉格学派的另一位创始人雅可布逊,以整个交际过程为背景,进行了全方位模式化,语言哲学家奥斯汀则按多层次方式处理行为意义,所有这些先期研究成果成就了系统功能语言学关于概念、人际、语篇三种高度概括的元功能思想(彭宣维 2015c)。功能多元性可以解决小句构成成分的分析问题,如由语序变化带来的主语问题:在 my aunt was given this teapot by the duke、this teapot the duke gave to my aunt 和 by the duke my aunt was given this teapot 中,传统语法认为,第二、三句中的 this teapot 和 by the duke 是倒装,18、19 世纪一批法国和德国学者反对这种缺乏任何实质内容的解说方式,认为三句中的 the duke、this teapot 和 my aunt 分别是各句的逻辑主语、心理主语和语法主语(当然前两句中的 my aunt 和 the duke 也是相应句子的语法主语;第二句中的 the duke 也是逻辑主语)。但韩礼德认为,它们不是主语的三个次类,而是三种不同的语义范畴(Halliday 1994:32)。王力把"在北京城里有座故宫"中的介词短语看作状语、"北京城里有座故宫"的第一个成分看作主语;这在系统功能语法中就不是问题(见彭宣维 2011)。

1.6　语言使用与模型设计的生态性

系统功能语言学的生态语言观的基础是维果茨基从社会认知角度确立的意义建构论(对比美国的社会认知观,如 20 世纪早期的乔治·米德(George Mead,如 1932/2002)和 80 年代以来的泽鲁巴维尔(Eviatar

Zerubavel,如 1997，2004）以及萨丕尔—沃夫的语言相对论），以别于传统上的以下认识：意义是现成的，等待语言符号去表达；或者，语言不断演化，不断根据使用环境优化自己，从而成为反映世界的工具。韩礼德认为，语言并非一个基于某个基础的超级结构，而是意识与物质彼此影响的结果，是人类的物理存在和意识存在相互冲突的结果，所以语言具有塑造意识的力量，将自己置身于历史过程的塑造之中：语言是现实的一部分——调节物质实践、建构社会关系；语言还是现实的塑造者——确保并限制其演化方向；语言更是现实的隐喻——通过自身的内在系统—过程、以多重分形组合的方式，重构语言自身建构而成的冲突与互补关系。据此，现当代社会的语言使用存在很多问题。例如，科技语篇大量使用名词化，以固定、确定、离散和抽象的方式，塑造一个接一个的独立王国，确保学者的优越感和优势地位，逐渐远离流动、不确定、具有连续性的深层现实；它们为专家自身构筑了一道屏障，与非专业人士隔离，异化了现代科技话语，用语法解构了现实。此外，人们通过语言制造偏见、性别歧视、种族歧视、社会不平等关系和各种冲突。还有，人们通过特定的语法组合方式，诱导各种不恰当甚至不合理的过度消费行为，赚取利益最大化，给社会带来许多认识误区，导致社会生态与环境生态严重失衡（Halliday 1990）。而进行语言学研究本身也是一项高度政治化的活动，即一种行为，一种介入社会和政治过程的方式，一种干扰研究对象（如科学本身）的行动，一种实现某种意识形态的途径，进而支配人类生存的生态—社会条件（Halliday 2001）。系统功能语言学的这种生态语言观，关注语言使用的人文生态和自然生态效应，体现了一种具有认识论意义的生存危机感和社会责任意识（黄国文 2016）。

1.7　词汇语法的互补性

最后，在系统功能语言学中存在多种互补性；对此，韩礼德全面讨论了三对范畴：语法与词汇、语言系统与语篇、口语与书面语（Halliday

2008）。其中，口语与书面语的互补性甚至连续性早有研究（如 Gregory & Carroll 1978），韩礼德给予了进一步论述，系统与语篇的互补性前文已有提及，这里概述词汇与语法的互补性。其实，两者分野是传统语法留给我们的财富：它虽然太过简单，但毕竟方便易行。其中，词汇仅指词汇系统中那些带有经验特征的词语，故称实词或词汇词，从而把识解逻辑关系意义的词语，即虚词或语法词排除在外。不过，有两点需要提醒初学者：任何一个词项，无论是实词还是虚词，都是词汇系统的一部分，尽管虚词的数量在一种语言中相对很少；而即便是实词，同样蕴涵了语法属性，如按照使用习惯，英美人说 commit an error 和 make a mistake，前后两个动词不宜换用。这种搭配限制看似庞杂，但在语篇实例中仍然有规律可循，为系统研究提供了概率线索；而在进一步的结构化过程中，虚词或语法词则明确相关逻辑语义关系。可见：（一）两类词语的语法关系，均为语篇的横组合过程，提供了结构化和组织化的语法依据，只是语法词的语法特征相对明确，而词汇词的语法特征相对隐晦，词汇和语法正是在这个意义上构成了一个统一的措辞层次；（二）词汇词提供经验意义单元，语法词除了提供逻辑关系，还会构筑一个整体意义单位，往往大于各个经验意义成分之和。正是词汇的这两个方面，构成了词汇词和语法词在功能上的互补关系。但系统功能语言学框架内的词汇语法研究是一个全方位的途径，涉及"从上面"（根据语场选择词汇语法手段）、"从下面"（从词语的既有使用现象归纳意义特征）、"从周围"（从概括到具体）三种方式，避免了传统语法仅从下面入手从而带来的观察、描写和解释上的不足。

1.8　发展走向

上述过程表明，系统功能语言学的学理与范式，使它自身具有许多突出的理论和应用优势。同时，由于它涉及语言内外的各个层面与维度，因而为语言事件的分类、解释、转述和重构提供了不同详略程度的范畴依据。例如，其多功能范畴及其词汇语法子范畴，可以从不同侧面在教学和翻译实践中进行语言事件的转述与重构;而其语篇类型意义上的语域(俗称语类)概念,不仅是重构相应语境的分类手段,更是不同语义单位的组织方式,为翻译风格和特殊用途语言教学研究,尤其是学科英语教学研究(见 Halliday 2004),提供了颇具实用价值的范畴依据。但系统功能语言学毕竟是在特定历史环境下、在一定程度上针对生成语言学的演绎方法及其第一代认知科学基础而并行发展起来的,在从语义到词汇语法的体现中,虽然有一致式和非一致式的选择路径,毕竟缺乏语用学那样系统梳理成类的用语原则和策略,更没有后来认知语言学运用涉身经验来解释有关语言结构的观察思路;英国传统的语言研究项目之一是词汇,系统功能语言学是在集中关注语法的前提下展开的,因此系统与功能关照下的词汇研究始终是一个弱项,需要从英国传统和认知语言学汲取有效营养。此外,它的出发点是社会学和社会语言学,尤其是后者涉及的权势与同盟关系,对此韩礼德也有进一步的理论阐述(Halliday 1978a:第9—12章),但至今没能在其模型建构中发展出相应的词汇语法范畴及其相应语义系统(见前文)。系统概念是基于计算流程构拟的,但系统功能语言学视角下的计算语言学研究在中国至今仍然是一个弱项。如此等等。总之,不同功能模块各有所长,彼此互补。从理论范式的兼容性与独特性看,不宜直接将它们并置一处来说明语言全景,但采用系统功能语言学自身的学理与方法来研究尚未涉猎、论述不系统或欠充分的语言行为现象,在参照其他学派研究成果的条件下,既必要,也可行,应该尝试,以补充相应不足;而在现有框架内对有关现象的深入研究,则是风险系数最低的入门路径。

第二章

词汇语法的上限级阶——语篇

"(Text as) Wording" as Wording in Text Size: Stretching Lexicogrammatical Rank Hierarchy from Clause to Text[①]

2.1　Introduction

It is noticeable that, in a series of papers published in the 1990s,

---

① 本章分 English Morphemic Constituents Working for Discourse Wording: Extending Rank Scale from "Clause (Complex)" up to "Text (Type)" 与 "'(Text as) Wording' as Wording in Text Size: Stretching Lexicogrammatical Rank Hierarchy from Clause to Text" 两文, 原文分别刊载于 *International Journal of English Linguistics* 2016(3): 38 – 60 和 *WORD* 2017, 63(2): 136 – 172. The content of this chapter comes from the presentation delivered at the 40th International Systemic Functional Congress held at Sun Yatsen University, China, 15 – 19 July 2013. Thanks to Professors Halliday and Ruqaiya Hasan who raised critical questions and made cordial comments on my speech. They even faxed to me evaluating that "this is an important paper for SFL" after they read one of the early drafts. Professor Geoff Thompson wrote to me that this paper "identified a grey area in SFL" and kindly offered a number of important suggestions and comments. It is great sadness that Ruqaiya and Geoff can no longer read this paper in print. Last but not least, I should thank the reviewers and the editors for their kind suggestions and comments.

Halliday uses the expression "(text as) wording" along "(text as) meaning" in Systemic Functional Linguistics (SFL for short; see Halliday 1992b, 1993a, 1995; all in Halliday 2005a). What does this "(text as) wording" thesis really mean? What is its top categorical extent? No full elaboration can be found. There is only a general characterisation that "(text as) wording" is the instantiation behaviours of their lexicogrammatical system to make "(text as) meaning", apart from an associated claim as similarly made before (Halliday 1981, 1982a): "The ranks are the structural units of the grammar (clause, phrase, group, word; each with its associated complex)" (Halliday 2005a: 254).

My personal consultation with Halliday himself confirms that "(text as) wording", though charaterised as the counterpart of "(text as) meaning", should still be clausal in terrain (see also Halliday 1961, 1966b, 1978a, 1981, 1982a, 1994, 2008; McGregor 1991; Martin 1992; Halliday & Matthiessen 2014). It is clause (complex), as well as those ranks below, that "realises" or "encodes" corresponding "text meaning", the latter being a socio-semantic unit between context or "extra-textual features" and language or lexicogrammar (Halliday 1978a). In my own words, text wording is embodied in stretches of lexicogrammatical units that realise text meaning, the maximal range of each unit being the clause (complex).

However, the "(text as) wording" thesis can be understood in an alternative way: "text wording" may be textual or discursive in categorical extent. That is, the lexicogrammatical hierarchy of a language as a whole should be a super-clausal phenomenon. Text wording in this sense should be the top rank of lexicogrammar: discourse size in scope and in constitution. That is, discourse process should be comprised of text-sized wording as well as text-sized meaning, the latter two being generated concurrently along the course of realisation from meaning to wording and along the course of instantiation from system to instance.

For that hypothesis, the present study attempts to discuss two interrelated points, focusing in particular on the wording side, with description of the meaning side very sketchy to be fully developed elsewhere.

- First, from the system angle, how shall morphemic and lexical items, to be sorted out by morphemic systems and word classes, be deployed to **function** for constructing such grammatical units as, respectively, words, word groups/phrases, clauses, clause complexes and text?

- Second, from the instance perspective, with the basic rank units of morpheme, word, group and phrase and clause in mind, how can "text wording", by illustration, be organised into the same size of categorical extent as that of "text meaning"?

These two questions will be answered in Sections 2 and 3 below from both the system and instance angles respectively, followed by a summary and further theoretical argumentation in Section 4.

The first issue will be addressed from the perspective of the functions that morphemes and words play for rank scales. Here, the notion "function" is used in the two analytical senses: grammatical (i. e., wording) and contextual (meaning). The former refers to the roles smaller linguistic items play in larger units in text whereas the latter refers to those roles of lexicogrammatical items that act in " sociocultural context " to construe ideational, interpersonal and textual meanings (Halliday 1961, 1970a, 1978a, 1994; Halliday & Matthiessen 2014).

For the second issue, the essay will proceed by applying three general working principles for discourse generation: unidirectionality, trace onlinedness and layered constitution (see Peng 2015b: 119 – 150). Unidirectionality accounts for the temporality, also called sequentiality or linearity, of meaning components replacive along the "surface" of discourse. Trace onlinedness observes the shuffling traces of meaning components being aligned by their respective categories, a process that associates and gives rise to a wording texture; here, "trace" refers to any semantic entities that have occurred before the current ones for discourse production and "onlinedness" refers to the constant semiotic association and interdependence of the past and the present components to generate the wording texture. Layered constitution observes how "visible" unidirectionality and onlined elements on the "surface" of discourse co-work to build up a multi-dimensional construct of text meaning underneath as "a socio-semantic unit" (for this last idea, see Halliday 1978a).

In regard to this multi-layered perspective, text or discourse studies so far have witnessed three generalised sets of approaches, as being either (i) **structural** at the underlying level (e.g., Pike & Pike 1983; van Dijk 1979; Longacre 1979, 2007; Hoey 1983; Cloran 1994, 1995, 2010; see also Cloran et al. 2007; Hengeveld & Mackenzie 2008); or (ii) **organisational** with reference to texture and cohesion (e.g., Halliday & Hasan 1976; de Beaugrande & Dressler 1981; Giora 1983; Stoddard 1991; Ghadessy 1995; Hoey, 1991a & b, 2001, 2005, 2007); or (iii) **both** structural and organisational from the perspectives of genre (register or text type), texture and cohesion (see Halliday 1978a: 133 - 134), an integrated approach followed by Hasan and her colleagues (see, e.g., Hasan 1978, 1979, 1984, 1985a, 1985b, 1993, 1994, 1005, 2000, 2001; Williams & Unsworth 1990; Martin 1992, esp. Chapter 6 regarding the layered conceptions of hyper- and macro-theme and macro- and hyper-new; Rothkegel 1993; Butt et al. 2007; Wegener 2011; Webster 2002; Forey & Thompson 2008; Matthiessen 2013; Halliday & Webster 2014; Pace-Sigge 2013; Lukin 2013, 2016; Bowcher 2016).

Of these three, the last view of text is preferable to the present study because it is able to give one an entire picture of text or discourse in context. In addition, the vantage point from the present perspective will be able to reveal a continuum between pure structural and pure organisational since cohesion in both of the "organic" and "structural" respects, such as "adjacency pairs" on the one hand, and "parallelism" and "theme-rheme development" on the other (see Hasan 1985a: 82; also Martin 1992: 434 - 488; Ghadessay 1995), has a strong structural nature that converges with the areas of generic structures of text, in particular when generic structures manipulate the selection of the aforementioned cohesive devices to generate organisational patterns (cf. Hasan 1985a & b).

Here, a brief explanation is in order for some of the key terms used and to be used.

First, according to Halliday (1995), language instance is topographically split off from language system (cf. Halliday 1978a). Then "meaning" is used in its narrow sense: the "actual" rather than "potential" aspect of language function. It is a socio-semiotic act or event construed in particular context of use by means of due lexicogrammatical configurations (see Halliday 2008: 14, 188; also Halliday 1978a).

Second, Halliday and Hasan elaborate the view that lexis and grammar form a continuum that sees no line of distinction in between; and lexis and grammar are complementary in function (Halliday 1966c, 2008; Hasan 1987; Matthiessen 1991; Cross 1992, 1993; Tucker 1997, 2007; cf. de Saussure 1998). Here, "complementarity" simply means that basic linguistic entities, such as lexemes, contribute to structuring and organising both discourse meanings and wordings.

Third, the terms "text" and "discourse" are the same thing but profiled from alternative angles: "'Discourse' is text that is being viewed in its sociocultural context, whereas 'text' is discourse that is being viewed as a process of language" (Halliday 2008: 78). The idea of discourse or text as process, as against discourse or text as product, is taken from Hjelmslev (1943/1961), but understood in the Hallidayan sense as a logogenetic course with two coexistent dynamic aspects: (i) the "deep" or "underlying" process of meaning-making (Halliday 1966d, 1971) and (ii) the "surface" course (Halliday 1966d; Hoey 1983) that hangs together "the lexicogrammatical units representing a text" by "cohesion" (Hasan 1978: 229), both of which are generated by selection within instantiated sub-systems of options (Halliday 1966d).

Other relevant concepts, such as appraisal, information, transitivity and syntagm, will be introduced where necessary for reference convenience.

2.2　Functions of "morphemes" and "lexemes" for rank scales: a systemic illustration

This preparatory section is a general account for extending the area of rank scale of lexicogrammar up to "text" that comprises both meaning and wording as complementary. In particular, it identifies the metafunctional features that morphemes have been conventionalised to bear, and the lexicogrammatical roles both morpheme and lexis play as their potential functions for making discourse process.

2.2.1　*Metafunctional features of morphemes*

This sub-section discusses two points: a systemic description of morphemes and their semantic functions. It begins with the types of morphemes in English that constitute word. Take as example the first sentence in *Headless Angel*.

(1) Beth was three months pregnant when we went to France on our honeymoon.

Morphemes are "forms which can only appear as part of a larger form or larger sequence of morphemes" (Matthews 1991: 210), as *head* and *-less* in *headless*, *be* and *-ed* in *was*, *month* and *-s* in *months*, and *we* and the genitive form that envelops *we* as *our*, where *-less*, *-ed*, *-s* and the genitive variant are bound morphemes and the others are base morphemes.

Bound morphemes are divided into derivational and inflectional, such as *-less*, *-ed*, *-s*, and the genitive form in *our*; they may either be in zero form (Φ) or non-zero form (X), as suggested by the plural variation of *write* (inflectional) or the zero morphological form of the verbal *focus* or *progress* and the nominal *focus* or *progress* (derivational) (Φ), or suggested by the third singular form *writes* (inflectional) or *writer* (derivational) (X). Base morphemes are either Free (maybe also Root; for derivational) or Stem (for inflectional) (Bussmann 1996: 453). The systemic network under discussion is drawn as Figure 2 - 1, where " { " stands for AND relation and " [" for OR relation; and the curved arrow overhead means recursiveness by repetitive operation for generating lexemes.

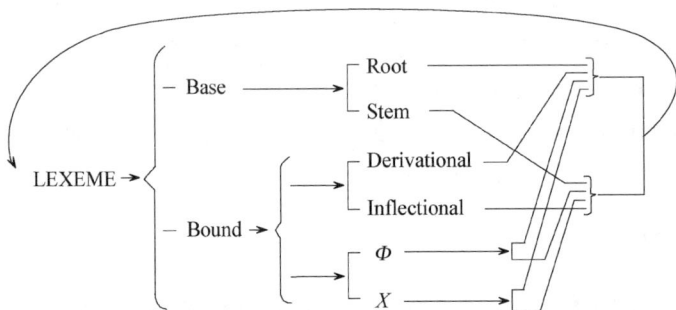

Figure 2 - 1: Systemic network for morphemic items

One, bound morphemes may function to work for any rank along the hierarchy of the lexicogrammatical, or meaning-wording, continuum (Mcgregor 1991). On the one hand, for inflectional bound morphemes, they are specified, by Crystal (1997: 93), into 8 types of grammatical categories, which are cited below for their importance to highlight the main point of this sub-section (cf. Halliday's (2008: 172) summarisation of 5 types in English: number, person, tense, aspect and case) :

 (i) aspect (verb) : (a) completeness, habituality, continuousness, duration, progressiveness; (b) perfect(ive) , imperfect(ive) ;

 (ii) case (nouns, pronouns, adjectives) : (a) actor, possession, meaning, location, motion towards; (b) nominative, vocative, accusative, genitive, partitive;

 (iii) gender (nouns, verbs, adjectives) : (a) male, female, sexless, living; (b) masculine, feminine, neuter, animate, inanimate;

 (iv) mood (verbs) : (a) factuality, possibility, uncertainty, likelihood;

(b) indicative, subjunctive, optative;

(v) number (nouns, verbs, pronouns): (a) one, two, more than one, more than two, more than three; (b) singular, dual, trial, plural;

(vi) person (pronouns, verbs): (a) speaker, addressee, third party, fourth party; (b) first person, second person, third person, fourth person;

(vii) tense (verbs): (a) present time, past time, future time; (b) present, past, future;

(viii) voice (verbs): (a) who did action, what was acted upon, what caused action; (b) active, passive, middle, causative.

There are three facts about the classifications. First, those under (a) are the "typical meanings conveyed" and those under (b) are the "typical formal contrasts" or grammatical functions. Second, as for their respective semantic features, all or most are experiential, but those under (iv), e.g. mood, (vi), e.g. person, and (viii), e.g. voice, should and may be interpersonal (speech function/interactive and modal/appraisal; see Halliday & Matthiessen 2014: 134 – 210; Martin & White 2005) and some under (vi), e.g. person, may be textual as well (i.e., conventionalised given information potential in system; see below). Third, all these terms have a more grammatical rather than semantic weight for their categorisation purposes, that is, to "grammaticalise" into different stretches of structural units: word by case, gender, number and person; word group by aspect, tense, voice and number (e.g., *three* bridges; *a **tertiary** class*) ; and clause by mood and person (they *go* vs. she *goes*; *I* go vs. *we* go).

On the other hand, for the derivational bound morphemes, they are grammar-oriented as well, but have more or less weight on the semantic pole at the same time, and may all or either be (i) experiential (*interesting* vs. *interested*; *intercellular* vs. *intracellular*; *evolve* vs. *evolution*; *arrival*; *bilingual*; *unhappy* vs. *happy* [antonymy]; *image* vs. *imagery*; nominal and verbal *progress*: φ morphemic variation), and/or (ii) interpersonal (modal/appraisal: *affordable* ["reaction" in appreciation: *did I like it?*], *speechless* ["normality" in judgement: *how special for human behaviour? +* "security" in affect: *surprise or diffidence at environment +* "deny" in engagement: *negation*], **un**happy [deny], *beauty* [quality] vs. *beauti**ful*** ["epithet" in nominal group or "attribute" in predicate, both being "reaction" of appreciation in attitude], *book* vs. *book**ish*** [negative "tenacity": *how dependable?*]).

Two, base morphemes work to a large extent for conveying meanings, which may either be pure experiential, as *nation* in *national* and *international*, and *form* in *formality*, *informal*, *reform* and *deform*; or both experiential and evaluative/interpersonal, as *claim* (meaning *cry* or *shout*: experiential uttering + appraisal of "normality" and "distance": explicit authorial distancing from "attributed materials") in *acclaim*, *declaim*, *exclaim* and *proclaim*, and *clar-* (meaning *make clear*: experiential act + positive "tenacity" in appraisal) in *clarify*, *clare*, *clarion* and *declarative*. (For details of Appraisal, see Martin & White 2005; Martin & Rose 2007.)

These grammatical categories can be summarised in systemic network under the headings of base and bound, both of which can be associated with their respective metafunctional potentials (see Figure 2 - 2).

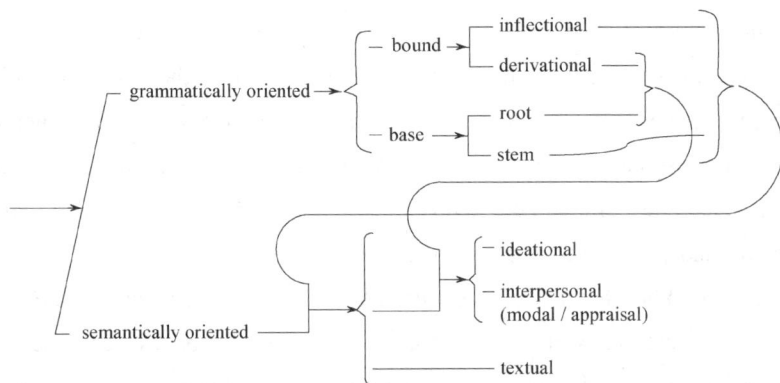

Figure 2 - 2: Potential metafunctions of morphemes

Note that both inflectional and derivational morphemes may have logical features too, as *John's book* (possessive) and *the wooden bell* (premodifier), apart from their experiential features (deictic and classifier respectively [classifier referring to taxonomic function]; see Halliday & Matthiessen (2014: 365 - 374, 377 - 378). Also, the figure employs a topological (or prototypical) way of presenting lexicogrammatical functions (see Lemke 1987, cited in Matthiessen et al. 2010: 230 - 232), as indicated by the slant square system at the beginning, since almost all lexical items, whether semantically or grammatically oriented in categorisation, contain both grammatical and semantic features: either is just a matter of degree but all grammatical categories are semantically based, as suggested by the curve lines extended from "base" and "bound" in the top sub-system to those terms in the bottom sub-system.

2.2.2 Lexicogrammatical functions of "morphemes" for rank scales

To this end, all the morphemes are sorted out from the sample text according to their lexicogrammatical functions and listed in Table 2 - 1 (Appendix). They are all grammatically oriented as they each perform certain structural or syntagmatic functions at their respective ranks; but at the same time they are more or less meaning-characterised, whether with "implicit meaning orientation" (the left column) or with "overt meaning change" (the right column). From this perspective, it is hard to make discrimination between their lexical and grammatical roles, a fact that has been fully elaborated (Halliday 1961, 2005a; Halliday et al. 1964; Hasan 1987).

Let me clarify in a very brief way some of these presented in the table. Consider the first two sentences of the sample text, with the second cited as (2).

(2) The trip represented our promise not to let the baby change who we were, not to forget that there was so much world, all around, waiting.

First, there are morphemes that represent different occasions at the **word** rank, some of which are concerned with experiential features, others with interpersonal and still others with textual. The word *around* in (2), for example, may be replaced by *round* with little experiential meaning changing; however, the presence or absence of the prefix *a*- is attuned with interpersonal goal: "definite" with *round* and less so with *around* in Britain, and formal with *around* and informal with *round* in America (Pearsall 1998: 1618). This *a*- is an example of bound morpheme. Meanwhile, there are free morphemes in (1) that involve explicit experiential meaning change. The word *honeymoon*, for example, has two free morphemes *honey* and *moon*; and the meaning of this compound word is not comprised of the sum of the meanings of the two parts: *HONEYMOON* ≠ *HONEY* + *MOON*. That is, the meaning of the word changes from the sum of their constituents. The same goes to most of the items listed in the second cell under the word rank in Table 2 – 1. Regarding this case, Halliday (2008: 59 – 61) lists a number of typical examples, clarifying the changes of the grammatical functions.

Second, some morphemes may work directly for the rank of **word group** and **phrase**, guided with either experiential or/and interpersonal or/and textual functions. For example, *-s* at the end of *month* is associated with the word group *three months* as it is attached to *month* for agreeing with the specific plurality manifested by the premodifier/numerative *three* in that context, which is experiential for specifying the length of the time concerned. Some context does not have such a particular premodifier as *three*, and the "head" carries with it such a plural form as well, a case required for message particularisation, where an enumerative item may not be necessary, such as *men*, *suits*, *walls*, *spires*, *hands*, *generations*, *elbows*, *wings* and *feet* in the latter part of the sample discourse. A further illustration may be given in terms of the pair of examples absent from the sample text cited above: *a beautiful magazine* vs. *a beauty magazine*, the former being "epithet" (here subjective evaluation) while the latter "classifier" of nominal group. Also involved in the nominal group rank is *our* in *our honeymoon*, which implies a possessive relationship between *we* (inclusive of both *Beth* and *I*) and the thing called *honeymoon*, a grammatical construction by which the genitive case aligns different items for "thematic" purpose (and here "given information" as well) (see Halliday & Matthiessen 2014: 387 – 388). Other items, including *was*, *went*, *represented* and *were*, are verbal groups (in lexical form, though), where the finite morpheme *-ed* suggests the general temporality meaning in the specific text type, a discourse property to be exemplified shortly.

Third, some morphemes are clearly **clause**-oriented. Consider for example the morphemes in the first cell at the "clause" rank in Table 2 – 1, most of which work for interpersonal, in particular for interactive/speech function, meanings by virtue of mood element "subject + finite", even though finites also help realise experiential temporality (see below). For example, the finite morpheme in *were*, which can be analysed as *be + -ed +* plurality, has a clausal construction relationship with the plural subjective *we*, known as subject-predicate agreement in the Indo-European linguistic tradition. This implicit *-ed* (compare the *-ed* in *represented* in Sentence 2 and also in the nominal group *untouched bread and cheese* in Sentence 11) works at the same time for governing a nominal group and a verbal group and is therefore clausal in function.

Others, such as *herself* in Sentence 7 and *her* in Sentence 19, are "complement" in the respective clauses, as they are commanded by the relevant verbal parts of the residues (residue being one constituent of Mood Structure, and the other being Mood; Mood + Residue makes a unit of mood structure, as (*John -s*) and (*love Mary*) in *John loves Mary*; see Halliday & Matthiessen 2014: 139 – 143). Also, each in the second cell has a clausal function too because it is the clause that transforms it into the form as it is. Here, they have a strong transitivity nature: *pregnant* in Sentence 1, *horrible* in 4, *oblivious to* in 9 and *hungry* in 11 are all "attribute" (i.e., adjectival ascription) of the relational processes respectively, that is, processes of classifying (e.g., *John is a teacher*) or identifying (*John is the teacher*; see Halliday & Matthiessen 2014: 265); that is, their suffixes have been deployed for serving the attribute function. But of course, they can all be utilised as epithet in nominal groups, a systemic nature that suggests their bi-functional roles again. Note that the word *pregnant* is in the adjective form, a morphological alternative to *pregnancy*; the variation arises from the "attribute" status of participant in the clause concerned. To be specific, it is a kind of "quality" compared with what the nominal form *pregnancy* represents, namely, a "thing". Since a "quality" is not equal to a "thing", the lexical items *pregnant* and *pregnancy* are inconsistent in both semantic and grammatical categorisations. It is this quality that goes to the functional slot of attribute in the clause construction per se.

Incidentally, the attribute function can be confirmed with the affix *a-* (cf. *a-* in *around*), which is absent from the sample text. One of the grammatical functions of this *a-* lies in its unique use as what has been called "predicate" adjective or adverb, as in *abed*, *ashore*, *asunder*, *aside*, *afire*, *asleep*, *alike*, *aweary*, *aloud*, *aflutter*, *a-ringing*, *abuilding*, *a-hunting* among others. They exclusively collocate with a relational process element like *be* or *go* or *remain* or *keep* or *seem*, as in *the two vases* look alike. Once again, some such formations may be both clausal and group-natured, as *aloof*, for example, in *an aloof house* (group) and *she always remained aloof from her family members* (clause), although such cases are not frequent to come up with.

The morpheme *-ing* in the last word in (2), that is, *waiting*, serves to constitute the rank of **clause complex**. That is, it implies a syntagm of a clause: *so much world was waiting (for us)*, which is dependent on *there was so much world* the dominant clause; or it has a similar grammatical function as that of an embedded clause ("relative clause" in traditional grammar): *(there was so much world) that was waiting (for us)*. Meanwhile, the sample text has no instance for the second cell under "clause complex", but there are some examples at hand, such as *stop to do* and *stop doing*, *remember to do* and *remember doing*, and *forget to do* and *forget doing*. That is, the *to* and *-ing* markers make difference in logico-semantic meaning: those with *to do* represent a purpose (enhancement feature: purpose) whereas those with *-ing* construe the Range of material or mental process (the outer or inner flow of experience) (see Halliday & Matthiessen 2014: 213 – 214).

Therefore, all those morphemes in the first cell under clause complex indicate logico-semantic and interdependency relations. First, all of them express a hypotactic or dependent feature. Second, the three infinitives, (*not*) *to let*, (*not*) *to forget* and *to enter*, realise the logico-semantic meaning of "cause": purpose; and the two after *saw*, with *to* being covert, are mental 'phenomenon': what one saw. Third, the relevant process components represent embedding (*waiting*, *reaching*, *polished*), temporal enhancement (X while Y: *strolling*) and positive addition of extension (one thesis added to another: *yelling*, *hugging*, *staring*; *broken*, *worn*) (see Halliday & Matthiessen 2014: 557 – 592).

Finally, there is one typical case implying that some morphemes may work directly for the process of **text**. For example, tense morphemes, apart from their finite functions for making the clause, may play such a role. To be specific, from the perspective of grammatical function, tense is a clausal conception (as in *John loves Mary* vs. *both John's love Mary*; see also above), although their expressions fall within the domain of verbal group (Halliday & Matthiessen 2014: 396 – 419); and from the contextual angle, the choice of tense morphemes is at the same time bound to the relevant context of discourse and/or the speaker's personal decision (see Table 2 – 1, where tense morphemes are grouped in three ranks). For example, the expressions *had* (*trembled*), *was remembering* and *had killed* in Sentence 7 and *had happened* in Sentence 9 are all relevant tenses: "past in past" (i.e., past perfect) and "present in past" (i.e., past continuous); and it is the ongoing context of each that translates it as what it is according to the general temporality requirement of the text under discussion. In other words, the use of English tense is a case out of register or genre (i.e., text type in the Hallidayan sense; see Halliday 1978; cf. Martin 1992) because different text types may give rise to different tense frequencies. The text under discussion belongs to literary genre, with all the propositions of the text being in the general past tense (simple past, past in past and present in past).

Meanwhile, it has long been acknowledged that a text of literary genre may utilise "historical present" (Romaine 1998), so as to achieve stylistic/ aesthetic effect, a characteristic that only appears in text and is hard to explain fully within the domain of the clause or verbal group. Generally, present tenses amount to the highest in descriptive, instructional, expository and argumentative discourses as unmarked. However, there are disciplinary exceptions, as in, for example, psychology and sociology journal articles, which tend to use simple past to make their discourses sound more objective.

What has been discussed so far can be visualised as Figure 2 – 3.

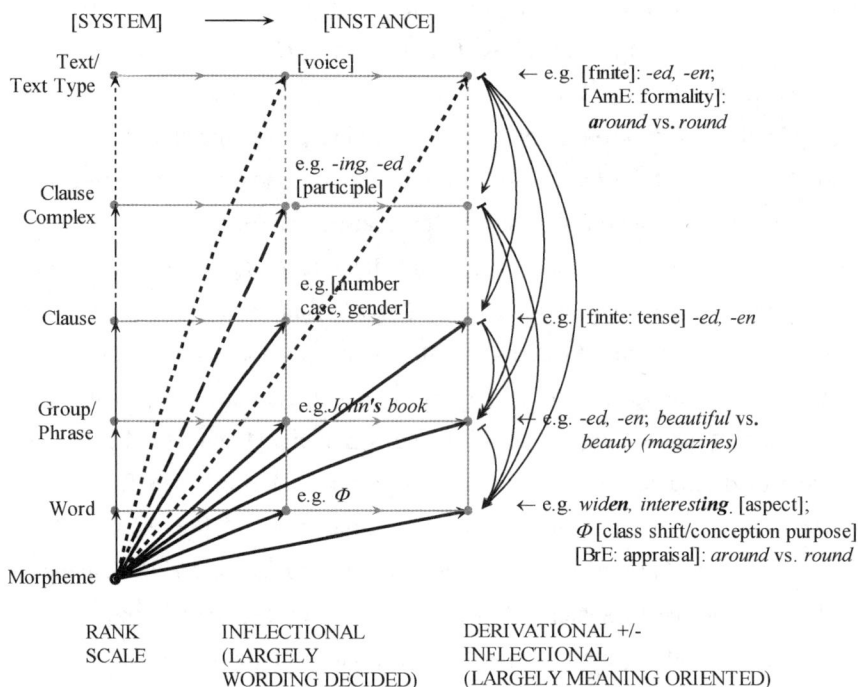

Figure 2 – 3: Lexicogrammatical functions of morphemes for text/text types

A little explanation is needed for the figure. First, the arc arrows downward on the right suggest choices of orientation and constraint: what possibilities there are and there are not by convention (for the idea of "probability", see Nesbitt & Plum 1988; Bateman & Paris 1991; Halliday 2005a; see also the collections edited by Fontaine et al. 2013; O'Grady et al.

2013). Second, the grey straight arrows from the left to the right represent the relevant grammatical constructions (functional slots in structure) deployed for morphemic items to fill in, a process of co-working or collaboration. Third, the arrows upward on the left side have two typical types: concrete and dotted, symbolising prototypical structural and organisation nature each; the line mixed with short lines and dots from clause to clause complex means that clause complex is both structural and organisational, since it has "structural" patterns ($\alpha + \beta$ and $\beta + \alpha$) on the one hand and also has "organisational" flexibility in position alternation ($\alpha + \beta$ or $\beta + \alpha$) according to contextual demands of various kinds, such as cohesion and coherence on the other. It is therefore a transitional area from the typical structural ranks to the typical organisational ranks (cf. Hoey 1991a: 215). However, structural ranks and organisational ranks are no longer in stratum or level distinction between meaning and wording, but in that they are continuum at the same stratum of lexicogrammatical hierarchy.

In one word, morphemes may function lexicogrammatically to make up word and to construct group (phrase) within the domain of clause (complex); but it is text (type) that decides their choices, e.g., whether in past or present form, and their probabilistic distribution in text.

2.2.3 *Lexicogrammatical functions of "lexemes" along rank scales*

This part treats lexis as a basic system that works to fill in slots at, and hence embody, those grammatical ranks above them for making meanings and text wordings.

The terms "word", "lexis", "lexeme" and "lexical item" need clarification. From the grammatical perspective, "word" and "lexis" have been alternatively used, either (i) as an umbrella term or (ii) as any variation of an item. For example, all the morphological forms of *go*, such as the different lexical items or lexemes *go*, goes, *went*, *gone* and *going*, are the same word *go*; or the other way round (cf., e.g., Crystal 1997: 90; Cruse 2001: 239). This study embraces the former view, which is in line with the SFL notions of the two terms: "word" refers to the grammatical rank between "morpheme" and "group" while "lexis", the general term for lexemes or lexical items, is part of the formal level concerning morphological variants (Halliday 1966c, 2008: 21 – 76; Hasan 1987).

The discussion treats lexis as a basic system that works to fill in slots at, and hence embody, those grammatical ranks above them for making meanings and wordings. To begin with, lexemes in the sample text will be grouped under the "lexical" (LX), "lexicogrammatical" (LG) and "grammatical" (GM) headings according to the 14 word classes Halliday singles out (see Halliday 1994: 214; Halliday & Matthiessen 2014: 427). They will be so grouped for their prototypical grammatical and contextual functions. That is, the "lexical" and "lexicogrammatical" headings command those that manifest contextual and grammatical roles; and those under "grammatical" are chiefly featured with their structural and organisational functions, even though semantic features of one kind or another are not ignorable all through.

The 14 word classes are further generalised into three types: nominal, verbal and adverbial. Under "nominals" are (i) common noun, (ii) proper noun, (iii) pronoun, (iv) adjective, (v) numeral, and (vi) determiner; under "verbals" are (vii) lexical, (viii) auxiliary, (ix) finite verbs, and (x) preposition; and under "adverbials" are (xi) adverb, (xii) linker, (xiii) binder, and (xiv) continuative conjunction. The sample text has 13 classes in all, with the case of "continuative" (under "adverbial") absent. The analysis is presented in Table 2 – 1 in the Appendix. On that basis, a model of lexicogrammatical functions of lexis for making text is worked out (see Figure 2 – 4; cn.: common noun; pn.: proper noun; prof.: pro-form; adj.: adjective; det.: determiner; nu.: numeral; lv.: lexical verb; ft.: finite; aux.: auxiliary; ad.: adverbial; prep.: preposition).

Here the three areas of LX, LG and GM interact in that lexical items by word classes work to fill up the relevant grammatical function slots whereas

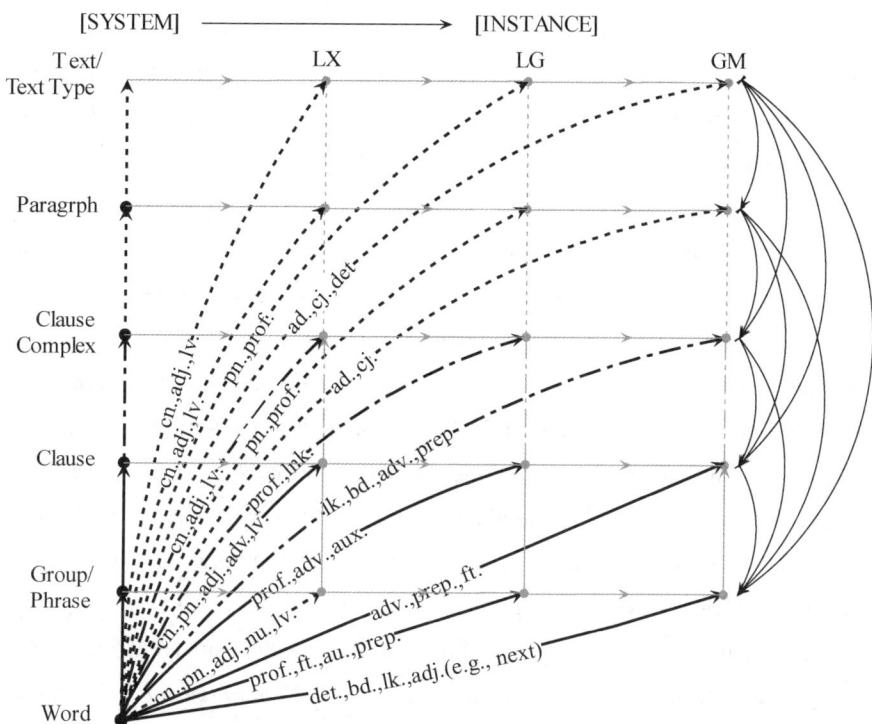

Figure 2 – 4: Working areas of "lexis" for rank scales

the grammatical forms, i.e., group (phrase), clause, clause complex and above — "text" and even "text type", orient and constrain the selections of lexical items, where the concept of "colligation" or "collocation" comes in.

Let me illustrate the point in what follows, though very briefly.

I begin with the common and proper nouns. They work in nominal groups, functioning as "head" (e.g. *2 the **trip**, our **honeymoon**, 8 **Beth** and I, 13 all **year** round, the **Seine**, 19 **generations** of elbows*) and "classifier" (e.g. *5 the **rag-doll** body, 15 the **abbey** road, 16 the **morning** mist, 20 **angel**'s wings*). They may also be constituent within prepositional phrase and clause without modifier (e.g. *3 strolling down to the beach for **lunch** and 5 **People** ran to the rag-doll body ...*).

Some word classes work for word group (phrase) and even above. Adjectives and numerals may serve nominal groups, as in *4 a **gorgeous*** *sunny day*, her **younger** *sister*, 17 **roofless** *walls*, its **childlike** *hands*, 1 **three** *months*, 2 *so* **much** *world*, 3 **fourth** *floor* and 9 **two hundred** *feet*. They may also be immediate clausal constituents, such as *4 it was* **horrible**, *6 it was* **hopeless**, *16 the river flowed* **slow** *and* **perfect**, *21 vacation's almost over*, and *Ye are* **many** *— they are* **few** (Percy B. Shelley: *The Mask of Anarchy*). Verbs typically go to word group. Lexical verbs may work as constituent of nominal group, as in *9 in tiny* **bathing** *suits*, *11 the* **untouched** *bread and cheese* and *19 a* **decapitated** *marble*; or that of a verbal group, as *be* and *go* in *1 was* (*be* + -*ed*) and *went* (*go* + -*ed*); *kill* in *7 had killed*; *be* in *21's* (*be* + -*s*); and *have* in *22 have* (*have* + ∅). Finite and auxiliary verbs go to the verbal groups too, as *will* in 10 and *have to* in 22. Here *have to* has the same status as the single word *must*: it is comprised of two lexical items but functions as one word; or it should be a case between typical word and word group. Adverbials find their grammatical function in nominal group (as postmodifier/qualifier: *9 two hundred feet* **away**); in adjective group (as premodifier: *2 so much, 11* **very** *hungry* and *21* **almost** *over*); in clause (as circumstance: *3* **down**, *4* **out**, *7* **before**, **here**, *22* **soon** and *23* **home**); in clause complex (*11* **though**; *19 the front of its bare feet broken off* **and worn** **as smooth as** *a windowsill*); and even in text, as, e.g. *[t]hen* in 3, which is a simultaneous time marker, indicating the time during which they stayed in Normandy; *[b]ut* in 6 concedes to what 5 has expressed, and *10* **finally** responds back to the series of reactions from sentences 4 to 9.

Next, the grammatical function of prepositions is to form prepositional phrase ("contracted clause"), such as *3 on* (*the side walk*), *5 for* (*the police*), *8 to* (*the shore*), *12 off* (*the Atlantic*), *15 along* (*the Seine*), *in* (*a courtyard*) and *by* (*generations of elbows*), serving Circumstance in the respective processes. Furthermore, they may function as " qualifier" at the postmodifier position of nominal groups, as that in *9 [y]oung men in tiny bathing suits*; they may also work across independent clauses.

(3) In spare time — between politics and classics there was little spare time — he began to read a few books of theology. By the middle of

1925 he had fairly clear convictions about Catholic Christianity. In his third year (1925 – 6) he went to private confession for the first time. **For** that purpose he went to Edward Wynn ... (Text A68 in *BNC*)

This is meaning-oriented; but it is also coherent in lexicogrammar: thematic progression on the one hand and cross-clausal nominal in logico-semantic relationship on the other, the latter being a kind of generalisation (see Halliday & Matthiessen 1999: 165 – 319; Halliday 2008: 71 – 72) that some people such as Schmid (2000), Aktas and Cortes (2008), Caldwell (2009) and others call "shell noun", as the general word *the trip* in 2 that points back to the journey event (*we went to France*), a relationship Hoey (1991a) terms "complex paraphrase".

Finally, pro-forms (pro-nouns, pro-verbs, pro-adjectives, pro-adverbs) and determiners are "phoric" in nature and work in the areas of clause, clause complex and discourse (co-referential), in particular the last two. For example, *their* in the clause *[b]oth programmes are the largest of **their** kind in the country* (Text A00 in *BNC*) is related to the subject *[b]oth programmes*; *they* in the clause complex *[h]er daughters have however been contacted so I agree to keep her company until **they** arrive* (Text A00 in *BNC*) refers back to *[h]er daughters* at the beginning. There are also those that refer to an entity in previous independent sentences, as *our* in the second sentence that associates itself with *we* in the first sentence: a cross-sentential referential phenomenon pertinent to the area above the clause: "text". Furthermore, the definite article *the* in 2, and *it* in 4 and 6 are anaphora (the first sentence suggests an "exophoric" narrator *I* by the plural *we*). The next two *it*'s in the text stand for the scene that a woman committed suicide by jumping out off a window and people's reaction after seeing the incident, respectively. Therefore, although expressions like 10 *both of us* occur in a prepositional phrase, *both* and *us* are deployed for cohering their co-textual entities.

Meanwhile, *we* and *our* in the first two sentences are lexicogrammatically united by textual grammar of given information, apart from their

第一部分 理论范式探新

simultaneous referential function of experience, as afore-mentioned. This bi-functional use suggests a model of "pro-form" system. To be specific, for referentiality, such pro-forms are experiential; but for phoricality, they are informational as well, in the domain of text above the extent of the clause (complex). Or, it is text or discourse process that engenders relevant lexical items to be replaced with their corresponding pro-forms to refer back or forth for economicality (see Peng 2005). Therefore, pro-forms should be the most typical "lexicogrammatical" category in textual size. Figure 2 – 5 describes the clausal and textual functions of pro-forms, where "m-w" stands for "meaning" and "wording" and the concrete arrows from word to clause mean, again, "structural" while the dotted arrows "organisational".

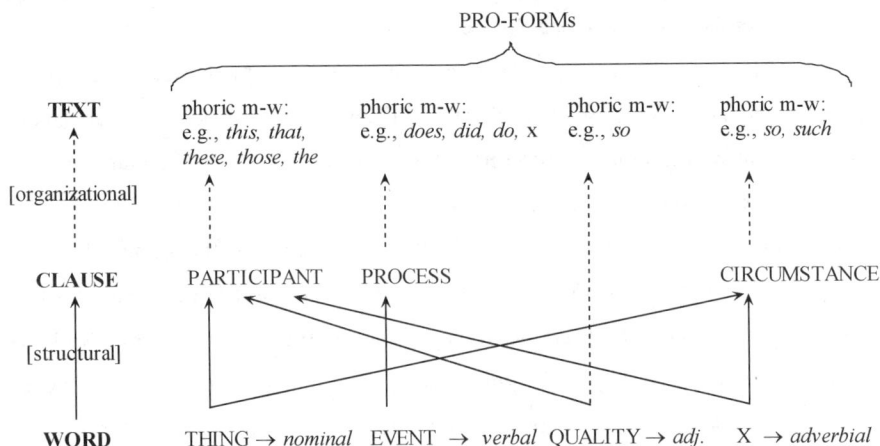

PRO-FORMs

TEXT	phoric m-w: e.g., *this, that,* *these, those, the*	phoric m-w: e.g., *does, did, do,* x	phoric m-w: e.g., *so*	phoric m-w: e.g., *so, such*
[organizational]				
CLAUSE	PARTICIPANT	PROCESS		CIRCUMSTANCE
[structural]				
WORD	THING → *nominal*	EVENT → *verbal*	QUALITY → *adj.*	X → *adverbial*

Figure 2 – 5: Textual nature of PRO-FORMS

To sum up, word classes such as pro-forms, determiners, adverbials, conjunctions, common nouns and lexical verbs are discourse-oriented in selection and distribution (Halliday & Hasan 1976; Hoey 1991a).

It is then reasonable to draw out the whole theoretical framework here. Figure 2 – 6(a) illustrates the ways by which the three metafunctions are associated with different typical ranks of lexicogrammar and Figure 2 – 6(b) indicates the constructing and orienting relations among different ranks (the curve lines along both sides); and both suggest the ways that meaning —

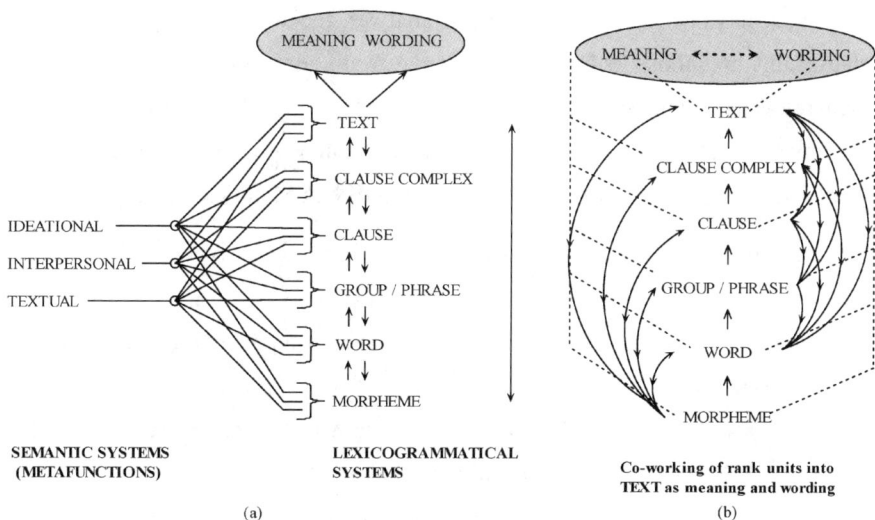

**SEMANTIC SYSTEMS
(METAFUNCTIONS)**

**LEXICOGRAMMATICAL
SYSTEMS**

(a)

**Co-working of rank units into
TEXT as meaning and wording**

(b)

Figure 2 – 6: English morphemes for constructing rank scales

wording unity may be produced in instantiation, as noted by the shadowed area. The distinctions into metafunctional components at different ranks are but analytical; in fact, these components serve the backbones in terms of which different ranks upward to text are constructed.

2.3　From morpheme to text: an instance illustration

　　The discussion so far have in a very general way focused on the potential semantic and lexicogrammatical functions of "morphemes" and "lexemes", with reference to the extension of the "rank scale" hierarchy up to "text". This section exemplifies the idea, though not merely from the morphemic and lexical perspectives; it will also take into account word group/phrase and clause to attend to all typical cases that work to create text as meaning and wording of the same size in complementarity. To be specific,

第二章　词汇语法的上限级阶——语篇

with what has been assumed above, it analyses the ways the components of clause unit and those below are oriented toward text wordings, along with their relevant meanings as socio-semantic units behind. As there are so many grammatical categories in SFL, only four particular areas are chosen for the demonstration (see Halliday 1994: 36; Halliday & Matthiessen 2014: 85):

(ⅰ) the "segmental" displacements of finite tense types in ideational grammar ("morphemic" to a large extent);

(ⅱ) the "prosodic" movements of appraisal components in interpersonal grammar (chiefly "lexical");

(ⅲ) the "culminative" flow of information in textual grammar (mainly "group and phrase"); and

(ⅳ) the "segmental" displacements of transitivity process types in, again, ideational grammar (principally "clausal").

The domain of constituent terms in each of the four cases (specified as "morphemic", "lexical", "group/phrasal" and "clausal") are but representative of the due kind; and there are other units as well, even though in minority.

Three points need emphasis. First, "meaning" takes the Hallidayan sense that systemic options are instantiated from their respective general systems, a selective process that specifies grammatical delicacy from general to particular to produce an integrated semantic unit out of all wording (Halliday 1978a). Second, the concept of "wording" here stands for the texture out of the sequential order of foregrounding entities on the one hand and the aligning of categories that advance their own lines of development on the other. "Temporality" is understood as a perspective that brings about the sequential order of relevant constituents being distributed and woven back and forth along their due categorical lines. Third, the "state-and-transition" methodology from Computational Linguistics is applied to describing the displacements of relevant items along text generation. It highlights how lexicogrammatical options are rendered into facets of discourse under the orientations of grammatical ranks next to and all above the relevant rank(s).

Therefore, the description will focus on the forward progression of discourse rather than the backward cohesion, as the former should entail the latter (see Hasan 1984; Martin 1992).

2.3.1 *From morpheme to text: the "segmental" displacements of finite tense types*

This sub-section provides a specific categorical exemplification for the illustration; that is, how the lexicogrammatical features of tense morphemes are structured into groups and clauses and organised into discourse from both meaning and wording aspects. This is one of the "segmental" displacements in the ideational grammar (Halliday & Matthiessen 2014: 85).

The choice pattern of tense finites should be discourse-oriented. That is, finite morphemes help make up verbal groups, which, with finite lexemes, are aligned and disposed by the relevant clauses and co-text. In fact, all finite elements in a text, whether morphemic (most of them of course) or lexical (in minor percentage), are chosen for constituting as well as representing one ideational facet of discourse wording and meaning.

Consider the first two sentences of the sample (see citations 1 − 2 above), which have 5 finite verbs (5 tense morphemes): *was*, *went*, *represented*, *were* and *was*, listed in the order as they occur in sequence. The sequentiality, as described in Figure 2 − 7, is suggested by the left-to-right overhead arrows. The small circles symbolise the state of each position in discourse and the arrows symbolize the transition, displacing from one state of entity occurrence to another.

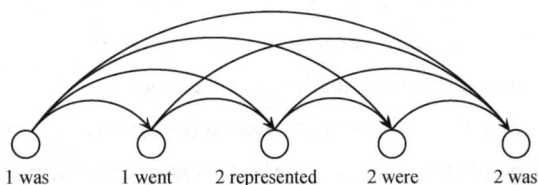

Figure 2 − 7: Tense morphemic displacements along sentences 1 − 2

The overhead arc arrows imply that all the items are associated to form a plane of their own in the local area. In fact, this correlation is a characteristic of any like categorical items in text: they are associated or onlined with one another in net and bond (Hasan 1984; Hoey 1991a & b).

In describing longer text, such a chain like Figure 2 – 5 would look rather clumsy and miscellaneous if all arrows and the entity circles are present. So the model should be simplified. Figure 2 – 8 is such an attempt that visualises the tense presentation of the text. This is the wording side of the temporality because it is characterised with linearity as formal characteristic on the "surface of discourse". In this figure, projecting and projected elements are indicated with parentheses "[ ]". The number at the beginning of each item stands for the sentence sequential order; the capitalised elements in "( )" are those omitted along the text process; each dotted arrow beginning with a cross dash head (therefore in "T" shape) means start or continuity of identical category whereas each concrete arrow beginning with a small circle stands for the due entity or feature, that is, the state of that moment of discourse continuity: it is no longer drawn in the arc shape; and its general displacement implies logogenetic sequentiality unfolding as being temporal. When category continuity line and sequentiality continuity line conflate, only the latter is manifested for visual obviousness.

The text is permeated with "past" time construal, a general frame projecting other tense types by embedding (Sentence 7) and by verbal or mental projections (Sentences 7, 9, 10, 13, 21 and 22).

Narrative genre may proceed with pure present tenses as can be evidenced, for example, with another flash fiction text entitled *Centerfold* (Appendix). The tense types are a kind of grammatical metaphor (i.e., incongruent way of meaning realisation), resulting from personal interest; they should all be in the past form when unmarked, but all are presented in the general present, a metaphorical mode of encoding.

There are also texts in which tense types are determined by subject matters, as in the third flash fiction text *The Human Pyramid* (Appendix). The tenses are lexicogrammatically congruent with the events that take place.

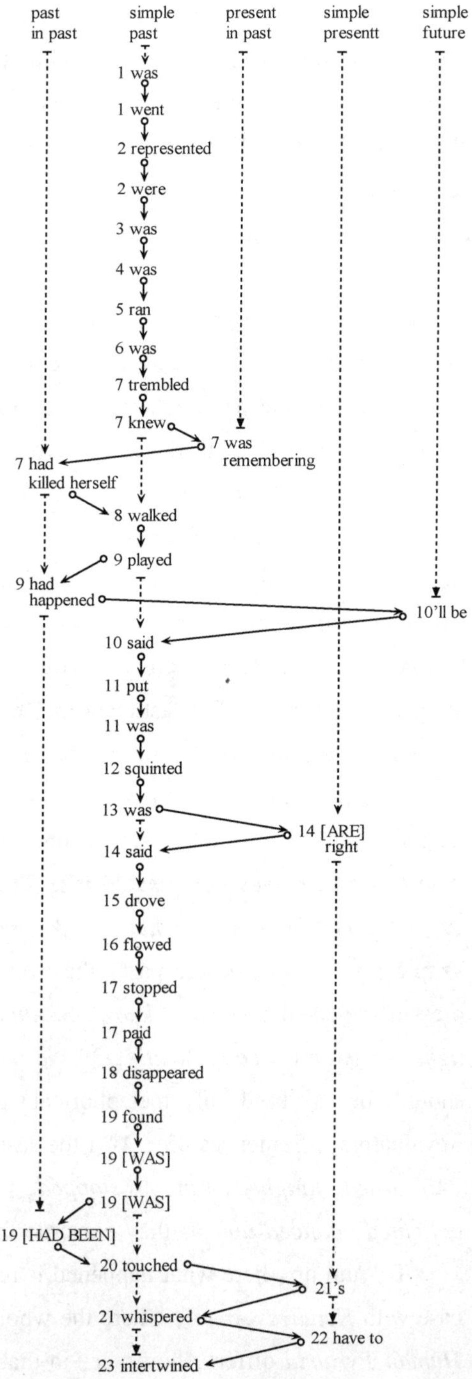
past in past
simple past
present in past
simple presentt
simple future
1 was
1 went
2 represented
2 were
3 was
4 was
5 ran
6 was
7 trembled
7 knew
7 was remembering
7 had killed herself
8 walked
9 played
9 had happened
10'll be
10 said
11 put
11 was
12 squinted
13 was
14 [ARE] right
14 said
15 drove
16 flowed
17 stopped
17 paid
18 disappeared
19 found
19 [WAS]
19 [WAS]
19 [HAD BEEN]
20 touched
21's
21 whispered
22 have to
23 intertwined

Figure 2-8: Tense morphemes and lexemes working for text wording

The first clause of the text (*These neighbors of mine* ***are driving*** *me nuts*) describes an ongoing, "current" condition in which the narrator is suffering, where the tense is present in present ("present progressive"). The two clauses in the second sentence are in simple past, narrating how the situation came into being (*it* ***was*** *a matter of clothing, then it* ***got*** *out hand*). The second and third paragraphs (Sentences 3 − 10) present the general state of what the first clause describes, and all the clauses are in simple present (3 *walks*, 4 *there're*, 5 *there're*, 6 *wear*, 7 *keep*, 8 *that's*, 8 *can*, 8 *wears*, 9 *trains* and 10 *can't*). The next three paragraphs (Sentences 11 − 17) are concerned with the past, where the tenses are past-oriented in general, and the presents are all embedded by verbal projections as *asked* (11 *what's*, *what's*), *said* (12 *am guessing*, 13 *get*) and *said* (15 *[IS]*). The paragraph that begins with *Now* (Sentences 18 − 23) shuffles with the alternations of simple present (18 *don't*, 20 *like*, 22 *that's*; 23 [IS]), past in present (19 *I've got*; traditional "present perfect tense") and simple past (21 *wasn't*, *became*, 22 *started*) as the events construed are related to the present and to the past respectively. The last clause in this paragraph, namely, sentence 23, omits its predicate, which should be simple present too as it identifies the current state, in a metaphorical way though: *naked-human pyramids*. Sentences 24 − 30 are all in simple present that conveys the constant present state (24 *try*, *comes*, 25 *it's*, 26 *it's*, 27 *have to*, *they're*, 28 *knows*, *need*, 29 *[NEED]*, 30 *that's*, *what's*). But sentences 31 − 43 are in alternative simple present and simple past: the events take place in the past, with the present projected (32 *don't know*, 35 *thanks*, *no thanks*, 36 *how about*, 37 *tight shorts and a cap*, 38 *it's*, 39 *we're*, 41 *can*, *can*, 43 *get*). 33 *could* should be a kind of metaphorical use, which is modality-oriented (evaluative). Sentences 45 − 47 (the last paragraph) are all in simple past (45 *turned*, *laughed*, *ran*, 46 *stopped*, *watched*, *fell off*, *seemed*, *tumbled*, *delighted*, *danced up*) as they construe the state of the past.

To sum up, here what happened is represented as it was. This is also the case with *Headless Angel*, where the whole situation is set up in the past. *The Human Pyramid* differs, however, in that it contains all spans of time: past, present and future, although the simple future (in sentence 42) is modality-natured again.

Figure 2 - 9 is the model of displacements on the "surface" of the discourse. For space limitation, both the simple future in 42 and the present

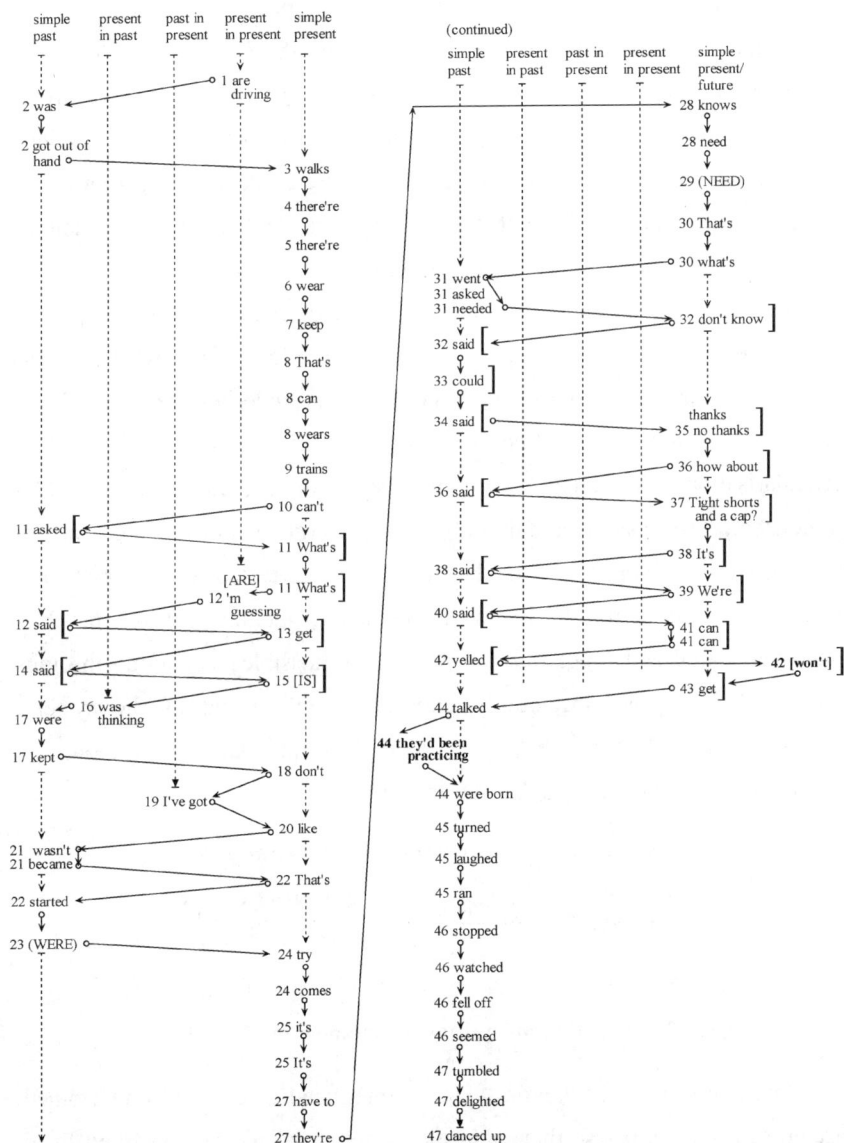

Figure 2 - 9: Unmarked tenses in *The Human Pyramid*

in past in past in 44 (traditional "past perfect" or "pluperfect" tense) are not singled out with proper vertical category lines from those of the simple past and simple present respectively, but they are bold-faced for distinction.

Note that all that have been figured out are grammatical in the SFL sense as they are presented so in terms of their respective syntagms.

So far in this section I have been illustrating the view that the deployed tense morphemes, along a few lexical items, are structured into word groups and clauses and organised into text, with clause complex in the middle bearing both structural and organisational natures. Meanwhile, morphemic choices are oriented with text types: different text types may demand different ways of organisation of tense items.

Now, a schematic description of the underlying meaning aspect to support the wording texture is presented above. In fact, from what has been contented so far, the whole systemic network that underlies the generation of tense wording texture may be described as: (i) time domain + (ii) particularisations by delicacy + (iii) sequentiality, all being in AND relationship. The system contains all those general factors that generate the meaning and wording aspects of the discourse. Intertextually, all practical or potential discourses in different social contexts, including those that have already appeared and those that are potentially possible, constitute the tense systems of 36 types; instantially, however, only some of the systemic options occur each time that work towards sequential organisation. The relevant systemic network looks like that in Figure 2 − 10.

Figure 2 − 10: The temporal unit of meaning in *Headless Angel*

This is no longer sequential, but an integrated categorical unit from the instantiated options per se that yield all the temporal pieces construed by the relevant finite clauses.

However, this figure blurs two aspects of temporality meaning behind the two-dimensional wording plane presented in Figure 2 - 7. This can be explained from two angles.

One, the respective temporality domains witness a process of due accumulations: present in past appears 1 time (3. 03%: 7 *was remembering*); past in past 3 times (9.09%: 7 *had killed herself*, 9 *had happened* and 19 *[HAD BEEN]*); and simple past amounts to 29 times (87.99%), three of which (10 *said*, 14 *said* and 21 *whispered*) in turn project 3 times of simple present (14 *[ARE] right*, 21's and 22 *have to*), and one of which projects 1 time of simple future (10'*ll be*).

All these figures can be described with a pie chart with the different distributions; however, the pie chart comes to its current shape by a course of accumulation from the first categorical components to the last ones. The accumulation process can then be visualised as a cone to advance the discursive categorical progression, a model that starts from one categorical component and then switches to another and so on till the text reaches its full fledge and ends there. At this stage of concern, a discourse is a course of accumulation along tense texturing as wording in the foregrounding sense on the one hand and a vertically expansion cone with the alternative relevant temporal categories as meaning on the other. Since the latter is not able to be directly "observed", it is then said to lie behind the "surface" plane of discourse, gathering the relevant temporality domains from the currently ongoing tense elements (see Figure 2 - 11).

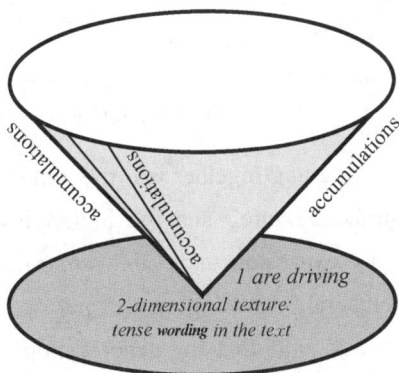

Figure 2 - 11: **Accumulation model of temporal meanings**

Here the bottom plane stands for the tense texture that was presented in detail in Figure 2 - 7; and the up-growing cone stands, analytically, for the expanding process of the respective domains of temporal meanings out of their tense texturing. The cone is no longer understood as a 2 - dimentional pie chart, which is the final stage of accumulation, overlooking the accumulation process, which concerns the ever increasing process in each domain of temporality meaning. Note, however, that the projected tenses are not separately presented for the purpose of brevity; in fact, they form a domain of their own attached to the meaning unit of the past.

Two, PAST in this text is the underlying meaning unit of the entire text, which should be one at a more abstract level that lies further behind the accumulations. This can be treated as the other way round of the growing process. That is, it is a course of generalisations and integrations from the semantic assembling by attending all the way to its holistic motif (s) of the speaker or writer. In fact, it is this motif that guides the discourse to proceed as it appears to be in the expansion. This is also a concomitant process along the interwoven surface texturing and the immediate underlying categorical domain accumulating. The model can also be envisaged as a cone, but in the opposite direction (see Figure 2 - 12).

the meaning unit
of PAST

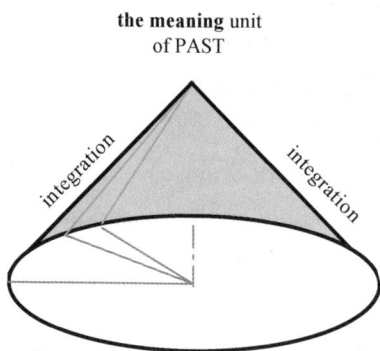

Figure 2 - 12: The integration process of meaning-making

Putting together all the three aspects of the text, namely, (i) the surface texture, and the underlying spindle of meaning-making process of (ii) expansion and (iii) contraction, then the textual mechanism of the temporality making model per se can be drawn as something like Figure 2 - 13. Note that the general motif built into the contraction process is here singled out and placed beside the spindle and texture for analytical purpose: In fact, a motif becomes a motif only along the process during which the speaker or writer is creating his text; one does have something beforehand in the mind, but that is usually vague and unconscious and is able to be concretised only after it is realised by lexicogrammatical means, whether laid out by medium modes or not.

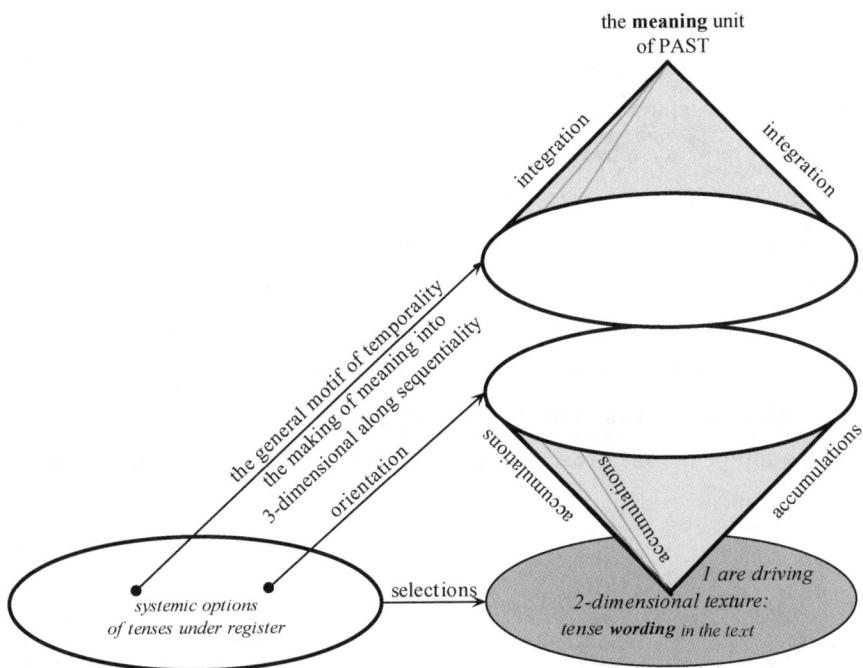

Figure 2 - 13: Making temporality along sequentiality by general motif

The bottom level of the model symbolizes the 2 - dimensional wording plane, which in turn amasses the temporality categories into the increasing cone upward toward a plane, the two of which in turn enable the general motif realisation into the ever-contracting cone up to a point.

Centerfold has simple present (e.g., *goes*, *leaves*), present in present (*is bleeding*) and past in present (*has disappeared/vanished*), all focusing on the PRESENT as the underlying socio-semantic unit of the text (see Figure 2 - 14).

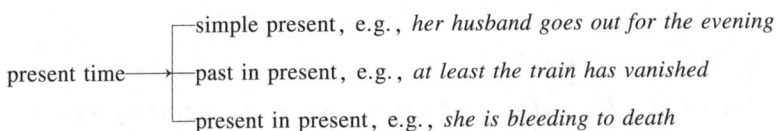

```
                    ┌─ simple present, e.g., her husband goes out for the evening
present time ──────→├─ past in present, e.g., at least the train has vanished
                    └─ present in present, e.g., she is bleeding to death
```

Figure 2 - 14: The temporal unit of meaning in *Centerfold*

A multi-dimensional model like Figure 2 - 13 can be visualised as well for this text *Centerfold*, which is omitted here for saving space.

The Human Pyramid appears to have both the present and the past; but, with the "present" as the perspective from which the "past" is implicitly projected, the temporal meaning of this text is still PRESENT. Altogether, there are 6 primary tenses: past in past (past perfective; 1 time, 1.64%), simple past (32 times, 52.46%), projecting 1 time of present in present (present progressive), 14 time of simple present and 1 time of simple future, present in past (past progressive; 1 time, 1.64%), present in present (1 time, 1.64%) and simple present (25 times, 40.98%). These accumulate respectively their due temporality domains, as envisaged in Figure 2 – 13. The bottom point refers to the first temporal element in the text: *are driving*; and the top point, the general "present", is the end that has contracted from all the temporality domains (see Figure 2 – 15).

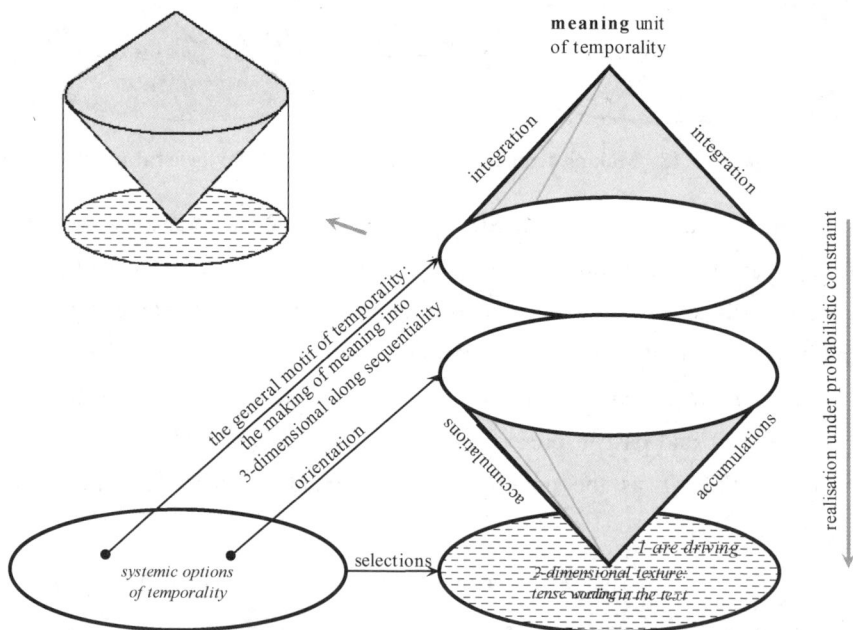

Figure 2 – 15: Accumulating and integrating of temporality along texturing

To sum up, repetitive uses of finite morphemes and the relevant lexical items gather their systemic potentials (recursive patterns) whereas systemic options are in turn chosen to orient the production and comprehension of temporality meanings as the integrated socio-semantic unit out of the ongoing tense types in use. The two aspects in terms of selection and orientation depend on each other for making the logogenetic process with the selected options in system(s) underlying the sequence of the foregrounding level, the two sides of which form a unity of their own and contribute to each other in collaboration, hence complementary: the separated presentation in the figure is analytical for clarity.

2.3.2 From word to text: "prosodic" movement of appraisals

The appraisal aspect of interpersonal meaning is the area that embodies one of the most typical complementarities between lexis and grammar because appraisal components, though characteristically loaded with emotive potentials, are themselves grammaticalised in the sense of colligation or "mutual expectancy" (Halliday 2008: 70, 172).

The appraisal is that aspect of language function that represents the speaker/writer's (inter) subjective presence in text. It has three general categories: Attitude, Engagement and Graduation (Martin & White 2005). Altogether, they can be specified into 26 sub-categories.

Attitude contains three main sub-types of feelings: Affect, Judgement and Appreciation. Affect refers to "the emotional charge between the interactants — a parameter that has been explored in terms of sociometric roles in sociology and social psychology" (Matthiessen et al. 2010: 47). It concerns [1] Inclination (e.g. 2 *promise*, 11 *hungry*), [2] Happiness (1 *honeymoon*, 2 *remembering* [evoked, or temporarily realised in indirect way], 9 *what had happened* [evoked], 21 *lover*, 23 *intertwined* [evoked]), [3] Satisfaction (absent from the sample; see Martin and White's "ennui", "displeasure"; "interest", "pleasure"), and [4] Security (4 *horrible, shock*, 7 *trembled*, 18 *disappeared*). Judgement is "the source ... in terms of some parameter of people, typically of their behaviour" (ibid., pp. 130 – 131). It includes [5] Normality ("how special?"; e.g. 3 *dive* [evoked], 10 *all right*, 12 *squinted*, 19 *palm-to-palm in prayer*), [6] Capacity ("how capable?"; examples absent from the sample; but, e. g. *intelligent*), [7] Tenacity ("how dependable?"; 2 *change*, *forget*, 3 *die*, 5 *ran*, *yelling*, 7 *killed herself*), [8] Veracity ("how honest?"; absent; but, e.g. *honest*), and [9] Propriety ("how far beyond reproach?"; 9 *play volleyball* [evoked], *oblivious*). Appreciation is the " source for evaluating phenomena in 'aesthetic' terms, either subjectively ('I like it') or objectively ('it is pleasing')" (ibid., p. 56). It associates [10] Reaction (impact: "did it grab me?"; quality: "did I like it?"; e. g. 4 *gorgeous*, *sunny*, 12 *glare*, 13 *cold*), [11] Composition (balance: "did it hang together?"; complexity: "was it hard to follow?"; e. g. 16 *perfect*, 17 *ruin*, *roofless*, 19 *decapitated*, *broken off*), and [12] Valuation ("was it worthwhile?" e. g. 5 *doctor* [evoked], 6 *hopeless*, 19 *angel's wing*, 21 *vocation*, 22 *home*).

Engagement is "the resource for speaker/writer to engage with others in the process of evaluation" (ibid., p. 88). It has 8 sub-categories sorted into two general categories: (i) Contract — [13] Deny (e.g. 2 *not*, 7 *never*) and [14] Counter (6 *but*, 11 *though*) under Disclaim; [15] Concur (14 *right*), [16] Pronounce (10 *I said*) and [17] Endorse (absent; but *the report demonstrates/shows/proves that* …) under Proclaim; and (ii) Expand — [18] Entertain (10 *I'll*, 21 *almost*), [19] Acknowledge (14 *she said*, 21 *whispered*) and [20] Distance (absent; but, e. g. *X claimed that* …).

Graduation is "the resource for grading or scaling", up scaling or down scaling attitude and engagement (ibid., p. 108). It concerns [21] Number (2 *much*, 10 *both*), [22] Mass/Presence (9 *tiny*), [23] Extent (1 *three months*, 2 *so*, 2 *around*, 3 *across the street*, 7 *before*), [24] Quality (degree: 7 *never*), [25] Process (Vigour: absent; but *slightly disturb* — *greatly disturb*; *like* — *love* — *adore*), and [26] Focus (2 *all*, 13 *all*, 21 *almost*).

Note that appraisal realisation is typically associated with lexical items, and that is what the sub-title is designed to convey; but it is not the whole story as word groups, phrases, clauses/clause complexes and even paragraphs with parallel patterns may also be engaged in enacting evaluative meanings, in particular in the areas of engagement and graduation, as shown in Martin & White (2005).

A word is in demand for this figure. First, the numbers before and after the entities are sentence sequential and categorical respectively. Second, the ongoing process indicated by those arrows with a small circle at the start is the unidirectionality of the discourse, which is oriented and shuffled by vertically dotted arrows with cross dash head implying the start or continuity of like categories, the two of which, i.e. unidirectional advance and back-and-forth alternation, reflect the application of the principle of trace online. When category line and the temporality line conflate, only the latter is manifested in concrete arrows. Third, some items branch off, suggesting simultaneity of two kinds of appraisal features, which split linearity into 2 - dimensional progression in local areas, as those in sentences 4 (*nowhere*), 7 (*never*), 10 (*'ll*), 14 (*right*), 17 (*searching for the sky*) and 21 (*almost*) each, forming a local feature of netting and bonding. Note that this is a type of textual organisation by which cohesive ties are embodied in the sequential displacements of the semantic components (see Hasan 1985b).

However, recall that Hasan treats a texture like this as part of text meaning (Hasan 1978: 228); the present illustration shows that texture like this should be text wording because it is the displacive movement in unidirectionality or linearity that weaves discrete grammaticalised appraisal options into a texture as syntagmatically enacted "on the surface of discourse". That is, the texturing process resembles to the syntagmatic course of transitivity configuration in that they share a similar course of alternative component replacing linearization, which has a noticeable formal characteristic; the difference rests with the fact that, for the former, the categorical components are simultaneously sorted into respective homogeneous categorical strings, the result of which is 2 - dimensional in organisational constitution, whereas the latter is 1 - dimensional in structural nature.

AFFECT	JUDGEMENT	APPRECIATION	ENGAGEMENT	GRADUATION

1 three months [23]

1 pregnant [12]

1 honeymoon [2]

2 promise [1]

2 not [13]

2 change [7]

2 not [13]

2 forget [7]

2 so [25]

2 much [21]

2 world [12]

2 all [26]

2 around [23]

2 waiting [10]

3 dive [5]

3 fourth floor [21]

3 die [7]

3 right [26]

3 acorss the street [23]

4 horrible [4]

4 shock [4]

4 nowhere [13]　4 nowhere [25]

4 gorgeous [10]

4 sunny [10]

4 [23]

5 ran [7]

5 yelling [7]

5 doctor [12]

5 yelling [7]

5 police [12]

6 but [14]

6 hopeless [12]

7 trembled [4]

7 never [13]　7 never [25]

7 before [23]

7 I knew [16]

7 remembering [2]

7 killed herself [7]

8 hugging [7]

8 hard [24]

9 tiny [22]

9 played
volleyball [9]

9 oblivious [9]

9 what had
happened

9 200 feet away [23]

10 'll [18]

10 'll [25]

10 all right [5]

10 I said [16]

10 finally [23]

10 both [21]

11 untouched [13]

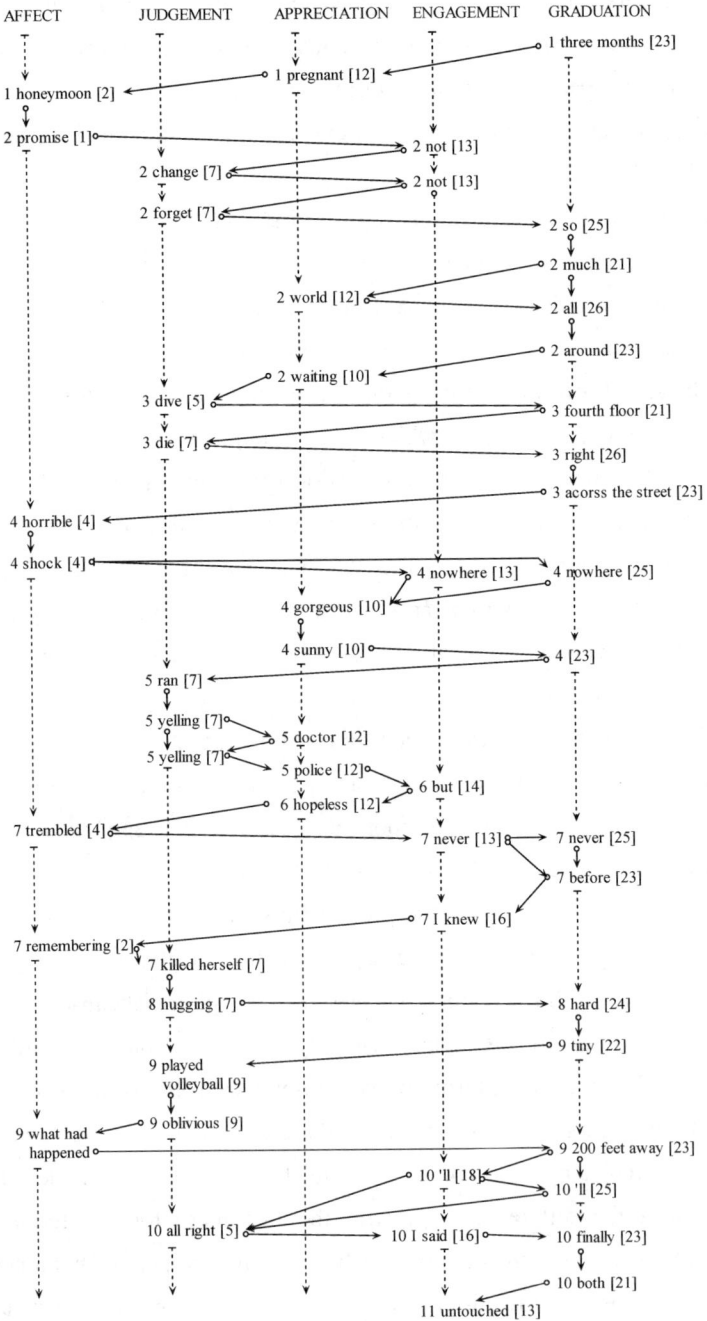

(To be continued)

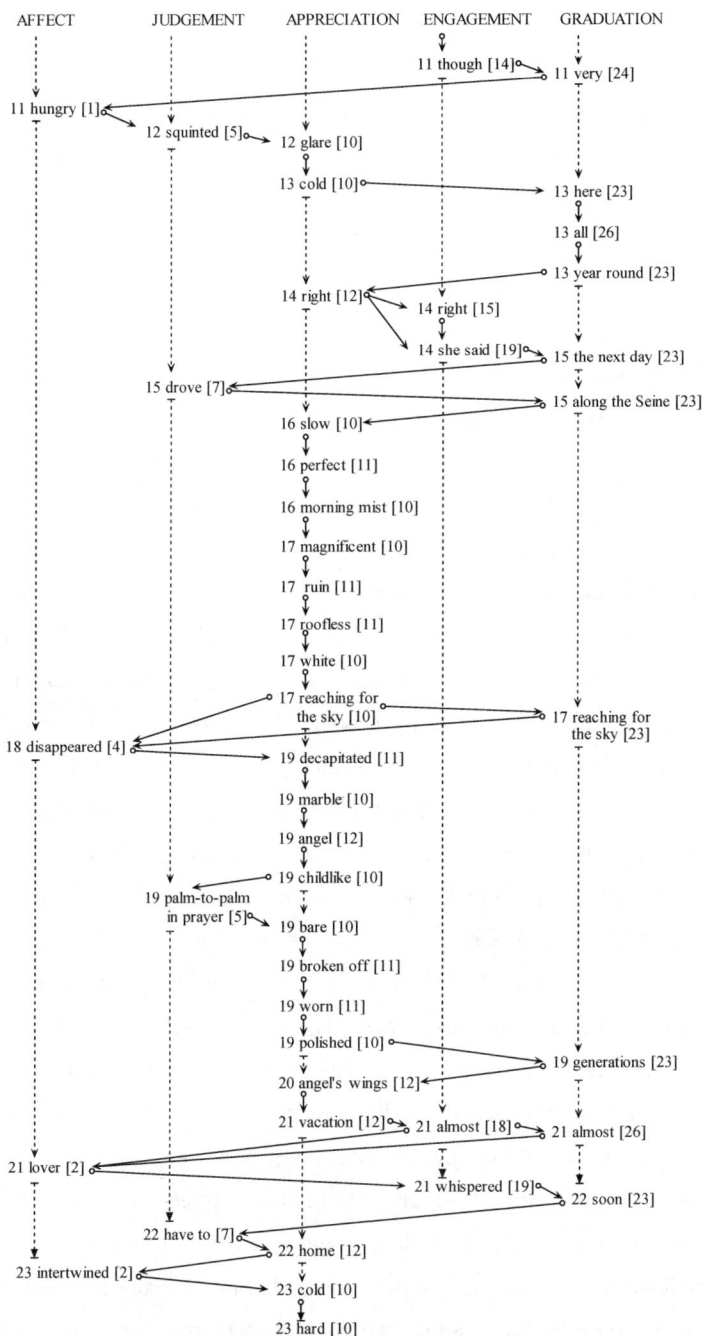

Figure 2－16: Prosodic movement for appraisal texture in the text

Another reason for this wording argumentation lies in that, the three general categories, i. e., attitude, engagement and graduation, stand in layered relations, with engagement and graduation manipulating attitude in alternative ways. However, the texture is generated by sequentiality, disregarding their AND relation, which proves that it should be formal in nature.

Now we move on to outlining the underlying meaning-making process, outlining because this is after all not the focus of this chapter. It is outlined along the surface texturing description for the purpose of showing what backs up the surface texture and how it looks like.

There are two co-working ways for making text meaning, one being Expansion by accumulating and the other being Integration by generalising, abstracting and/or metaphorising.

Expansion in this case is a course being displayed by considering the appraisal meanings of the different kinds in accumulating. The accumulating process is realised with the relevant categories and their sub-categories gathering their respective forces by probabilistic distribution and integration, the ultimate shape of which can be visualised as a cone. Take the text of *Headless Angel* as an example. The total occurrences of the appraisal features in this text amount to 101 times, with Affect 11 times (10.89%), Judgement 16 times (15. 84%), Appreciation 33 times (32. 67%), Engagement 13 times (12. 87%), and Graduation 28 times (27. 72%). Of these, the appreciation items have the highest frequency because the text involves considerable object descriptions at the stage expressed by the sentences from 16 to 21 (see Figure 2 - 3). Next to it is graduation, i.e., the up- or down-scaling operation of the attitude and engagement in the text. Here a pie chart can be used for describing the distributions; however, this is but a static observation of the result of accumulation. The expansion course is in fact understood as an increasing cone-like growing process from the first appraisal component *three months* (i.e., extent of graduation) to the last one 23 *hard* (reaction of appreciation), along which each category grows onlined. Note that a pie chart presentation is only the end look of the expanding cone, with the accumulation process ignored.

It should be clear that the increasing process has two prototypical extremes, one being summation and the other blending, a point that requires lengthy elaboration; but the numerous discourse analyses by applying the RST (e.g., Halliday & Webster 2014), for example, are good cases in point: the logico-semantic relations of elaboration, extension and enhancement (EEE) for making expansion process display the three typical types of integration (EEEs), all contributing to the summation presented above.

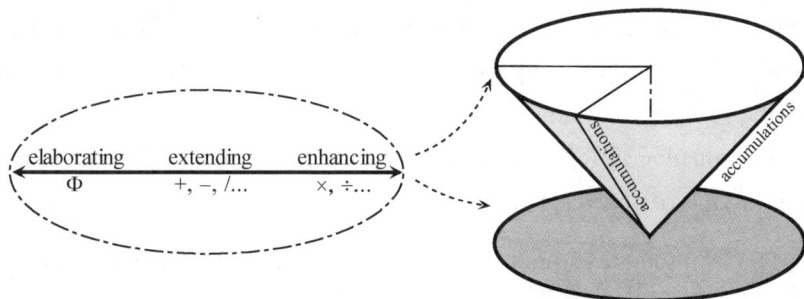

Figure 2 - 17: EEEs: three typical types of integration behind the surface summation

Integration is the other way around: along the process of all appraisal components being textured and coned to distill and observe the general evaluative motif of the whole text. This can be visualised as a cone-making process too, but in the opposite direction. To be specific, all those appraisal domains singled out above serve at the same time to point towards a general "underlying theme" of judgement: a kind of condition in which human beings stay. That is, the text is committed more to implicit judgement about the morality of the human world than to the surface appreciative description, a case that shows meaning-wording disparity of attitude in their due stratum of organisations.

Since the process of expansion is easier to understand, let me illustrate that of integration. Consider the last sentence of the text:

(4) 23 Our fingers intertwined on the cold, hard stone.

A contrastive feature can be obtained here: the *cold* setting and the characters' loving and optimistic behaviour.

On the one hand, the earthly world was selfish and indifferent:

(5) 9 Young men in tiny bathing suits played volleyball on the sand, oblivious to what had happened two hundred feet away.

It reminds one of two images narrated in history. One association is the scene Cain answered God's question where his brother Abel was after Cain, for being jealous, killed Abel and hid the body: "I know not: Am I my brother's keeper?" (*Genesis*, 4: 9). The other association is the famous painting entitled *Landscape with the Fall of Icarus* by Pieter Brueghel (1525 – 1569), which criticises people who are cold, merciless and apathetic to others' sufferings.

The situation in (3) is echoed by further description of the old Atlantic water, a kind of apperception with analogy:

(6) 12 I squinted against the glare off the Atlantic. 13 The water was cold here, all year round.

The case of (4) and the related circumstances suggest the social environment in which the disaster happened, as set up at the beginning of the text:

(7) 3 Then in Normandy, strolling down to the beach for lunch, we saw a woman dive from a fourth-floor window and die on the sidewalk, right across the street.

On the other hand, however, that is not entirely what the world was. In fact, some people were conscientious to their companies:

(8) 5 People **ran** to the rag-doll body, **yelling for a doctor**, **yelling** for the police.

This represents another side of the human nature. In fact, the intimacy expressed in Sentence 23 comes from the interaction between the two opposite sex parties, a positive relation that gives rise to reproduction power that maintains human love in ensuing generation. In fact, that Beth was conceiving posterity, at a stage of early pregnancy in particular, does suggest one cardinal tie among human beings, as evidenced with the reactions after the death event:

(9) Bodily support: 7 Beth trembled **against** me in a way she never had before ... 8 **Hugging each other hard**, Beth and I walked to the shore.

(10) Spiritual encouragement: 10 "It'll be all right," I said finally, to **both** of us; 14 "Right," she said.

(11) Go on enjoying planned journey (routine life): 15 The next day we drove the abbey road, along the Seine ... 17 We stopped at the Abbaye de Jumièges and paid to enter the magnificent ruin, roofless walls and white stone spires reaching for the sky.

All these, including the last sentence cited as (4), work for making an invoked meaning of "tenacity", behaviour reliable and dependable for living the human life. It is at least a natural necessity to guarantee the upcoming successfulness of human beings, i.e., the hope and reason for survival, as against whatever the social surroundings might be. In other words, people should support one another.

Taking together both sides, the hopeful, positive attitude should have a more purposeful advocating value than what the word *hopeless* (line 6) is represented to suggest, as the end weight (the last sentence; see citation 2) pronounces it. In fact, the last part of the text says more about it:

(12) 20 Beth touched the angel's wings. 21 "Vacation's almost over, lover," she whispered. 22 "Soon we have to fly home."

Therefore, an invoked "tenacity" meaning as the general motif or meaning unit of *Headless Angel* can be generalised out of the text: to hold positively to life and to each other to live on, which sounds encouraging and sympathetic and promising. The negative aspect, on the contrary, functions as a counterpart to help highlight the positive value, the latter of which should be what Hasan (1967, 1985c) calls the "underlying" theme or the "symbolic articulation" as verbal art (cf. Halliday 1966d). This is a case of generalisation and abstraction, with no metaphorisation committed.

Now the accumulation and integration model of the underlying appraisal meaning as well as the surface wording texture (Figure 2 – 3) can be schematically put together as an organic whole (see Figure 2 – 18). This is a multi-dimensional model that embodies the principle of layered **constitution**.

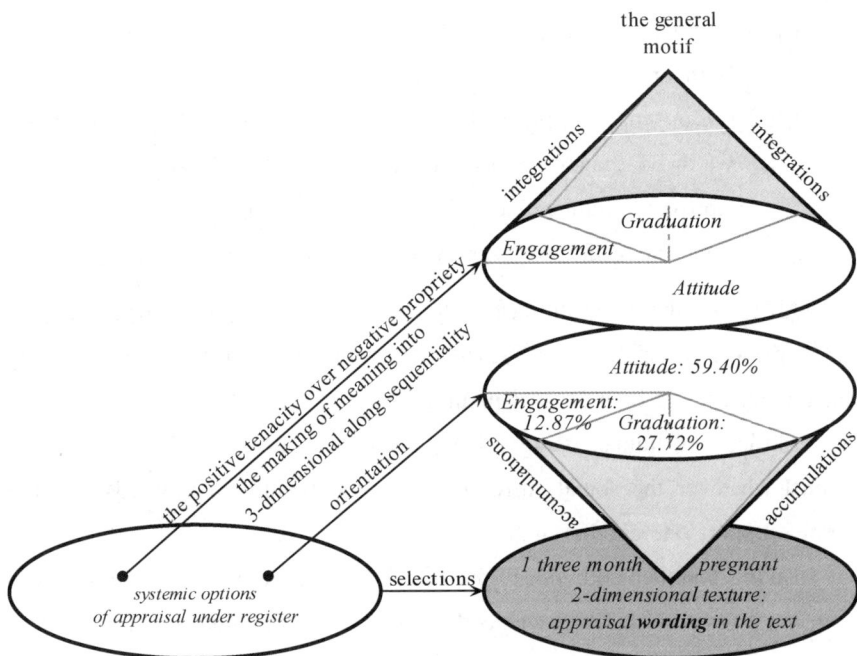

Figure 2 – 18: Appraisal meaning and wording in *Headless Angel*

This is a content triangle through selection expression: (i) options of semantic categories in different metafunctions, (ii) wording textures out of selection expressions and (iii) ever increasing and also integrating textual meaning unit(s) from the former two. The first belongs to the sub-systems of semantics at stake whereas the latter two belong to instance. Textures are visibly foregrounded wordings whereas selection options and meaning unit(s) are the correspondent underlying or "deep" operational objects that can only be worked out through experienced reading; but they should stay in constant awareness of the speaker or writer to make a text sensible.

It is apparent that (i) whatever the extent of the meaning unit of a text is, the wording should be the same size in category; (ii) the meaning and the wording aspects cannot be distinctly set apart: they are complementary and supportive to each other in their interwoven processes; and (iii) in consequence, the classical belief that text is only a socio-semantic unit should be no longer tenable (see Halliday 1978a, 1961), which will be argued in Section 4 below.

2.3.3 *From group/phrase to text: "culminative" flow of information*

There are two independent aspects of message configuration: Thematisation and Information. Since thematic progression in text has been fully explored (e.g., Fries 1981, 1995a & b, 2002; Kies 1988; Francis & Kramer-Dahl 1992; Rashidi 1992; Martin 1992: 434 – 448; Hasan & Fries 1995), the present attempt focuses on the information aspect. But it must be conscious that the two co-work to construct stretches of messages for text generation.

According to Halliday (1994: 299; Halliday & Matthiessen 2014: 120), thematisation is "speaker-oriented" while information is "listener-oriented"; but both are "speaker-selected". The theme-rheme selection repeats the "point of departure" of each unit of message, which starts with a big end and gradually declines, described as "diminuendo"; and the given-new selection usually renders the message the other way around, stopping with a big end (the focus), a process of "crescendo" (Halliday 1994: 337). In logogenetic process, such a model of thematic-diminuendo and information-crescendo unification occurs culminatively for making a text, along which each unit that occurs recedes to the status of basis for what to come next; and, on occasion, any one of those that is in the background may be brought up to close association, both locally and globally, with the newly appeared, such as *we* in the first sentence, and *our* in the second and the last sentences of the text; they are local theme within the relevant clauses and nominal group, and remain "given" even in long distance, guaranteed by the due co-text.

> (13) 1 Beth was three months pregnant when **we** went to France on **our** honeymoon ... 23 **Our** fingers intertwined on the cold, hard stone.

This is a typical case; and there may be other possibilities that locate between the typical Given and typical New. In order to observe the intermediate newsworthiness, we refer to Prince's (1981) taxonomy, regardless of theoretical differences for the moment (cf., Fries 1981, 1995a & b, 2002; see also Brown & Yule 1983: 182 – 184).

(i) GIVEN—

    (a) Situationally Evoked: ***Lucky me*** *just stepped in something.*

    (b) Textually Evoked: *Susie went to visit her grandmother and* ***the sweet lady*** *was making Peking Duck.*

    (b – 1) Current: *to the left of* <u>*the red line*</u> *about half a centimeter above* ***it***

    (b – 2) Displaced: *draw* <u>*a black triangle*</u> *... underneath* ***the triangle*** *...*

(ii) SEMI – GIVEN and SEMI – NEW—

    (c) Inferrable:

    (c – 1) Containing Inferrable: *Have you heard* ***the incredible claim that the devil speaks English backwards?***

    (c – 2) Noncontaining Inferrable: *I went to the post office and* ***the stupid clerk*** *couldn't find a stamp.*

(iii) NEW—

    (d) Unused: ***Rotten Rizzo*** *can't have a third term.*

    (e) Brand new:

    (e – 1) Brand-new Anchored: ***A rich guy I know*** *bought a Cadillac.*

    (e – 2) Brand-new Unanchored: *I bought* ***a beautiful dress.***

By applying this detailed model, the author makes an exhaustive analysis of the sample text and presents the result in Table 2-2 (Appendix), where the numbers at the beginning are sentence orders while those in " [ ] " are information entities sorted out and arranged in sequence, which obtain the property of grammatilisation. Note that pro-forms are systemically Given; but when they are laid out sequentially in the second part of an information unit, it may attain importance in the given-new interaction, such as, typically, (*to*) *both* (*of us*) in 10; however, most of such items are directly allocated to the textually evoked categories for their introductory and foundational role to lead up to what is meant to be unknown to the implied reader. Therefore, the relevant parts that contain such components are underlined in the unused and brand new groups.

With these individual elements, the "culminative" flow of information for the text can be described as Figure 2 – 19.

The texture describes one aspect of message culmination of the text, interwoven with the relevant thematic progression being omitted here. It is a kind of wording that displays the writer's personal perspective for the enabling process. However, it has its own uniqueness in that Given and New occur in an almost alternative way and that is how the general Given and New are close in number, the situation of which differs from that in the ideational or the interpersonal facet that may concentrate on some categories for comparatively long distances in occasion.

Now we focus on the meaning aspect of the information texture, in particular the expansion and the integration. We begin with the expansion side. The text has altogether 134 items of information, with 135 features in total (note sentence 19 with both textually evoked: current and containing inferable features): situationally evoked 4 times (2.96%), textually evoked (current) 32 times (23.7%), textually evoked (displaced) 13 times (9.63%), containing inferable 17 times (12.59%), noncontaining inferable 2 times (1.48%), unused 15 times (11.11%), brand-new anchored 18 times (13.33%) and unanchored 34 times (25.19%). All these form a pie chart of their own. Figure 2-20 is a 2-dimensional look of the accumulating process laid out with degree of newsworthiness weight to highlight the communicative attractiveness.

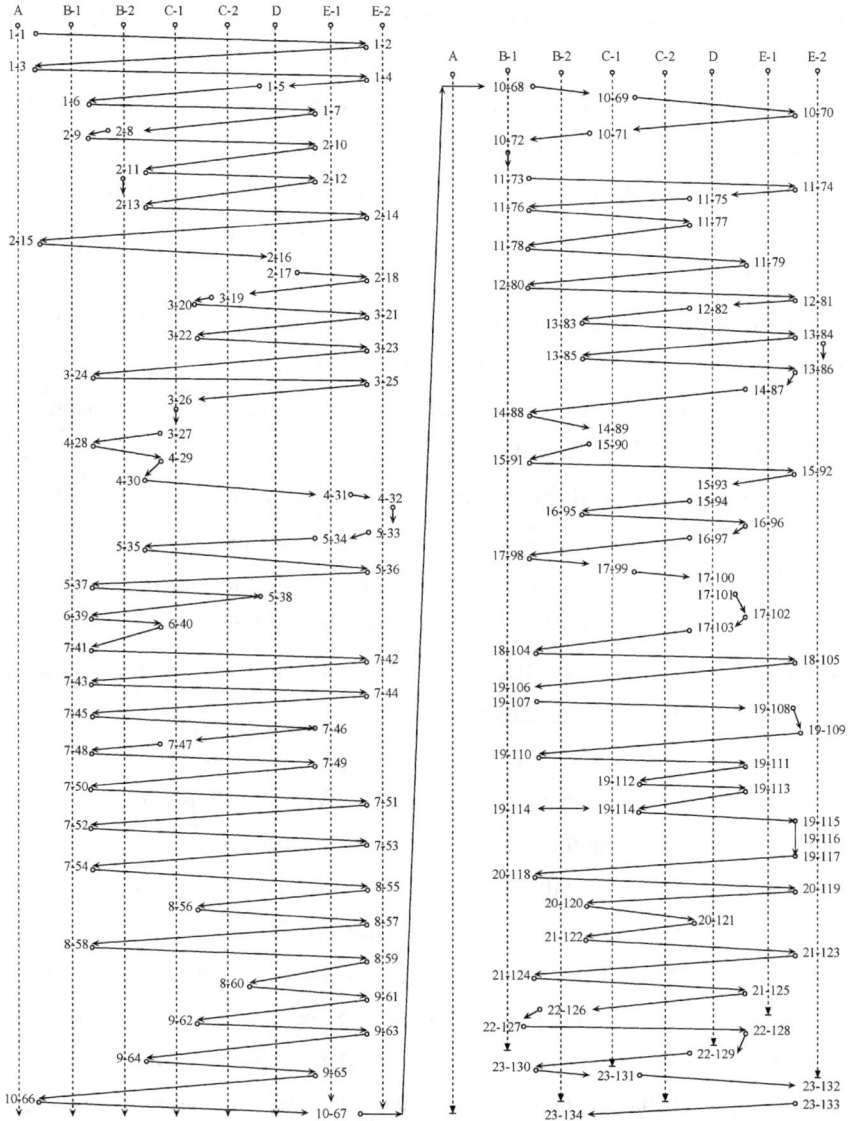

Figure 2‐19: "Culminative" information flow in the text

GIVEN SEMI-GIVEN / SEMI-NEW

NEW

50.36%

36.29% 14.07%

49.64%

15.19%

13.33%

11.11%

1.48%

12.59%

9.63%

23.7%

2.96%

e-1 e-2 d e-1 e-2

accumulations
accumulations
accumulations
accumulations
accumulations
accumulations
accumulations

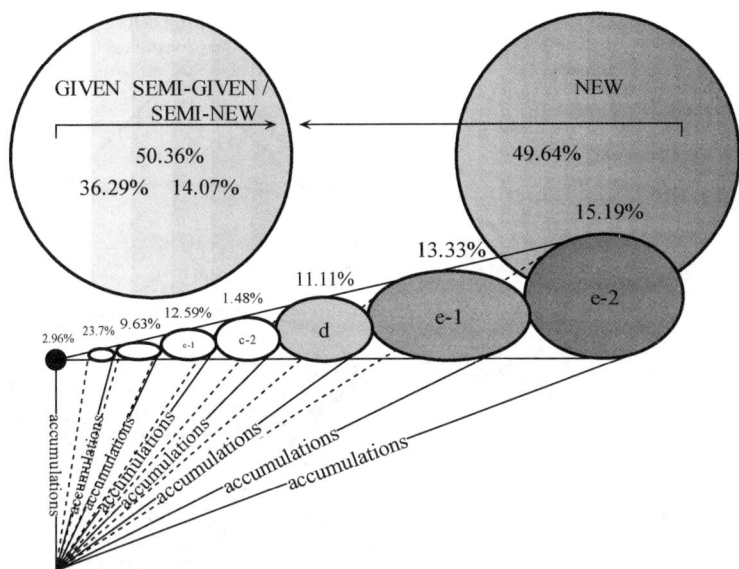

1 Beth: GIVEN-THEME

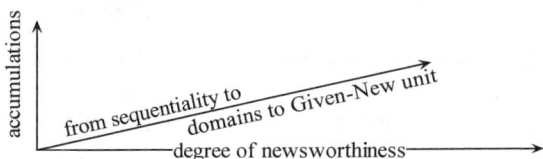

accumulations

from sequentiality to domains to Given-New unit

degree of newsworthiness

Figure 2 − 20: A specification of the accumulating process

In reality, however, the process, along the texturing, should be multi-dimensional, a cone-like form again as that of appraisal, along its generalisation and contraction. Figure 2 − 21 is the whole meaning-wording architecture in the dynamic, constructing sense. Martin's conceptions of hyper-new and macro-new should be in the lower cone in the ever-growing course because they are committed to a layered idea by recognising something hyper and macro, which are not configured on the surface of the general information flow of a text.

The Given-New model has attempted to claim that newsworthiness should be a matter of degree against the background of discourse. However, if a three-place criterion is used, that is, the first three as Given, inferable as Semi-Given/Semi-New and the other three as New, then the number of each

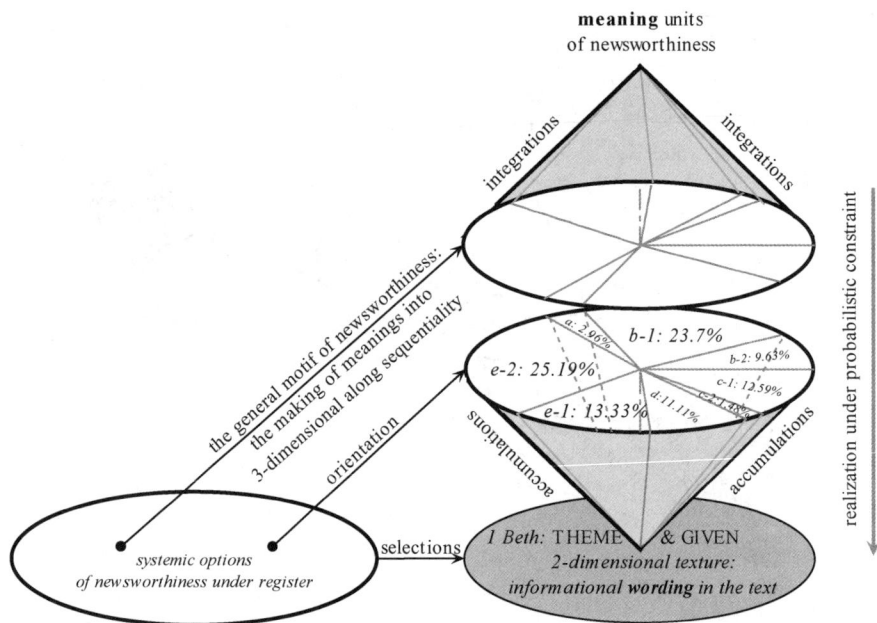

Figure 2 – 21: **Information flow into a multi-dimensional architecture**

of these three should be 49, 19 and 67; but from a two place angle as inferable is something that can be "recovered", the Given and the New are equal in number: 68 and 67. This suggests that a text must have enough Given for introducing newsworthiness and at the same time needs to have a comparable amount of New to maintain readers' curiosity. It is also noticeable that Given and New appear almost alternatively; in fact, only through repetitive alternations can a text in the informational respect satisfy the addresses' demand for story (see also Martin 1992: 452). These two perspectives explicate the reasonable binary division between Given and New elaborated by Halliday (1967 – 68, 1994; Halliday & Matthiessen 2014).

2.3.4 From clause to text: " segmental " displacements of processes

This last sub-section is concerned with a case within the domain of the clause, that is, the organisation of transitivity units and the underlying organic whole. The sample text, *Headless Angel*, has all the six types of transitivity processes: Material, Mental, Relational, Verbal, Behavioural and Existential (Halliday 1994: 106 – 144; Halliday & Matthiessen 2014: 213 – 220). All of them are specified into their categorical components according to their syntagmatic roles (Hasan 1987) and the result is presented in Table 2 – 4 (see Appendix).

The relevant wording process in terms of which a transitivity texture takes shape is described as Figure 2 – 22, where the focal parts of the respective local participants are attached.

The meaning aspect of the text can be constructed like what we did above. There are 55 transitivity processes, among which material amounts to 26 times (47. 27%), mental 6 times (10. 91%), relational 13 times (23.64%), verbal 2 times (3.64%), behavioural 7 times (12.73%) and existential 1 time (1.82%). This agrees in general with previous statistics (e.g., Peng 2000: 340 – 342; Matthiessen 1999, 2007: 807 – 814; Halliday & Matthiessen 2014: 215). Therefore, the ever-increasing cone to form a pie chart stands against the ever-contracting cone as the subject matter of this text: "incident in France travel", as described in Figure 2 – 23.

It is interesting to note that there should be a contextual strategy that manipulates the organisation. It is embodied in the way similar to "projection", a notion adapted from Halliday who uses it to describe the naming and content introduced by verbal and thinking acts (see Halliday & Matthiessen 2014: 508 – 549). Projection in the present sense, however, is concerned with whatever that is set off from a point of departure. The sample text, as a first-person narrative, is set off from the projector *I* who *saw*, *knew*, *decided*, *felt*, *heard* and *did* what are laid out respectively. Figure 2 – 24 presents each of these and their sub-cases to reveal the structural layers that underlie the texture of the text. In fact, this should be the contextual generic structure that determines the organisation of the text (cf. Hasan 1985a). It is built into the semantic unit under discussion.

第
一
部
分
　
理
论
范
式
探
新

MATERIAL	MENTAL	RELATIONAL	VERBAL	BEHAVIOURAL	EXISTENTIAL

1　was
(Beth, pregnant)

went
(we)

2　represented
(trip, promise)

let...change
(the baby,
who we were)

forget
(WE, that...)

was
(there, world)

[WAS]
(all, around)

waiting
(world/all)

3　strolling
(WE)

saw
(we, a woman)

dive
(WOMAN)

die
(WOMAN)

4　was
(it, horrible)

[CAME]
(shock)

5　ran
(people)

yelling
(people)

yelling
(people)

6　was
(it, hopeless)

7　trembled
(Beth)

never had TREMBLED
(she)

knew
(I, X)

was remembering
(she, X)

had killed
(sister, herself)

8　hugging
(WE, each other)

walked
(Beth and I)

9　played
(young men,
volleyball)

[WAS] oblivious to
(young men, X)

10　happened
(what)

will be
(it, all right)

said
(I, Y)

11　put
(I, X)

was
(I, hungry)

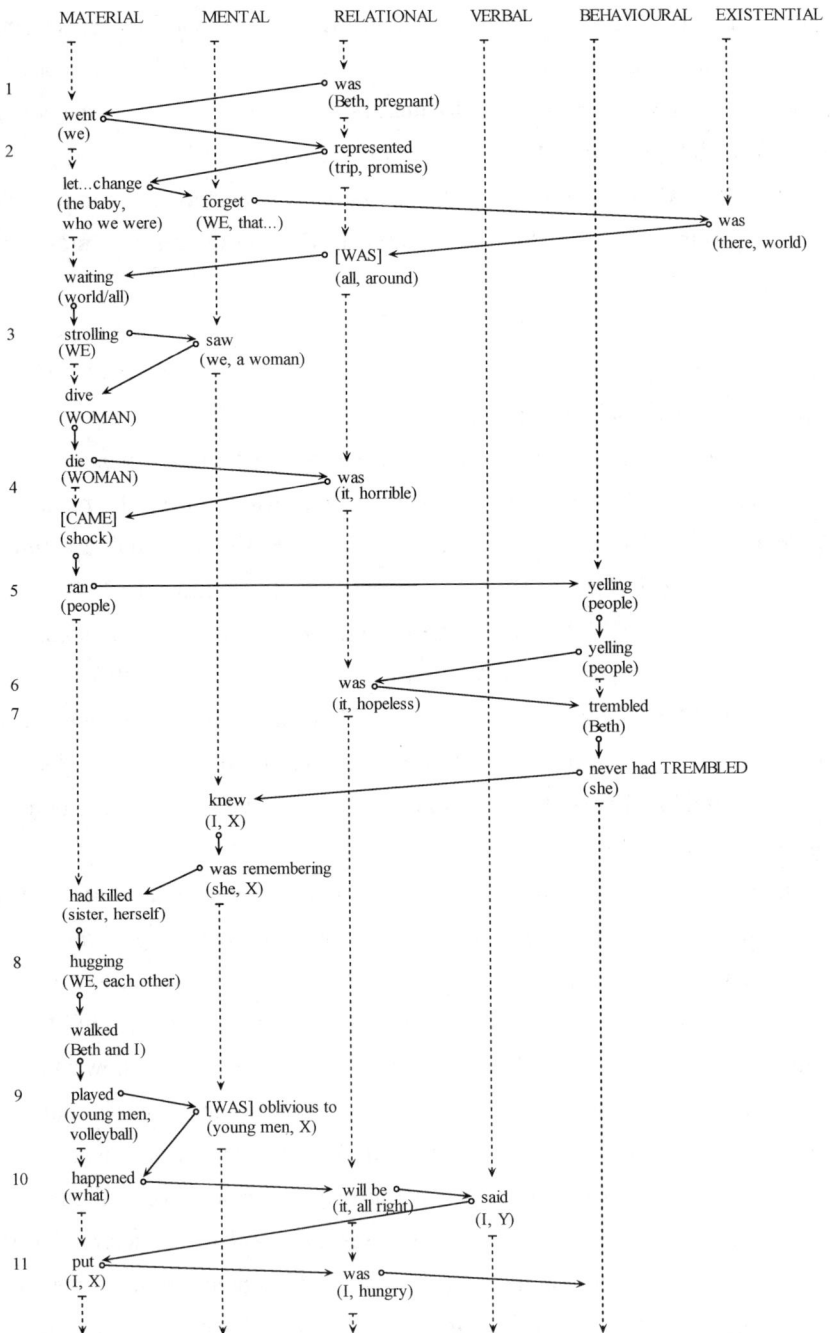

(To be continued)

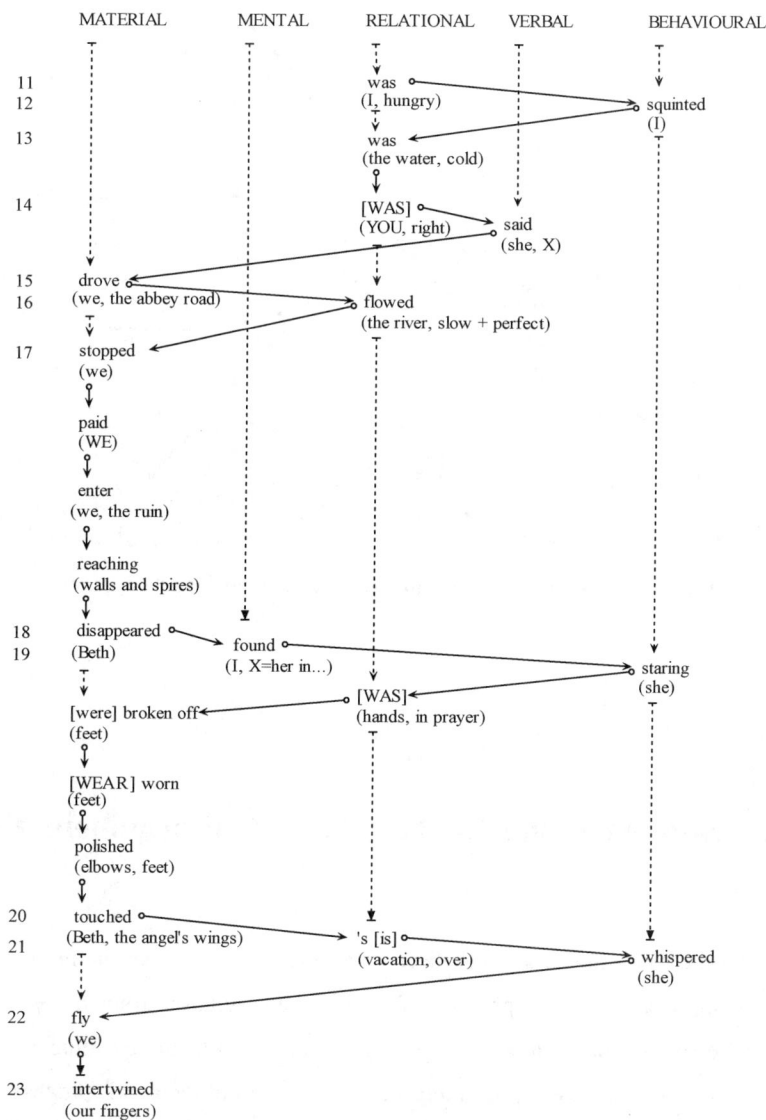

Figure 2 − 22: Displacements of "segmental" processes for discourse

第二章 词汇语法的上限级阶——语篇

第
一
部
分

理
论
范
式
探
新

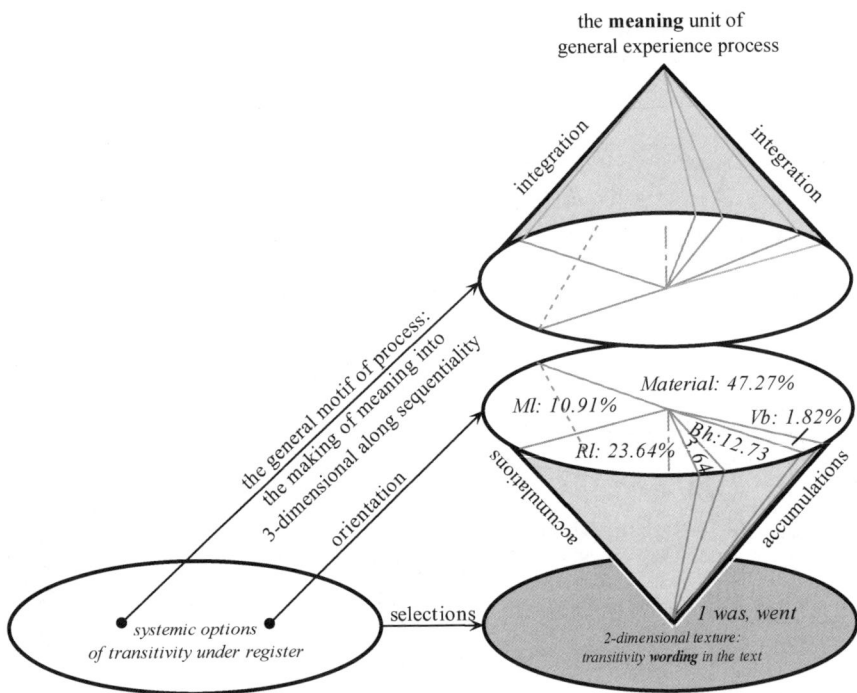

Figure 2 – 23: Transitivity and process accumulations and integrations

2.4　Summary and further theoretical argumentation

　　All the four chosen aspects discussed so far, that is, morphemic tenses, lexical appraisals, group/phrase information and clausal transitivity, may now give rise to the vision of a more generalised multi-dimensional model, similar to any of those presented above: one unidirectional process that makes up a 2 – dimensional texture as wording, both of which in turn work towards a 3 – dimensional, spindle-like unit of meaning. Note once again that the 2 – dimensional texture is characterised as grammatical for its linear

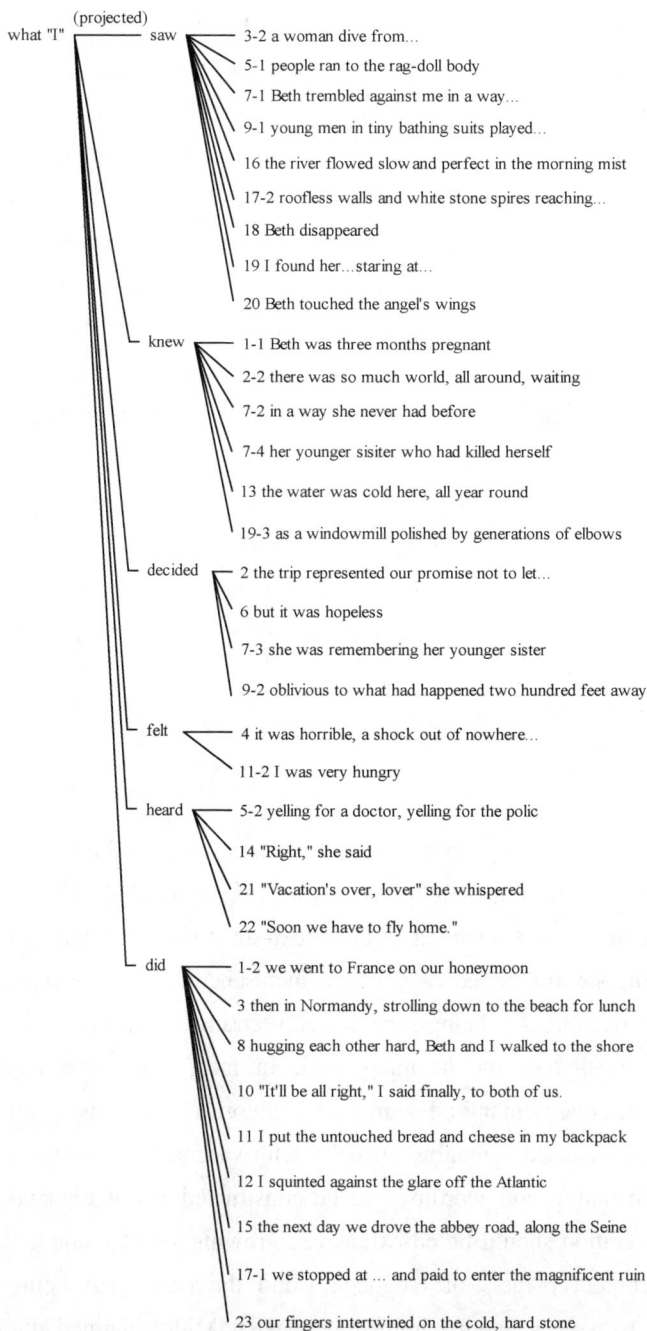

what "I"

(projected)

saw
- 3-2 a woman dive from...
- 5-1 people ran to the rag-doll body
- 7-1 Beth trembled against me in a way...
- 9-1 young men in tiny bathing suits played...
- 16 the river flowed slow and perfect in the morning mist
- 17-2 roofless walls and white stone spires reaching...
- 18 Beth disappeared
- 19 I found her...staring at...
- 20 Beth touched the angel's wings

knew
- 1-1 Beth was three months pregnant
- 2-2 there was so much world, all around, waiting
- 7-2 in a way she never had before
- 7-4 her younger sisiter who had killed herself
- 13 the water was cold here, all year round
- 19-3 as a windowmill polished by generations of elbows

decided
- 2 the trip represented our promise not to let...
- 6 but it was hopeless
- 7-3 she was remembering her younger sister
- 9-2 oblivious to what had happened two hundred feet away

felt
- 4 it was horrible, a shock out of nowhere...
- 11-2 I was very hungry

heard
- 5-2 yelling for a doctor, yelling for the polic
- 14 "Right," she said
- 21 "Vacation's over, lover" she whispered
- 22 "Soon we have to fly home."

did
- 1-2 we went to France on our honeymoon
- 3 then in Normandy, strolling down to the beach for lunch
- 8 hugging each other hard, Beth and I walked to the shore
- 10 "It'll be all right," I said finally, to both of us.
- 11 I put the untouched bread and cheese in my backpack
- 12 I squinted against the glare off the Atlantic
- 15 the next day we drove the abbey road, along the Seine
- 17-1 we stopped at ... and paid to enter the magnificent ruin
- 23 our fingers intertwined on the cold, hard stone

Figure 2 - 24: The generic structure of *Headless Angel*

weaving into a fabric, with no concern of the integration of the relevant discrete semantic components into respective meaning events; it is produced by sequential knitting. The 3 – dimensional, spindle-like unit is meaning in nature because it is synthesised entity out of the semantic components along the texturing. Since both the 2 – dimensional texture and the 3 – dimensional unit share the same sets of grammaticalised meaning components, the two sides are organically associated into an integral whole. This suggests that the demarcation of meaning and wording should be only a matter of analytical thinking, not something truly separated, as the content plane and expression plane are (cf. Miller 1985; see also Chapter 6 below, where the nature of Subject Construction is elaborated).

Now let us reflect on the approaches to text or discourse examination sorted out in Section 1. It is apparent that our classifications of them into structural, organisational, and both structural and organisational are acceptable, and our proposal is comprehensive enough to cover what all of them have discussed.

On that basis, we now move on to make a general theoretical argumentation that the top rank of lexicogrammatical hierarchy should be "text" in categorical extent.

To begin with, since meaning is the meaning of wording and wording is the wording of meaning (Hjelmslev 1943/1961; Firth 1957/1968), it would be impossible for text meaning to be a text-sized construct like a wall while text wording be comprised only of distinct schematic clause-sized stretches like bricks without also being schematically arranged into the same size in its own right as that of the meaning wall. In fact, "selection expressions" configure discrete semantic features or categories (in paradigmatic order) into conventionalised syntagms (usually with variations of course), in terms of which meaning and wording are co-constructed in interdependence; the two in generation should be co-extensive, growing side by side as being part of the "content plane" of language (and the other part being systemic paradigms), a view against immediately what Miller claimed that meaning and wording should be separately generated.

A debate may arise here. One would argue that there is something that holds the distinct schematic stretches together, that is, the underlying meaning unit. It follows that the clauses and clause complexes and those rank units below in text would look like porcelain pieces inlaid into a plasticine-like wall of meaning that has not yet been constructed, except that the wall of meaning "are already given", a view that nobody would acknowledge (see Halliday 2005a: 252). In fact, distinct schematic clausal porcelain pieces are incapable of formatting (grammaticalising or coding) the meaning wall per se. The relationship is to some degree also like that between water glass and water: the size and shape of a water glass decides the size and shape of an amount of water. In that regard, individual water glasses in the normal size and shape are incapable of holding the amount of a river or an ocean in the usual size and shape of the latter, except that the glass has the exact size and shape of a riverbed or ocean bed. To use another metaphor that may be more appropriate. Nobody would deny that a forest is made up of individual trees. However, if the individual trees themselves in an area do not form a large shape different from those individuals, then the conception of "forest" is not able to make sense at all. In other words, the category of forest (text meaning) takes shape only on the condition that the individual trees in the whole form that shape (text wording). It is right in this sense that Systemic Functional Grammar is called a meaning- or function-based grammar (Halliday 1994; Hancock 2005).

It is therefore arguable that any constitutions arising out of semantic features, semantic categories, and/or even chunks of semantic units along instantiation and realisation, by means of cohesive devices against genres or text types, should be unities or syntagms of both meaning and wording, whatever categorical size they are. However, this is usually understood just as such syntagmatic cases as: (i) **word**, as in *helpful*, *uneasy*, *feet* (*foot* + pl), *greenhouse*; (ii) **word group** or **phrase**, as in *green house*, *wooden stool*, *three houses*, *the train*; *the man on the burning deck*; *a cup of tea*; *in my view* and *in brief*; (iii) **clause**, as in (*the*) *lion* + *chased* + (*the*) *tourist* + *lazily*; and (iv) **clause complex**, as in (*if winter comes*) + (*autumn will* *be left behind*) and (*John came in*) and (*Mary went out*), and (*John came in*) because (*Mary went out*) (see, e.g., Halliday & Matthiessen 2014: 211–591; see, also, Jespersen 1940–1949; Quirk et al. 1985; Biber et al. 1999; Hunston 2013; Hunston & Francis 2000; Hunston & Thompson 2000; among others).

The present author believes that unities or **syntagms** of larger sizes should be included as well. Let us consider what Halliday has cited for demonstrating text meaning structures in both spoken and written modes (Halliday 1981):

(i) Structural stages of buying and selling language in Cyrenaican Arabic (Mitchell 1957):

Salutation ^ Enquiry as to object of sale ^ Investigation of object of sale ^ Bidding ^ Conclusion Auctions: Opening ^ Investigation of object of sale ^ Bidding ^ Conclusion;

(ii) Narrative structural formula (Labov & Waletsky 1967):

Abstract ^ Orientation ^ Complication ^ Evaluation ^ Resolution ^ Coda;

(iii) Retail sale structure, as structure "in all registers" (Hasan 1985a):

((Greetings ·) Sale initiation ^) ((Sale inquiry ·) (Sale request ^ Sale compliance) ^) Sale ^ Purchase ^ Purchase closure (^ Finis);

(iv) Structural formula of persuasion (Martin 1981; see also Martin 1995, 1996, 2012a):

Set ground ^ State problem ^ Offer solution ^ Evaluate solution (^ Personalise solution)

I would add to the list Hoey's (1983) observation of the organisation sequence patterns "on the surface of discourse", here as (v), (vi) and (vii), where connection symbols "-" is replaced with " ^ ":

(v) Problem-solution patterns:

Question ^ Answer;

Situation ^ problem ^ response ^ result ^ evaluation;

Cause ^ Consequence;

Instrument ^ Achievement;

(vi) Matching patterns, such as parallelism over independent clauses and/ or complexes; and

(vii) General-particular patterns, e.g.,

Generalisation ^ *Example*; and

Preview ^ *Detailed relations*.

All these, among others (for dialogic cases, see, e.g., Tsui 1994; Brazil 1995; Schegloff 2007; for the immediate data of problem-solution patterns familiar to the SFL community, see Martin 2013; for clause-text analogy, see Pike & Pike 1983), have been said to be semantic, a view that has carried away people too far to be aware of their true wording nature.

For my understanding, the characteristic of texture cannot be claimed to be "semantic" simply for its semantic constituents, as transitivity is also made up of semantic components (participant, process and circumstance). In other words, if one should follow that logic, that is, semantic sequence be semantic, then all those patterns at the rank of clause (complex), and even those ranks below, should also be meanings at most (i.e. figures and elements), not wording either, because they are as well comprised of semantic chunks, and here semantic categories are deployed from relevant systems, the same way as those text structures aforementioned (see below, where the usual connection symbols "+" is rewritten as "^" too to show their sequential order).

(viii) *Theme* ^ *Rheme*; *Given* ^ *New*; *Mood* ^ *Residue*; *Participant* ^ *Process* (^ *Participant* ^ *Circumstance*); *Process* ^ *Medium* (^ *Agent*).

This analogy immediately counters against one's commonsense of the nature per se. That is, they share the nature of "sequentially" on the surface of discourse, as all those textures figured out in Section 3 above; and the only difference rests with that those represented in Section 3 account for the local temporality whereas these cited sequences are global. In other words, if different parts in each of those textures in the previous section are termed with more general names, they form similar sequences as those listed here as (i – viii). For example, from the ideational perspective, the sample text can be generalised into a sequence like (ix) below, where Structure *a* is specific and Structure *b* is very much skeletal, two ways of generalisation dependent on alternative purposes.

> (ix) a. Onset: General Background Setting for the Whole Story (Sentences 1 – 2) ∧ Local Accident Setting, Plot 1 and Surrounding Reactions (Sentences 3 – 9) ∧ A Balanced Assessment of the Human World (Sentences 10 – 14) ∧ Local Background Setting for Plot 2 (Sentence 15) ∧ Plot 2 (Sentences 16 – 22) ∧ Coda: Further Positive (Sentence 23).
>
> b. Onset ∧ Plots ∧ Coda.

It should be noted that sequences at the clause rank, like (viii), are possible in all lexicogrammatical respects, but their linearity cross the domain of the clause, such as those presented above, are not likely to be worked out as (ix) because the former two in the present sample are componential organisations that have no comparatively distinct schematic stages on the surface progressions of the discourse. That is, only the ideational strand of (ix) is a good case for our point here.

Therefore, all syntagmatic sequences should be wordings in nature that have their respective "underlying" meanings. In theoretical terms, once selection statements configure semantic options that are deployed from paradigmatic sets into syntagmatic structures and organisations, however big or small they are, the statements generate meaning and wording at the same time.

In this regard, the nature of meaning unit should be free from "sequence", the latter of which is exclusively the characteristic of wording. For example, *the lion* and *the tourist* in both active and passive voices are constant Actor and Goal: **the lion** *chased* **the tourist** vs. **the tourist** *was chased by* **the lion**, regardless to their word order difference. That is, both clauses share the same semantic unit of "THE LION CHASED THE TOURIST" event. Likewise, any textual sequence constituted out of whatever size of semantic chunks, should be syntagmatic in nature. To be straightforward, sequence is a property of syntagm departing from paradigm, as both Hjelmslev (1943/1961) and Halliday (1978a) hold; and semantic sequencing is the process of formalization or grammaticalisation. On the contrary, text meaning or social semantic unit is an organic or integral whole of landscape out of sequential orders by means of elaboration, extension and enhancement. Of course, this does not deny the process of expansion and contraction, as shown above: sequence is different from process. In one word, syntagmaticalisation is grammaticalisation when the latter construes semantic options into meaning and wording, whether textual or clausal.

To sum up, "text wording" should, in logic, be the same size as "text meaning" in the categorical sense, the two together making a unity of verbal act or event in context; and when clause complexes and those rank units below unite to make text meaning, they stretch themselves homogenetically into larger forms of their own above the domain of the clause (complex), along which text meaning is created. This is the target of a discipline that has been called "text grammar, text linguistics, text semiotics and textology" (see Coote et al. 1989: xii).

2.5   Concluding remarks

Three general conclusions can be drawn. First of all, lexical items and grammatical units co-work to create text meaning and wording along instantiation and realisation; they are complementary in that the meaning aspect concerns the accumulations and integrations whereas the wording aspect is responsible for aligning them into structures and textures in alternative aspects. These two aspects are indeed one of continuum with no clear distinction in between. It is now reasonable to claim "text" as a rank of lexicogrammar, or in particular, the topmost rank of the scale hierarchy,

第
一
部
分

理
论
范
式
探
新

which can be simply described as: morpheme → word → word group/ phrase → clause → clause complex → (paragraph → chapter → book →) text (type) , with those in the parenthesis to be accounted for in further argumentation.

Furthermore, morpheme-text rank scale should be a continuum too with the following as representative ranks in the middle: word, group and phrase, clause and clause complex, each being a prototypical construction unit, with continuous phenomena in between that are highly intricate in constitution (Peng 2011: 7 - 15). This can be evidenced in particular with those units that contain rank shift. For example, a down-graded unit may be a lexeme (*something* **interesting**) , a group or phrase (*something* ***highly probable***; ***three months*** *pregnant*; *a **gorgeous sunny** day*; *the front **of its bear feet***) , a clause (*Beth trembled against me in a way **she never had before***) , or even a clause complex (frequent in complicated expository texts). The matter may be further twisted and hedged by cases in formal style full of nominalisation, which, as Halliday points out, simplifies the grammar but complicates the lexis (Halliday 2004). Therefore, from morpheme to text is continuum by virtue of lexicogrammatical complexity. It follows that, seen from the " system " angle, the continuum comprises prototypical options of word **classes**, clause **patterns** and text **genres/types**, alongside other (semi-) ranks of constructions, all embodying the sense of systemic powerhouse of lexicogrammar available for making meaning and wording of text.

Finally, the three principles, that is, unidirectionality, onlinedness and layered constitution, should be fundamental to modeling text or discourse process as a whole in the logogenetic sense based on phylogenetic and ontogenetic resources of language, a theme to be fully developed.

Appendix

The sample texts (with each sentence labeled with sequential number in the first and third texts) :

0 *Headless Angel*, by Tom Hazuka

    1 Beth was three months pregnant when we went to France on our honeymoon. 2 The

trip represented our promise not to let the baby change who we were, not to forget that there was so much world, all around, waiting. 3 Then in Normandy, strolling down to the beach for lunch, we saw a woman dive from a fourth-floor window and die on the sidewalk, right across the street. 4 It was horrible, a shock out of nowhere on a gorgeous sunny day. 5 People ran to the rag-doll body, yelling for a doctor, yelling for the police. 6 But it was hopeless. 7 Beth trembled against me in a way she never had before; I knew she was remembering her younger sister who had killed herself. 8 Hugging each other hard, Beth and I walked to the shore. 9 Young men in tiny bathing suits played volleyball on the sand, oblivious to what had happened two hundred feet away.

10 "It'll be all right," I said finally, to both of us. 11 I put the untouched bread and cheese in my backpack, though I was very hungry. 12 I squinted against the glare off the Atlantic. 13 The water was cold here, all year round.

14 "Right," she said.

15 The next day we drove the abbey road, along the Seine.

16 The river flowed slow and perfect in the morning mist. 17 We stopped at the Abbaye de Jumièges and paid to enter the magnificent ruin, roofless walls and white stone spires reaching for the sky.

18 Beth disappeared.

19 I found her in a courtyard staring at a decapitated marble angel, its childlike hands palm-to-palm in prayer, the front of its bare feet broken off and worn as smooth as a windowsill polished by generations of elbows.

20 Beth touched the angel's wings. 21 "Vacation's almost over, lover," she whispered. 22 "Soon we have to fly home."

23 Our fingers intertwined on the cold, hard stone.

Centerfold, by John Briggs

When her husband **goes** out for the evening, he **leaves** her, now even months pregnant, at loose ends. She **decides** to clean out drawers. In the bottom drawer of his bureau she **finds** a several-months-old men's magazine. She **opens** to the "Dream Girl Centerfold." It**'s** a nude photo of herself lying seductively on a beach.

Her legs **stretch** out in a V across the pages. Her elbows **prop** her up from the sand as she **reclines** in a pose that **causes** her pelvis to tilt out and her breast to arch back a little unnaturally. She **smiles** fetchingly along her shoulder at the camera. Behind her a fat blue wave **curls** itself into a glassy tube about to shatter against the shore.

On the next double page this image **repeats** exactly, except for a red line beginning to show between her legs. On the following pages the stain **grows** larger. She **is bleeding** to death.

As she **turns** the pages, the provocative pose and her smile never **change**, but the stain **reaches** past her feet. Throughout, the wind **blows**, lifting the ends of her hair.

Eventually, elbows still propping her up, her head **lolls** at a grotesque angle and her body **rots**. Her skin **turns** to rags. The wind **gusts** her hair.

When the last of her flesh **has disappeared**, presumably picked off by gulls and ants, she **remains** as a skeleton propping herself up on the beach with the waves arching over.

As least the stain **has vanished**. Her bones **gleam** sleekly in the sunlight. The figure of her skeleton **cuts** a stylish composition against ocean and sky.

She **doesn't** exist on the magazine's last two pages. The beach **looks** pleasant and inviting. The waves **strike** a cool, clean blue.

The Human Pyramid, by Neno J. Perrotta

1 These neighbors of mine are driving me nuts. 2 At first it was only a matter of clothing, then it got out hand.

3 The big woman, the one with short hair, walks around naked talking on a cordless phone. 4 there're always at least four or five little kids hanging on her legs or tagging along. 5 The ones over there, they're naked, too. 6 Babies wear diapers, thank God.

7 And four ponies and a llama they keep inside an electric fence. 8 That's where you can always find the other woman, the one that most of the time wears at least underwear. 9 She trains the ponies. 10 I can't even guess what she does with the llama.

11 I asked the mailman, "What's with those people over there? What's their story?"

12 "Circus, I'm guessing," he said. 13 "But they both get unemployment checks and letters to the kids from all over the world."

14 "Yeah. Sure," I said. 15 "A world-renowned, nude circus." 16 And to be honest, I was thinking lesbians, too. 17 But, since there were so many kids, I kept my mouth shut.

18 Now don't get me wrong. 19 I've got nothing against nakedness. 20 And I like kids and ponies as much as they next guy. 21 it wasn't until a few weeks ago that the carnival-like goings on became too much for me. 22 That's when they started with the human pyramids. 23 To be specific, the naked-human pyramids.

24 Every time they try, the whole thing comes crashing down. 25 With those diapers on top it's a snow-capped mountain of naked flesh. 26 It's a miracle no one ever gets hurts.

27 So, now I have to worry that they're not too bright. 28 Hell, everyone knows you need at least one strong man to anchor a human pyramid. 29 Maybe more.

30 That's what's driving me crazy. 31 I even went over and asked them if they needed help. 32 "I don't know about the nude business," I said. 33 "But I could wear a bathing suit."

34 "Thanks," said the naked woman. 35 "But, no thanks."

36 "How about a cape?" I said. 37 "Tight shorts and a cape?"

38 "It's a family thing," said the "bra and panties" woman. 39 "We're all in one, big happy family."

40 "Okay," I said. 41 "But kids can get hurt. Somebody can get hurt."

42 "No we won't," yelled all the kids. 43 "We never get hurt." 44 They talked at the same time, like they'd been practicing since the day they were born.

45 When I turned to go home the kids laughed and ran to ride the ponies. 46 I stopped and watched while some of them fell off and seemed to crack their heads on rocks. 47 One of the babies tumbled onto the electric fence, laughing and delighted by the steam that danced up from her soggy diaper.

Table 2 – 1: Lexicogrammatical functions of MORPHEMES in *Headless Angel*

		Not meaning oriented (implicit meaning orientation)	Meaning characterised (overt meaning change)
1	Word	2 (so much world) all around	0 head**less** 1 **honey**moon 2 **represent**ed [*vs.* present], **pro**mise [*vs.* mise] 3 **wo**man, side**walk**, a**cross** 4 **no**where 5 **rag-doll** 7 **ne**ver [*vs.* ever], **be**fore [*vs.* fore] 9 men, suits, volley**ball** 11 **un**touched, back**pack** 15 a**long** 17 walls, spires 18 **dis**appeared, dis**appeared** 19 court**yard**, **de**capitated, child**like**, hands, prayer, its bare **feet**, window**sill**, genera**tions**, genera**tions**, generations, elbows 20 wings 21 vaca**tion**, 21 **al**most [*vs.* most], lover 23 inter**twin**ed
2	Group/ Phrase	1 **our** honeymoon [*deictic*] 2 **our** promise [*deictic*] 7 against **me** [*compl.*], **her** young**er** sister [*classifier*] 9 you**ng** men, tiny bath**ing** suits [*class.*] 11 untouch**ed** bread and cheese [*class.*], **my** backpack 17 the magnificent ruin [*epithet*] 19 a decapitat**ed** marble angel [*class.*], **its** childlike hands, **its** bare feet [*deic*] both of **us** [*compl.*] 20 angel**'s** [*deictic*] 23 **Our** fingers [*pl.*]	1 **was**, **went**, three months [*head*] 2 represent**ed**, **were**, **was** 3 **saw**, a fourth-floor window [*num*] 4 **was**, a gorge**ous**, sunny day [*ep*, *cl*] 5 **ran** 6 **was** 7 trembl**ed**, **had**, **knew**, **was** remembering, had**killed**, 8 walk**ed** 9 play**ed**, had**happened**, tiny bathing suits, two hundred feet **a**way [*h*, *q*] 10 **said** 11 **put**, **was** 12 squint**ed**, glare [*v.→n.*] 13 **was** 14 **said** 15 **drove** 16 flow**ed** 17 stop**ped**, **paid**, roof**less** walls [*classifier*] 18 disappear**ed** 19 **found** 20 touch**ed** 21 Vacation**'s**, whisper**ed** 22 **have** to 23 intertwin**ed**

第一部分 理论范式探新

(continued)

		Not meaning oriented (implicit meaning orientation)	Meaning characterised (overt meaning change)
3	Clause	1 **we** [*subj.*] 2 **we** <u>were</u> [*subj.* + *pl.*], 　there **was** [*sgl.*] 3 **we** saw [*subj.*] 4 **It** (was) [*subj.* + *sgl.*] 6 **it** was (hopeless) [*subj.* + 　*sgl.*] 7 **she, I, she** [*subj.*], 　**her**self [*goal*; *compl.*] 8 **I** [*subj.*] 10 **It**'ll [*subj.* + *sgl.*], **I** 　[*subj.* + *sgl.*] 11 **I** [*subj.*], **I** [*subj.*] 12 **I** [*subj.*] 14 **she** [*subj.*] 15 **we** [*subj.*] 17 **We** [*subj.*] 19 **I** [*subj.*], **her** [*compl.*] 21 **she** [*cf.* her] 22 **we** (have to) [*subj.* + *pl.*]	[tense finites cited in the previous cell] 1 preg**nant** [*vs.* pregnan**cy**] [*attr.*] 4 horrib**le** [*attr.*] 6 hope**less** [*attr.*] 9 obliv**ious** to [*attr.*] 10 final**ly** [*circ.*] 11 hung**ry** [*attr.*]
4	Clause Complex	2 not **to** let, not **to** forget, 　wait**ing** 3 strol**ling**, (saw X) [to] 　dive, [to] die 5 yel**ling**, **yelling** 8 Hug**ging** 17 **to** enter, reach**ing** 19 star**ing**, **broken, worn,** 　polish**ed**	[stop **to** do vs. stop do**ing**; remember **to** do vs. remember do**ing** forget **to** do vs. forget do**ing**]
5	Text		[tense finites listed in 2 Group/Phrase]

Table 2 - 2: General lexicogrammatical functions of WORDS in *Headless Angel*

Here (ⅰ) "lexical" (lexico-) stands in particular for playing socio-semiotic function apart from their wording tasks; (ⅱ) "grammatical" for wording even though it may help render its own contextual meaning out of its constituents; and (ⅲ) "lexicogrammatical" for both.

GC	Case	Lexical	Lexico-grammatical	Grammatical
1	Common	1 months, honeymoon 2 trip, promise, baby, world 3 beach, lunch, woman, fourth-floor, window, sidewalk, street 4 shock, day 5 people, rag-doll, body, doctor, police 7 way, sister 8 shore 9 men, suits, volleyball, sand 11 bread, cheese, backpack 12 glare 13 water, year 15 day, abbey, road 16 river, morning, mist 17 ruin, walls, stone, spires, sky 19 courtyard, marble, angel, hands, prayer, front, feet, windowsill, generations, elbows 20 angel('s), wings 21 vacation 21 lover [vocative] 23 fingers; stone		
2	Proper	1 Beth, France 3 Normandy 7 Beth 8 Beth 12 Atlantic 15 Seine 17 Abbaye de Jumièges 18 Beth 20 Beth		
3	Pronoun		1 we; we[our] 2 we[our], who, we; there [existential] 3 we 4 it 6 it 7 me; she, I, she, she[her], who, herself 8 each other, I 9 what	

(continued)

GC \ Case		Lexical	Lexico-grammatical	Grammatical
3	Pronoun		10 it, I, both, we [us] 11 I, I[my], I 12 I 14 she 15 we 17 we, it[its] , it [its] 19 I, her 21 she 22 we 23 we[Our]	
4	Adjective	1 pregnant 4 horrible, gorgeous, sunny 6 hopeless 7 younger 8 hard 9 young, tiny, oblivious 10 right 11 hungry 13 cold 14 right 16 slow, perfect 17 magnificent; roofless, white 19 childlike, bare, smooth 21 over 23 cold, hard		15 next
5	N	1 three 2 much 9 two hundred feet		
6	Determiner			2 the, the 3 the, a, a, the, the 4 a, a 5 the, a, the 7 a 8 the 9 the 11 the 12 the, the 13 the 15 the, the, the 16 the, the 17 the, the, the 19 a, a, the, a 20 the 23 the

GC \ Case		Lexical	Lexico-grammatical	Grammatical
7	Lexical	1 go 2 let, change, forget, wait 3 stroll, see, dive, die 5 ran, yell, yell 7 tremble, have, knew, remember, kill 8 hug, walk 9 bath, play, happen 10 say 11 put, untouch(ed) 12 squint 14 say 15 drive 17 stop, pay, enter, reach 18 disappear 19 find, stare, decapitate, break off, wear, polish 20 touch 21 whisper 22 fly 23 intertwine	1 be 2 represent be be 4 be 6 be 10 be 11 be 13 be 16 flowed 21 be	
8	F		10 will ('ll)	
9	A		22 have to	
10	Preposition			1 to, on 3 in, to, for, from, on, across 4 out, of, on 5 to, for, for 7 against, in 8 to 9 in, on, to 10 to, of 11 in 12 against, off 15 along 16 in 17 at, for 19 in, at, in, of, by, of 23 on

第二章 词汇语法的上限级阶——语篇

（continued）

Case GC		Lexical	Lexico-grammatical	Grammatical
11	Adverb		2 not, not, around 3 down 4 out, nowhere 7 never, before 7 away 10 finally 11 very 13 here, all, round 19 palm-to-palm 21 almost 22 soon, home	2 so, all 3 right 10 all
12	Linker		3 then	3 and 6 but 8 and 11 and 16 and 17 and, and 19 and, as … as
13	Binder			1 when 2 to, to, that 11 though 17 to

Note: 1 – 6: nominals (3: the pronouns are listed here for their referential function, excluding their morphological variations at the clausal rank; 5 N: numeral); 7 – 9: verbals (F: "finite", which has but one element that is lexical *will* [*'ll*] as the other are all morphological; but note that the relevant lexical items remain in the previous square); 10 – 12: adverbial ("continuative" absent) [*our* in 1, 2 and 23; *her* in 7; *my* in 11; the two *its* in 19; and *angel's* in 20 under "Determiner" are all morphological deictics and are not included here, but included in braces to suggest their relations to the present list and for later use.]

Table 2 – 3: Information analysis

(a) Situationally evoked:

1 *Beth* [1] was three months pregnant when *we* [3] went to France

2 *there* [14] was so much world

10 "*It* [66] 'll be all right"

(b) Textually evoked:

(b – 1) Current:

1 on *our* [6] honeymoon

2 represented *our* [9] promise; who *we were* [12]

3 *we* [24] saw a woman dive

4 *It* [28] was horrible

6 *but it was* [39] hopeless

7 *Beth* [41] trembled against *me* [43] in a way *she* [45] never had before, *I* [48] knew *she* [50] was remembering *her* [52] younger sister who had killed *herself* [54]

8 *Beth and I* [58] walked to the shore; *I* [68] said finally

10 *I* [69] said finally, to both of *us* [72]

11 *I* [73] put the untouched bread and cheese in *my* [76] backpack, though *I was* [78] very hungry

12 *I* [80] squinted against the glare off the Atlantic

14 "Right," *she* [88] said

15 The next day *we* [91] drove the abbey road

17 *We* [98] stopped at the Abbaye de Jumièges

18 *Beth* [104] disappeared

19 *I* [106] found *her* [107] in a courtyard

19 *its* [110] childlike hands palm-to-palm in prayer

20 *Beth* [118] touched *the angel*'s [120] wings

21 *she* [126] whispered

22 "Soon *we* [129] have to fly home."

23 *Our* [130] fingers intertwined

(b - 2) Displaced:

2 *The trip* [8] represented our promise not to let *the baby* [11] change who we were

4 *a shock out of nowhere* [31]

5 People ran to *the* rag-doll *body* [35]

8 Hugging *each other* [56] hard

9 oblivious to *what had happened* [62] two hundred feet away

13 *The water* [83] was cold *here* [85]

16 *The river* [95] flowed slow and perfect in the morning mist

21 "*Vacation's* [122] almost over, lover,"

22 "*Soon* [128] we have to fly home."

23 Our fingers intertwined on the cold, hard *stone* [134]

(c) Inferrable:

(c - 1) Containing:

3 then in *Normandy* [20], strolling down to *the beach* [22] for lunch; dive from a fourth-floor window and *die on the sidewalk* [26], right *across the street* [27]

4 it was *horrible* [29]

6 it was *hopeless* [40]

7 in a way she never had *before* [47]

8 Beth and I walked to *the shore* [60];

9 Young men played volleyball on *the sand* [62]

10 I *said* [69] finally, *to both of* us [72]

11 I put *the untouched bread and cheese* [74; cf., 3 for lunch] in my backpack

12 I squinted against *the glare off the Atlantic* [82]

14 "Right," she *said* [89]

15 *The next day* [90] we drove the abbey road

19 <u>its childlike *hands*</u> [112] palm-to-palm in prayer, *the front of its bare feet* [114] broken off

23 <u>Our *fingers*</u> [131] intertwined on the cold, hard stone

(c-2) Noncontaining:

3 *then* [19] in Normandy

(d) Unused:

1 we went to *France* [5]

2 not to forget that there was *so much world* [16], *all around* [17]

5 yelling for *the police* [39]

11 I put the untouched bread and cheese *in my backpack* [77]

15 The next day we drove *the abbey road* [93] , along *the Seine* [94]

17 We stopped at *the Abbaye de Jumièges* [100], 17 paid to enter *the magnificent ruin* [101], roofless walls and white stone spires reaching for *the sky* [103]

20 Beth touched the angel's *wings* [120]

22 "Soon we have to fly *home*." [129]

(e) Brand new:

(e-1) Anchored:

1 we went to France on <u>our *honeymoon*</u> [7]

2 *represented* our *promise* [9], *not to let* the baby *change who* we were [13], *not to forget that* there was so much world, all around, waiting [18]

5 People ran to the *rag-doll* [34] body

7 *in a way* she *never had* [46] before, I *knew* [49] she *was remembering* her *younger sister* [51] who *had killed* herself [54]

9 oblivious to what had happened *two hundred feet away* [65]

10 "It'*ll be all right*, [67]" I said *finally* [70]

11 I put the untouched bread and cheese in my backpack, though I was *very hungry* [79]

12 I *squinted against* [81] the glare off the Atlantic

14 "*Right*," [87] she said

15 The next day we *drove* the abbey road [93]

16 The river *flowed slow and perfect* [96] in <u>the morning *mist*</u> [97]

17 We *stopped* at the Abbaye de Jumièges [100] and *paid to enter* the magnificent ruin [101], *roofless walls and white stone spires reaching for* the sky [102]

19 its *childlike* [111] hands *palm-to-palm in prayer* [113]

21 "Vacation's almost over, lover," she *whispered* [125]

22 "Soon we *have to fly* home." [128]

23 Our fingers *intertwined* [132] on the cold, hard stone

(e-2) Unanchored:

1 Beth was *three months pregnant* [2], *went to* France [5]

2 there was so much world, all around, *waiting* [17]

3 *strolling down* [21] to the beach *for lunch* [23], we *saw a woman dive from a fourth-floor window* [25]

4 a shock out of nowhere on *a gorgeous sunny day* [32]

5 *People ran* [33] to the rag-doll body, *yelling* [36] for *a doctor* [37], *yelling* [38] for the police

7 Beth *trembled* [43] *against* me [45]

8 *Hugging* each other *hard* [57], Beth and I *walked to* the shore [60]

9 *Young men in tiny bathing suits* [61] *played volleyball* [62] on the sand, *oblivious to* [65] what had happened *two hundred feet away* [66]

10 I said *finally* [71]

11 I *put* [74] the untouched bread and cheese in my backpack

13 The water was *cold* [84] here, *all year round* [86]

18 Beth *disappeared* [107]

19 I *found* her *in a courtyard* [110] *staring at a decapitated marble angel* [111], the front of its bare feet *broken off* [117] and *worn* as *smooth* [118] as *a windowsill polished by generations of elbows* [119];

20 Beth *touched* the angel's wings [123]

21 "Vacation's *almost over* [125], lover"

23 Our fingers intertwined on the *cold, hard* [133] stone

Table 2-4: Transitivity: clausal constituents out of groups and phrases made up of words and morphemes

Participant: Nominal, Adjective & Adverbial Group	Process: Verbal Group	Circumstance: Nominal & Preposition Group; P. Phrase
1 Beth, we; three months pregnant 2 The trip, we; so much world, the baby; who, our promise, all around	1 was, went 2 represented, let ... change, were, forget, was, waiting	1 to France, on our honeymoon 3 in Normandy, 3 to the beach, for lunch, from a fourth-floor window,

第
一
部
分

理
论
范
式
探
新

(continued)

Participant: Nominal, Adjective & Adverbial Group	Process: Verbal Group	Circumstance: Nominal & Preposition Group; P. Phrase
3 we, a woman	3 strolling, saw, dive, die	on the sidewalk, right across the street
4 It, a shock; horrible	4 was, [came/was out of nowhere]	4 out of nowhere, on a gorgeous sunny day
5 People	5 ran, yelling, yelling	5 to the rag-doll body, for
6 it; hopeless	6 was	a doctor, for the police
7 Beth, she, I, she, who; her younger sister, herself	7 trembled, had [trembled], knew, was remembering, had killed	7 against me, in a way, before
8 Beth and I; each other, hard	8 Hugging, walked	8 to the shore
9 Young men, oblivious, volleyball	9 played, had happened	9 in tiny bathing suits, on the sand, to what, two hundred feet away
10 It, I; all right	10 'll be, said	10 finally, to both of us
11 I, I; the untouched bread and cheese very hungry	11 put, was	11 in my backpack
12 I	12 squinted	12 against the glare, off the Atlantic
13 The water; cold	13 was	13 here, all year round
14 she; Right	14 said	
15 we; the abbey road	15 drove	15 The next day, along the Seine
16 The river; slow, perfect	16 flowed	16 in the morning mist
17 We, roofless walls and white stone spires; the magnificent ruin	17 stopped, paid, enter, reaching	17 at the Abbaye de Jumièges, for the sky.
18 Beth	18 disappeared	
19 I, its childlike hands, the front of its bare feet a windowsill; her, smooth	19 found, staring at, [were], broken off worn, polished	19 in a courtyard, at a decapitated marble angel, palm-to-palm, in prayer by generations of elbows
20 Beth; the angel's wings	20 touched	
21 Vacation, she; almost over	21 's, whispered	
22 we	22 have to fly	22 Soon, home
23 Our fingers	23 intertwined	23 on the cold, hard stone

第三章

语言的过程

四个维度及其工作记忆加工模型①

3.1 引言

韩礼德在《语言系统的并协与互补》中指出，

> 系统有赖于记忆：有赖于每一个说话人铭刻在大脑中的内容，尤其是共享记忆，从而确保一定数量的、切实可行的不同说话人——大脑具有足够的共享基础，连续而无断裂。共享的不仅包括语法和语音系统网络，还有量化类型——我一向主张的盖然性模式，即上述系统自身的内在特征。（Halliday 2008：15）

本章拟在这一指导思想的基础上，将系统功能语言学先前的二维模式推向四维模式。在扼要介绍系统功能语言学基本思想及其范畴的基础上，报道本章作者构拟的、和语言系统相对的语言实例，即语言过程模式：一是从先前的二维推衍到四维，涉及时-空一体化视野：从系统（离线）走向实例（在线）、从静态回到动态、从历时-共时分野到两者一

---

① 本章原载于《北京师范大学学报》（社会科学版），2013 年第 4 期，第 33—48 页。这里有改动。

体的泛时语言观;二是为语言的社会性补足应有的认知属性,出发点是笔者提出的现在主义认识论,基础就是记忆理论的最新发展,即工作记忆原理。

"过程"这一概念源于叶尔姆斯列夫。他根据索绪尔的语言和言语概念把语言区分为系统与过程(Hjelmslev 1943/1961)。但他没有对两个概念做明确界定。从具体内容看,过程指语篇的产生流程;系统是过程背后的常量和前提,包括语音、语义和语法诸方面。从共时维度看,过程源于系统,新的语篇依据系统而生成,所以语篇的"过程"涉及两个侧面:在系统中的选择过程以及话语"表层"随时间流程的次第更新与生成过程(见前一章)。值得注意的是,叶尔姆斯列夫在论及系统时还不时用"语言"代替"系统",因此这个意义上的语言就是和言语或语言实例相对的语言系统;韩礼德以此作为基础之一创立了系统功能语言学。

语言的过程指语言体现相关社交功能的工作记忆加工阶段,涉及语言发生的整体性、过程性和在场性,是一种现在主义基础上的语言观:人类在交往中积累起来的一切语言系统成分都可能从离线状态经由长时工作记忆、被调用到当下在线的短时工作记忆中来进行加工处理;因此,语言过程是语言实例的特点之一,语言的过程性是语言在场性的一种体现方式,是由整体观确立的;语言系统是意义潜势,从共时角度看是基础,是"建筑材料",语言过程是由交际动因驱使和制约的选择过程,是在工作记忆支撑下发生推进的。

语言的过程主要涉及以下先期成果:(一) 韩礼德关于语言的经典模式;(二) 韩礼德于1995年提出的扩展模式;(三) 语言在社会属性之外的认知属性以及认知语言学和语用学的基本发现;(四) 记忆理论,尤其是工作记忆理论;(五) 建立在涉身哲学基础上的现在主义认识论及其语言观。这些来自语言学和非语言学的功能模块,将整合于认知神经工作机制之下。这里从三个方面加以综合介绍:(一) 背景:韩礼德的经典语言模式和扩展语言模式;(二) 语言过程的四个维度:理论上的进一步思考;(三) 工作记忆原理、现在主义认识论基础上的语言认知机制及其创造性。

3.2 背景：系统功能语言学的经典与扩展模式

下面从韩礼德的语言模式演变入手。1961年，韩礼德提出了系统功能语言学的早期模式（Halliday 1961），包括情景（超语篇特征）、语境、词汇和语法、语音和书写系统、语音和书写实体五个层次；其中第一个和最后一个层次在语言之外，而"语境"是语义性质的，相当于人们常说的"上下文"。1976年，韩礼德用"语义"取代了"语境"，并在兰姆（Lamb 1966）的层次语法启示下，阐述了各层次之间"体现"和"被体现"的关系：语境→语义→词汇语法→语音/书写系统→语音/书写实体，箭尾范畴由箭头范畴体现，逐层加以代码化（Halliday & Hasan 1976：5）。对于中间三个层次，韩礼德同时分别用了三个替换性的非正式称谓：意义、措辞和声音。这就是读者早先接受的系统功能语言学经典模式。

首先是语境概念，包括情景语境和文化语境，最初是由功能人类学家马林诺夫斯基提出来的：文化语境决定并寓于情景语境中，语篇生成离不开相关情景语境和文化语境。

这一观点为伦敦语言学派创始人弗斯接受，并把它和语言系统做了明确关联："情景语境指一种纲要式的结构，特定地应用于社交过程中典型的'重复性事件'。它也是检验语篇是否具有共同惯用性的保障，从而排除偶然的、个人的、特有的特征进入注意范围。"它包括三个方面：（一）参与者：人、个性以及相关特征：（1）参与者的言语行为，（2）参与者的非言语行为；（二）相关物体、非言语和非个人事件；（三）言语行为的效果（Firth 1957/1968：177）。

韩礼德对情景语境做了更为具体的解释。情景指一种社会符号结构，即关于言说或书写行为中发生在周围环境里的相关事件，可以是远离言语行为的物理环境，包括一组情景类别，是从构成相关文化的社会符号系统中派生而来的意义群集（Halliday 1978a：33，109）。具体而言，"语境指语言形式和情景（语言运作环境）中非语言特征之间的关系，也指不在注意范围内的语言特征：它们统称为'超语篇特征'"（Halliday 1961：243－244）；但"社交语境"不只是"社会化与文化传递形式，也与角色关系、权势结构和社交控制方式、符号系统、价值系统、普遍知识"有关（Halliday 1973：63）。

其次是语域。从内涵上看,语域指语义配置的不同变体,是连接情景和语义层的中介,语篇是其实例表现,从而把文化性要素与特定情景类别联系在一起;它是特定社交语境中可资调用的语义潜势。从外延看,它关涉同一社团内各种不同情景的语言使用类别,诸如广告、法律、新闻、商业、政治、经济、学术、论辩、指导、描述、日常交流、小说叙事、诗歌戏剧以及妇女、工人、学者用语和黑帮行话等,它们具有不同的语义特点,所以也称语类(或体裁、篇类)。

语域之上是语境。从分类看,韩礼德将语境概括为三个变元:语场（Field of discourse）、语旨（Tenor of discourse）、语式（Mode of discourse）。"语场指语言片段出现的规约性场景,不仅包括交谈话题,还包括场景中说话者或参与者的所有活动[另加:还包括其他参与者的活动]……";语旨"指参与者之间的关系……不仅指语言使用正式程度的变化……而且指……诸如这种关系的运作与否,关系中的情感量值……";语式"指言语活动所采用的交流渠道,不仅是口头和书面媒介的选择,还有更为具体的选择[另加:'与语言在情境中的作用相关的其他选择']……"（Halliday 1978a：33, 115）。

对此,马丁（Martin 1992：496）把语域直接与情景语境等同。这显然与韩礼德的本意不符。但出于操作上的方便,人们在使用语域概念时大都沿用马丁的处理方案。同时,马丁首先把语篇类别意义上的语类概念(在韩礼德那里与语域同质)外推到意识形态和语域之间,是一个有语言参与而带目的、分阶段的社交过程概念,与索绪尔说的文化体制(包括语言体制)接近;意识形态和语类构成文化的内涵。于是有:意识形态⇆语类⇆语域⇆语义⇆语法⇆语音（Martin 1992：496）。向后的箭头表示体现和制约关系;向前的箭头则指向情景和文化因素。后来,他又直接把语类和意识形态等同看待(见 Martin 2012a),甚至认为他最大的遗憾是引入了意识形态这一术语(学术报告)。

这里需要明确"意识形态"的内涵,因为文献中的大多数论述都不做具体解释。此术语源于马克思,指的是跟社会阶级和社会冲突有关的观念上层建筑,是一种阶级冲突的核心概念,一种对"真实"的扭曲表征。之后,意识形态逐渐形成一个中立范畴,指"基于一定的社会地位而形成的思想观点"(胡辉华 2001)。巴赫金把它进一步概括为一种社会符号,一种构成所有社会关系的、具有本质意义的符号媒介,一种与社会领域更为广阔的对抗力量相关联的物质力量和社会实践(Gardiner 1992:8)。

第三,语域变量指语义三元:概念、人际和语篇;语篇是组织概念和人际意义的"手段"。需要明确的是,韩礼德的意义概念指语义成分,呈聚合关系,形成系统网络。例如,对于威胁,韩礼德分为两类:物理性威胁和非物理性威胁。前者涉及两组情况:(一)实施威胁的主体具体与否,如果具体,他可能是说话者本人,也可能是他人;(二)对于其中任何一种情况,条件是否明确。在明确的条件下又分两种并存情况:一是重复性威胁或持续威胁,二是条件属于主从类还是并列类;并列类又可分为命令或者禁止两个次类。非物理性威胁,要么是心理惩罚,要么是行为限制(Halliday 2003:238-239)。显然,人类通过经验获得的关于威胁的认识在这里被类别化和范畴化了。事实上,其他经验也可以通过类似方式加以描述。这就是系统语言学的特点:把连续体识解为可以进一步处理的语义特征和范畴,便于词汇-语法手段进行意义重构。

第四,三类语义系统经过词汇语法组合,变成实例化的词汇语法结构关系。(一)概念意义,包括经验意义和逻辑意义,由及物性、时制和归一度体现。词项范围内的经验意义分别是:事物(名词)、事件(动词)、品质或特征(形容词)、数量(数量词)、关系(英语系词、介词、连词;汉语结构助词)等;在小句级阶上,这些成分被结构化,构成及物性、时制①和归一度。归一度指命题的肯定与否定两个极端,如"张三(没有)追赶李四";处于两个极端之间的情态范畴也有经验意义,可以直接用"级差"来统称②。下面对及物性做扼要说明。如(1)张三在追赶李四,(2)张三看见李四了,(3)张三就是李四,(4)张三跳舞了,(5)张三说自己又长胖了,(6)他家门前有一条小河,它们分别代表及物性的六个过程类别。

---

① 夸克等人划分了16种英语时态,但韩礼德根据逻辑递归原则演绎出36种(涉及逻辑关系)。见韩礼德著《功能语法导论》(第二版),彭宣维等译,北京:外语教学与研究出版社,2010年,第六章。"逻辑-语义关系"可见该书第七章,包括扩展和投射两个大类。

② 这跟评价理论说的"级差"是一回事,但评价理论侧重其评价功能,这里则关注其经验意义侧面。也就是说,相关现象同时具有评价意义和经验意义两种特征。例如,"活泼"既是一种积极判断态度,也具有描述性格特点的经验特征。

（1）是物质过程："张三"和"李四"均作参与者："张三"是动作参与者，"李四"是目标，"追赶"是过程本身，前两者受过程支配。（2）是心理过程："张三"是感觉者，"李四"是现象。（3）是关系过程："张三"是载体，"李四"是属性。（4）是行为过程："张三"是行为者。（5）是言语过程："张三"是言说者，后面是言说内容。（6）是存在过程，它跟（4）一样，只有一个参与者：存在者。它们体现的都是经验过程意义。

（二）人际意义由语气和情态体现。韩礼德针对英语的情况指出，英语小句的语气由语气成分加剩余部分组成；语气成分又由主语和定式成分组成，从而构成两种总体语气：祈使和直陈。直陈分陈述与疑问；陈述又分感叹和言说；疑问包括特指问和是非问。这些语气类别，可以体现四种互动性的人际语义范畴（也称言语功能）：给予（我们帮一把可以吗？）、索取（把东西给我吧）、提问（你去过天津吗？）和陈述（我去过三次）。胡壮麟（1994：第八章）指出，汉语的语气主要由声调和语气词体现。

（三）语篇意义由主位化体现，具体包括主位结构、信息结构和衔接。主位结构指主位和述位一起构成的消息组织方式，如"张三打了李四"和"张三给李四打了"中的"张三"是主位，即小句表达的消息中第一个成分，是一则消息表述的出发点。信息结构指由已知信息和新信息构成的功能结构关系，如"（——你看到谁了？）——我看到了张三了"，其中"张三"是新信息；"我看到了"是已知信息。总体上，衔接包括照应、省略、连接和词项衔接四个大类，相关成分把一个又一个语义片段连接成为更大的单位，使这些片段具有内在的连贯性。

在上述基础上，马丁从语篇是一个社交语义单位的见解出发（Halliday 1978a），运用韩如凯的衔接和谐思想（Hasan 1984），从协商（人际互动意义）、识别（照应）、连接与连续（语篇的逻辑意义）、概念（词项衔接）、语篇组织五个角度，探讨语篇组织。可见，语义层不仅包含语义成分的系统网络，还涉及由这些成分组织而成的整体及其随时间变化的过程。那么，既然语义是聚合性的，词汇语法是组合性的，组织性的话语属于语义层还是词汇语法层？据韩礼德和马丁的见解，它仍然是语义性的。如此，话语性质的语义组织在此前的语言学模式中当居何处？

为此，韩礼德把此前有关语义层的两个观点（（一）语义层是一个聚合性的网络关系；（二）语篇是语言的实例，是一个社交语义单位）、把索绪尔认定的语言和言语、叶尔姆斯列夫的系统和过程联系起来,区分语言系统和语言实例,推出了下面的扩展模式。

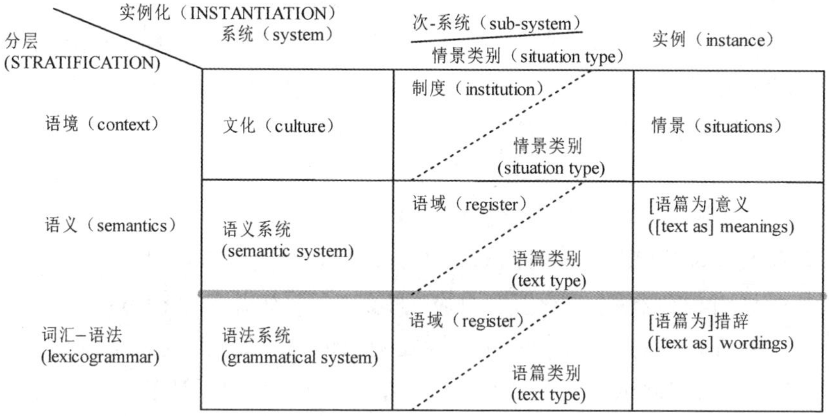

分层 (STRATIFICATION)	实例化（INSTANTIATION） 系统（system）	次-系统（sub-system） 情景类别（situation type）	实例（instance）
语境（context）	文化（culture）	制度（institution） 情景类别 (situation type)	情景（situations）
语义（semantics）	语义系统 (semantic system)	语域（register） 语篇类别 (text type)	[语篇为]意义 ([text as] meanings)
词汇-语法 (lexicogrammar)	语法系统 (grammatical system)	语域（register） 语篇类别 (text type)	[语篇为]措辞 ([text as] wordings)

图 3－1：韩礼德的扩展语言模式

这样,左边的系统成分网络与右边的组织关系就可以统一到语义层之下了;不仅如此,词汇语法层涉及类似关系(另见 Halliday 1973：101);而语音层同样涉及系统和实例问题,在"作为意义的语篇"与"作为措辞的语篇"之外,还有"作为声音的语篇"(text as sounding)。

3.3 语言过程的四个维度：理论上的进一步思考

为此,经典模式提出的一系列范畴及其性质就需要重新加以考虑。笔者将在尽可能不改变原有范畴、同时吸取其他功能学派有关思想的基础上,以这个扩展模式为出发点来重新做出规划。首先,韩礼德早先的两个核心观点,即(一)语篇是一个社交语义单位以及(二)词汇语法的上限是小句(复句),就需要做出相应调整;也就是说,(三)语篇不仅是语义性质的实例组织,也是词汇语法的实例组织;(四)词汇语法的上限级阶不再是小句,而是语篇;(五)语音系统的实例性组织也不再是语调单位,而应该是语篇单位性质的。笔者将依据图 3 - 1 讨论前四点,即根据相关专题做概述。

下面从语式、人际性、主位化的内涵开始。这一议题是第一次论及,所以多说一些。把"人际性"放到这里,对于熟悉经典模式的读者来说,似乎南辕北辙,其实不然——经典理论的语式概念,其内涵不应该是所谓的"语篇性",而应该是人际性的,与主位化没有必然联系。

根据前文引述的定义,语式涉及两层意思:(一) 口头和书写媒介;(二) 典型的口语和书面语类别及其连续性。两者属于两个不同的领域:媒介涉及互动方式:是面对面对话还是非面对面交流与独白(非面对面交流如电话、网络聊天);究竟启用哪一种方式,往往并无选择自由,而是由外在人际环境决定的。例如,在电话发明以前,跟远方的友人交流往往通过书写实施;在通讯发达的当代,手机短信、微信和电子邮件又常常让人缺乏回避余地;人与人面对面撞上了,不可能改用文字打招呼;在集体聚会上发言,也不可能只有书写材料而不开口讲话;而要严密论述自己的看法,书面方式在时间和空间上游刃有余,于是显得特别重要。当然,在当今社会选择交流媒介的途径还是有相当自由空间的。例如,我们有时选择直接打电话而不是短信或微信,但有时正好相反,有时又选择电子邮件;这些社会行为均涉及人际的心理因素和处理问题的方式。因此,经典模式中的语式概念,是一种确定、限制、支配人际交往方式和交际效果的重要手段,应该划归语旨的范围,即在经典语旨定义之后另加"也涉及交际目的和由交流媒介决定的交往方式"。

经典语式理论的第二层意思,即语言在典型口语和典型书面语之间的连续特征,同样应该体现一个人际功能次范畴。这个次范畴就是笔者确立的权势意义,跟人与人之间的等级差异、社交场合以及心理距离连在一起。韩礼德在《作为社会符号的语言》第 8 章"城市社会里的语言"中对此有初步论述,并在随后第 9—13 章中或多或少反复提及。其实,在该书中韩礼德区分了两种语言变体:一是与语篇意义联系在一起的语域概念,即由使用场合决定的语言变体(语义);二是社会变体:由城市言语社团决定的语言异质性和多样性。"在等级社会结构中,这(异质性)是我们文化的特点,我们赋予语言变体的价值,是社会性的价值,变体是社会结构的符号表达",是"社会的索引"。他举的例子是"*I saw the man who did it, but I never told anybody*"(我看见那人干了这事,但我从来没有告诉过任何人)与"*I seen the bloke what done it, but I never told nobody*"(我瞅见那家伙干这事儿来着,可我从没跟人提过)。据韩礼德的看法,这种"高值"与"低值"变体就是语体①:

> 说话人可以在正式语境中使用高值变体、在非正式语境中使用低值变体:我们把这种匹配叫做一致型。但它也可使用非一致型,即在语境确立的标准之外使用。这样做能获得一种前景化效果,根据不同环境可以是幽默的、令人吃惊的、嘲弄性的或许多其他情形。这一实施方式的重要性在于:这样的变体是有意义的。一个特定实例中的一个特定选项的意义,是整个复杂环境因素的一个函数,这些环境因素一起在某种层面上决定体现相关社会体制的意义交换。

韩礼德进一步指出:"压力之下的社会群体,明白其自身的语言规范会受到其他社会群体贬低,通常会使用微妙的复杂形式来从事言语游戏,这样的言语会受到特有的高度评价",所以相对于整个制度化了的社会等级结构而言,整个语言系统均以这种方式被赋予相应价值;"鉴于社会群体在特定社交语境中选择意义的方式彼此有别,带有特定意图的语体就成为社会价值的赋值对象,而这些社会价值是依附于这些社团本身的",于是有"标准"和"非标准"变体,与"社会身份"密切相关。这是一种制度,一种社会结构的载体与象征符号(Halliday 1978a:157,160–162)。韩礼德为我们清楚地确立了语体及其相应的社会体制范畴,并对后者做了充分阐述。我们要研究的是:(一)这种社会体制该如何定性和称谓;(二)如何按照正统的系统功能语言学方式,对这种社会结构关系进行系统描写。

在早期,美国学者布朗和吉尔曼(Brown & Gilman 1960)从欧洲主要语言的代词系统出发,确立了两个重要范畴:权势(Power)和同盟(Solidarity)。第一,权势和同盟的定义:如果一个人可以控制另一个人的行为,我们就说这个人对另一个人具有权势地位;权势是一种关系,至少涉及两个人,是不平等的,两人不可能在同一行为领域都有权势,否则就会产生冲突;这个意义上的权势涉及体力、财富、长幼、性别,以及在教会、

---

① 这个术语和文体学使用的 style 系不同内涵;汉语拟分别使用"语体"与"文体/风格"以相区别;也见 Enkvist(1985)意义上的 style 概念以及彭宣维(2015b)。

政府、军队或在家庭内部所具有的体制化角色(同上)。同盟指彼此之间的社会心理距离,如由经历、职业、性别、年龄、兴趣、出身、信仰、种族等因素决定的共同性,以及由此结成的同盟和一致关系,潜在于所有人之间,有远近之别。第二,权势和同盟的关系:在权势上具有优势的人之间可能是近同盟,如父母、同胞之间,也可能不是,如人们很少见到的官员。同样,在权势上处于劣势的人之间可能是近同盟,如老管家之间;也可能像跟不熟悉的餐馆服务生一样疏远,属于远同盟(同上)。显然,这里的权势关系与韩礼德的有关论述基本一致,因为两者在关涉的对象及其范畴化方式与性质上是兼容的。这里正式采用"权势"来指称韩礼德描述的社会等级结构关系①。

但布朗和吉尔曼的模式存在若干分类问题。

第一,既然权势有高、中、低位,是一个连续体,那么除了最底层,往上面移动的任何一个等级地位上的人,对下面所有的人都应具有权势地位,是不平等的;处于同一层次上的人之间在地位上则是平等的。据此,笔者从系统描写的角度,把由社会角色-地位决定的语义特征区分为两类:等级地位(高、中、低)与相互关系(平等与不平等,不平等又可能是下对上与上对下的)。笔者拟把这样的社会关系,按照系统功能语言学的意义形式一体化原则,在词汇-语法连续体上统称为等级性。

第二,同盟关系的远近特征无法涵盖所有的社会心理距离。葛德指出,话语情景会涉及话语策略。例如,当不同社会地位的人之间处于冲突和对立状态时,彼此会尽可能拉大距离,手段是语言:社会地位低者会使用攻击性的粗俗语,以威胁对方;而不熟悉这种语言表达方式的高社会地位者则尽可能使用精心选择的词语,可能包含威胁和不明确的暗示。相反,在非冲突状态下,双方则可能尽量拉近距离,在语言上尽可能抹去过分显眼的不平等用语;如居高位者可能使用亲切的举止和言辞,低地位者则尽量使用正式用语(Gaitet 1992:14-15)。这种情况可称为投合性。从分析角度看,冲突与否构成一个选择系统。两种情况之间还有中间状态,可称之为中和性。三者构成一个与距离性有关的系统,且称为融洽性;它和同盟之间是合取关系。因此,距离性={同盟性(远/近)+融洽性

---

① 也见前文韩礼德关于情景的论述:社交语境与角色关系、权势结构和社交控制等有关。

［对立/非对立（投合/中和）］｝。距离性的连续体在词汇-语法层可称为亲密性。

此外，每一个社会层次上的人之间都有远近程度；按照布朗和吉尔曼的观点，即权势和同盟有交叉关系，据此这里涉及六种典型的可能情况：优势+亲近、优势+疏远、平等+亲近、平等+疏远、劣势+亲近、劣势+疏远。

同时，特定场合对权势与社会距离也有调节作用。它有两个方面。第一，物理环境的，这一点跟体制化程度有关。例如，本来具有平等关系的人，他/她如果走向台前讲话，其他人就需要倾听，不管倾听的人在体制化了的社会等级关系中具有何等重要的地位；而在私底下的非制度化场所，他们又会恢复常规关系。第二，观念认知的，是行业领域还是日常话题，跟行业性相关。笔者把体制化和行业性两类彼此相关的词汇-语法现象统称为庄重性。

鉴于"社会角色-地位"、"社交场合"、"社会等级距离"均与权势有关，这里扩大布朗和吉尔曼说的权势概念的外延，包括上述所有三种情况，即把"权势"作为一个统摄三者的上位概念。三个权势子系统体现为"等级性"、"庄重性"和"亲密性"三个词汇-语法范畴（对比Poyton 1990）。

现在来看典型口语和典型书面语及其连续性。格列高利（Gregory）在朱斯（Joos 1967）确立的五种语体类别之上，构拟了一个连续体。该连续体上有一些相对典型的变体范畴。在言说一端有即兴与非即兴之分：即兴包括（一）交谈与（二）独白；非即兴有（三）"朗诵"与（四）说出写好的东西。后者和书面语一端联系在一起，两者协作产生以下可能性：（五）写出来为了说但感觉不到是提前写好的变体；（六）写出来为了说的变体；还有一种不必是为了说的变体，又分（七）当作言谈（像是听说的）或思想（像是无意间听到的）来读和（八）纯粹为了阅读（Gregory & Carroll 1978：47）。

这些典型情况在理想化的语体轴上构成一个连续统；在语言使用的具体分布上，可能存在两种情况：语体成分涉及的意义，有些是连续的，有些则是离散的。例如，*Intelligent vs. brilliant vs. talented vs. wise vs. apt vs. bright vs. shrewd vs. clever vs. smart vs. witty vs. quick vs. sharp vs. brainy* 等体现智商高的成分，表达的是连续的意义，甚至相互覆盖。汉语中有"勇"或"勇敢"这一高值语体成分，对应的低值成分是"敢"和"大胆"等；

第三章　语言的过程

其间缺乏中性成分(尽管"敢"接近中值,但毕竟带口语特点)。于是,我们得到下面的系统模式及其体现关系(见下图)。

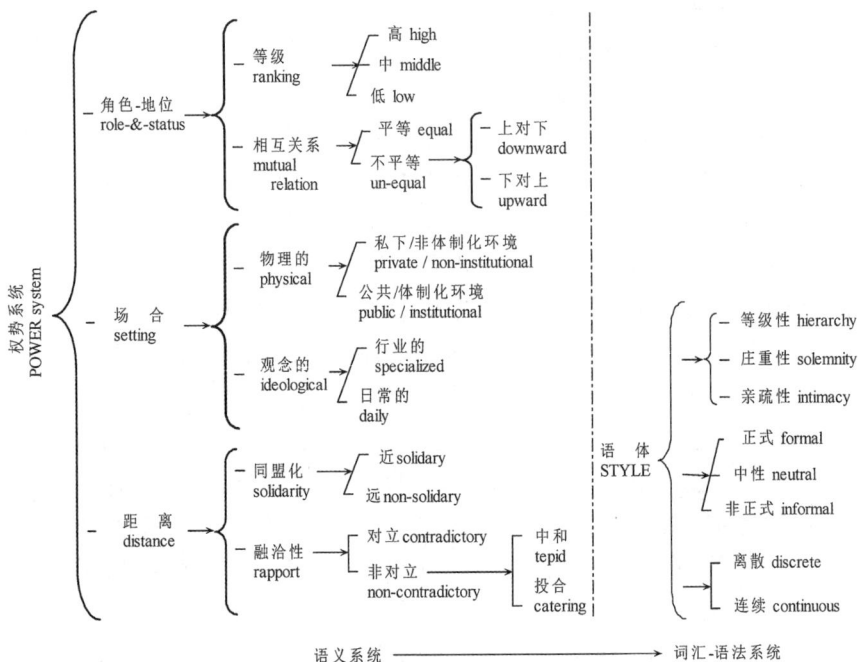

权势系统 POWER system
- 角色-地位 role-&-status
  - 等级 ranking
    - 高 high
    - 中 middle
    - 低 low
  - 相互关系 mutual relation
    - 平等 equal
    - 不平等 un-equal
      - 上对下 downward
      - 下对上 upward
- 场合 setting
  - 物理的 physical
    - 私下/非体制化环境 private / non-institutional
    - 公共/体制化环境 public / institutional
  - 观念的 ideological
    - 行业的 specialized
    - 日常的 daily
- 距离 distance
  - 同盟化 solidarity
    - 近 solidary
    - 远 non-solidary
  - 融洽性 rapport
    - 对立 contradictory
    - 非对立 non-contradictory
      - 中和 tepid
      - 投合 catering

语体 STYLE
- 等级性 hierarchy
- 庄重性 solemnity
- 亲疏性 intimacy
- 正式 formal
- 中性 neutral
- 非正式 informal
- 离散 discrete
- 连续 continuous

语义系统 ─────────────────→ 词汇-语法系统

图 3 – 2:人际性的权势意义及其词汇-语法体现模式

　　注意,角色-地位的高中低之间、相互关系的平等与不平等之间、私下与公开场合之间、亲疏关系之间以及语体的正式、中性与非正式之间,都是连续的,所以在表征上用斜线框,即合取关系;与之相对的是非连续性,用正竖线框表示,都是析取关系。于是,在人际相度上有以下模式:权势→语体。

　　这里需要补充费尔克拉夫(Fairclough 2001)的一个观点:一个语篇会涉及多个语域信息,这样,语篇表达的权势和语体变化幅度(程雨民2004)就可以得到合理解释(对比 Fairclough 1988)。

　　这里对作为整体的人际相度略作说明。根据韩礼德确立的体现模式:言语功能(命令、提供、疑问、陈述),即人际互动,是由语气和情态体现的,它们又由声调(1 降调、2 升调、3 平调、4 降升、5 升降)和调式(key:声调的复合方式,如 13、53)来体现。但马丁和他的同事一道,在语旨这个大的人际情景范畴之下,分离出另一个人际功能次范畴,这就是评价意义,并把情态纳入其中。笔者为评价意义提供的形式范畴术语是"评判"(Assessment;对比 Halliday & Matthiessen 2004:608-612;2014:679-685):体现评价意义的词汇语法范畴,包括语素(如否定性的前后缀-less 和 un-,即介入的否定性)、各类词项、词组和短语(英语中的 my pot[我的罐子]与 that pot of mine[那只我的罐子,相对于"那只你的罐子"]:对比级差意义)、小句(如倒装句、强调句、宾语前置句、部分被动句、汉语中的"连"字句、"得"字句和动补式/动结式等)。评价意义也可以通过声调或/和调式来体现(如调式表达的反驳、抗议、可能性、断然性等意义)。至此,我们得到一个包括三组人际次相度在内的体现模式:

语旨→
    (言语功能/互动意义 → 语气 +
    评价 → 评判 +
    权势 → 语体)→
            声调与调式。

余下两个问题:(一)语式的内容被移到人际相度后,原先语式的位置留下了一个空位,应如何处理?(二)主位化性质为何?我们拟在解决第二个问题之后来回答第一个问题。

在经典理论中主位化涉及主位结构、信息结构和衔接关系。这里暂时不谈衔接问题。韩礼德对主位的定义是:"主位是消息的出发点,是小句赖以展开的基础,所以小句的一部分意义取决于哪个成分被选作它的主位"(韩礼德 2010:41);而余下的部分就是述位。信息结构通常由已知信息和新信息构成(有时只有新信息,如"从前有座山"):说话人设定的、听话人可以恢复的信息是已知信息,不可恢复的是新信息。例如,"——你看见谁了?——我看见张三了!","我"是主位,"我看见"是已知信息;"看见张三了"是述位,"张三"是新信息。

韩礼德是把主位结构和信息结构所体现的意义作为语篇的组织功能看待的,原因是它们与衔接纽带一样,都是组织语篇的手段。笔者的理解有所不同。第一,衔接发生在所有语言层次、语言相度以及词以上的语言级阶上,所以它不是一个单纯的语义现象。例如,语篇语音组织的衔接问题,是语音层本身的(见胡壮麟 1994),跟词汇语法和语义没有直接关系。第二,主位结构和信息结构涉及消息展开的角度问题,是由说话人选择、语篇表达的视角；认知语言学对类似现象使用的是同一术语。显然，消息展开是一回事，确立消息展开的角度则是背后的支配性因素①。根据兰盖克的定义，"视角指观察者与被'观察'的情景之间的整体关系"，是一种观察性设置；最明显的就是假定的观察点（Langacker 2008：73）。这一点近乎于语用学原则与策略。第三，"语篇"自身是"被/受"组织的，而不是组织主体；主体是具有动机的个体：只有主体才具有选择和组织能力。韩礼德指出："主位是我，即说话人，所选择的发话点。已知信息是你，即听话人，已经了解或者可以推知的内容。主位+述位结构以说话人为准，已知信息+新信息则以听话人为准。……但两者当然都是说话人做出的选择。正是说话人指派了这两种结构，使彼此映射，从而为话语提供一种复合组织，并与周围环境联系在一起"（Langacker 2008：341）。

据此，先前的"语篇功能"其实是一种"个体功能"（Personal function），即说话者个人在话语过程中赋予信息片段以消息价值的交际功能，确定消息表征的角度（从而吸纳其他学派的研究发现），并随时给予调节，同时影响概念意义和人际意义的词汇-语法化；但这不仅是先前说的组织化影响，也是互动性影响，即协作共处的相互关照——同时考虑三类语义的识解，这一点符合经典理论界定的"配置"内涵，至少并不冲突。再者，个体特征的引入并非说个体的主动性就像这个术语本身显示的那样具有完全的自由意志；据韩礼德，虽然个体是选择主位和信息的主体，但同时受听话人左右，这就和人际功能连成一体了。

从社会符号层面看，将个体特征纳入系统功能语言学的模型，可以满足个人对话语的支配与调节作用这一重要的交际侧面，与人际功能构成互动和互补关系：在个体与群体之间取得协作。马丁（Martin 2006）在讨论体现、实例化与个体化及其与意识形态和主体间性的关系时，构拟了一个有关个体化的渐变模型。该模型包含储备库到惯用组目，中间有系统、编码方式、个性风格、个体。语言使用的这一个体化侧面，决定了与他人存在差异的理论机制。笔者据此为马丁提倡的个人化（Persona）提供进一步的理论支持和落脚点——纳入系统功能语言学的元功能范围，这样可

---

① 米勒（Miller 1985）指出："虽然'意识中心'、'视点'或'聚焦'等词语可能是当今的叙事理论不可或缺的……（但）任何小说里都没有观察或者聚焦，而只有用文字表达出来的虚拟幻象。"这说明视角是一个存在于语篇过程中的策略性意义。

以尊重和确立说话个体在语言符号系统中的认识论地位,确保个体在交际中的重要性。

因此,语言模式其实只是一种总体方向①;意义生成的具体过程是受个人因素支配的;既有严格执行者,也有越轨异类,中间是各种可能的复杂状态。这其中最关键的是交际动机,会使编码方式、个性化风格以及个体的临时因素发生很大变化,从而出现从常规到非常规的语言使用现象。

这一点在韩礼德的著述中是可以找到理论依据的。他在讨论人的社会属性时确立了两个范畴:个体与群体,作为个体的人类通过语言组成人群,再经过语言的作用由人群成为个人,而个人由语言构成社团,个人在社团中通过语言获得个性(Halliday 1978a:12-16)。据此,个体包含人类、个人和个性诸多带有共性特征的个性差异,也存在不同体质、心理、健康状况、生活阅历、经验知识以及人生观、价值观和意识形态。而正是这种差异才会针对同一议题产生互有差异甚至彼此迥异的语篇组织方式与相关内容,从而带来不同的语用效果。经典系统功能语言学只注意到了和群体有关的社交互动特性;马丁对人际的评价立场给予了补充;其有关论述再一次让我们看到了先前所谓语篇功能这一称谓的局限(见 Leech 1983:61),因而需要补充模型中忽略个体这一重要侧面的空位。

这里保留"语式"这个术语,内涵是基于能使功能的个体选择途径。直言之,它是一种语篇语义范畴,是语篇组织的个体因素,是作者或说话人确立叙述视角的相关动因。因此,它不再是经典系统功能语言学关于口语-书面语媒介及其语言变体的连续统,也不同于叙事学中关于讲述和展示带来的中介距离这个意义上的语式概念。

据此,语篇相度的核心体现模式则是:

语式→

　　语篇功能/能使功能:表述起始点+信息价值 →

　　　主位化(主位结构+信息结构)→

　　　　调核化②。

---

① 系统功能语言学一向对"规则""规章"持消极态度,因为其基本观点是:语言使用带有选择性和概率性;因此,纳入个体化概念可以缓解这种抵触情绪。

② 调核化指调核重音或调核突出的声调群单位的形成过程。调核位置是重音所在,标示信息焦点;相关区域为新信息;余下的是已知信息。

最后是概念相度。经典模式是把主语作为语气成分的一个构成要素的,即"语气成分＝主语+定式成分"。如 *John has been cutting the piece of wood since the morning* 中,作为主语的 *John* 与作为定式成分的 *has* (*been …ing*)一起构成语气成分;识别方式是在句末添一个附加问句:*isn't he*? 主句中的 *John* 在附加问句中被代词化为 *he*;故 *John* 应为主语。

这让笔者想到了传统语法识别主语的两条基本标准:(一) 附加问句中被代词化的那个成分;(二) 和动词有性数格一致关系的那个名词词组,英语中的性和格已经不明确了,但保留了数范畴。传统语法的问题是,这两条标准虽然在大多数情况下是兼容的,但对于存在句则无能为力,因为对存在句做附加问,其代词化成分是 *there* 的直接复制,而不是对其中那个有数的一致关系的名词词组的代词化。如 *there were three dogs in their house,weren't there*? 其中,*dogs* 在这里就不是主语。照此,经典系统功能语言学也没有解决历史遗留下来的问题;有学者的回应是,数的问题在英语中已经不典型了,可以忽略不计(Halliday & Matthiessen 2014:147–150)。但笔者有不同看法,作为一种现象,如果通过忽略不计的方式加以"忽略",这不是解决问题的理想办法。笔者认为,那个名词词组的主要功能的确是主语,但这个主语并不是人际性的。笔者认为主语及主语结构是体现及物性语法关系的更为抽象的句法结构:后者是从前者概括而来的一个词汇语法范畴(具体讨论见本书第 4—6 章;也见彭宣维 2011:第九章)。

对于经典模式对过程的分类,笔者也有不同理解(具体讨论见本书第 4 章)。首先,先前确立的关系过程显然与物质过程和心理过程是交叉而非互斥关系;而这一点在《功能语法导论》(第三版)中已经有所体现。这让笔者有机会重新审视三者的关系。正如韩礼德所说,物质和心理是两种不同的经验类别:一种是关于外在的,一种是关于内在的;而关系是对物质或心理经验的一种表征方式,如"张三现在北京"(物质-关系)、"张三似乎很郁闷"(心理-关系)。与此相对的有一类现象,如"李四昨天没上课,开小差了"、"李四坐在那里根本没听讲,开小差了"。两句都有"李四开小差了",但表征的现象一类是物质经验,一类是心理经验。这一类现象且叫做作为关系:主要表征过程的行为特征,这是非关系性质的。而先前的言语、行为和部分存在过程基本上可以划入物质-作为类。如此,我们得到四个新的及物性过程类别：物质-关系、物质-作为、心理-关系、心理-作为。笔者的具体研究表明，关系与作为、物质与心理之间存在重叠现象（见下一章的理论阐述）。

表 3-1：及物性新模式

	关　　系	作　　为
物质	张三很漂亮/张三是老师 张三现在北京/圣诞节是周二 张三有三套房/钢琴是张三的	李四在追赶王五 李四在不断打喷嚏 李四说他在城里
心理	张三很高兴/大海让张三兴奋 张三在兴头上 张三有爱心	李四感觉腿发软/李四想念王五 李四看见王五在跑/桌面摸起来很光滑 李四在想问题/李四着迷了

下面是我们理解的概念相度；关于及物性的构成，具体讨论见后面第四、五、六章：

语场 →

概念功能（经验＋逻辑）→

及物性（过程模式→作格模式→主语模式）

最后，我们需要对人际意义部分的词汇语法范畴"语气成分"的构成做一补充：主语移走之后，原先主语位置上发挥相应交际功能的成分需要一个术语来指称，姑且称之为"互动语"（Interactant），涉及存在句中的 there 与非存在句中和动词的数有一致关系的那个名词词组。即是说，在非存在句中，与动词有数的一致关系的那个名词词组身兼二职：形式化的主语（概念相度）和形式化的互动语（形式相度）。其实，无论是在英语中还是汉语中，对话中依靠新信息来维系人际关系与交往的发展也很常见。据此，体现人际互动意义的词汇语法手段，以"互动语+定式成分"这样的结构成分来体现，但这只是多种方式中的一种；汉语缺乏这样的成分，主要靠语音和语气词来体现（见本书第六章）。

此外，时制在传统语法中究竟用来做什么，缺乏足够的理论阐述和明

		语境（情景语境和文化语境）			
	语域:	语篇语义学：意义单位		语篇语法学：词汇语法/措辞	语篇语音学/语篇书写学
	语义配置	所指→			能指
语境	语式→	语篇意义	出发点	主位化→	调核化
			新闻性	信息化→	
	语场→	概念意义	过程性	及物性（过程模式→作格模式→语态模式+主语模式）→	语调化
			级差性		
			时间性→	时制→	
	语旨→	人际意义	互动性→	语气→	声调化
			评价性→	评估→	
			权势性→	语体→	
→	链接	代码化、结构组织化、实例化、体现			

图 3-3：语言过程涉及的基本范畴

确认识。这里根据夸克等人的观点，认为它是体现时间意义的词汇语法手段，一同由语调这个中性范畴来体现："时间→时制→语调"。

这些范畴构成一个三维立体模式：（一）竖向维度——词-篇连续体，即从语素到词、词组或短语、小句或复句、段、节、章直至篇，是一个连续体，中间是代表性级阶；（二）横向维度——从语境到语义、词汇语法、再到语音，它们之间是被体现和体现的层次关系，后者体现前者；（三）纵深维度——概念、人际和语篇性质的意义及其相应的措辞与声音/书写（见图 3-4；另见彭宣维 2011：33）。

虽然笔者明确提到了词-篇连续体上的典型范畴，但在实际分析时不一定能够获得相应的分析性单位，这一点尤其表现在语素级阶上；再者，即使可以划分出这样的单位，就现在的认识水平看，还没有合适的术语来逐一代之。因此，这是一个理想化的认知模型，可能随不同语言而有所变化，但总体上具有普遍性。

语言过程就是这个立体模式中三个空间维度在时间流程中的延伸。因此，如果考虑时间因素，这应该是一个四维模式，时间基于空间而发挥作用。这是接下去要讨论的问题。

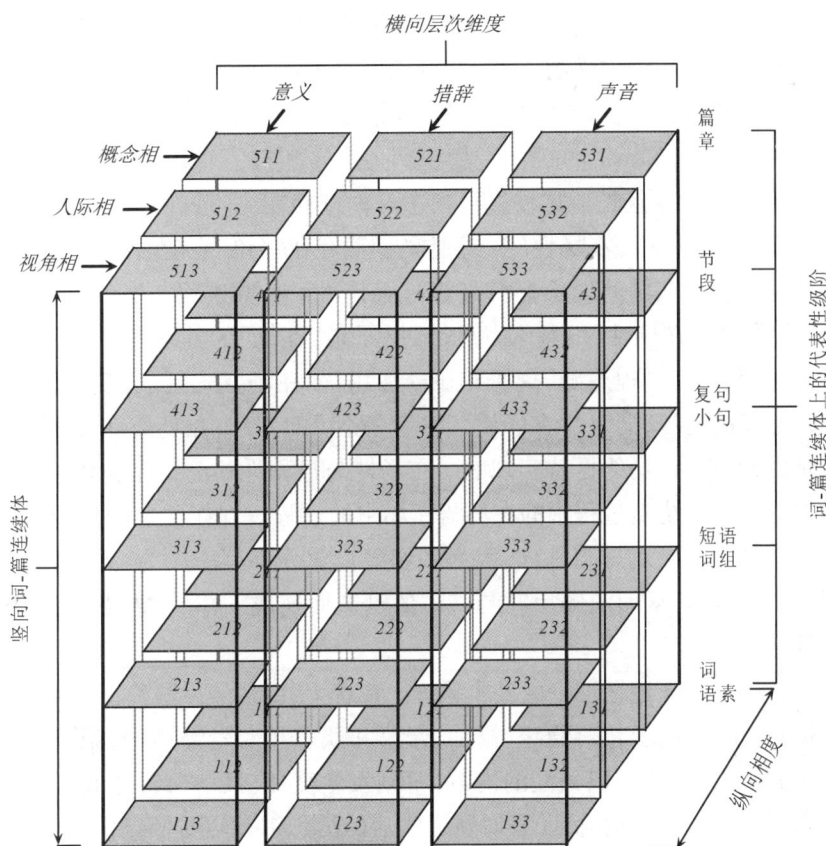

横向层次维度

意义　措辞　声音

概念相 →

人际相 →

视角相 →

竖向词‑篇连续体

纵向相度

词‑篇连续体上的代表性级阶

篇章
节段
复句 小句
短语 词组
词 语素

511　521　531
512　522　532
513　523　533
411　421　431
412　422　432
413　423　433
311　321　331
312　322　332
313　323　333
211　221　231
212　222　232
213　223　233
111　121　131
112　122　132
113　123　133

图 3‑4：语言过程涉及的立体维度

3.4　语言的记忆加工过程及相关因素

　　上面扼要介绍了语篇可能涉及的各个主要范畴及其体现模式,这里还需要说明语篇生成的动态性。该议题是针对韩礼德模式集中关注语言系统而提出来的,也是此前有关论述已经涉及和具备但尚未如此定性的一步工作。而这样来定性也是学界早有的认识,这里只是提到意识日程

上来而已。下面主要阐述三点：（一）语言的生成过程；（二）过程模式
与认知语言学和语用学的关系；（三）语言编码中的不确定因素。语言过
程可用现在主义认识论加以解释；操作上则与工作记忆关联。

现在主义（Nowism）关注一切（"外在"与"内在"）过程的现时性，即
"此即此在"的在场性。这种过程状态可称作存在的"现在性"，它有三个
基本着眼点：（一）在场性——主体的明确存在感知，这是基础；（二）过
程性——基于在场的现象更替；（三）整体性——融过程与在场于一体。
"过程性"是"在场性"的基本特点，"过程"是"在场"的基本存在方式：在
场由过程表征，过程追随、寓居并显现在场，以在场方式延展、变化，从而
丰富在场的内涵；同时，"在场性"是"过程性"的基础，在场成就过程：过
程是由无数个在场的更替实现的。在场性与过程性的前提是整体性：整
体的泛时视角统括过程中的在场与在场中的过程。现在主义的基本思想
是语言过程的出发点和基础，因为一切潜势成分都可能成为当前信息加
工的待选因素，从而消解历时与共时的割裂而连成一体、进入当下（见彭
宣维 2015b）。

然后是工作记忆理论的基本原理。传统上，记忆分为两种：长时记忆
和短时记忆。前者相对稳定，添加、修改和遗忘相对较慢；短时记忆则是
注意的焦点，也是意识关注的内容，时刻发生变化。后来，百德利和赫奇
提出了工作记忆的概念，一种对新近激活的信息进行临时储存的功能，这
些信息占据着意识，可以进行操作，也可以导入和排除短时记忆（Baddeley
& Hitch 1974；Baddeley 1986，2000[1999]）。再后来，人们发现对于专家
或者并不太难的语篇（尤其是文学语篇）的解读来说，读者并没有如经典
记忆理论说的、需要花费相当时间从长时记忆中提取信息进行识别加工；
相反，这一过程似乎非常容易。于是，肯奇等（Ericsson & Kintsch 1995；
Kintsch et al. 1999）不再把工作记忆和长时记忆对立起来，而是看作横跨
短时记忆和长时记忆的一种共享特征，从而区分短时工作记忆和长时工
作记忆，后者属于长时记忆的一部分，与短时工作记忆中[1]正在加工的内
容联系在一起，随时等待提取，排除了"意识"状态与工作记忆的必然联系。

---

[1]　此前，工作记忆与短时记忆基本一致，只是定义的角度不同；但在这里，短时工作
记忆与短时记忆是什么关系？他们没有明确论述；笔者认为还是此前的短时记忆
和工作记忆的关系。

进而,他们阐述了长时工作记忆的工作原理。长时工作记忆是根据短时工作记忆提供的线索动态生成的,前者体现了后者的变化情况。短时工作记忆中通常包含3—5个活跃的字符节点;它们会"照亮"长时记忆中的相关信息节点(先前存在的结构关系,诸如概念、框架、格式塔和图示),而这些节点又和长时记忆中没有被"照亮"的其他节点连接在一起(连接是长时记忆的特点)。因此,长时工作记忆包括被照亮的节点,外加与它们连接而没有被照亮的节点。信息加工可以在所有这些节点之间提取信息而无需外来的引导信息介入。可见,工作记忆涉及两个部分:短时工作记忆中的提示性信号和长时工作记忆中的节点,后者和整个长时记忆相连。在语篇解读过程中,短时工作记忆不断分析处理新的字符信号,后者会不断激活长时记忆中的相关信息并形成新的节点;长时工作记忆则不断得到充实与复杂化。随着短时工作记忆中信息的更替,那些关注较多、加工水平较高的信息就进入长时工作记忆,而其他信息随即遗忘;但整个阅读过程都是长时工作记忆中新节点增加、长时记忆中其他节点之间连通的过程。而这正是现在主义思想在认知加工中的体现。

据此,笔者提出语言功能的加工模式。依据是韩礼德扩展模式的实例化概念以及语言在工作记忆中的在线加工特点,目标是语言的生成过程:一切相关信息呈现于当下,是现在主义性质的(见图3-5;对比 Levelt 1989:9;Leech 1983:58-63)。

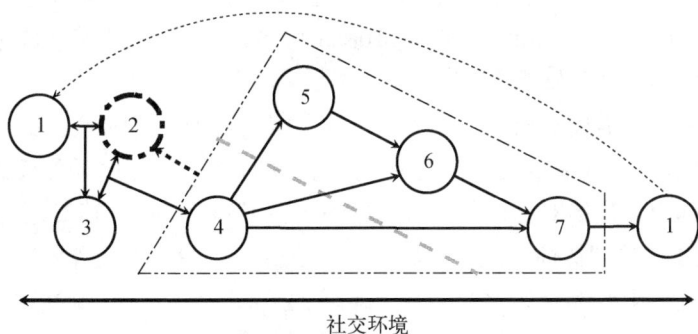

图 3-5:语言加工过程示意图

该过程涉及长时工作记忆和短时工作记忆,即"4+5+6+7"的整个区域;而"2-7"属于认知神经范围,系相关在线信息的居所。交际意图激活长时记忆("2")中的相关信息,形成长时工作记忆("4"),包括随时等待调用的语义、词汇语法、语音/书写等系统成分;这些成分与处于离线状态的其他长时记忆中的信息("2")具有联通关系,所以后者可以随时被激活、被调用。在长时工作记忆支持下,短时工作记忆("5+6+7")进行语义("5")、词汇语法("6")以及语音/书写("7")的结构化"编码"。因此,短时工作记忆是在线加工的一端,也是注意端;长时工作记忆则处于另一端,在很大程度上是无意识的。加工后的表达信息("7":语音/书写单位)由外在媒介("1",即韩礼德说的"语音或书写实体")进一步体现:它既可能作为外部刺激信号由言说者本人"输入",以调节言说内容、方式与质量,也可以为听话人作为"输入"信号而激活长时记忆中的信息,从而形成长时工作记忆并进行解读。"3"是感知识别系统,应该是"1"和"2"互动产生的;"2"和"3"互动形成长时工作记忆"4"。从工作记忆("4+5+6+7")向"2"的反向虚线箭头,表示语篇生成的加工过程可能受到足够注意而存入长时记忆;其他信息则随即消失。相关加工机制与前面提到的解读过程在功能上应该是一致的:经过加工处理的主要信息可以形成相关认知语境,并为进一步信息加工提供引导和限制,保证语篇生成的连贯性。

这里沿用认知语境概念(对比前文马林诺夫斯基、弗斯和韩礼德的定义):不论外在语境的影响力度有多大,均需在激活储存于长时记忆中的相关经验知识后、新"输入"的信息通过被激活的信息得到感知识别,然后才对语言"编码"和"解码"发挥作用(对比 Sperber & Wilson 1995: 15-16)。同时,语篇的创建与解读也是语篇语境的建构过程(见 Threadgold 1988; Halliday 2007a; Hasan 1995, 1999),前提是人类积累的既有经验知识和认知水平。

这里我们需要对语言编码中的不确定因素给予扼要阐述。图3-5这样的生成模式,容易给人一种批量生产意义的错觉,即经由类似模式生成的意义都应该是绝对一样的(Fish 1980;另见 Fish 1973)。其实,上述过程涉及"选择"的创造性。这一点韩礼德早就给予了相关阐述,涉及意义在实例化过程中的综合性、奢侈性、不确定性、非自足性与变量性(Halliday 1997)。以不确定性为例,在语篇生成的具体过程中,哪一个意义片段安排在哪里,往往并没有事前准备,而是在总体动机参照下,随机而临时成就的。我们都有这样的经验:对于同一个主题,如果同一个人在不同时间和场合来表达、不同的人针对同一主题在同一场合表达,无论是组织方式还是具体内容,都会有或大或小的差别。这种随机性是不可预测的,如语篇过程中何时、在哪里、相距多远出现相关成分,作者在写作之前并不知道,阅读过程也无法预料。因此总体目标的可预测性与具体表述的不可预测性之间,存在一种张力,作者需要在两者之间维系一种平衡,否则具体表达的意义片段就会脱离总体主旨而"偏题"。这也是写作过程中作者会不时回过头去参照已经写下的文字才能继续下去的原因。"偏题"是在维系总体主旨过程中出现的与之"脱节"的现象,这可能有智力因素,如平时训练不够,也可能有健康、情绪等原因。

上述过程大都出于理性设计;也有不带理性的,如行文中随意加入与正题无关的词句的案例。于是,这里涉及另一个级差模式:理性与非理性编码。理性总是和带目的的动机联系在一起;非理性往往缺乏应有的动机,具有随意性。

上述诸现象(或许还有其他情况)是在语言过程中三维之外的时间维度上发生的,编码动机支配整个过程,因而在意义链生成的不同阶段(不同的现在),任何语义成分、词汇语法单位、语音或书写要素发生改变,都可能引起意义的局部甚至整体改变。

于是,前文呈现的四维立体模型,在这里找到了动态加工的内在环境,从而使图 3-4 得到过程特性。韩如凯指出:功能模式关注语言的动态性,这对所指与能指之间的关系性质具有内在价值(Hasan 1988:46)。语言的过程维度强调语言的生成过程,即语言的动态性;正是这一在线加工特点,语言的交际功能得以实时发挥;其实,任何有语言发生的人际互动,均处于类似加工状态下。这是一个由多重互动关系构成的过程:内外互动、长-短时工作记忆互动、长时记忆中处于工作状态与非工作状态的信息互动、先"编码"的信息与后"编码"的信息互动、感觉-运动神经与交际意图互动、"输入"与"输出"互动等。

3.5　总结

语言模式是一种系统,一种制度,一种共同体内各成员遵守的常规人文法则,类似汽车、火车、轮船、飞机运行的公路、铁路、航空航海线,或者牵着风筝高飞的绳子及其放风筝的人。但这些法则的具体实施多有变数,随意性、随机性、不可预测性、不定性时有发生;而这正是语言实例的特点,是语言使用的本来面目,体现了使用者的主动性、动机性、创造性、灵活性,因而具有明确的人文特点。不过,上述众多"变数"中包含了一种历史的必然性。这里的观点与模因论并不冲突:其三个特征之一"复制忠实性"中包含了变异和创造因素;唯嫌对后者的平衡对立价值强调不够。毕竟,计算机病毒复制与文化传播(复制)有本质不同:前者是机械自动的完全复制;后者受兴趣、智力、记忆能力支配,有创造性因素介入,所以利科把类似现象称为"创造性模仿"(Ricoeur 1983:31)。把计算机病毒复制与大脑传承文化的机制混为一谈,是一种把大脑和计算机等同的机械论。

第二部分

及物性模式重构

第四章

及物性过程模式重构^①

本章及后面三章将对系统功能语法的及物性进行重构,包括对过程模式、作格模式和主语模式三个逐步概括化的句法现象深入讨论。其中,作格模式又分作格关系和语态关系两个次层次,它们的生成受制于消息推进的影响。

4.1 问题的提出

及物性(Transitivity)是系统功能语法的核心内容之一,具体涉及物质、心理、关系、言语、行为和存在六个过程,前三者为主要范畴,后三者为次类,分列于主类两两之间,构成一个连续的、具有互补/析取关系的系统。对此,本书作者有不同看法。首先,在经典及物性系统中,关系过程是在有关"内部"(心理)与"外部"(物质)经验的基础上确立的,因此前者与后两者的界定基础不同,这不符合范畴分类原则;我们认为,关系和物

---

① 本文在第九届中国功能语言学学术研讨会上报告过(2005 年 10 月,河南开封),后与许西萍合作刊发于《外语教学》2017 年第 4 期,第 18—24 页。

质-心理不是并行的互补关系,而是交叉关系;据此,及物性过程类型应该怎样看待? 其次,物质和心理既然涵盖了所有的经验类别,言语和行为范畴又该如何处理? 第三,存在句呢? 是否仍为一个相对独立的过程类别?

下面将据此对及物性过程做重新分类和解释:(一) 经典模式中将物质、心理和关系看作并列互补范畴(析取关系)存在的问题;(二) 识解的本质与及物性新模式;(三) 对言语、行为和存在现象的重新归类。

4.2　及物性过程重新分类的必要性

现今的及物性模式成型于 20 世纪 60 年代末(Halliday 1969/1976)。韩礼德在先前尝试(Halliday 1964/1976, 1967 – 1968;王力 1947;另见 Peng 2015a)的基础上将过程划分为三类:物质(Material,之前用的是 Action:作为)、心理(Mental)和关系(Relational)。后有三个分支。一个来自韩礼德本人:他增加了三个次类(Halliday 1969/1976),被广泛接受(Halliday 1985/1994;Halliday & Matthiessen 2004, 2014;也见 Eggins 1994/2004:206 – 253;Bloor & Bloor 1995:107 – 134;Thompson 1996/2004/2013;Martin et al. 1997:10 – 113;Butt et al. 2000:45 –83)。第二个分支源自福赛特(Fawcett 1980, 1987):他坚持韩礼德早期(1967 – 1968)的作格观和三分原则,即作为、关系和心理;后来他提出了六个过程,但角度不同:作为、关系、心理、环境(Environmental)、影响(Influential)和事件关联(Event-relating),均为析取关系(Fawcett *forthcoming*)。此外,马丁(Martin 1992:279)将韩礼德的六个次类归纳为三对析取范畴:作为:物质和行为;含义:言语和心理;存在:关系与存现。注意:关系范畴出现在所有分支模式中。

然而,经典理论对物质和心理范畴的界定与对关系范畴的界定,出发点是不一样的,即将关系和物质或心理并行看待,有违科学分类的一致性原则,因而有重新分类的必要。看以下两组实例(粗体为原文,下划线为本书作者所加)。

（1）AT&T's stock **slid** 14 percent Tuesday as the company **issued** its first profit warning under chief executive C. Michael Armstrong, <u>**fueling**</u> worries about whether his radical remake of the nations' largest long-distance company **will succeed**. The disappointing forecast, which **came** as AT&T **posted** first-quarter results that met most expectations, <u>**dampened**</u> the enthusiasm **created** by last week's initial public offering of ＄10.6 billion worth of stock in the company's wireless business.（Halliday 2004：196）

（2）a. I think mum's <u>more upset</u> than he is.

b. She's <u>not very interested</u> in the food.

c. he <u>is afraid</u> of snakes 　　（同上，221 页）

d. she <u>gets really annoyed</u> with a doctor's name

e. it <u>seemed encouraging</u>

f. you <u>look pleased</u> 　（同上，224 页）

g. I'm <u>very distressed</u> 　（同上，226 页）

前一组均被看作物质句,后一组均为关系句。问题是：其中加下划线的小句均与内部经验有关,可否都看作心理句？从理论上说,既然关系范畴是在物质和心理经验的基础上划分出来的,又何以认定它同其他五个范畴一起构成一个封闭的、具有连续统性质的人类经验体系、彼此互为析取关系呢(见 Halliday 2004：172 直观图:"'经验语法'：英语过程类别"及 173 页上的系统网络图)？

据韩礼德,划分物质和心理范畴的依据是人类的经验知识类别,有关"外在"世界的经验称为物质,"内在"世界者为心理。请看韩礼德本人的有关理论阐述(同上,170 页)：

我们在很小(三至四个月)的时候就意识到,在内部与外部经验之间存在基本差别：我们感受周围世界所发生的一切以及内心意识世界所发生的一切(包括知觉、情绪和想象)。有关"外部"世界的原型形式就是作为和事件：事情发生、人或其他动作者做事或使之发生。"内部"经验难于确定,但它要么是对外部世界的某种重现、记录、反应、反射,要么是有关我们存在的一种分离意识。语法在这两者之间确立一种非连续体：外部经验和内部经验之间的界限十分明

确,而由此确立的就是那些有关**物质**和**心理**过程的语法范畴。(粗体系原文,下同)

在此,我们需要对两种经验做一点说明。首先,语言所表达的从本质上讲无疑都是大脑的认识。因此,物质与心理过程之间的分别,并没有质的差异,只是经验类别不同而已。这一点在 20 世纪的学术界已得到广泛认可。具体而言,物质和心理都是经验性的(也见 Halliday & Matthiessen 1999),唯加工对象不同而已:物质经验是工作记忆加工中有关"外在"事物和事件的经验,可能真的存在(如"北京城"或"张三走了 60 公里"),也可能是假想的("龙","鬼吃人");心理经验则是一种有关"内部"状态、事件或活动的自我意识,涉及意识或潜意识状态下内心事件或活动的过程,包括情感、知觉、意愿和认知(Halliday 2004:208 - 210;这最后一个范畴仅仅是一个狭义概念,处于广义认知的最高层)。在许多情况下,尽管心理过程是对他人心理行为、事件或状态的描述,但均与说话人的自我意识有关:这是说话人在语言发展中形成的、具有自我参照特点的想象性心理行为。因此,物质经验是现象性的,心理经验则带有元现象的特点。

有了上述认识上的准备,下面转向所谓的第三大过程类别:关系。我们仍将从先前的定义及相关理论阐述入手(以下引译文的下划波纹线为笔者所加)。

> 除了物质和心理过程(即我们经验的外部和内部方面)外,我们还要提供第三个成分,从而构成一个具有一致性的经验理论。我们学习归纳和概括,将一个经验片段与另一个经验片段联系在一起,说明彼此相同,或此片段属于彼片段。在这里,语法确立起第三类过程,即那些识别和分类过程,我们称为关系过程句……(同上)
> ……这一点揭示了"存在"在典型配置时所具有的重要特点:经验"权重"在于两个参与者之间,相关过程则仅仅是连接两个参与者的高度概括性的成分……(213 - 214 页)
> ……这种配置……开启了一种语法潜能,来诠释这种带有类属关系的成分及其识别所具有的抽象关系,范围涉及所有经验领域。(214 页)

显然,这里的范畴化方式与前面提到的两种经验的范畴化方式不同:它是在上述两种范畴的基础上的进一步加工。换言之,该范畴化方式所揭示的,是对相关物质或心理经验的选择识解与结构化,从而变成语法关系。在这里,小句在识解经验范畴、生成概念语义关系的过程中,确立一个图景:一些经验范畴被选择出来,而其他范畴则用来说明这些经验范畴之间的识别或分类关系。因此,一种神经通路在原有激活水平的基础上得到进一步选择加工。据此,关系过程实则是一种经验性的选择识解和重新配置,基础是那些已经激活的物质或心理概念成分。这是一个已经被激活并经由进一步加工所获得的概念,与相关物质或心理经验有交叉关系。其实,韩礼德本人对这一点是有认识的:

> ……我们已经看到,"物质"小句是有关我们对物质世界的经验的,"心理"小句是有关我们对自己意识的经验的。两种经验均可识解为"关系"小句,但由此生成的不是"做"或"感知",而是"是"……(211 页)

> ……在该过程的展开中,"关系"小句很像"心理"而非"物质"……如果一个过程的识解随时间而延伸,并且这是唯一的选择,那么"关系"和"心理"小句看起来像是同一过程的两种变体;这其实就是某些理论(尤其是哲学)将它们看作"状态"的原因。(212 页)

> ……"心理"和"关系"小句之间存在交叉关系,像 I was scared(我吓了一跳)一类的小句可做两种解释。(224 页)

或许,这种相似性源于形式判断,至少从两者均有两个参与者的角度看是这样。其实,关系不只与心理经验有关,也与物质经验有关,如 London is beautiful/a beautiful city 以及 Sydney is an Australian city 所描述的,都是外部经验(对比 I am happy/upset)。可见,识解的结构化过程可能出现"关系",与进入这一过程的物理或心理经验之间,均有交叉关系。

关系是与物质-心理有关的现象,但这只是加工识解中的一类;还有一类非关系性的物质和心理现象。事实上,这一点韩礼德早就看到了,他甚至还使用"参与者"和"目标"这一对分析物质过程的术语来分析心理过程(Halliday 1968:181):

> 我们在两种过程即作为(action)和归属(ascription)之间做出了区分。作为范畴包括物理的和抽象的过程,还包括各种有生命的感知、认知及其他心理过程,如 Mary washed the clothes, John threw the ball, John sold the books, the prisoners marched, the boy fell down, it rained, John

saw the play, Mary spoke French。归属则是属性(attributes)归附问题,如 *she looked happy* 以及 *it cost ten shillings*。无论是作为还是归属,在英语中都作过程看,即它们均需在时态和情态方面做出选择;当然它们也存在诸多不同,如归属句中的属性必须出现。

在这里,韩礼德不仅注意到"作为"与"物理"(后来的"物质")/"心理"过程有交叉关系(对比 Halliday 1967(3)),而且在"作为"和"归属"(后来扩展为"关系")之间做出了区分,而后者福赛特(Fawcett 1980:138)阐述为"非作为"过程。

因此,本书作者将"作为"(Actional)当作一个术语使用,表示韩礼德(Halliday 1967(3):38)描述的"作为和事件"现象(actions and events)(当然同时涉及物质和心理现象;注意:action 在心理学中也常用来描述心理活动);而与此相对的"关系"(Relational),则指"状态和关系"(states and relations)(Halliday 1970:146;也见 Fawcett 1987:131),意义是分类与识别(Halliday 1985/1994;Halliday & Matthiessen 2004/2014)。下面将对作为和关系方式所识解的经验类别进行阐述,从而确立及物性过程分类的新模式。

4.3 识解的本质及具有复合特征的及物性新模式

我们将会看到,识解是一个具有相对选择自由的体现过程(对比 Langacker 1991;Talmy 2001a:169-172),在这一阶段上,物质或心理经验,在很大程度上既可以被识解为作为性质的结构,也可以是关系性的,由此体现的语法关系既可能是一致式,也可能是隐喻式。即是说,这些识解方式源于相关社交动因(见上一章),在第二加工阶段上,通过语法隐射(即由词汇-句法关系识解)而生成结构关系。

对比以下各组例句,其第一句都是从(1)中摘取出来的,其他例句则据此重新组合而成。各例均有多重特征(":"表并列特征),如(3a)是

心理∷作为∷隐喻∷及物;(3b)为心理∷作为∷一致∷及物;
(3c)心理∷作为∷一致;(3d)心理∷关系∷归属;(3e)心理∷关
系∷属有;(3f)心理∷关系∷处所∷隐喻。注意各组最后的存在句。

（3）a. AT&T's stock … was **fueling** worries about …

　　b. AT&T's stock made him worry more and more about …

　　c. as for AT&T's stock, he was worrying more and more about …

　　d. the worries that AT&T's stock had been fueling is that …

　　e. owing to AT&T's stock, he had more and more worries about …

　　f. because of AT&T's stock, he was in worries about …

　　g. there was worries in him about …

　　……

（4）a. the disappointing forecast … **dampened** the enthusiasm

　　b. the disappointing forecast made people feel more and more depressed

　　c. people who had been in high spirit now were feeling more and more depressed about

　　d. what people were depressed about is that …

　　e. people … had more and more a depressing mood about the disappointing forecast

　　f. people were in depressing mood about …

　　g. there was a depressing mood in people about …

　　……

（5）a. the enthusiasm had been **created** by last week's initial public offering

　　b. last week's initial public offering had made people feel enthusiastic

　　c. people became enthusiastic about last week's initial public offering

　　d. people were in enthusiasm aroused by last week's initial public offering

　　e. people had got the emotion of enthusiasm by last week's initial public offering

　　f. what people felt enthusiastic about is last week's initial public offering

    g. there was an enthusiasm in people about last week's initial
       public offering

    ……

    例(2)中所引各例也可进行类似重组转换。以其中第一小句为例,足可说明这种选择识解的灵活性。

(6) a. I think mum's more upset than he is.

    b. … mother has been occupied with an upset mood …

    c. … an upset mood is dominating mother …

    d. mum has an upset mood

    e. mum's in upset mood

    f. what mum has is a mood of upset

    g. there's an upset mood in mum

    ……

    显然,没有必要对物质经验的选择识解也做类似转换演示。读者想必已经明白这里的意图:如果暂不考虑可能存在的别扭感觉(许多规约用法都是从类似用语方式开始的),无论是物质还是心理经验,在语言加工过程中均可能以任何一种方式出现。

    历时地看,语言发展到今天,无论是作为特征还是关系特征,均可运用于对正在或即将识解的经验进行加工操作;从发生论的角度可以推知,作为和关系最初基本上是对外部经验的处理;隐喻化手段的使用则将这两种方式运用到内部事件和状态的识解上。尽管这些隐喻特征仍然存在,但经过长期使用便形成了一种非标记现象,如 she is happy。

    不过,虽然选择体现方式将物质和心理经验形式化,但识解方式本身所体现的也是经验性的。事实上,两种识解方式对概念/经验潜势(即被激活而即将进入体现阶段的经验图式或经验范畴系统)的选择同样融入了小句概念/经验意义的建构中,并成为决定性特征,使语义潜势变成词汇语法现实。在这一过程中起支配作用的,是工作记忆中的中央执行系统,伴随实施语言原则和策略。

    至此,我们将有关模式总结如下。注意,新模式中的"过程"是一个具有双重特征的概念。这里保留了韩礼德有关及物分析的相关参与者术语,但需留意各类过程的物质或心理经验类别及其在小句生成过程中的动态识解方式。

表4-1：及物性过程新模式

方式 类别	识解/体现(Construing/Realizational)	
	作为(Actional)	关系(Relational)
物质经验 (Material)	**物质-作为过程：动作者+目标** (**Material-Actional Process：Actor + Goal**) - she sat with her knees up to her chin - she was pounced upon by Lady Palsworthy - history has witnessed everything - now her father said she must not go - he sighed heavily - there comes a bus from the other end of the road	**物质-关系过程：载体+属性** (**Material-Relational Process：Carrier + Attribute**) - he was tall and dark and handsome - his name was Peter - Ann was twenty-one and a half years old - you've got a bicycle - his voice now had lost its ironies - there was a young man in love
心理经验 (Mental)	**心理-作为过程：感觉者+现象** (**Mental-Actional Process：Senser + Phenomenon**) - she was pleased and a little flattered - she discovered that with a start - shamefaced curiosities began to come back into her mind - he's a great worker, and you can depend on him. - she said to herself … - there lingered a passion in her to embrace him	**心理-关系过程：体验者+体验** (**Mental-Relational Process：Experiencer + Experience**) - I never was so happy before - I am in love with him - her soul was full of the sense of disaster - she had a number of fragmentary impressions of Alice - she gained his belief again - there was an enjoyable mood around

还有两点需要明确。第一,心理-关系过程是在物质-关系过程的基础上确立的,也有两个功能成分:体验者和体验。它们与左前框内的范畴具有共同性:均涉及情感、感知、意愿和认知四个次范畴(见前);但作为一对相对独立的范畴,这里有必要使用这一对新术语。一方面,它们不再叫做感觉者和属性是有充分理由的:相关主体与心理-作为方式中关涉的

主体在功能上有差别：前者是具有相关心理体验的主体，故称"体验者"。而体验与物质-关系句中的"属性"的区别在于，属性是有关载体的特性，是主体归附于载体的属性，而体验则是对相关体验者的心理状态的描述。另一方面，我们仍可以采用韩礼德的包孕（Intensive）、环境（Circumstantial）和属有（Possessive）三个次范畴做具体分析（对比 Fawcett 1987, forthcoming）。

第二，这里的模式明确揭示了语法隐喻产生的机制。即是说，如果将别的范畴（不管是在同一过程内部，还是在不同过程之间）作为源范畴使用，就会出现隐喻现象。试比较（引例来自 H. G. Wells 的小说 *Ann Veronica*；下文之引例无出处者均同此）：

(7) "Let us walk across the Park at least," he said to Ann Veronica.

(8) "Why should I ever come back?" she said to herself, as she went down the staircase.

前一例在现行模式中是一个典型的言语物质-作为句（见后文），(8)所表达的则是一种心理活动，一种内部经验（参阅 Chafe 1994：41－42），因此，这是一个心理-作为句。不过，(8)可能同时涉及内、外两种行为，于是在两种经验范畴之间便产生一个连续统（对比 Halliday 2004：170）。

据此，韩礼德说的 *the fifth day saw them at the summit* 则是以心理-作为过程为源范畴的物质-作为隐喻句；而 *the importance of impression management is most visible with these individuals*（Halliday 2004：652）则是以心理-关系过程为源范畴的心理-作为隐喻句（相应的一致式可表述为 *these individuals can clearly see the importance of impression management*）。

又如，当我们描述一个女孩子长得漂亮时会说 *she is beautiful*，这是一致表达式（包孕-属性）；也可以环境式为源范畴：*she is like a flower*；还可以同一包孕类中的识别式为源范畴：*she is a flower*。

这后两种关系句的跨类耦合现象，也能解决传统修辞学遗留下来、而莱可夫等人（如 Lakoff & Johnson 1980/2003, 1999; Lakoff 1987; Johnson 1987）的认知隐喻理论没有办法解决的问题。传统修辞学将后两例分别叫做明喻和暗喻，认知隐喻理论只关心经验格式塔尤其是抽象范畴形成的隐喻认知机制，但并没有考虑两类小句产生的语言机制及其意义差别，事实上很多隐喻性的抽象范畴都是经由语言手段形成的。韩礼德的语法隐喻同时涉及级转移、类转移以及相关功能转移,它们在经典模式中都是语法隐喻;前两者显然是狭义的语法隐喻(也见前面 Halliday 的例子);*she is like a flower* 及 *she is a flower* 之间的差异正是语法层面上的,属于同一过程内部不同次类之间的语法隐喻现象。

此外,读者或许已经注意到,我们将经典模式中的言语和行为句放到了第一个框内,而存在句则分布于四个框内,这便是我们下面要讨论的议题。

4.4　对经典模式中行为、言语和存在过程的重新归类

根据前面确立的标准,典型的行为和言语过程均应归入物质-作为过程。看经典定义:

……在"物质"与"心理"之间的是行为过程:那些表征内部活动的外部表现,即那些将意识过程(如 *people are laughing*)以及生理状态(如 *they were sleeping*)表现出来的行为。(Halliday 2004:171)

……在"心理"和"关系"之间的是言语过程范畴:那些在人类意识状态下建构的、以语言形式确立的象征关系,如言说和意指行为(如言语句 we say,或对所说内容做介绍:*that every fourth African is a Nigerian*)。(同上)

比较这两"种"过程。广而言之,它们均与生理活动有关,其中行为过程带有更多的生理性,因为它并不直接表明任何心理动机(如 *he sighed, she breathed heavily*)。因此,两者均为生理行为性质的经验范畴:可以看到或感觉到的"外部"行为事件(也见 Thompson 1996:97, 99 – 101)。而这一点正是我们划分物质和心理经验的依据。

有人会反驳说,大多数行为和言语动作与事件均受心理动机支配。这一点毫无问题,但这些物质过程也受心理因素支配。这里只考虑外在

的、可用五官感知的行为举止。这一点还可从其他物质活动得到印证。以下实例均引自韩礼德(Halliday 2004),并在各例后标明了页码。

(9) We're all eating now. (179 页)

(10) He's always here; he's living up there now. (180 页)

(11) the lion sprang (180 页)

(12) the tourist was caught by the lion (182 页)

(13) they played games (193 页)

(14) In fact, shares of the new AT&T Wireless Group also fell Tuesday even as three major brokerages initiated coverage of the stock with a 'buy' recommendation. (196 页)

(15) the boy was kicked (196 页)

各例表明,相关动作者均"以外部表现揭示内部工作状态",或者调用和关涉有关主体的"意识"活动。因此,行为和言语过程不宜作为相对独立的过程范畴来看待,而是生理性的物质-作为过程,可区分为:"非言语/行为"。

接下来我们看经典理论说的存在过程。其原始定义为:在"关系"与"物质"之间的是与存在有关的过程,即存在过程,这里相关各种现象可直接作"存在"看待——存在或发生(如 *today there's Christianity in the south*)。这一理论描述看起来很有说服力,因为总的说来,这一类现象有一个固定的小句类型来表达,至少在英语中是这样。但从我们确立的标准看,上引括号中的例子仍需作物质经验看,我们不应受表达形式的影响。又如,

(16) ... in the circular glow of the green-shaded lamp there lay, conspicuously waiting, a thick bundle of blue and white papers tied with pink tape.

此例无论从哪个角度看都像一个典型的物质-作为过程,即它所描述的是一个可视事件。

不过,仅仅依据这一例会让人误以为所有的存在句均可归入物质-作为过程;其实不然。

(17) There sprang from that a vague hope that perhaps she might extort a capitulation from her father ...

（18）There was just a minute's hesitation before they gave her a room.

（19）It is not, my dear Veronica, that I think there is any harm in you; there is not.

（20）Miss Miniver thought that there was no true sincerity except in love, and appealed to Ann Veronica.

（21）There came a wild rush of anthropological lore into her brain, a flare of indecorous humor.

（22）Before this there was a sort of restraint — a make-believe.

（23）When Capes glanced up at them for a moment, Manning seemed to be holding his arms all about her, and there was nothing but quiet acquiescence in her bearing.

（24）She would never love him as she loved Capes, of course, but there are grades and qualities of love.

（25）… and then Capes … ventured to be perverse, and started a vein of speculation upon the Scotchman's idea — that there were still hopes of women evolving into something higher.

各例中加下划线的成分表明,它们均与心理活动有关。可见,存在过程也涉及心理经验:它们也具有描述心理事件和状态的作用。

总之,(16)—(25)中各例均涉及作为和事件,或状态与关系,即关涉所有外部与内部活动、事件、状态和关系的经验。

可以推知,存在句从本源上讲是用来描述外在世界里的事物、事件或事实的经验的,然后才隐喻性地用来描述有关内在活动或关系的意识状态(对比 Lakoff & Johnson 1980, 1999; Johnson 1987)。而就当代英语而言,这后一种情况已成为一种表达物质和心理经验的常用手段:任何过程类别均可采用这种表达模式,至少在"已知-新信息"的常规配置原则支配下没有可资利用的已知信息来引入新信息时如此。

那么,存在句究竟应当归入关系还是作为类呢? 福赛特(Fawcett 1987)将存在句作为一类处所句看待,如 *there's a sheep over there, there aren't any unicorns (anywhere in the world), and there followed an angry debate (after that)*(157 页),理由是任何一个英语存在句均可将前面的 there 去掉而改成一个典型的处所句。

不过这里我们仍需小心。下面一组实例引自亨利·詹姆斯的小说 *Roderick Hudson*,这些例子(斜体为我们所加)除了关系特征,似乎同时带有作为特征。

(26) But before he had uttered the words, there *rang* through the studio a loud, peremptory ring at the outer door.

(27) It was a generous dark gray eye, in which there *came* and *went* a sort of kindling glow …

(28) As he was turning to leave her, there *rose* above the hum of voices in the drawing-room the sharp, grotesque note of a barking dog.

(29) There *stirred* in his mind an odd feeling of annoyance with Roderick for having thus peremptorily enlisted his sympathies.

(30) It was perhaps for this very reason that, in spite of the charm which Rome flings over one's mood, there *ran* through Rowland's meditations an undertone of melancholy, natural enough in a mind which finds its horizon insidiously limited to the finite, even in very picturesque forms.

(31) For forty-eight hours there *swam* before Rowland's eyes a vision of Roderick, graceful and beautiful as he passed, plunging, like a diver, from an eminence into a misty gulf … Beyond this vision there faintly *glimmered* another, as in the children's game of the "magic lantern" a picture is superposed on the white wall before the last one has quite faded.

这些例子看起来都像作为方式,因为过程成分均带有作为性。或者我们可以说带这一类过程成分的存在句可以看作是同时具有关系和作为特征的跨类耦合现象。而(26)—(28)和(29)—(31)的不同之处在于,前三例为物质-关系句,而后三例为心理-关系句。

此外,此类句中的标志成分 *there*,正如福赛特(Fawcett 1987: 156)所说,"对及物性不起作用",而只是"一个主位表达程式"(thematic pattern)。据此,(26)—(31)可转换为以下作为句:

(26') a loud, peremptory ring rang through the studio at the outer door

(27') a sort of kindling glow came and went in the eye

（28'）the sharp, grotesque note of a barking dog rose above the hum of voices

（29'）an odd feeling of annoyance stirred in his mind with Roderick

（30'）an undertone of melancholy ran through Rowland's meditations

（31a'）a vision of Roderick swan before Rowland's eyes

（31b'）another vision glimmered beyond this one

这些例证表明,转换后的各例都是物质-作为句,或者说同时带有作为和处所关系特征。

因此,以下两例为心理-关系句,只是其中的参与者 *a minute's hesitation* 及 *one irrelevant qualifying spectator* 不再分别叫作属性和感觉者,而是心态和体验者。

（32）There was just a minute's hesitation before they gave her a room.

（33）At the back of her mind there seemed always one irrelevant qualifying spectator whose presence she sought to disregard.

下面是另一组实例,用以说明它们的关系属性,同时揭示它们所具有的物理或心理经验事实。

（34）There is something <u>sound</u> in that position …

（35）There is something <u>heavy</u> about him; I wonder if it's his mustache?

（36）There was a very white-faced youngster of <u>eighteen</u> …

（37）There is something <u>brave</u> in your spirit, as well as penetrating in your eye … —— Charlotte Bronte: *Jane Eyre*

（38）There was something <u>glad</u> in your glance, and genial in your manner, when you conversed … —— Ibid.

（39）… there was something <u>ludicrous as well as painful</u> in the little Parisienne's earnest and innate devotion to matters of dress.

这些实例可以归入关系栏。其中前三例是物质-关系句,随后三例为心理-关系句,均为系包孕中的属性式。因此,存在句一方面关涉物质和心理经验,另一方面可能是关系性的,或者说同时具有作为特征。

总之,存在句可以看作是同时兼跨四种过程特征的现象。从我们提供的视角看,这一现象需做详尽的语料分析。

4.5　总结

本章从经典系统功能语法的及物性过程分类中存在的问题入手,提出了重新分类的具体方案,并给予论证。首先,经典模式采用两种分类标准,这不符合范畴分类的一致性原则。然后,我们从第一加工阶段的角度离析出能够从整体上概括所有人类经验的物质和心理类别,并以第二阶段的加工为着眼点考察由此发生的两种选择识解方式,即作为和关系,伴随二者的是一致式和隐喻式两种选择途径;但无论哪种识解方式,其本身也是经验性的,也是在选择操作支配下结构化的,与物质和心理经验一起,进入词汇语法生成过程。

现将新的及物性整体模式用系统网络的方式加以描述(见下图):

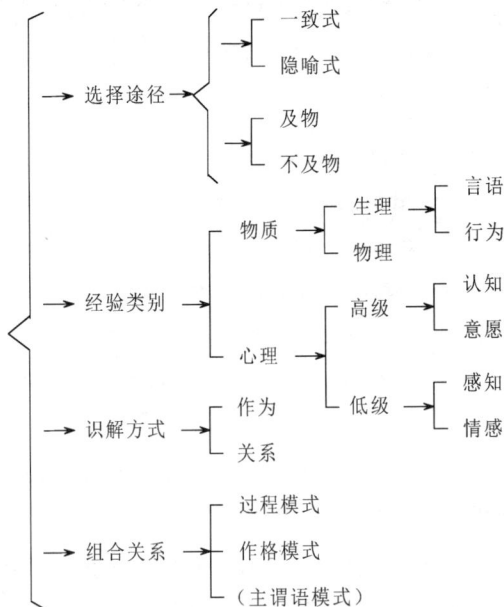

图 4 - 1: 及物性新系统

注意,我们从全面性的角度把"主谓语模式"放到了系统中,旨在表明这是及物性组合的一种方式。这个问题在后面第六章做深入讨论。

第五章

及物性作格模式重构与消息推进[①]

5.1 引言

在经典系统功能语法(经典理论)中,及物性(Transitivity)包括及物分析(Transitive Analysis)和作格分析(Ergative Analysis)两个方面,是小句概念语法的核心内容,是组织经验意义的两种词汇语法模式。作格分析受"±施动性"(±Agency)支配,因而有不带施动性的中动语态(Middle)以及带施动性的非中动语态(Non-middle)(又称施效性语态 Effective Voice),后者又分施动(Operative)与受动(Receptive)两类。中动、施动、受动三者涉及的现象统叫作格关系,所配置的参与者范畴有施事(Agent)、中介(Medium)、范围(Range)和受益者(Beneficiary)(见Halliday 2004:280-305,尤其是297页的系统模式)。

但经典理论中存在几个问题需要解答。第一,韩礼德最初提出作格

---

① 本章原分"SFG 作格分析的地位及其系统配置新探"与"作格关系、语态类别和信息推进——从认知加工阶段看信息范畴的概念功能属性"两文,分别刊载于张克定等主编《功能·语用·评价》,北京:高等教育出版社,2007 年,第51—64 页与《外语研究》2007 年第 3 期,第41—48 页。这里有改动。

理论时,它在地位上先于及物分析,对后者有支配关系;但后来又改变看法,认为作格分析是在及物分析基础上的进一步概括,与当初的认识相反。哪一种更接近事实? 第二,对于上述作格系统,两个精密度阶上的范畴该以语态相称吗? 语态和作格关系是否一回事? 如果不是,语态和各精密度阶上的作格关系是否在同一语言层次上? 这些作格关系与作格参与者之间是什么关系? 两者是否存在选择的先后顺序? 经典理论中施动和受动关系的划分没有给出任何理由和依据,因此其标准是什么? 基于以上问题,现有作格分析的系统模式又该如何重构?

为此,本章拟讨论以下基本问题:第一,作格模式的重构;第二,作格模式与消息推进的关系。我们遵循韩礼德的基本假设:作格经验模式是在过程模式之上的进一步概括。

5.2 作格分析的地位及其系统配置

5.2.1 作格分析和及物分析的地位关系

这里讨论韩礼德对两者地位关系的改变以及本书的处理方案。

韩礼德在 20 世纪 60 年代后期(Halliday 1968)最早对系统功能语法的作格分析做了系统论述。当时,作格分析作为一个相对独立的范畴,是与及物分析相区别的;而此前它是及物分析的一个特征(Halliday 1967(3))。作格的独立性在于起因关系(Causation;也见 Fawcett 1987:143;对比 Lakoff & Johnson 1980:69-76,1999:170-234;Lakoff 1987:54-55;Talmy 2001a:407-549;b 各处;Shibatani 2001:66)。起因关系在后来的相关阐述中有进一步讨论,唯早先的一个参与者,即受事(Affected)(另一个为施事 Agent),后来变成了中介(Medium),因为中介具有更强的概括性(但 Fawcett 1980,1987,forthcoming 保留了早先的这两个术语)。

虽然相关术语及其内涵自此保留下来,但作格分析与及物分析的关系发生了变化。例如,在韩礼德的早期论述中,施事和受事是两个支配动作者和目标(及物分析术语)的概念(如 Halliday 1967(4))。请看以下阐述(Halliday 1967(4);另见 Fawcett *forthcoming*:136):

> 英语小句的基本组织模式似乎应首先考虑起因与结果,而不是动作者和目标……这两种组织模式可分别称为"作格"和"及物"。在英语中,作格与及物并存……但起支配地位的模式是作格。(182页)作格……是将小句组织成为过程和参与者的一个更为概括的形式,它支配语态系统(中动与非中动)及主要小句类型。(189页)

后来,韩礼德改变了上述看法。正如福赛特(Fawcett *forthcoming*:136)指出的那样:"'施事'一类的概念,在其他流派中的地位……与我们所说的'语义结构成分'相当。我们不以这种方式看待时,它们则更接近或位于形式'表层'。"

韩礼德本人的明确论述可以在以下引文中看到(波纹线为我们所加)(Halliday 1970:157-158):

> 这一点说明,作格模式(其过程带有一个必要的参与者和一个可能的促动者 causer)比动作者和目标更易于概括。它涵盖行为过程和心理过程,甚至还有关系句……因此,作格在现代英语的及物性模式中表达出更为概括的模式,一种可供讲英语的人谈论所有过程的表达选项。

这在新版《功能语法导论》(如 Halliday & Matthiessen 2004:282)中表述为:"……在英语和其他许多语言中,及物模式对不同过程类别做出区分,而作格模式则在这些不同的过程类别的基础上做出概括。"

可见,施事和中介的性质自始至终均基于起因关系。或者说,与及物分析强调过程的"行为和扩展"相比,作格分析所强调的则是"起因与结果"(Halliday 2004:288)。显然,韩礼德关于作格和及物在地位关系上的改变,是与这种"概括性"一致的(见292页)。而对于作格分析的这两种前后对立的看法,笔者接受后一种的认识。下图是我们描述的示意图(引自彭宣维 2011:306):

"及物分析" 所得参与者   "作格分析" 所得参与者

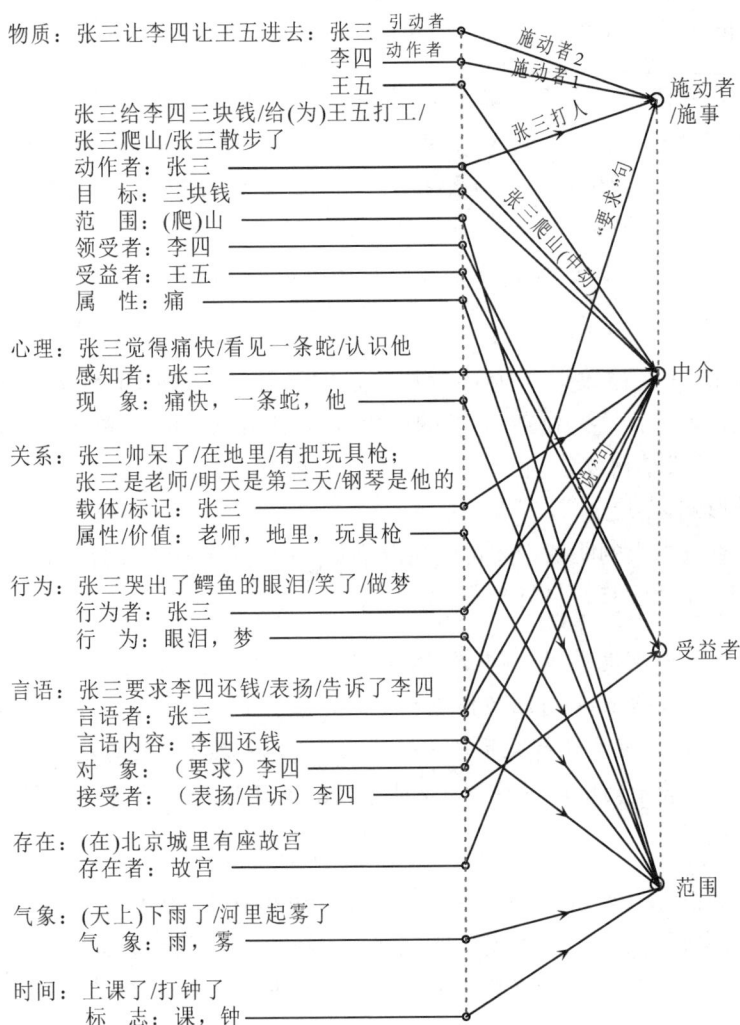

物质：张三让李四让王五进去：张三 —— 引动者
    李四 —— 动作者
    王五

施动者2
施动者1

施动者/施事

张三给李四三块钱/给(为)王五打工/
张三爬山/张三散步了
动作者：张三
目　标：三块钱
范　围：(爬)山
领受者：李四
受益者：王五
属　性：痛

张三打人

"要求"句

张三爬山(甲动)

心理：张三觉得痛快/看见一条蛇/认识他
感知者：张三
现　象：痛快，一条蛇，他

中介

关系：张三帅呆了/在地里/有把玩具枪；
张三是老师/明天是第三天/钢琴是他的
载体/标记：张三
属性/价值：老师，地里，玩具枪

"给"句

行为：张三哭出了鳄鱼的眼泪/笑了/做梦
行为者：张三
行　为：眼泪，梦

受益者

言语：张三要求李四还钱/表扬/告诉了李四
言语者：张三
言语内容：李四还钱
对　象：（要求）李四
接受者：（表扬/告诉）李四

存在：(在)北京城里有座故宫
存在者：故宫

气象：(天上)下雨了/河里起雾了
气　象：雨，雾

范围

时间：上课了/打钟了
标　志：课，钟

图 5-1：过程参与者与作格参与者的关系

5.2.2 语态和作格关系分离的必要性

这里阐述语态的本质及其和作格范畴的关系。

之前,系统功能语法的语态理论始终是和作格关系联系在一起的:作格关系(中动、施动和受动)和语态类别(中动、主动和被动)是一致的。如在韩礼德的早期论述中,两组术语交替使用:"受动(被动)句"(Halliday 1967(3):45,60),"语态中的主动与被动、施动/受动选择"(1968:205)。这表明它们是相当的。这在他后来的有关论述中也有所体现,例如(Halliday & Matthiessen 2004:297);也见先前的两个版本(1985:150和1994:168):"语态系统的工作方式如下。不带'施动性'的小句既非主动也非被动,而是中动;带施动特征的小句则为非中动或施效性语态。因此,施效性小句要么是施动语态,要么是受动语态。在施动句中,主语就是施事,过程由主动动词词组体现;而在受动句中,主语为中介,过程由被动动词词组体现。"

可是,以上处理方案在相关论述中出现了相互抵触的情况。例如,韩礼德在《导论》中使用了"中-受动"(medio-receptive)表示一种"特殊类别"的"语态"(如 Halliday & Matthiessen 2004:289)。即是说,这是一种与"真受动"相对的语态。有关真受动的实例如 *the glass was broken by the cat*(290页);中-受动的例子如:*songs were sun by the choir, the music was enjoyed by the audience*(同上)以及 *the bed hadn't been slept in by anyone*(298页),后者又称"范围-受动:中动(即中-受动)"(range-receptive),但没做任何解释。问题是,这个以范围开始的现象何以能既是受动的又是中动的? 该范畴是介于典型的中动和真受动之间呢,还是一种"特殊类别"的中动? 对于下面这两个分别以被动和中动形式出现、所表达的却是主动和被动意义的例子,又该如何处理呢:*he hasn't been finished with the job* 以及 *the clock winds at the back*(引自 Quirk et al., 170)?

笔者认为,作格关系和语态类别并非一回事,两者应该区别开来:作格关系和语态类别同属于词汇语法关系,但彼此仍然存在抽象程度上的不同。事实上,韩礼德(Halliday 1967(4):217)已经认识到了这一点:"可供选择的成分是'受动',但有被动动词词组的可能表被动,也可能不是;动词的被动性绝非体现受动的必要条件……"。可见,即便仅仅把语态看作一个词组而非小句现象,我们把作格关系和语态形式按照抽象程度区别开来也是有依据的。做出这一区分,不仅可以解决实际问题,也可让我们从一个新的角度看待经验意义的模式化,尤其是存在抽象度的不同(另见 Halliday 1978a：117；Fawcett 2000；对比 Miller 1985，他认为语义和语法是独立生成的）。

与此相关的另一个问题是：各语态类别所体现的语义关系是否就只有作格关系呢？其实，韩礼德曾明确指出：语态类别产生的原因是消息配置上的需要（Halliday 1969/1976）：

> 在施动和受动语态之间，即影响说话人在 *Wren built this gazebo* 和 *this gazebot was built by Wren* 之间做出选择的，并非及物性因素，而是主位；两者之间的意义差别是语篇性的……不过，中动与非中动之间的区别确实会带来及物性意义上的差别；这种差别使我们能够对当今英语语义结构中体现的主要行为类型做出划分。

显然，语态的产生源于消息配置（Message Configuration），涉及主位结构（Thematic Structure）与信息结构（Information Structure）。语态类别同时涉及作格关系和消息推进方式，这是本章要处理的议题之一。

在韩礼德后来的阐述中，尽管上述观点没有再出现过，但我们看不出作格关系与消息推进之间有任何对立性。事实上，对消息推进的要求可以看作是作格关系产生的重要原因。简言之，由"±施动性"确立的各范畴是受消息推进需要产生的，它们在本质上仍然在经验语法的范围内。

既然施动、中动和受动三种作格关系的概括性低一些，那么语态系统中既有的主动（Active）、中动（Middle）和被动（Passive）三个术语，则可以作为更为概括的关系范畴使用，一是因为后者有广泛的接受范围，二是它们作为修饰语所限制的仍然是句法性的。

这些句法关系可以做如下理解。当代英语有六个主要的形态和句法范畴，它们协作确立主语-谓语结构（Corbett 2000：178-218），即一个高度概括的概念形式范畴。这六个范畴是：一致关系（Concord；即数和格）、管辖关系（Government；格等）、时态、体、语序和动词词组被动式（也见 Fawcett 2000：227-229）。主谓语结构可以看作一个由上述范畴复合而成的句法关系，它们协同体现由此确立的底层概念结构。语态的分类正是在这样一个平台上确立的。因此，我们说的主动语态是一个小句级上的句法现象，具体由一致和管辖关系说明：一致关系与底层的经验过程有直接关系，而管辖关系则在一定范围内说明经验过程的延伸范围和详细程度，不管是作格句还是非作格句。与此相对，中动语态则只关涉一致关系①,所体现的只是非作格句,此时没有施动特征出现。而被动语态则必须涉及动词词组的被动结构"*be + -en*"及相关变体,同时关注一致关系,体现底层的施动性,但施事没有关涉性的信息地位,且只是间接参与者,不管是显性还是隐性(对比 Fawcett 1980,1987,2000)。据此,语态系统中的句法变体,与及物系统中的及物与不及物一样,不再是一个词组现象,而是小句性的。这一点施巴塔尼(Shibatani 1994:4938)和特劳格特(Traugott 2002:198)有明确论述。

为了避免底层的施动、中动和受动关系和体现它们的"表层"语态类别(主动、中动和被动)在术语使用上发生混淆,这里就前三者在术语使用上做一点相应的变化,即把由"±施动性"确立的两种作格关系分别改称为"无向关系"(Neutral)(先前的"中动")和"有向关系"(Non-neutral)(先前的"非中动"),与后者有关的施动和受动关系则分别改称施向关系和受向关系,英文称谓不变。理由是,如果排除其他方面的差异,我们在词汇语法层的进一步分层尝试与经典理论的相关概念是一致的,只是在这里将作格关系一分为二了;这样一来,相关术语及内涵的微调是必要的。不过,作格关系仍受"±施动性"支配,这一点跟韩礼德认识一致;而消息是和作格关系同时生成的,彼此之间有对应关系,二者均位于词汇语法层上。

5.2.3　作格分析中的参与者:施事、中介、范围和受益者

首先看施事和中介。在先前的分析中,及物和作格具有相同数量的主要范畴:及物分析的参与者包括引发者(Initiator)、动作者和目标,而作格分析中除了施事和中介外,还有一个促动者(如 Halliday 1985/1994)。这样来认识作格参与者,不便表明两者在分析功效上的差异:两种分析视角都涉及三个主要参与者,如何合理说明作格分析具有更为"概括"的特点呢?最近,韩礼德(Halliday & Matthiessen 2004,2014)取消了促动者。这一改变可使作格分析的概括性得到体现。这不仅与及物分析有所区

---

① 注意,系统功能语言学的中动语态与认知语言学、语言类型学说的中动语态不是一个概念:前者指看不出施动和受动特征的小句类别,即"自发的"(见后文);后者特指被动意义的非被动表达。

别,也表明及物分析的必要性(学界一般只有作格分析)。

韩礼德在 2004 年版《导论》中有以下论述(290 页;也见 2014 年版): "……小句的表征方式要么是自发的(self-engendered),即缺乏单独的施 事;要么由外部促成,此时有一个发挥施事的参与者。"可用韩礼德使用过 的例证来说明: the glass broke, the baby sat up 以及 the boy ran 都是非作 格句,而以下是作格句: the heat broke the glass, Jane sat the baby up 及 the lion chased the boy。

笔者发现,非作格句中的中介概念可进一步划分为两个次类: 中性 (Unconcerned)和受事,后者是韩礼德早先用过的(也见前文),福赛特 (Fawcett 1980, 1987, 2000)则坚持沿用"受事"。例如作格句 the clothes were washed by Mary 中的 the clothes 是受动性的。它被看作受事,因为它 受到了来自施事或"外因"的操作处理或承受了它的负面影响,这种影响 可能很明显,也可能是隐含性的。坚持这一点既有理论意义,更有实际价 值。说它有理论意义,因为承认受事范畴有利于说明前面阐述的"受向" 作格关系;说它有实际价值,原因在于可以用来明确标示上例中 the clothes 的确切作格特征。

这里谈的情况,尤其是 Mary washed the clothes 中的 Mary,和 he walked out of the room 中的 he 不同,因为后者的 he 既不对别的参与者施 发行为,也不接受类似处理,这与前一例中的 the clothes 相对。因此,这样 的参与者可确定为作格意义上的中性,即零作格特征。而在受事和中性 两极之间还有过渡情形。例如,在以下各例中,the clothes washed well, the book reads easily, the table touches smooth, the wall fell down, the glass broke,所有中介都带受动特征。但这一点与 he walked out of the room 中的 he 有区别: 后者是中性的。注意,作格特征与相关参与者的行 为是否受意愿支配的情况有别(对比 Talmy 2001a: 523 - 527 所说的自动 现象 Self-Agentive,如 the girl rolled across the field 以及 the man jumped off the cliff)。

据此,及物性作格维度上的主要参与者系统可用图 5 - 2 加以描述:

施动句可同时带有施事和受事中介(如 John beat the bushes with a stick),故在进入" +施动性"后,施事与受事为合取关系;在"-施动性"后, 或作受事(the wall fell down/the clothes washed well),或作不带受负面影 响的中性(John is a student of linguistics),两者为析取关系。右端的竖向

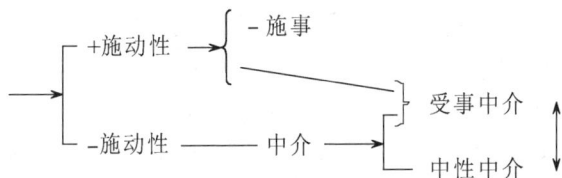

图 5-2：作格系统中的主要参与者系统

双向箭头表可能的连续性。该图表明，施事与受事之间的分别，不是来自它们自身，而是外在施动性，即超越及物分析维度之上的外在原因。

此外，受益者和范围是另外两个同时被纳入作格范围的参与者（Halliday & Matthiessen 2004：293－295；对比 1985：131－137；1994：144－149）。受益者是及物小句中除施事和中介之外的第三个参与者，如以下各例中加下划线的成分（除最后一例外均引自 Halliday 1994：145－146）：*I give my love a ring that has no end*，*Fred bought a present for his wife/bought his wife a present*，*John said to Mary that …*，*John asked Mary a question*，*he persuaded Fred that …*，*he convinced Fred that …*，*it cost him a pretty penny*，*she made him a good wife* 和 *she showed him an open heart*。

而就范围看，这是一种更为普遍的现象。据韩礼德的说法，范围在物质过程中为界域（Scope），在行为过程中为行为（Behaviour）（对比行为者 Behaver；Halliday 2004：251），在言语过程中为言语内容（Verbage），在心理过程中为现象（Phenomenon），在关系过程中为属性（Attribute）或价值（Value）（见 Halliday & Matthiessen 2004：294 的表5(43)）。显然，范围成分既可能出现在作格句中，也可能出现在非作格句中。

范围和受益者在某些情况下与施事和受事之间可能有交叉关系。例如，类似 *John shot Mary a bullet* 的意图，也可以 *a bullet was shot into Mary by John* 的方式出现。前一句中的范围 *a bullet*（子弹）在后一句中同时肩负受事角色：子弹不可能自己射出伤人。可见，该成分具有复合参与者特征。我们还需留意的是，*Mary* 作为受事中介，还可能理解为带有负面意义的受益者。如果这一观点基本成立，那么该成分也具有双重角色。又如，在 *John was told an interesting story by Mary* 和 *an interesting story was told by Mary* 中，尽管前一句中 *John* 和后一句 *an interesting story* 分别为受益者和范围，但两者均有受事特征。

有一点韩礼德始终没有给予说明,这就是作格关系的生成机制及其和作格参与者的关系。笔者发现,作格参与者本身是一种语义成分,随着选择陈述被赋予相应的作格地位:在作格句中,如果施事获得中心地位,整个小句的作格关系就是施向性的,而施事为直接参与者;如果受事获得中心地位,其作格关系则是受向性的,此时施事为间接参与者,可显可隐;在非作格句中,中介始终处于中心地位,其作格关系始终是无向的;因此,对作格参与者中心的选择决定了作格关系的类别。它们受制于消息配置。

读者或许已经注意到,前面的分析还没有涉及韩礼德模式(如Halliday 2004:297)中描述的施动-受动特征,即我们改称的施向和受向关系。这是接下去要讨论的问题。

5.2.4 "±施动性"和作格关系:作格特征系统及其可能的结构配置

这里将主要通过作格特征系统来揭示整体作格关系(即施向、无向和受向范畴)与上述四个参与者以及"±施动性"的关系。事实上,整体作格关系是伴随相关参与者出现的另一组作格范畴。具体而言,施事和中介这两个语义范畴涉及有关操作的参与者类别,它们与受益者和范围一样,都是"前语法阶段"被激活的、在第二加工阶段被识解出来的经验范畴。而施向-受向关系与小句中的施事和中介有关。一个小句有显性施事和中介,但并不一定就能保证整个小句的作格关系就是施向或受向范畴。除了其他情况外(如Jespersen 1924:167),作格关系受制于语篇连贯原则,而保证这一点的重要条件就是相关成分的信息性/新闻性。注意,我们仅仅谈到了施向和受向关系,没有涉及语态,尽管前两者均由语态进一步体现。

现将这些特征可能涉及的配置情况列于下表,每一种配置之后各举一例,并在参与者后加注了英文缩写称谓(Ag:施事;Aff:受事;Rg:范围;Bf:受益者;Un:中性中介;参与者角色放在( )内,受"±施动性"支配的共现参与者在[ ]内,":"表支配关系,"/"表作格关系)。

及物性中的作格系统

1 —— 11 + 施动性
　　　 12 - 施动性

11:[(211+2122)/321], e.g. *John chased Mary*

11: [(211+2122)/321], e.g. *Mary was chased by John*

2 —— 21 —— 211 施事
　　　　　　　 212 中介
　　　　 2121 中性
　　　　 2122 受事
　　　 22 —— 221 范围
　　　　　　　 222 受益者

12: [(2121)/321], e.g. *John is running*

11: [(211+222/2122+221)/321], e.g. *John shot Mary a bullet*

11: [(222/2122+221+211)/322], e.g. *Mary was given a book by John*

3 —— 31 无向
　　　 32 有向 —— 321 施向关系
　　　　　　　　　 322 受向关系

12: [(2121+221)/31], e.g. *Mary laughed a loud laugh*

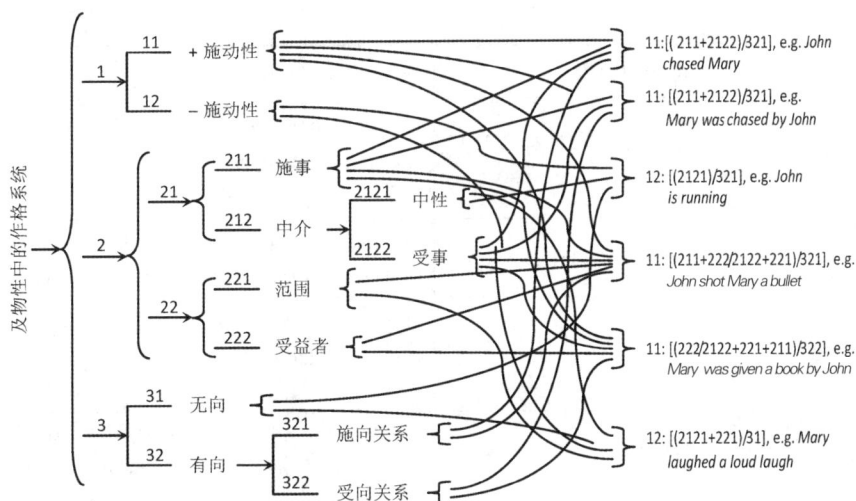

图 5-3：作格特征系统的网络模式

表 5-1：作格特征的可能配置一览表

	可能的配置关系	例　　证
1	11：［（211+2122）/321］	*John（Ag）chased Mary（Aff）*
2	11：［（2122+211）/322］	*Mary（Aff）was chased by John（Ag）*
3	11：［（211+222+2121）/321］	*John（Ag）gave Mary（Bf）a book（Un）*
4	11：［（222+221+211）/322］	*Mary（Bf）was given a book（Rg）by John（Ag）*
5	11：［（221+222+211）/322］	*a book（Rg）was given to Mary（Bf）by John（Ag）*
6	11：［（211 + 222/2122 + 221）/321］	*John（Ag）shot Mary（Bf/Aff）a bullet（Rg）*
7	11：［（221/211+2122/222）/321］	*a bullet（Rg/Ag）shot Mary（Bf/Aff）*
8	11：［（2122/222 + 221 + 211）/322］	*Mary（Bf/Aff）was shot a bullet（Rg）by John（Ag）*
9	11：［（221/2122 + 2122 + 211）/322］	*a bullet（Rg/Aff）was shot into Mary（Aff）by John（Ag）*
10	11：［（211+2122$_1$+2122$_2$+221）/321］	*the old lady（Ag）has made her son（Aff$_1$）marry his daughter（Aff$_2$）a billionaire（Rg）*

第五章　及物性作格模式重构与消息推进

（续表）

	可能的配置关系	例　证
11	11：［（2122_1+211+2122_2+221）/322］	A（Aff_1）has been made by B（Ag）to marry his daughter（Aff_2）a billionaire（Rg）
12	11：［（21+2122+222+221）/321］	the doctor（Ag）made Mary（Aff）conceive George（Bf）a stout baby（Rg）
13	11：［（2122+222+221+211）/322］	Mary（Aff）was made to conceive George（Bf）a stout baby（Rg）by the doctor（Ag_2）
14	11：［（221/2122+211_1+222+211_2）/322］	a baby（Rg/Aff）was conceived by Mary（Ag_1）for George（Bf）owing to the doctor（Ag）
15	11：［（222+221+211_1+211_2）/322］	George（Bf）has been born a baby（Rg）by Mary（Ag_1）owing to the doctor（Ag_2）
16	11：［（211/221+2122）/321］	a shadow（Ag/Rg）scared Mary（Aff）
17	11：［（2122+221）/31］	Mary（Aff）was scared by a shadow（Rg）
18	12：［（221/2122+211）/322］	Mary（Rg）was loved by John（Un）
19	12：［（2121）/31］	Mary（Un）laughed/dreamed/smiled
20	12：［（2121+221）/31］	Mary（Un）laughed a loud laugh（Rg）/the book（Un）has only 2 pages（Rg）/A loved B
21	12：［（2121+222+221）/321］	Mary（Un）told John（Bf）a story（Rg）
22	12：［（222/2122+2121/211）/322］	John（Bf）was told a story（Rg）by Mary（Un）
23	12：［（221/2122+222+211）/322］	a story（Rg/Aff）was told to John（Bf）by Mary（Un）

　　显然,施动性和非施动性促成施事-中性-受事特征,而与此并行的则是无向和有向关系,后者又分施向和受向关系,作格关系和作格参与者之间是同时生成的。这一组范畴是整体性概念,因为它们关涉的不仅是有关"±施动性"和参与者,还与过程类型(由动词词组表达)有关,因此是一个小句而非词组概念,更不是参与者概念。但两个维度都是作格性质的,进一步的"表层"语态则提供明确的形式标记。

在上述基础上,本章接下去几个小节拟探讨以下议题:第一,对消息及消息推进的认识;第二,消息推进与作格范畴的关系;第三,消息推进和语态类别的关系。

5.3 作格关系、语态类别和消息推进

5.3.1 消息及消息推进

在经典理论中,消息(Message)主要体现在两个方面,一是主位-述位结构(Theme-Rheme Structure),二是已知-新信息结构(Given – New Information)。对于前者,笔者(2002)指出韩礼德主位概念的形式特征,即小句的第一个成分为主位。对于信息结构,其中的语义成分涉及新闻性或新闻价值(Newsworthiness),这就是韩礼德说的"±可恢复性"(±recoverability)(即已知和新价值;如 Halliday 2004:91;也见 Chafe 1994各处)。通常,信息的主题主位范围和已知信息为同一成分,例如(引自Halliday 2004:97),

(1) John's father wanted him to give up violin. His teacher persuaded him to continue.

其中的 *John's father* 和 *his teacher* 为已知信息,也是主题主位①。

不过,这一点并非充分条件,因为新信息也可能被选择而成为主题主位。例如,

(2) Along the road walked an old man. (Thomas Hardy: *the Return of the Native*)

这里 *an old man* 是主题主位,而 *walked along the road* 则是延伸内

---

① 这里的讨论只关注经验性主位成分,不考虑人际和语篇主位成分(见 Halliday 1994:53 – 55)。

容。据此,传统语法常说的倒装,除其他情况外(Jespersen 1924:167 - 168),则源于非标记性的消息配置原则,即从左向右、由最低信息价值到最高信息价值的交际动力原则(Firbas 1964)。诚然,已知信息和新信息仅仅是语篇过程中有关信息价值的两种极端情况,中间可能存在等级梯度(Prince 1981;Chafe 1994:71 - 81),主题主位的性质也可能如此。

总之,消息是结构化加工阶段获得的交际地位及相互关系。交际地位包括两方面的因素:一是哪些经验成分被加工成一则消息的出发点,即谈论对象,即一类特殊的主题主位;哪些是交际的目的,即对主位信息做延伸或详述的述位。二是这些经验范畴的新闻价值,即信息性。主位和述位相互作用,构成一则消息的两个基本功能;已知信息和新信息则是一则信息单位中相关经验范畴被赋予的新闻价值。据此,消息推进(Message Progression;Daneš 1974),或称消息流动(Message Flow;Chafe 1994;Halliday 2004),指语篇过程中由主位和述位的配置方式构成的消息单位之间的更替。

前面指出,消息范畴尤其是主位-述位功能的确立,需要参照作格关系。但"参照"的内涵为何?它们之间究竟如何发生联系?下面拟首先讨论消息和作格之间的关系,从而说明决定消息范畴的第三个条件:及物性经验基础。

5.3.2 消息推进与作格范畴的关系

作格分析涉及三组同时生成的范畴:±施动性,作格关系(施向、无向和受向)以及作格参与者。对于消息和作格而言,这里将有两对彼此对应的范畴,一是作格参与者中心与作格关系,均系作格范畴;二是出发点与序列性,与消息有关。我们将说明,它们都是第二加工阶段选择和识解出来的、彼此对应的范畴,进而揭示作格经验范畴和消息价值在生成中的参照关系和同时性。

首先,消息出发点和作格参与者中心是同时生成的。消息出发点(Point of Departure),即主体的兴趣焦点,指一则消息在加工识解中的配置方式,即以哪一个经验范畴作为谈论对象。需要说明的是,这里的出发点概念指一则消息的第一个成分,如(2)中的 *along the road*;而 *an old man* 只是潜在主题主位,它是否变成主题主位需看语篇的发展走向。这与视角有关(Perspective,如 Langacker 1987:117, 120 - 132)。

与此相关的是作格参与者中心。"中心"(centredness)这一概念受福赛特(Fawcett 1980)的"施事中心"(agent-centred)和"受事中心"(affected-centred)启发;在本书中它指作格参与者在第二阶段的加工识解中被赋予的作格地位(Ergative Status),从而确定整个小句的作格关系:如果居中心地位的是施事,那么整个小句的作格意义就是施向关系,施事则为相关过程的直接参与者(Direct Participant);如果居中心地位的是受事,其作格意义就是受向关系,此时的施事为间接参与者(Indirect);如果居中心地位的是中性中介,其作格意义则是无向关系。总之,作格系统中的"中心"范畴,是赋予参与者作格地位、确立作格关系的关键概念,是受消息配置支配的:"出发点"的确立和序列性的生成(消息配置)带动了参与者的作格地位及作格关系的生成。直言之,主题主位的确立必然同时涉及以哪一个参与者为作格中心的问题。在 *Mary washed the clothes* 中,Mary 是消息出发点,但它也是一个作格中心,即相关作格关系中的施事被选择为直接参与者;而在 *the clothes were washed by Mary*(两例引自 Halliday 1967(3))中,消息的出发点是受事 *the clothes*,相关施事则被选择为间接参与者。

因此,消息出发点与作格参与者中心之间有一致关系:两者涉及的是同一个成分。但彼此角度不同:出发点是消息性的,其内涵是有关消息片段的基本谈论对象;作格参与者中心是一个经验语义范畴,它是确立作格关系的条件之一。

其次,上面的叙述同时涉及另外两个概念,即作格关系和序列性。序列性指一则消息的构成成分之间的功能配置:主位在前、述位在后,但对于信息来讲,要么是已知信息在前,这是非标记现象;要么是新信息在前、已知信息在后;也存在已知或新信息在一则信息片段中间的可能性。

可见,作格关系和序列性有共同之处:两者都是整体概念。作格关系是以某一参与者为中心而确立的、有关整个小句及物性的作格特征;序列性是指以出发点为基础的消息功能及互动关系。它们分别为作格意义和消息意义的代表:作格关系所代表的是由作格分析确立的作格经验模式,与及物分析确立的经验模式相对;序列性所代表的,是相关消息片段的交际功能价值,包括它的谈论对象和新闻性。

作格关系和序列性也是同时生成的。作格关系是受参与者的地位决定的。是施事还是受事被选择为主题主位,意味着整个小句的经验作格关系类别的不同:如果是施事被加工为主题主位,这就说明相关施事被识解为整个作格关系的中心,该作格关系就是施向性的;如果受事被加工为主题主位,整个小句的作格关系则是受向性的;当然,如果一个小句不存在施动性,如例(2),那么这就是一个无向关系小句,中介 *an old man* 为潜在主题主位。此外,施向和受向之间的选择变体对过程类别本身并不产生影响,但它们和消息配置是联系在一起的,并且可能产生经验意义上的差别,如大家熟知的以下被动句就可能和相应的主动句之间出现意义上的差别:*I was taught physics by Einstein*。该句可以看作是其主动句 *Einstein taught me physics* 的变体,也可能是别人而非 *Einstein* 本人教我 *Einstein* 的物理学(另见 Goldberg 1995)。鉴于作格关系的确立同时意味着消息序列性的生成,因此,彼此之间存在函数性质的互动关系。

当然,就参与者中心而言,除了施事和受事两个主要中心外,还可能有范围(Range)中心和受益者(Beneficiary)中心,如在 *the teapot was given to my aunt by the duke* 和 *my aunt was given the teapot by the duke*(引自 Halliday 2004)两句中,前者以范围 *the teapot* 为整个作格关系的中心,后者以受益者 *my aunt* 为中心。它们均为各则消息片段的主题主位。

总之,对消息出发点的选择,决定了整则信息的序列性;这同时意味着由参与者中心决定的作格关系类别,都是在第二加工阶段上生成的。其间的关系可用下表揭示;图后是有关示例分析。

表 5－2:作格与消息

类别 / 范围	作　　格	消　　息
局部	作格地位:参与者中心的确立 施事,中介,范围,受益者	出发点:主位的经验特征基础 (施事、中介、范围和受益者)
整体	作格关系: 施向,无向,受向	序列性:主位+述位结构的经验特征基础 已知与新信息的可能序列

(3) a. *Mary* washed the clothes.(施事中心/施向关系::施事主位/施向序列)

b. *The clothes* were washed by Mary.(受事中心/受向关系：：受事主位/受向序列)

c. *The teapot* was given to my aunt …(范围中心/受向关系：：范围主位/受向序列)

d. *My aunt* was given a teapot …(受益者中心/受向关系：：受益者主位/受向序列)

e. Along the road walked *an old man*.(中性中介中心/无向关系：：中介潜在主位/无向序列)

有了上面的探讨,我们就可以为消息范畴确立第三个条件,即支撑主题主位地位的经验基础。也就是说,无论是以出发点为前提的主题概念,还是主位加述位的序列关系,均与作格范畴发生直接关联:信息是直接以作格范畴(包括作格关系和作格参与者)为依托的,而作格范畴则离不开消息的序列配置方式。当然,消息和作格虽然是同时生成的,但它们之间是通过出发点和参与者中心两个概念发生对接关系的。

5.3.3　消息推进和语态类别的关系

下面拟说明,消息配置与作格关系是句法性质的,在此基础上的进一步抽象则是语态,后者体现前两者。

语态和消息的关系人们很早就注意到了,但 20 世纪早期的马泰修斯(Mathesius)是进行相关理论阐述的第一人。他在 19 世纪相关研究成果(尤其是 Weil 1844/1978：32, 37)的基础上,以"句子的实际切分"(Actual Division of Sentence)为理论框架,将语态,尤其是被动语态,作为一种揭示"表达出发点"(expression departure)的形式标志看待(Mathesius 1929/1983, 1939/1989)。在此基础上,韩礼德(Halliday 1967(4)：217)对表达出发点理论做了改造,把它看作一个纯粹的句法范畴,即小句的第一个成分,即以位置为导向的主位概念(Theme；Halliday 1967(4)：211 - 223；2004 第 3 章；Brown & Yule 1983：126；彭宣维 2002)。即便如此,这一术语的消息特征仍然明确(彭宣维 2004)。在这里,被动标志作为一种典型的句法现象,其生成也受消息的配置原则支配。韩礼德(Halliday

1968：183）指出：

> 对受向范畴的选择，部分是受制于施事的消息地位的：要么施事明确表征新信息，通常是对比信息——此时，施事以介词短语的形式出现在句尾，此为常规情况，并为调核；要么（说话者当作）可以完全恢复的信息，于是被全部省略。

用我们的话说，其他情况除外，无论是主动、中动还是被动语态，三者的配置均出于同一目的：为句子消息设置一个出发点，确立主题地位。具体而言，这个以参与者身份出现的消息范畴具有关涉意义（aboutness）；不管它所在的小句是哪种语态，它都可能是主位的一部分。

从施向、无向和受向关系以及主位-述位配置方式，到主动、中动和被动语态，都可能因隐喻而出现错位情况。例如，*the clock winds up at the back* 在语义上是一则受动消息，但语法上是中动语态（Quirk et al. 1985：170 称为"实义被动", notional passive）。相反，夸克等人提供的以下例句均为被动式：*by the time she got there, her friend was gone, grandfather was sat in the rocking chair, I've been stood here for about ten minutes* 以及 *I'll soon be finished with this job*。其中前四例为无向序列，最后一例系施向序列。

底层的作格和消息范畴与表层的语态类别的体现和配置关系，可用下表体现出来。其中第一列为局部作格范畴，从消息的角度看则是出发点；中间一列是消息序列范畴，以作格关系作垫衬；最后一个是语态；后两项不一致者即为语法隐喻现象（见 Goatly 1997）。

表 5-3：作格与语态的配置关系

与过程句/非作格句直接相关的消息范畴及其体现：	
出发点序列语态类别	例　　　证
1. 中介中心：无向：主动态	*the book has two hundred pages, Mary said that …*
2. 中介中心：无向：中动态	*Marry laughed, Mary walked out of the room*
3. 中介中心：无向：被动态	*Mary was gone, I've been stood here for about ten minutes*
4. 中介中心：受向：主动态	*Mary suffered a loss, Mary lost a watch*
5. 中介中心：受向：中动态	*the clock winds up at the back*

与过程句/非作格句直接相关的消息范畴及其体现：	
出发点序列语态类别	**例　　证**
6. 中介中心：受向：被动态	*Mary was scared of/overjoyed with it, Mary was loved by John*
7. 范围中心：受向：主动态	*the bed could sleep four people*
8. 范围中心：受向：中动态	*the bed sleeps comfortable, a pop song sings easier than a classical one*
9. 范围中心：受向：被动态	*the bed hasn't been slept yet, a story was told to Mary by John*
10. 受益者中心：无向：主动	*John heard a story*
11. 受益者中心：受向：被动	*Mary was told a story by John*
与施动句/作格句直接相关的消息范畴及其体现：	
12. 施事中心：施向：主动态	*John chased Mary, John killed the cow*
13. 施事中心：施向：被动态	*I'll soon be finished with this job*
14. 施事中心：施向：中动态	*(–what did John and Mary do?) –they kissed*
15. 中介中心：受向：被动态	*Mary was chased by John*
16. 受益者中心：受向：主动态	*Mary received a book from John*
17. 受益者中心：受向：被动态	*Mary was given a rose by John*
18. 范围中心：施向：主动态	*the bullet shot Mary's eye, the heat broke the glass*
19. 范围中心：受向：主动态	*Mary's eye received a bullet*
20. 范围中心：受向：中动态	*there plants a willow in the garden*

5.3.4　消息推进和语态类别的关系：实例分析

从施向和受向范畴的角度看消息，在一定条件下也可能与相关经验成分被选择出来做主题主位的心理机制有关，至少在某些语境下是这样。正如韩礼德（Halliday 1967（3））指出的那样，作为小句的一个整体特征，施向和受向的划分在某些情况下必定受信息价值的配置支配,因为无论哪种关系均受制于社交目的(即非标记性的交际动力原则)以及语篇过程中消息流动的关涉性(主题主位)与具体化方式(述位)等的选择动机。看下面的例子(斜体为笔者所加):

(4) *The two sisters* worked on in silence, *Ursula* having always that strange brightness of an essential flame that is caught, meshed, contravened. *She* lived a good deal by herself, to herself, working, passing on from day to day, and always thinking, trying to lay hold on life, to grasp it in her own understanding. *Her active living* was suspended, but underneath, in the darkness, *something* was coming to pass. (D. H. Lawrence: *Women in Love*)

鉴于非标记性的交际动力结构要求已知-新信息序列,因此主位成分,如*[t]he two sisters*,*Ursula* 和*[s]he* 分别被配置在各信息片段首位。尽管*[h]er active living* 和 *something* 并非全新信息,却是"可推知信息"(inferable;Prince 1981):*she* (属格形式)的作用是引介性的,有人也称"易及信息"(accessible; Chafe 1994:71 – 75)或"可恢复信息"(recoverable;Halliday 2004:298)。此外,这些名词组在认知上均被作为出发点,并被置于各信息段的起始位置。

我们也注意到,镶嵌小句 *that strange brightness of an essential flame that is caught, meshed, contravened* 以及最后一句中的 *her active living was suspended*,两则信息都是受向性的,即两个关涉成分 *that strange brightness of an essential flame* 和 *her active living* 也位于句首,从而确定整则信息为受向类。显然,这些成分都接受了被动化而得以谈论。即便主位成分是新信息,它们也很容易根据语境获得加工识别,全新信息成分因此而后置。

可以肯定的是,在一定条件下,被动形式的出现是主题主位配置上的需要,同时也为了维系语篇过程中的关涉连贯性:或者是出于替换的目的,或者有对比方面的原因。请斟酌哈代(Thomas Hardy)在《苔丝》(*Tess of the D'Urbervilles*)开篇说的第一段话(斜体为笔者所加):

(5) On an evening in the latter part of May *a middle-aged man* was walking homeward from Shaston to the village of Marlott, in the

adjoining Vale of Blakemore or Blackmoor. *The pair of legs* that carried him were rickety, and there was *a bias in his gait* which inclined him somewhat to the left of a straight line. *He* occasionally gave a smart nod, as if in confirmation of some opinion, though *he* was not thinking of anything in particular. *An empty egg-basket* was slung upon his arm, *the nap of his hat* was ruffled, *a patch* being quite worn away at its brim where *his thumb* came in taking it off. Presently ***he*** was met by an elderly parson astride on a gray mare, who, as he rode, hummed a wandering tune. "Good night t'ee," said *the man with the basket* …

在有意安排主题主位成分 he（粗斜体）出现以前，整个话语片段中各小句，无一例外集中在第一句配置的主位上，即 *a middle-aged man* 及其相关身体部位：*[t]he pair of legs*, *a bias in his gait*, *[h]e*, *he*, *[a]n empty egg-basket*, *the nap of his hat*, *a patch* 以及 *his thumb*。之后是两个关涉性成分交替出现。可见，正是主位连续性或主位推进（语篇性）引发了被动形式（以镶嵌方式出现）。这一点在下面这个语段中更为明显，相关被动式均为不定式。

（6）He had caught both substance and shadow — both fortune and affection, and was just the happy man he ought to be; talking only of himself and his own concerns — expecting <u>to be congratulated</u> — ready <u>to be laughed at</u> — and, with cordial, fearless smiles, now addressing all the young ladies of the place, to whom, a few weeks ago, he would have been more cautiously gallant.（Jane Austen：*Emma*）（下划线为笔者所加）

我们引述了多个别的小句，以便表明周围环境里的主要关涉对象。这一实例足以说明，正是相关语境中的主题主位连续性导致了被动化。因此，无论是施向-无向-受向意义，还是主动-中动-被动语态，它们都是语篇现象。

根据以上讨论，我们得出三个推论。第一，任何一个语言理论，如果它仅仅着眼于句子范围，要想实现观察的充分性是很困难的。第二，这也可以从一定程度上解释为什么施事有时可有可无或毫无意义,而有时又必不可少(见 Jespersen 1924；Quirk et al. 1985：164－165；Halliday 2004：295)。第三,这还能部分说明语态出现的原因(也见 Dik 1997；Butler 2003)。因此,如果没有被动现象或受向关系的配置需要,就不可能有对语态范畴的理性认识,更不可能促使人们进行主动－被动的范畴划分。

5.4 小结

通过以上分析我们有如下发现。第一,作格分析和及物分析之间的确存在概括化程度,两者均为词汇语法层的范畴：语态为抽象度更高的句法范畴。第二,语态同时受作格关系和消息配置影响；作格关系受"±施动性"支配；语态和作格范畴之间也是体现和被体现的关系。第三,作格关系和作格参与者在经典理论中存在选择的先后顺序；本章则认为,作格关系和作格参与者是在第二加工阶段中伴随"±施动性"的识解方式同时进入选择过程的：对参与者的作格地位的确立则意味着作格语法关系的生成。这样,就有三组作格范畴：±施动性,作格关系[无向和有向(又分施向和受向)]以及作格参与者[施事、中介(中性加受事)、范围和受益者]及其作格地位。我们在行文中还讨论了语态同时和消息流动有关,而后者又与作格关系有关。我们看到,表层句法性的语态除了表达经验过程外,还用来表达信息价值范畴。此外,被动句和相应的主动句之间可能表达不同经验意义的事实表明,语态类别和底层语义范畴之间不可能总是一一对应的,由此也揭示出语义和语法的区别与联系。总之,作格是基础,是消息范畴的来源和依托,两者连成一体；语态是作格关系之上更为抽象的句法手段。至此,我们得到下面的表征模式：过程模式→作格模式→语态模式。

第六章

主语是人际性的吗？
——论主语结构的概念性形式特征①

经典系统功能语言学将主语（Subject）看作小句人际性的语法范畴，即语气成分（Mood Element）中除了定式操作语（Finite Operator）之外的一个成分；但我们认为，主语以及主语—谓语结构（主语结构 S - Construction），应当看作体现小句概念意义的一种语法形式范畴。我们的基本假设是：主语结构是在及物性过程模式和作格模式之上的进一步概括：过程模式→作格模式→语态模式+主语模式，三者都是词汇语法范畴。

这里只涉及陈述句，不涉及疑问句和祈使句。虽然三类基本句子都发挥人际性的言语功能，即社交意义（Interactional），但陈述句的基本功能还同时传递概念意义，而疑问句和祈使句的基本作用是人际性的。下面我们将具体涉及两个方面：（一）韩礼德的语气理论以及主语识别中存在的问题；（二）主语的语法形式特征及相关理论阐述。

---

① 本章原分"试论主语及主语结构的概念形式特征"与"主语是人际性的吗？"两文，分别刊载于《中国外语》2006 年第 1 期，第 22—28 页与《外语与外语教学》（后者与尚慧敏、刘娟、刘芳合作）2007 年第 3 期，第 8—11 页。这里有改动。

6.1 韩礼德的语气理论以及主语识别中存在的问题

6.1.1 经典理论的语气理论和主语范畴

这里暂不涉及韩礼德在 1970 年及以前的观点,只介绍此后比较定型的看法。韩礼德关于主语的基本观点是,主语是语气成分的一个基本构成要素(另一个是定式操作语),它们和剩余部分(Residue)一起,构成小句的人际语法范畴语气(Mood),相关语境范畴是语式(Tenor)。这一有别于传统语法的处理方案,似乎不仅能满足其模式建构的理论需要,还有充分的依据。

首先,语气理论中需要一个功能成分,以便解释它如何维系和推动言语交往。一方面,韩礼德(Halliday 2004:107-108)将有关人际意义"言语功能",即社交意义,归纳为两种交换关系:一是商品交换(Commodity exchange),包括物品—服务(goods-&-services)与信息(information)交换;二是角色交换(Role exchange),包括给予与索取交换(giving and demanding)。这两种变量在选择中可以生成四种语义范畴:

(i) ["物品—服务"+给予]→提供(offer):*would you like this teapot?*;

(ii) ["物品—服务"+索取]→命令(command):*give me that teapot*;

(iii) [信息+给予]→陈述(statement):*he's giving her the teapot*;

(iv) [信息+索取]→询问(question):*what is he giving her?*

前两种被概括为提议(Proposal),其功能是物品—服务交换,因而有如下体现模式:"物品—服务"交换→提议(提供+命令);后两种是命题(Proposition),功能是信息交换,体现模式为:信息交换→命题(陈述+询问)。与命题和提议相应的语法范畴就是语气。

另一方面,他将语气的构成具体化,包括"语气成分"和"剩余部分";而维系和推动言语交往的核心成分,则是其中的语气成分。例如(同上,第 69 页;下划线为笔者所加),

（1）Speaker：　　　　　　　 Listener（becoming Speaker in his turn）：

　　<u>Would</u> you like his teapot?　Yes，I would. No，I wouldn't.

　　<u>Give</u> me that teapot!　　　All right，I will. No，I won't.

　　<u>He's</u> giving her the teapot.　Oh，is he? Yes，he is. No，he isn't.

　　<u>What</u> is he giving her?　　A teapot. I don't know；sha'n't tell you.

　　即是说,正是小句中那些"在一系列修辞性交换中被颠来倒去的"部分,发挥了相关交际功能（111 页）。这一点集中体现在主要以类似成分交替出现的言语交往中,如 I would, I wouldn't, I will, I won't, is he, he is, he isn't 等。在韩礼德看来,这个核心成分正是人们普遍接受的"主语"和"定式成分"；说话人使用主语来行使一定职责,使小句作为交际事件而发挥作用。说话人将其交际意图负载于"主语+定式操作语"这一结构上,"要求听话人予以承应。"（117 页）其测试手段是附加疑问句：被复制到附加疑问句中的代词化和定式成分就是主语和定式操作语①。至此,一切历史遗留问题似乎就得到了完满解决。

　　其次,当韩礼德将主语确认为一个人际语法范畴时,其立足点是功能定性和理论传统。一方面,他试图给主语指派一个语义性的功能地位（112 页）：

　　　　"主语"这一术语与早先的"语法主语"一致；但在这里我们拟从功能的角度给予重新解释。主语不是一个纯粹的形式范畴；像其他语法功能一样,从根源上讲它是语义性的。

　　他进一步说：主语为一则命题的形成提供某种东西,即相关命题内某种可以被肯定或否定的东西（117 页）。于是,将主语看作人际性的语法范畴似乎便有了充分理由（110 页）：

　　　　当语言被用来交换信息时,小句以命题的形式出现。于是,命题就成了某种可以争论的东西——某种可以肯定或否定的东西,还可以被怀疑、反驳、强调、有保留地接受、限制、调节、悔恨等等。

　　这一点似乎显得尤为有力,因为有整个西方传统作支撑。而无论是

---

① 传统语法在主语的识别上采用了两条基本标准：（一）与相关动词有数的一致关系的名词组,（二）在附加疑问句中以代词化的方式被复制（见随后一节）。韩礼德在这里实际上是放弃了前一条标准,只沿用了后一条。

从语言学还是从哲学的角度看,这一传统至少在亚里士多德(Aristotle)时期就开始了。例如,亚里士多德在论述肯定命题和否定命题以及全称命题与非全称命题时,就提到了"断言或否认"所关涉的"可能性、不可能性、偶然性、必然性"(《亚里士多德全集》第一卷 69 页;简称《全集》)。这似乎就为韩礼德将主语重新解释为一个人际性的语法范畴、对命题实施各种操作的手段,提供了理论来源。

然而,上述观点对我们认识有关语言现象实际上是误导。笔者的基本问题是:为什么不能将"语气+剩余部分"分析为一个独立于主语结构的范畴而主语结构另作解释呢?下面首先说明两者分离的事实依据,然后指出经典系统功能语言学以命题作为出发点存在的问题。

6.1.2 经典模式中主语识别存在的问题分析

韩礼德说小句的语气成分是由主语加定式操作语构成的;但在具体分析中"主语结构"和"语气结构"则被分别处理为两个层次,即(一)主语结构:"主语+定式操作语+谓语+补语+状语",(二)语气结构:"语气成分+剩余部分"。我们以为,如果将两者看作一体,会显得很牵强:这显然是两种彼此独立的结构关系。尽管有不少系统功能派学者对"主语+定式操作语"的人际性,从不同角度做过阐述,但何以将两者看作一体而仅仅体现社交功能?此外,巴特等人(Butt et al. 2000:91)指出:"语气和语气成分是给予主语、定式范畴和归一度的称谓"(the name **given** to the Subject and Finite plus the polarity)(黑体为笔者所加;也见 Eggins 1994 第6章)。因此我们就有可能在主语结构和语气结构之间划分一条界线,因为"给予"这一行为可能完全是人为的。

从韩礼德的分析看,是"主语+定式操作语"被看作语气范畴的内在构成成分的。但笔者认为这只是巧合:英语中仍然存在主语和语气成分中相关构成范畴分离的现象。而将语气成分中名词组所体现的范畴看作主语,其实是将两种性质不同的范畴混为一谈了。

这里涉及主语的识别问题。一方面,按照传统语法,作主语的名词组与谓语定式动词之间有数的一致关系(如 Biber et al. 1999:180-192;这个问题很复杂,可另见 Sun 1979)。据此,以下句子中加下划线的成分即为相应各句的主语①。

(2) The schedule leaves a wide margin of time for self-study, doesn't it?

(3) There were two caterpillars on the leaf, weren't there?②

(4) In the garden are planted three orange trees, aren't there?

但另一方面,"主语在附加疑问句中以代词的形式复现"(Quirk et al. 1985: 725; 也见 Lakoff 1987: 547)。这样就只有(2)一类的句子才同时符合两条标准;(3)和(4)都有问题:据前一标准,两个名词组为各句的主语;据后一条,there 为(3)的主语,但(4)呢?

为此,一些语言学家提出了补救措施。例如,耶斯帕森(Jespersen 1949VII: 109)将存在句中的 *there* 看作准主语(Quasi-)。夸克等(Quirk et al. 1985: 1403－1406)则叫做语法主语(Grammatical),与名词性实义主语(Notional)相对,如(3)中的 *two caterpillars*。但仅仅贴上一个标签,并没有从理论上解决问题:如果主语存在"语法"和"实义"之别,那么"主语"应该是一个什么样的范畴呢?无论哪一种定性说明都成问题;*there* 与所谓的实义主语之间,缺乏像"先行主语"(Anticipatory)和"后置主语"(Postponed)那样的内在关系,例如,

(5) It was on the news that income tax is to be lowered.

此外,我们找不到别的直接语义关系。所以,我们很难将(3)中的 *there* 与 *two caterpillars* 以及(4)中的 *in the garden* 与 *three orange trees* 均看作同一类范畴。

那么,附加疑问句的功能是什么呢?附加疑问句有升、降两种语调,分别体现两种功能。升调是说话人指望听话人对相关陈述的命题做出真实与否的决断;如果是降调,说话人则希望听话人对相关陈述给予肯定回答,因而具有感慨而不是疑问的功能(Quirk et al. 1985: 811)。因此,无论是升调还是降调,其基本功能都是人际性的,促动听话人参与话语交际并

① 三例均系作者自拟,并分别得到三名被询人(英语为本族语,分别来自英国、加拿大和澳大利亚)认可。此外,他们还一致认为,对于(3)的附加疑问句,除了 *aren't there* 之外,还可以说 *don't we* 或 *don't they*。

② 有人向我指出,用存在句的"例外"情况来反驳底气不足,理由是这只是一个孤例。笔者的看法是,这里所举的确只有一例,但存在句广泛存在:(2)所代表的是一大类语言现象,且相当复杂(如 Lakoff 1987 等),在笔者看来,有关问题还远未解决。

做出相关应答。这正是语气成分所体现的基本人际功能。据此,笔者主张将带有附加疑问句的句子看作两个相对独立的小句:前面的陈述句同时发挥概念和人际功能,而后面的附加疑问句,除了隐喻用法,如以疑问传递信息,则只有人际意义(对比 Fawcett 1999)。

这样看来,传统语法中由识别主语的两条标准所确立的语法范畴,应该是两个不同的概念。换言之,以名词组与相关动词的数的一致关系为标准所确立的范畴,与以附加疑问句作为测试标准所识别的语法范畴,是两个概念而非同一范畴。一方面,韩礼德采用了后一条标准,这样识别出来的范畴就是人际性的,而由此确立的、关于语气的整体框架则合理地解释了有关现象,这是他的重要贡献。但附加疑问句中那个复制成分所回指的,并非总是主语! 另一方面,由一致标准确立的是一个什么样的语法范畴呢? 这个问题的确存在,因为传统语法一向关注的这一类现象,经典理论并没有给出合理解释;2004 年以前韩礼德将这个十分重要的问题忽略了。虽然新版《导论》补充指出,相关动词的人称和数的格标记在当代英语中已基本消失(Halliday & Matthiessen 2004:119),不足为训①;但任何一个懂英语的人都知道,有关第三人称单数的动词后加-s 的情况,仍然普遍存在;如果将德语、法语和俄语等其他印欧语考虑在内,无论何种人称都存在类似标记现象。

下面是有关德语、法语和俄语的例子,并配相应的汉语译文;目的是试图表明这些语言中句子主语的性、数、格与谓语动词的形态变化之间存在对应关系。

先看德语。德语中主语与谓语的对应关系非常严格,谓语动词受不同人称(我、你、他/她/它、我们、你们、他们、您/您们)的制约,谓语动词必须随主语变化。例如:

(6) *Ich* **komme** zu dir.(我到你这儿来)

(7) *Er* **kommt** zu mir.(他到我这儿来)

---

① 其实这个问题与经典理论一向主张的"概率"问题有关。这虽然是经典理论的基石之一,但这并不意味着:概率就是一切,Halliday 也从来没有这样说过或暗示过;而据笔者所知,语言学界也没有任何其他人说过"概率"就是确立范畴的首要和唯一条件。其实,历时语言研究中对许多范畴的构拟,从来都不是从概率出发的,相反,研究语言的历时发展进程的语言学家们,通常最担心(也是最小心)的,就是从现当代语言现象的概率出发来考察其历时演化过程。

（8）*Sie* **kommen** zu mir.（他们到我这儿来）

以上三个例句为现在时，谓语动词 *kommen*（来）随主语的人称变化而变化。又如，

（9）*Du* **kannst** zu mir kommen.（你可以到我这儿来）

（10）*Er* **kann** zu mir kommen.（他可以到我这儿来）

（11）*Sie* **können** zu mir kommen.（他们可以到我这儿来）

这三个例句也为现在时，但带有情态助动词 *können*（能、能够、可以），它与主要动词的不定式（即动词原形）一起构成复合谓语。情态助动词须随主语的人称变化而变化，主要动词以不定式的形式位于句末。

（12）*Ich* **bin** in Beijing angekommen.（我到达北京了）

（13）*Er* **ist** in Beijing angekommen.（他到达北京了）

（14）*Sie* **sind** in Beijing angekommen.（他们到达北京了）

以上三个例句为现在完成时，表示在说话之前动作已经完成，但与现在仍有关系。德语的现在完成时由"时间助动词 *haben* 或 *sein*（随主语人称而变化）+主要动词的第二分词"构成，时间助动词的选用须视主要动词而定。例句中的 *angekommen* 是主要谓语动词 *ankommen*（到达）的第二分词，要求的时间助动词是 *sein*。句中的 *bin*、*ist*、*sind* 是时间助动词 *sein* 与主语"我"、"他"、"他们"的对应变化形式。

再看俄语：

（15）*Мальчик* каждый день **опаздывает** на урок.（男孩每天上课都迟到）

（16）*Мальчик* сегодня **опоздал** на урок.（男孩今天上课迟到了）

（17）*Мальчик и девочка* каждый день **опаздывают** на урок.（男孩和女孩每天上课都迟到）

（18）*Девочка* сегодня **опоздала** на урок.（女孩今天上课迟到了）

（19）*Мальчик и девочка* сегодня **опоздали** на урок.（男孩和女孩今天上课都迟到了）

在俄语中句子的谓语动词与主语之间存在着严格的对应关系。它不但受到主语的性、数的制约，还取决于主语行为的时间和状态。例句（15）

中句子主语 *мальчик*（男孩）的行为是经常性的,所以与之相对应的谓语动词以完成体的现在时形式 *опаздывает* 出现。（16）中"男孩"的行为是已完成的一次性行为,所以使用的是谓语动词完成体的过去时 *опоздал*。（17）的主语是复数,其行为是经常性的,因此相应的谓语则是未完成体的现在时的复数形式 *опаздывают*。（18）中主语是阴性,故谓语动词是 *опоздала*,而不是 *опоздал*。（19）表示的是两个人已完成的一次性过去行为,所以谓语动词是 *опоздать* 一词的复数形式的过去时 *опоздали*。

法语虽然不及德语和俄语的变化丰富,但毕竟这种对应关系很明显。例如,

(20) *Je* **pars** pour l'Amérique avec quelques amis intimes.（我和几个好朋友动身去美洲）

(21) *Nous* **partons** d'un éclat de rire.（我们有时会突然大笑起来）

(22) *Elle* **est partie** à trois heures.（她三点钟走了）

以上三句话的谓语动词存在明显的形态变化,它们分别是 *pars*, *partons*, *est partie*,其实都是从同一个动词 *partir*（"离开"的原形）变化来的,因主语 *Je*（第一人称单数名词）、*nous*（第一人称复数名词）和 *elle*（第三人称单数名词）不同。事实上,法语中所有定式动词都要随主语数、性等的变化而变化;第三句是复合过去时,过去分词因主语是阴性而要加 *e*。

这些现象足以说明,小句中有一个名词词组与相关动词有内在联系;这个名词词组就是主语。按照我们的理解,即便其间没有上述形式标记,这种内在联系也能通过语义关系得到间接说明。因此,相关名词词组的功能不能避而不谈;存在句只不过是把相关功能揭示出来了。

但是,德语、俄语和法语中有关存在句的附加问,与英语不同,倒是与汉语接近,即前面的相关名词词组没有关系。例如,以下各对实例中的反疑问成分都一样(斜体成分为相应小句的主语):

(23) In Deutschland gibt *es* viele chinesische Studenten, **nicht wahr**?（es 为形式主语,viele chinesische Studenten 为宾语;翻译:在德国有许多中国大学生,是不是?）

(23') Sind *Sie* Stefan Holz, **nicht wahr**?（您是施特芬·霍尔茨先生,是吧?）

(24) У *них* ест ь много денег, **правда**?（他们有很多钱,是吗/不

是吗?)

(24') *Эта девушка* очень красивая, **правда**? (这个女孩很漂亮,
是吧?)

(25) Il n'y a plus de *doute* possible, **n'est ce pas**? (不会再有疑问了,
对不对/不是吗?)

(25') *Les concierges* ont toujours tenu une grande place dans la vie
parisienne dans la littérature, **n'est ce pas**? (《守门人》在文学作
品所描写的巴黎人的生活中总是占有重要位置,对不对/不
是吗?)

　　至于新版《导论》认为的"结构主义传统下的主语是一个纯粹的语法
成分,在句法层的操作中没有语义可言"(同上),则是另一回事;我们说的
主语是有语义的,即小句的概念意义(见下文)。就是说,与动词有数的一
致关系(无论显、隐)的那个名词组就是主语,附加疑问句中以代词身份出
现的那个成分不一定同时是主语,而那个代词本身的功能也并非主语。
主语结构和语气结构应当分离开来处理;即便多数情况下,复制代词就是
前面陈述句中的名词组(主语),但这只是重叠问题,此时相关名词组具有
双重功能:既协作构成语气成分,也作主语。试比较对(2)和(3)两例所
做的分析:

(a)

the schedule　　leaves a wide margin of time for self-study	
主　　语	谓　　语
语气成分	剩余成分

(b)

there	were	two caterpillars	on the leaf
谓		主　　语	语
语气成分		剩余成分	

图 6-1:韩礼德关于主谓语与语气结构分离的分析

　　此外,经典理论从命题的角度寻找理论依据也值得商榷;我们拟从根
源上来梳理这一点。其实,命题是一个同时具有概念性和人际性的复合
概念;韩礼德之所以将主语看作一个人际性语法次范畴,其理论出发点直
接与命题和提议有关。而这一点可以追溯到古希腊哲学家那里。例如,

亚里士多德在论述命题的基本类别时,涉及命题的肯定与否定、全称与非全称、简单与复合、矛盾与非矛盾等问题。这些均同时涉及命题的概念意义。以矛盾命题与非矛盾命题为例,亚里士多德有以下论述(在哲学领域subject 被译为"主项";出处同前,54 页):

> 如若两个命题的主项相同,肯定命题的主项是全称的,否定命题的主项不是全称的,那我们就把这两个命题称为相对立的矛盾命题,如"所有的人都是白的"和"并非所有的人都是白的",以及类似的命题。再如,"有些人是白的",在我所说的矛盾意义上,就与"没有一个人是白的"相对立。

矛盾命题牵涉的则是经验事理,后者与概念意义所体现的经验知识范畴有关,属于语场的范围(彭宣维 2003)。这一点在亚氏之后的语言学研究中屡有论及,如 19 世纪法国的威尔(Weil 1844/1978)在论及表达出发点时就是以命题的概念意义为依据的。

又如,肯定命题与否定命题,在系统功能理论中被概括和阐述为一种语义范畴,即归一度(Polarity);它同时与经验意义和人际意义有关;而与此相关的全称命题与非全称命题(ALL and NON-ALL Propositions),在当代诸多文献(包括 Halliday 理论)之中被进一步阐述为情态(Polarity),在系统功能语言学的理论阐述中同时涉及概念意义和人际意义(见 Halliday 2004:126 - 130;胡壮麟等 1989:71)。

此外,命题还与动词的时态有关,而这一点所体现的经验意义十分突出。如亚里士多德所述(《全集·解释篇》第 5 章 52 - 53 页):

> 所有命题都含有一个动词或一种动词的时态。甚至"人"的定义,如若不增加"现在是"、"过去是"、"将来是"或某些这一类的词,那么它根本无法形成命题……在各种命题中存在着简单命题,如肯定某事物的某种东西,或否定某事物的某种东西,另一种是复合命题,如由简单命题构成的命题。简单命题是一种有意义的表述,它肯定或否定某一事物在过去、现在或将来的存在。

这里除了命题的时间性外,还涉及简单与复合命题。这些阐述显然与小句的概念意义有关(参阅 Halliday & Matthiessen 2004、2014 第 6、7 章有关动词词组和复句的概念意义的论述)。因此,鉴于命题同时涉及概念义和人际义,我们就很难说与命题有关的主语一定就是人际性的了。

这里小结如下。第一,在多数情况下,那些作主语的相关名词词组,具有双重功能:一是韩礼德确认的人际性语法范畴,另一个则是笔者将要阐述的、体现概念意义的语法形式范畴。但这两种功能并非总是重叠在同一成分上的,如(3)和(4)。第二,命题是一个复合概念,至少亚里士多德笔下的命题如此;而在由此发展而来的系统功能语法中,命题就该同时是概念意义与社交性和评价性的人际意义。经典理论仅仅以命题的一个侧面为依据来确认语气成分的构成要素之一,显然有些经不起推敲。

那么,这里确立的主语究竟是一个什么性质的范畴呢?

6.2 主语的语法形式特征及相关理论阐述

6.2.1 主语的语法形式特征

这里拟说明,主语是一个语法形式范畴,起支配作用的是底层的概念结构。笔者将从两个方面来阐述这一点。第一,经典理论中缺乏这样一个形式范畴;第二,我们拟从语言学史上人们对主语的一些共识的角度,来梳理主语的语法形式特征。先看前一点。

把主语看作概念意义的语法形式范畴有理论上的需要。经典理论在分析词组和复句时,均涉及两个侧面;但在分析小句时只涉及一个侧面;主语结构正好可以填充这个空挡。

首先,韩礼德(Halliday & Matthiessen 2004 和 2014 第 6 章)在分析名词词组和动词组时,讨论了它们的经验结构和逻辑关系。以名词词组为例,他自拟了一个典型例子,能囊括名词词组内的所有基本语义范畴: *those two splendid old electric trains with pantographs*,其中的语义范畴分别为指别(*those*)、数量(*two*)、主观特征(*splendid*)、客观特征(*old*)、类别(*electric*)、事物(*trains*)和制约(*with pantographs*),并将由此组合而成的结构称为经验语义结构:指别+数量+主观特征+客观特征+类别+事物+制约。与上述语义成分相对应的是语法类别：限定词（*those*），数量词（*two*），形容词（*splendid/old*），形容词（*electric*），名词（*trains*）以及介词（*with*）和名词（*pantographs*），它们构成以 *trains* 为中心语、其前后成分均为修饰语的逻辑结构：前置修饰语+中心语+后置修饰语（对比 Bloomfield 1933/1955 第 12 章；也见后文）。

注意，其中的制约范畴与其他语义范畴不同：它不是由一个词而是由一个介词短语体现的。但介词的基本功能并非经验性的，而是体现经验范畴之间的逻辑语义关系的（认知语言学则看作体现认知空间关系）。因此，韩礼德此处说的经验语义结构，正是他在别处（Halliday 1973）说的概念意义，即经验意义与逻辑意义的总称（彭宣维 2003a：57－62）；他叫做逻辑关系的范畴，实际上是一个更为抽象的概念，一个也在语法形式的范围内，因为这是一个基于经验意义的抽象结构关系。即是说，他对词组的分析实际上已经涉及笔者说的语法的两个层面，即"第二阶段加工"过程中被识解的语法结构，以及由此进一步抽象产生的组合关系（也见上一章）。这种语法关系与传统语法所说的，在所指对象上基本一致，只是彼此的理论框架不同（见后文）。

其次，韩礼德对复句内部两个小句之间的关系也做了类似区分。其一是逻辑语义关系，其二是相互关系（Halliday & Matthiessen 2004 第 7 章）。笔者认为，前者名副其实；而后者同样是一个更为抽象和更为形式化的范畴，这也是传统语法涉及的基本议题之一，唯理论框架有别。因此笔者建议称之为逻辑语法关系；这也正是笔者理解的语法形式范畴（见后文）。

按照这一思路，介于词组级和复句级之间的小句，其概念范畴（及物性、级差性、时间性）及其结构关系，为何无类似逻辑关系（见 Halliday & Matthiessen 2004 和 2014 第 5 章）？笔者主张，主语结构与概念意义之间应有体现关系，只是主语结构是基于概念意义但已脱离了具体语义特征的、更为抽象的概括范畴，是一种概念形式（也见前文图 4－2 和图 5－1）：

[概念元功能/意义潜势]→[概念形式I：及物性+时间性+归一度]→
[概念形式II：作格关系]→[概念形式III：语态结构+主语结构]。

下面从柏拉图和亚里士多德的有关论述来梳理主流主语观的概念形式特征。斟酌以下引文（着重号系笔者所加）：

（i）陌：一个句子必须而且不能不有一个主语。费：是的……
陌：我给你说一个句子，由一个名词和一个动词把一个事物和一个动
作组合在一起。你得告诉我这个句子说的是谁。费：好的，我尽力而
为。陌：费亚提特坐着——句子不长。费：不长。陌：这个句子说的
是谁……你得告诉我这个句子说的主语是谁。费：是我；我是主语。

（ii）肯定判断是一个有关主语的事实的陈述，这个主语要么是
一个名词，要么是一个无名称者；肯定判断中的主语和谓语必须各自
指向一个单一的事物。

主语在这两段话里是多个概念的总称，从当代语言学的角度看，它至
少有三种相关但又不同的内涵：一是外在实体性范畴；二是与主题主位相
近；三是我们理解的语法形式特征。

第一种主语观是一个外在实体。根据当时的认知水平，*I am the
subject* 一句中的 *I* 是指特定情景中的说话人：鉴于 *I* 和 *subject* 是识别关
系，*subject* 也是外在的，因为前一引文中由"名词"和"动词"所组合的"事
物"和"动作"在柏拉图的认识中肯定不是两个认知范畴。如果这一理解
基本合理，那么这一主语观当然就很成问题。从当代认知语言学的角度
看，*I* 则是一个经过认知处理而获得的经验语义范畴，*subject* 也一样。

第二种主语概念在以后两千多年的历史过程中演化出了一个独立的
范畴地位，这就是相关信息片段中所谈论的那个基本对象。这一概念成
型于公元前一世纪狄奥尼修斯（Dionysius）有关词序功能的论述；到 18 世
纪的法国和德国时已有广泛讨论，如法国的狄德罗（Diderot, 1713 -
1784）、孔狄亚克（Condillac, 1714 - 1780）以及里瓦罗尔（Rivarol, 1753 -
1801），德国的博德默（Bodmer, 1689 - 1783）和赫德尔（Herder, 1744 -
1803）等（出自 Scaglione，载于 Weil 1844/1978：ix）；在 19 世纪中叶以后
得到充分发展（Weil 1844/1978；Gabelents 1868, 1891；Wegener 1885；
Ammann 1928；后三者出自 Sgall et al. 1986 与 Hajicova 1994）。美国的结
构主义学者霍凯特（Hockett 1958：201）则是明确区分语法主语和语义性
主题的第一人。

第三个主语概念是以相关经验范畴为基础的语法形式范畴，这一点
明确地贯穿于整个西方语言学史直至当代，如古希腊时代的斯多葛学派
（主要体现在关于词的"格"理论中）、亚力山大学派（如 Thrax &

Dyscolus)、古罗马时代的瓦罗(Varro)和普利西安(Priscian)、13 到 14 世纪的摩的斯泰学派(如 Thomas of Erfurt 关于 Dependency 与 Terminancy 以及 Suppositum/subject 与 Appositum/predicate 的相互关系)(见 Robins 1997)。20 世纪上半叶丹麦学者耶斯帕森的主语概念,本质上也是语法形式的(如 Jespersen 1949 III 各处,尤其是 206—208 页;另见陈脑冲 1993)。布拉格学派区分"句子的实际切分"和"句子的形式切分",后者就是指语法主语和语法谓语(Mathesius 1939/1989;钱军 1998:294 – 295)。类似主语概念也出现在当代其他学派的有关论述中,只是角度及理论框架相异。而夸克(Quirk et al. 1985:717 – 799)接受这一形式概念的事实,尤能表明经典理论之外其他学派的学者,一般都是把主语作为一个语法形式范畴看待的。

再回过头去看,如果说柏拉图和亚里士多德笔下的主语概念还显得有些驳杂和粗疏的话,那么此后学界确有一些学者明确地阐述过主语是一个基于经验意义的语法形式范畴这一观点。例如,马泰修斯(Mathesius 1975:100 – 101)指出:

> 英语倾向于选择某种具体的成分作句子主语,尤其是那些指人的词……在当代捷克语和英语中,主语可以实施以下功能:既可能是由述谓结构表达的施动者,也可能是动作的受动者,但其分布在这两种语言中有很大差别……

这里阐述了词序演变和语用目的的关系,但结合其"形式切分观"我们看到:第一,尽管这里强调的是功能词序观,但主语的本质并没有改变,仍然与关注对象概念相分别;第二,被保留下来的主语概念在于它体现经验性的语义范畴"施动者"和"受动者"。不过,"在英语中,动作者和主语并非总是一致的"(Hill 1958:267;另见 Weil 1844/1978:37)。这在当代一些代表性著述中也有回应;而且与主语对应的还不仅仅是施动者和受动者。例如,一些代表性学者(如 Quirk et al. 1985:740 – 747;Biber et al. 1999:123 – 124)在总结主语的有关特征时,均认为主语可能对应于多种经验语义角色,诸如"施动者,即一个动作的有意识的发动者","一个事件的无生命的外在启动者","某一施动者为了实施某种动作所使用的工具或手段",以及"好些非施动性的角色",如"接受性主语,用以指示一个有生命的个体,即一个被动接受者,或者某一动作或状态的经验因素"。总之,主语和谓语的部分来源于人们现今所理解的谈论对象和评述的内涵,但已经与后两者分离开来,发展和进化成为一对独立的语法概念。因此,无论是从系统功能语法理论完善的需要看,还是从语言学史上主流主语观的继承与发展历程看,主语都应当作为一个经验性的语法形式范畴来看待。

在系统功能学派内部,也已经有将主语结构作为一个语法形式范畴看待的。例如,韩礼德本人早先(Halliday 1970/1976:24)就是将主语结构和人际性的语气结构分离开来处理的:

	// the sun	was shining	on the sea //
概念:	受事 Affected	过程 Process	处所 Locative
人际:	语气 Modal	命题 Propositional	
语篇:{	主位 Theme	述位 Rheme	
	新信息 New		
	主语 Subject	谓语 Predicator	状语 Adjunct

图 6-2:韩礼德早期的主语分析

这里的主语和三类词汇-语法范畴没有任何直接关系;福赛特(Fawcett 2000:72)在引述该图时,于最后一个结构范畴前添上了 COMBINED(组合性的)这样一个总括性的称谓,并认为这里的句法分析为整合性分析(integrated analysis)。其实,我们完全有理由把它理解为一种更为抽象的形式关系,否则它何以游离于三个基本语法范畴之外?但这也可从侧面说明其理论建构中存在的人为因素,而后来的假设方案并非一定合理。我们完全有理由将主语结构的并行组合关系分离和抽象出来处理。

这一思路启发了福赛特(Fawcett 1999, 2000)。其主语概念指从系统网络中选择语义特征(对比 Halliday 2004)到纯粹的语法形式关系的说明(Exponence)过程,由一系列体现运算(Realization Operations)构成(如180 及 181-182 页),从理论上揭示了韩礼德模式中缺乏句法层(Syntax;韩氏甚至反对使用这一术语,如 1994:xiv)的局限。他的具体分析如下(上图出处为 2000:148,下图出处为 2000:247;上图中的句法范畴缩写符是:S(ubject), O(perator), M(ain verb), C(omplement), A(djunct)):

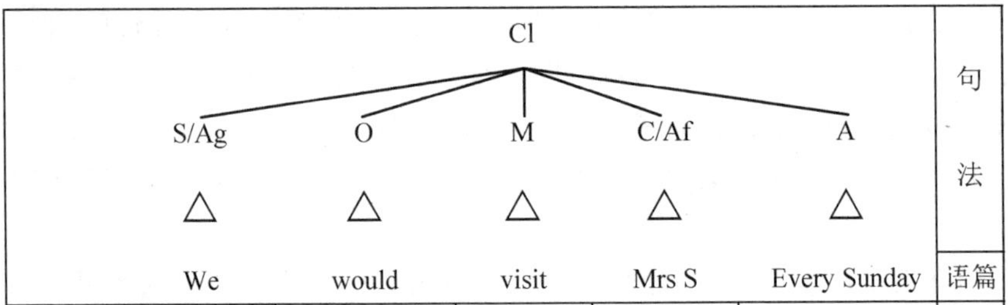

		Cl			句法
S/Ag	O	M	C/Af	A	
△	△	△	△	△	
We	would	visit	Mrs S	Every Sunday	语篇
经验	明确施事	重复性过去	社交行为	明确受事	周期性概率	语义

经验	明确施事	重复性过去	社交行为	明确受事	周期性概率
人际	信息提供者				
归一度		确定			
有效性		不确定			
主位	主语 主位				
信息					非标记新信息
(无"逻辑关系"或"情感"意义)					

He	would	visit	his gran	every Sunday
Subject	Finite	Predicator	Complement	Adjunct
主语	定式语	谓语	补语	状语

图 6‑3：福赛特对主语结构的分析

如果我们对比其中句法（Syntax）和语义（Semantics）的相互关系，即可看出主语结构的地位和性质（完成的主语结构见下图分析），即一种整合各种意义的功能结构。

对此，笔者从总体上是赞同的，但也有保留意见，包括语义、语法的性质，尤其是为了满足"计算"方便而削弱甚至取消"级阶"概念、从而使句法层表现出纯粹的线性过程的做法，值得讨论，因为这样在很大程度上容易使语言的一级结构（Harris 1998 称为 First Order Construct）和二级结构（Second Order Construct）偏离太远（不过这在很大程度上是一个具体的操作性问题）。但韩氏这种前后不同的处理方案表明，其中带有明显的人为痕迹。

总之，这里梳理的主语应当是一个句法概念，一种从底层概念意义基础上抽象而来的、纯粹的结构关系。这种分析性思考不仅可以回应"主语结构缺乏语义关系"的误识，对笔者来说还是十分必要的，因为这样能明确实例性词汇语法的多层次性。

6.2.2 进一步理论阐述

有三个相关理论问题需要做进一步解答：第一，语气成分中原先叫做主语的范畴究竟应该如何称谓？第二，定式操作语这一称谓所体现的语义功能又该如何确定？第三，我们所说的语法范畴的多层次性，其间究竟指的是什么？

就第一个问题而言，笔者主张将建构语气成分的、原先叫做主语的范畴称为"互动语"（Interactant），即实施社交互动的基本功能成分；而定式操作语是另一个功能成分；根据韩礼德的认识，两者合称为语气成分，体现话语的社交意义，从而达到物品—服务或信息交换的目的。按汤普逊（Thompson 1996：45）的观点："只要当前命题处于运作状态"，互动语就是"非协商性的"（non-negotiable）。笔者认为，这种非协商性是与定式成分的"有效性"相对而言的（见后文）。

这里扼要说明主语结构的构成。前面已经指出，英语的主语结构由六大主要句法范畴构成：一致关系（Concord，确立主语和谓语）、管制关系（Government，确定谓语和宾语）、时态（Tense，界定时间语义范畴）、体（Aspect，说明动词事件特征，同时体现时间意义）、语序（word order，如 John chased Mary 与 Mary chased John）以及被动语态的动词词组等。这些范畴中前四个均直接与语素相关（而部分实例因此体现出"格"关系），另外两个大致与位置和先后顺序有关；从功能关系上讲，它们均直接涉及句法结构，均在小句级上发挥作用。上述关系能表明由此确立的语法关系的抽象性（也见下文）。

此外，如果把支撑性 there（存在句）结合起来考虑，将先前叫作主语的那个范畴改称为互动语尤其符合逻辑。即是说，既然先行成分 there 是主语，即所谓的"傀儡主语"（Dummy subject）或"语义上空洞（或无指代）"（Quirk et al. 1985：740‒747；Biber et al. 1999：123‒124），那么从逻辑上讲，没有语义内容，又何来形式呢？因为体现程序是"意义→形式"。可见，存在性 there 并非主语，而是一个建构语气成分发挥交际功能的范畴。也就是说，there be 存在句型中只有与定式动词有一致关系的名词组才应该被当作主语;其他句型中作主语的名词组则同时发挥相关人际功能。在后一种情况下,同一个成分同时发挥两种语法功能:一是体现概念意义中的有关范畴,二是协同体现社交人际意义。据此,前面例(2)句首的 *there* 则是语气成分的构成要素"互动语";(3)附加疑问句中的 *there* 仍然可以看作是对前面陈述句中处所成分 *in the garden* 的复制,故 *in the garden* 为相关语气的互动语①。

这里顺带提一下现代汉语的语气成分问题。据调查,汉语的能愿动词以及在没有能愿动词情况下的实义动词同样可以被重复,从而维系话语推进及社交事件(interactive event)(彭宣维 2000:134 - 136);除了声调手段,实施语气的还有一系列词汇性的语法手段(胡壮麟 1994/1995;彭宣维 2000:136 - 142),就像《导论》新版提到的越南语、泰语和日语那样。

就第二个问题而言,定式成分也是双功能的,因为它能同时协作体现概念性的时间意义和人际性的社交意义。因此,我们需要区分定式范畴的语义功能,并确立相应的语法功能称谓(另见 Halliday 2004:115 - 116;Jespersen 1949IV 第 1、3 和 22 章)。一方面,定式操作语具有体现概念意义中时间范畴的作用,即时间性(Temporality),一种语法性的语义范畴(因为不少时态体现的并非外在时间,而是认识性质的);其语法功能则是协作构成时态范畴,因而定式操作语的这种语法功能可称为时态操作语或时态定式语。于是有以下体现模式:时间性→时态操作语/定式语。另一方面,定式操作语也是人际导向的:它同时发挥另一种功能,即协同体现社交意义,所以也称语气操作语。或如汤姆逊所说:定式成分引导"听话人推导相关命题所主张的有效性"(validity),"并将这种有效性与此时此地言语事件的现实性或者说话人的态度联系在一起"(Halliday & Matthiessen 2004:115)。因此有以下体现模式:社交性→语气[语气成分(互动语+语气操作语/定式语)+剩余部分]。

我们的目的是试图重新确认主语的语法功能性质以及原先叫做主语的那个范畴的称谓,附带涉及定式成分的语法和语义功能问题。而要使

---

① 此前学界认为存在性 *there*"不具备地点副词 there 的处所意义"(Quirk et al. 1985:1405),所以有处所性/指别性 *there* 与存在性/呈示性 *there* 之别(Adamson 1999/2002:606;Lakoff 1987:462 - 585;Bolinger 1977:90 - 123)。但从这里的具体情况看,*there* 并没有完全脱离处所特征,除非这里的 *there* 不作 *there be* 句型中 *there* 的理解。

前面的论证过程落到实处,还有一个重大的理论问题需要解答。这就是前面提出的第三个问题:如何从理论上说明概念语法范畴分层问题? 这一点之前已有讨论(彭宣维 2011),但不彻底。现将主要观点总结如下。虽然这里的观点是基于汉语分析取得的,但结论具有普通语言学意义。

米勒(Miller 1985)传统语法的评价是:传统语法的主要问题在于将语法和语义混在一起,两个层次是独立生成的(193 页)。我们认为,传统语法说的语义和语法,实际上正是系统功能语法的概念语法范畴的基础,但在这里它们是同一形式层次的不同次层次。第一,这两个层次是同时生成的:传统上说的语法是在音系成分序列化和结构化过程中同时生成的;而语义范畴在结构关系中的序列化,正是系统功能语法的形式范畴,如及物性和作格性,它们和主语结构一样,都是形式化编码过程中从经验语义范畴的组合结果;第二,及物性和作格性在体现过程中可能表征为为数较少的数种形式结构,这就是主语结构;第三,在大的语法层次上分层,它们之间只是抽象程度的不同,没有明确和硬性分界,或如学界常用的比喻,是一个硬币的两个面。

第一点需要很大的篇幅来阐述,此处只是引用结论;下面仅对后两点做扼要概述。笔者在讨论现代汉语中由语法结构确立的语义范畴时,涉及诸多语法形式范畴,包括"得"字结构(补语)、"连"字句、"把"字句、"被"字句、"领主属宾句"、兼语句、存在句、"形容词谓语句"、"名词谓语句"。我们看到,同一种语法结构对应于多种语义结构,即系统功能语言学的语法关系。例如,语法形式上的"把"字结构,对应于好几种语义结构,包括物质过程("他把那家伙揍了一顿"),心理过程("张三把这事又想了一遍")。又如"得"字结构,可能有物质过程("张三打得很重"),心理过程("这事儿张三想得太多了"),还有增强复句("张三打得儿子昏了好几次")(另见 Fawcett 1987;Zhou 1997)。又如,在英语的名词词组中,其语法形式结构,即第二级结构,要么是前置修饰语+中心语(如 *those trains*),要么还有后置修饰语(*those trains with pantographs*);但名词词组的语义结构范畴,即第一级结构,不仅在数量上远远多于前置和后置两个成分,在构成上也复杂得多。当然,也有一个语义关系对应于多个表达形式者(杨宁 1994),但这主要是信息配置的需要。因此,这些事实不仅能为本书的基本观点提供理论支持,也与认知语义学"意义-形式影射关系"(meaning-form mappings)或意义-形式"合成关系"(conflation)的观点基本一致(Talmy 2001a：11，25)。

总之,第一级结构是人的认知能力通过音系手段从语境启动的经验知识中提取语义特征、并经过入列条件的选择而生成的组合关系;第二级结构则是对第一级结构的进一步抽象化和结构化。抽象化就是概括化或象征化的认知过程;对语法层次的深入分析,有赖于语义结构(第一级结构),对语义结构的深入分析,有赖于有关语义成分及其选择陈述;而后者的隐喻化,就意味着表达陈述对经验范畴或多或少的认知"勾画"和重新处理,从而可能出现与经验事理相悖的语义关系,如 *the fifth day saw them at the top of the mountain*;这也正是 Halliday(1995b，1999)把上述过程看作对"经验"范畴的"重新整形"(reshaping)的原因。可见,第一二级结构关系之间并非对等,而应当从理论上区分开来。而从一级结构到二级结构,就意味着抽象程度的加大和范畴数量的减少。据此,将主语结构看作概念性的语法范畴,不仅符合前人有关主语性质的基本认识,而且能清楚地区别于语气成分的构成要素之一。

6.3 结语

这里将主语的功能属性总结如下。第一,主语是一个狭义的语法范畴;它与概念意义有关,是直接体现小句概念意义的最终形式层次。第二,主语与语气不发生任何关系,更不存在体现关系,连性质也不相同;同时,主语与谈论对象已经分化。第三,主语是主语结构的基本构成要素之一;另一个是谓语,包括定式动词、谓语、补语和状语等次范畴;此外,主语结构还应包括语态和时态等形式范畴。本章在引言中提到"提议"与主语无关;事实上,祈使句句首被省略的成分,就不宜再叫作主语。

至此,我们通过上面第四、五、六章讨论了及物性语法模式的三个层次:过程模式、作格模式、语态+主语模式。其实,概念意义可以根据需要体现为多于三个次要层次的经验模式;确立上述三个模式是根据有关传统进行的。

第三部分

应用研究

第七章

论英汉语中原因连接成分的信息导入功能

—— 一项以语料库为基础的实证研究[①]

7.1 引言

本章以系统功能语法的信息理论为立足点,以语料库为基础,对英汉语篇过程中原因连接成分所发挥的、引导已知信息和新信息的功能,进行一项实证研究。

已知信息和新信息是系统功能语法信息理论中的基本范畴。最初,韩礼德(Halliday 1956)是在"现代汉语的语法范畴"一文中使用这两个术语的。后来,他结合布拉格语言学派的"句子的实际切分理论"尤其是"主位理论",对它们进行了系统的理论阐述和具体分析(Halliday 1967 – 1968)。这不仅立刻引起了西方语言学界对布拉格学派语言理论的广泛关注,也引发了此后人们从不同角度对语言信息的深入探讨(如 Chafe 1976, 1994; Clark & Haviland 1977; Taglicht 1984:32 – 52; Lambrecht 1994; Dik 1997; Birner & Ward 1998 等);而韩礼德后来则对该理论做

---

① 本章与罗洁和曹意文合作,原载于《外语教学与研究》2007 年第 6 期,第 424—430 页。

了进一步发展和完善（如 Halliday 1978a，1985，1994；Halliday & Matthiessen 2004，2014）。

在系统功能语法中，信息理论的基本思想如下：一个声调群（tone group）确立一个信息单位（information unit）；它必须包含一个由调核（Tonicity）确立的新信息（New Information）以及可能存在的已知信息（Given Information）。新信息指说话人希望听话人关注的一则信息：这具有新价值，很重要，可能在先前的语境中出现过，但此时需要重新引起听话人注意。而由此划定并确立的已知信息则是：说话人假定在听话人注意范围内的信息，可以从语境中恢复，是新信息引入语篇过程的基础。

本章的基本目的是要通过上述信息概念，来考察原因连接成分在英汉语篇过程中发挥的、引入已知信息和新信息的作用。据此，这些原因连接成分就是一种话语标记成分（Discourse Marker）。例如，根据语感，我们觉得英语 *because* 是一个引导新价值的连接成分：*because* 所引导的小句所包含的基本内容是说话人假定听话人此前不了解的或者说话人还没有向听话人提及或说明的信息。但这样的假设仅仅是凭语感做出的判断。于是我们便有了以下疑问：英语的实际使用情况是这样的吗？如果是，这种用法占多大比例？据此，英汉语中原因连接成分（包括词和短语）中哪些通常是引导已知信息的？哪些引导新信息？如果它们能同时引导已知信息和新信息，各自的分布比例又是多大？

这里有两点说明。第一，我们说一个原因连接成分引导新信息，是指被引导的成分中含有新价值，因此我们是把被引出的部分与原因连接成分作为整体看待的，其中起支撑作用的已知信息暂不予考虑。第二，我们也不考虑普瑞丝（Prince 1981）和切夫（如 Chafe 1994）提出的有关新信息和已知信息之间的过渡价值：相关语境中的任何新价值，无论其交际动力如何，均归入新信息范围，余下的则直接划归已知信息。这样既便于操作，也符合本章的基本宗旨。

为此，我们从英汉语的实际使用入手，以语料库中的语篇为依据，对原因连接成分的使用情况做详尽调查。根据我们的经验，这一实证研究的结果，不仅有助于我们区分各个原因连接成分的功能，从而比较准确地把握语篇的信息发展脉络，而且对我们恰当使用相关原因连接成分也具有参考价值。

本章由两个主要部分构成。第 2 小节是引证性的：通过实验确立典型实例,说明原因连接成分的信息引导功能。第 3 小节主要通过量化手段来做定性说明,以确认相关成分的系统特征,并举例说明英汉互译中的应对情况。我们使用的语料来自中国外语教育研究中心研制的"英汉双语平行语料库",涉及文学作品和非文学作品两大语类,具体出处在引文后标出。

7.2 原因连接成分的信息引导功能:实例分析

这里需要首先明确调查对象。我们从英语的原因连接成分中选择了以下常见的 12 个: *because*, *as*, *for*, *since*, *now that*, *because of*, *as a result of*, *owing to*, *due to*, *thanks to*, *by reason of* 和 *on account of*;汉语中调查了 4 个: 因为,既然,由于,鉴于。我们发现,这些成分大都能同时引导已知信息和新信息,但有的只能引导已知信息。

需要说明的是,本小节使用的代表性实例是通过问卷调查确立的。调查对象是北京某大学外国语言文学学院英语语言文学专业语言学方向的一、二年级部分硕士研究生,他们在系统功能语言学方面接受过严格训练,对信息理论有透彻了解。调查问题是: 以下各例中的原因连接成分是否具有引导已知信息或新信息的作用? 如果有,请确定所引入的是:(一) 已知(信息);(二) 新(信息);(三) 难以确定。发放问卷共 17 份,收回 17 份。调查结果见附录表 7-1。为了获得直观认识,下面就相关成分的典型使用情况逐一举例做扼要说明。

(1) a. (... and he is lame.) **Because** he is lame, and consequently slow, they drive him with their guns — like this! (脚也瘸了走得慢,他们使用枪赶他——像这样!)(Charles Dickens: *A Tale of Two Cities*)[已知]

   b. **Because** the AIDS diagnosis is considered a death sentence, many do not seek treatment.(由于对艾滋病的诊断被认为是死刑判

决,许多人不去寻求治疗)(George Bush: *State of the Union Message*)[已知]

c. I do it **because** it's politic; I do it on principle.(我那样做是出于策略,出于原则)(Charles Dickens: *A Tale of Two Cities*)[新]

d. Suicide is a grave sin in Islam **because** it reflects a total lack of faith in God.(伊斯兰教认为自杀是非常严重的罪过,是对上帝完全缺乏信心的表现)(Vivi Yanti Zainol: *What Is a Muslim after 911?*)[新]

这里挑选的前两例中 because 引导已知信息,后两例中引导的则是新信息。(1a)的上文已经介绍过当事人脚瘸了,所以 because 引导的前一小句就是已知的;consequently slow 是可以推知的信息,但似乎带有一定的新价值。统计中有一人把整个部分都看作新信息,可能是忽略了引文前括号内的信息。(1b)中 because 引导的信息在一定范围内已成共识,可以断定为已知信息。(1c)中 because 引导的 politic 是全新信息,给出了当事人做事的理由。(1d)because 后的信息是在向人们介绍一种异域文化知识,所以是对前一句提供的补充信息。第一、三句为文学语类,二、四句为学术语类。

(2) a. At first, **as** already told, she had flirted fancifully with her own image in a pool of water, beckoning the phantom forth, and — **as** it declined to venture—seeking a passage for herself into its sphere of impalpable earth and unattainable sky.(起初,她像前面说的那样,异想天开地和映在水中的自己的倒影戏耍,招呼那映像出来,由于它不肯前进一步,她便想为自己寻找一条途径进入那不可捉摸的虚幻的天地中去)(Nathaniel Hawthorne: *The Scarlet Letter*)[已知]

b. **As** direct steamers to your port are few and far between, in most cases, goods have to be transhipped from Hong Kong.(由于到你方港口的直达船稀少,在大多数情况下,货物必须在香港转运)(*Business Lestters [7]: Terms of Payment*)[已知]

c. This was my second folly, far worse than the first, **as** I left but two sound men to guard the house.(这是我的第二次冒失行为,

而且远比第一次要恶劣,因为我这次只留下了两个健康的人守卫房屋)(Louis Stevenson:*The Treasure Island*)[新]

    d. It was unlucky that the wrong direction was chosen, but for most purposes it does not matter, **as** we think simply of an electric current, without needing to consider it as a stream of electrons. (不幸的是恰好选中了一个错误的方向,但在多数情况下倒无关紧要,因为我们只要简单地把它理解为一般电流,而无需将它看作一个电子的流束)(*What Is Electricity?*)[新]

    这里四句也按同样顺序排列。根据相关上下文,(2a)*as* 引导的句义是 *she* 的倒影不肯从水中出来,这既在前文提及,也是我们普通人的常识。该小句在此发挥衔接作用,引出下面 *she* 自己要走进去的理由。(2b)*as* 引导的小句,是在提醒贸易对方一个事实,双方都清楚,因此它在这里的语境中可作已知信息解。(2c)*as* 后面的信息是说明当事人在前面提到的自己冒失的原因,所以为新信息。(2d)*as* 引导的理由,听话人此前无从知晓,也是新信息。

    (3) a. "Yes, dearest Charles," with her hands on his breast, and the inquiring and attentive expression fixed upon him; "we are rather thoughtful tonight, **for** we have something on our mind tonight."("是的,最亲爱的查尔斯,"她用手抚着他的胸口,专注地、询问地凝望着他,"咱们今晚很有些心事呢,因为我们感到沉重")(Charles Dickens:*A Tale of Two Cities*)[已知]

    b. China must learn from America as well and escape her scholastic straightjacket, **for** academics is a means not an end …(中国也必须向美国学习,并从自己学究式的死板教学中解脱出来,因为教育是手段,而不是目的。)(*When Silence Is not Golden*)[已知]

    c. He had a good leg, and was a little vain of it, **for** his brown stockings fitted sleek and close, and were of a fine texture; his shoes and buckles, too, though plain, were trim.(这人长着一双漂亮的腿,也多少以此为豪,因为他那质地上乘的褐色长袜穿在腿上裹得紧紧的,闪着光,鞋和鞋扣虽不花哨,却也精巧)(Charles Dickens:*A Tale of Two Cities*)[新]

d. These stories might most logically be called "belief tales", **for** their usual effect is to give credence to folk beliefs.(这些故事从逻辑上讲可被称作"信仰故事",因为它们的通常效果是增加了民间信仰的可信度)(*Myths and Legends*)〔新〕

　　第一例中 *for* 所引导的是双方都明确的,即双方都有的"心事",这对听话人来说是已知信息。第二句 *for* 后的一句为已知信息,因为对于可能阅读这类文章的读者来说,*academics is a means not an end* 是常识。第三句 *for* 引入的是在说明当事人那双好腿好在哪里,那些信息在前面的语境中没有介绍,所以是新信息。最后一句 *for* 所引导的新价值不言自明。

（4）a. He did not like to look at the fish anymore **since** he had been mutilated.(他不忍心再朝这死鱼看上一眼,因为它已经被咬得残缺不全了)(Ernest Hemingway: *The Old Man and Sea*)〔已知〕

　　b. **Since** shares represent ownership of a company's dividend, profit, revenue, asset and cash flow, the ways to value shares will be based on these five categories of figures.(既然股票代表了公司的股息、盈利、营业额、资产及现金流的拥有权,评定股票价值的方法就将从上述这五个方面着手)(Hoe Soon: *Tools for Analysing Shares*)〔已知〕

　　c. They add nothing to the wealth of the world, **since** whatever they produce is used for purposes of war, and the object of waging a war is always to be in a better position in which to wage another war.(他们对世界财富并不增添什么,因为无论他们生产什么东西,都用于战争目的,而进行战争的目的总是争取能够处在一个更有利的地位以便进行另一场战争)(George Orwell: *1984*)〔新〕

　　d. **Since** the proletariat must first of all acquire political supremacy, must rise to be the leading class of the nation, must constitute itself the nation, it is, so far, itself national, though not in the bourgeois sense of the world.(因为无产阶级首先必须取得政治统治,上升为民族的领导阶级,把自身组织成为民族,所以本

身还是民族的,虽然完全不是资产阶级所理解的那种意思)
(*Manifesto of the Communist Party*) [新]

　　这里的第一句是在记叙老人与鱼搏斗的最终结果:只剩下一副鱼骨架了,所以此处的信息为可推导的已知信息。第二句 *since* 引导的是常识信息,也是已知的。第三、四句中 *for* 引导的信息无从恢复,均为新信息。

（5）a. **Now that** you have come, I think you will do something to help mamma, something to save papa.(现在你来了,我想你会有办法帮助妈妈和救出爸爸的) (Charles Dickens：*A Tale of Two Cities*) [已知]

　　 b. **Now that** it is operating in a different environment with fierce competition from new ports in neighboring countries, efficient service alone is on longer enough to retain customers.(随着时代的进步,周边环境的改变,邻国新码头的崛起,光在服务水平方面与时俱进,已经不足以吸引客户了) (Koh Lay Kheng：*Pragmatic Measures That Pay off*) [新]

　　此二例中 *now that* 引导的已知和新信息很明确,尤其是后一句,逐一举出了当时出现的三种新情况,具有新价值。

（6）a. **Because of** the position in which O'Brien was standing, Winston could not see what the thing was.(由于奥勃良站在那里,温思顿看不到究竟是什么东西) (George Orwell：*1984*) [已知]

　　 b. He was afraid, **because of** his great weakness, that he might fall in and drown.(他怕自己会由于极度虚弱,跌进去淹死) (Jack London：*Love of Life*) [已知]

　　 c. He crossed a small "branch" two or three times, **because of** a prevailing juvenile superstition that to cross water baffled pursuit. (他在一条小溪流上来回跨过两三次,因为孩子们普遍迷信来回跨水就会让人追不上) (Mark Twain：*Adventures of Tom Sawyer*) [新]

　　 d. The only difference here is that the danger arose **because of** the trustee's and the debtor's failure to correct the violation, not

because of the trustee's exercise of the abandonment power as in Midlantic.(这里的唯一不同就是,之所以出现危险,就是因为受托人和债务人没有纠正违法行为,而不是因为受托人行使了像米德兰特克案例中一样的放弃权)(*Environmental Law in a Nutshell*)[新]

第一句 *because of* 引导的信息,其新闻价值不大,这里可以作为引入新信息的支撑性已知信息。第二句相关信息是作补充说明的,前文已经说明他的身体状况,所以这里也作已知信息处理。第三句相关部分是说明读者不明白的原因的,作为新信息处理。第四句的两个 *because of* 非完全小句,试图辨别相关原因,把读者引到作者的交际意图上来,也是新信息。

(7) a. Farmers are attempting to produce transgenic livestock already, but not efficiently, **due to** the minimal ability to alter embryos genetically, as stated above.(农民正在尝试生产转基因家畜,但不是很有效,原因是像上面说的那样,遗传性改变胚胎的能力极小)(*Cloning Technology*)[已知]

 b. Variations from place to place are **due to** factors such as rainfall, evaporation, biological activity and radioactive decay.(由于受降雨、蒸发、生物活动以及放射性衰变等因素的影响,不同的海区海水盐度也不同)(*The Earth's Oceans*)[新]

这里的第一句中有 *as stated above* 这样的提示语,所以 *due to* 引导的自然是已知信息。第二句中的 *due to* 是为前面提到的 *variations* 提供条件的,而这些因素在上文未曾提及,是新信息。

(8) a. Equipped with an army, **thanks to** the efforts of his indefatigable wife, Ferdinand marched on the apparently impregnable city of Ronda, which is perched on a mountain beside a 600-foot gorge.(由于妻子坚持不懈的努力,费迪南拥有了一支军队,他向外部坚固的龙达城出发了,该城坐落在山上,一旁是600英尺深的峡谷)(*Ferdinand's First Victory*)[已知]

 b. Lately they've been doing that more and more, **thanks to** increased travel（which exposes people to fungi which they have no immunity）and to immunosuppressant drugs（which leave patients vulnerable to what would otherwise be innocuous fungal infections）.（近来,真菌的活动越来越猖獗,一大原因是旅游热(旅游使人类接触到了真菌,而人们对这些真菌根本没有免疫能力),另一原因是免疫抑制药物的使用(这类药物使病人易感那些可能是无害的真菌)（It's Not Just Athlete's Foot）[新]

首句所在的上文,已经从不同角度说明妻子对他组建军队所做的种种努力,所以 thanks to 在这里引入的是已知信息;后一句 thanks to 引导的原因成分是句子表达的重点信息,解释真菌传染蔓延的原因,具有很强的新闻性。

（9）a. … as all **on account of** the whiskey and the excitement, I reckon.（我想这都是因为威士忌在作怪,当时又很冲动）（Mark Twain：*Adventures of Tom Sawyer*）[已知]

b. Well, you see, I'm a kind of a hard lot, — least everybody says so, and I don't see nothing against it — and sometimes I can't sleep much, **on account of** thinking about it and sort of trying to strike out a new way of doing.（您瞧,我是个苦命的人,至少大伙是这么说我的,我也不反对——有时为了想这个问题,好改一改自己,结果弄得睡也睡不着）（Mark Twain：*Adventures of Tom Sawyer*）[新]

第一句中 on account of 后的名词词组包含定冠词,其实是对前文描写的、因喝酒而产生冲动这一事件的概括性重述,为已知信息。后一句中相关成分引导的无疑是新信息。

（10）a. The Impressionists used a very light palette and **as a result of** their influence, Manet's work lighted considerably.（印象派画家用色浅淡,因而在他们的影响下,马奈的作品在色彩上显著变淡）（Manet：*A Painter Ahead of His Time*）[已知]

b. Those who gain fame most often gain it **as a result of** possessing a single talent or skill: singing, dancing, painting, or writing, etc.(那些出了名的人们,绝大多数是因为有一技之长,如唱歌、舞蹈、绘画、写作等等)(*Fame*)[新]

短语 *as a result of their influence* 相对于随后一个小句来说,是前提,也是可以根据句首小句的信息推知的。后一例强调的是名人的一技之长使他们获得声誉,引导的原因使读者对一技之长有更具体的认识。

(11) a. I puts it all away, some here, some there, and none too much anywhere, **by reason of** suspicion.(我把钱全都存了起来,这儿存一点,那儿存一点,哪儿也不存得太多,以免引起人们的怀疑)(Louis Stevenson:*The Treasure Island*)[新]

   b. But the main — that's the big 'un, with the cloud on it — they usually calls the Spy-glass, **by reason of** a look-out they kept when they was in the anchorage cleaning...'(但主桅山———也就是被浓雾笼罩的那座大山———通常被叫做望远镜山,因为海盗在此停泊清理船身时,总是派人在那里瞭望放哨)(Louis Stevenson:*The Treasure Island*)[新]

在我们考察的语料中,*by reason of* 引导的都是新信息。(11a)与上文有联系,讲海盗在海上挣钱怎么花,说话者在讲自己的花法前,先提到大多数人都会把钱花光,而自己却存起来。原因信息在前文没有出现过。(11b)的情况与(11a)相当。

(12) a. **Owing to** their historical position, it became the vocation of the aristocracies of France and England to write pamphlets against modern bourgeois society.(由于他们的历史地位,法国和英国的贵族所肩负的使命,就是写一些抨击现代资产阶级社会的作品)(*Manifesto of the Communist Party*)[已知]

   b. While this illegal activity was once commonplace, it happens mush less frequently now, **owing to** active policing by the SEC.(这样的非法活动过去相当盛行,但由于证券交易委员会的积极监督,现在这种情况少多了)(*American Economy*)[新]

前一例中 *owing to* 介绍的是英法贵族的历史地位,叙述者和读者均知晓,是可以通过推断而恢复的信息。后一例的第一句说的是历史上的情况(过去时),第二个小句说的是现在(注意时态),接下来的那个不完全小句说明有关现状的原因。

上面引证了英语中表原因的主要连接成分的信息引导功能;下面来看看汉语中四个相关成分的信息引导功能。

(13) a. 辛楣**因为**韩学俞没请自己,独吃了一客又冷又硬的包饭,这吃到的饭在胃里作酸,这没吃到的饭在心里作酸,说:"国际贵宾回来了。"(钱钟书《围城》)[已知]

b. 事实上,惟有学中国文学的人非到外国留学不可,**因为**一切科目像数学、物理、哲学、心理、经济、法律等等都是从外国港灌输进来的,早已洋气扑鼻。(同上)[新]

前一句在表原因部分出现前就已经提到,此处只是作为引导后面新信息的基础,其信息可以通过语境恢复。后一例阐述"前果后因",将观点放在前面,以引起读者注意,但表示原因的后半句才是作者要申述的重点,故为新信息。

(14) a. **由于**这一切,**由于**上述各方面的成功,应当说,晋绥解放区现在是比过去任何时候更加巩固了。(《在晋绥干部会议上的讲话》)[已知]

b. 这是**由于**我党坚决地站在农民方面实行土地改革的结果。(《目前形式和我们的任务》)[新]

前一例带下划线的部分显然是纯粹的已知信息,后一例旨在说明有关"结果"的根源,即"土地改革",所以以"由于"引导的信息具有重要性。

"既然"和"鉴于"引导的都是已知信息。且各看二例:

(15) a. 你**既然**不肯结婚,连内助也没有,真是"赔了夫人又折朋"。(《围城》)[已知]

b. **既然**这样,怎么会改变对香港的政策呢?(《要吸收国际的经验》)[已知]

(16) a. **鉴于**这种情况,中国政府曾号召计划生育,提倡使用避孕药具。(《中国的计划生育》)[已知]

b. 拿中央的人事变动来说,我们历来对待这样性质的事总是过

分,**鉴于过去的经验教训**,我们这次用很温和的方式来处理这件事。(《中国只能走社会主义道路》)［已知］

可见,无论在英语还是汉语中,表原因的相关连接成分的确具有引导已知信息和新信息的作用。换言之,相关成分在语篇过程中所起的是衔接和连贯作用,但衔接和连贯所针对的则是信息价值的次第更迭,从而保证语篇对读者的吸引力。

7.3　分布概率及英汉对应比较：定性说明

上一小节以实例引证的方式,分析了英汉语中有关原因连接成分引导已知信息和新信息的功能;这些实例都是在问卷调查的基础上确定的。下面拟通过全面的分析和统计,说明英汉语中所选原因连接成分所具有的系统特征,即已经规约形成、可供选择的聚合关系特征。我们从语料库中搜索到所有相关用例,然后根据第 1 小节提到的标准先分别独立分析,然后逐一讨论核对。统计结果见附录表 2。

根据上表,我们可以得出以下结论。在英语和汉语中,

➢ *because* 总的说来是引导新信息的,这一点集中体现在非文学语类中;文学语类差别不明显,同时引导已知信息和新信息;

➢ *since* 主要用于引导已知信息,尤其是在文学语类中;而在非文学语类中也有体现,但差别不明显;

➢ *now that* 主要用于引导已知信息;

➢ *owing to* 和 *by reason of* 主要用于引导新信息;

➢ 其他成分可同时引导已知信息和新价值,其中有的偏向于引导新信息,如非文学语类中的 *for* 和 *because of* 以及所有的 *thanks to* 及 *due to*,但并不明显;*as a result of* 用于引导已知信息的时候较多,但对比差异也不明显;还有些成分,如 *as*, *on account of*,文学语类中的 *for* 和 *because of*,几乎各占一半。

➤ "因为"：在非文学语类中主要引导新信息,和英语的 *because* 用法相当,但远不及后者在非文学语类中分布特点突出;

➤ "由于"：和文学语类中的"因为"差不多,引导已知信息和新信息的比例相当,和英语的 *for, as, because of, on account of* 以及 *as a result of* 大致相当;

➤ "既然"和"鉴于"：用于引导已知信息,和英语的 *since* 大致相当,但前二者尤其是"既然"的出现几率相当高。

这里提到了相关成分在互译中的英汉对应问题。为了明确这一点,我们来看两个实例,即语料库中"既然"和 *because* 在翻译时所使用的原因连接成分(其他情况请参阅上一小节所引实例及译文)。先看"既然"。在《围城》中,"既然"一律被翻译成 *since*。且看二例:

(17) "我做父亲的太放纵你们了,你们全不知道规矩礼节——",翻着《验方新编》对方老太太道:"娘,三媳妇**既然**有喜,我想这张方子她用得着……""As a father I have been too lenient with all of you. None of you knows your manners-" and leafing through Proven Remedies, he said to Mrs. Fang, "Mother, since Third Daughter-in-law is expecting, I think she could use this prescription …"

(18) 好,你**既然**内行,你自己——将来这样送人结婚罢/All right, since you are such an expert, why don't you do that yourself the next time someone gets married?

在非文学语类中,除了有译 *since* 的,还有四种别的情况:

(19) 有些同志又认为,**既然**现在是社会主义阶段,"一切向钱看"就是必然的,正确的。/Others argued that since we are still at the socialist stage it was only natural and correct for people to "put money above all else." (《党在组织战线和思想战线上的迫切任务》)

(20) **既然**搞的是天翻地覆的事业,是伟大的实验,是一场革命,怎么会没有人怀疑呢? /We are undertaking a tremendous endeavour, a great experiment, a revolution — how could there not be

skeptics?（《拿事实来说话》）

（21）搞了八年了，**既然**是行之有效的方针政策，为什么要改变？ / Why should we change, when they have proved effective over the last eight years?（《中国只能走社会主义道路》）

（22）**既然**这样，怎么会改变对香港的政策呢？ /Such being the case, how can we change our policy towards Hong Kong?（《要吸收国际的经验》）

但反过来，从 *since* 翻译成汉语的情况看，对译成"既然"、"因为"和"由于"的情况分别是 19 次、31 次和 10 次，三个数字表明它们的出现几乎成等差分布。例如，

（23）**Since** I must say so, I know it./**既然**我非回答不可，我的回答是：知道。（Charles Dickens：*A Tale of Two Cities*）

（24）They add nothing to the wealth of the world, **since** whatever they produce is used for purposes of war, and the object of waging a war is always to be in a better position in which to wage another war./他们对世界财富并不增添什么，**因为**无论他们生产什么东西，都用于战争目的，而进行战争的目的总是争取能够处在一个更有利的地位以便进行另一场战争。（George Orwell：*1984*）

（25）But, **since** military and commercial rivalry are no longer important, the level of popular education is actually declining./但是，**由于**军事和商业竞争已不复重要，民众教育水平实际已趋下降。（同上）

我们再来看 *because*。首先，*because* 在文学语类中共出现 244 次，汉译时对应的成分为"因为"、"Ø"（无相关话语标记）、"为的是"、"由于"和"实际上"，分别是 172 次、56 次、1 次、9 次和 1 次。例如，

（26）Why don't you do it? It's **because** you're afraid./你老是吹牛不敢动手，哦，｜ Ø ｜我知道你害怕了。（Mark Twain：*Adventures of Tom Sawyer*）

（27）So far, we have spoken before these two, **because** it was as well that the merits of the cards should not rest solely between you and me./到目前为止,我们是在这两位面前说话,**因为**我这手牌的威力不能光让你和我知道。(Charles Dickens: *A Tale of Two Cities*)

(28) So all this row was **because** you thought you'd get to stay home from school and go a-fishing./原来你这么大叫大闹,**为的就是**你以为这样就可以呆在家里,不去上学去钓鱼呀。(Mark Twain: *Adventures of Tom Sawyer*)

(29) All past oligarchies have fallen from power either **because** they ossified or because they grew soft./过去所有的寡头政体所以丧失权力,或是**由于**自己僵化,或是**由于**软化。(George Orwell: *1984*)

(30) All the town was drifting toward the graveyard. Tom's heartbreak vanished and he joined the procession, not **because** he would not a thousand times rather go anywhere else, but **because** an awful, unaccountable fascination drew him on./全镇的人潮水般涌向坟地,汤姆突然不伤心了,也跟在后面。**实际上**他很想到别的地方去,但是却被一种可怕的、不可言状的魔力吸引到这里。(Mark Twain: *Adventures of Tom Sawyer*)

其次,在非文学语类中,*because* 翻译成"因为"、"Ø"、"由于"(包括"之所以……由于")和"所以/因此/因而",分别出现 219、65、89 和 32 次。非"因为"的翻译情况各看一例:

(31) Suicide is a grave sin in Islam **because** it reflects a total lack of faith in God./伊斯兰教认为自杀是非常严重的罪过,｛Ø｝是对上帝完全缺乏信心的表现。(Vivi Yanti Zainol: *What Is a Muslim after 911?*)

(32) A bond is a long term debt security. It represents debt **because** the investors actually lend the face amount to the bond issuer./投资者把钱借给发行债券的机构,**因此**债券也可说是种长期债务凭证。(Flavia Cheong: *Overview of What Is a Bond and Why They Are Seen to Be Sound Investments*)

(33) But **because** most of the infected cows were still healthy, the

epidemic appeared small./但是,**由于**大多数已感染的牛仍表现健康,因而流行的规模看起来不大。(*Cannibals to Cows: The Path of a Deadly Disease*)

可见,对应有一定规律;但变化能达到目的语表达的流畅性。

总之,本小节从统计的角度考察了英汉语中主要原因连接成分的系统特征以及翻译中彼此的对应情况。这里的量化结果足以说明我们在第一小节中提出的有关假设。

7.4 小结

本章依据系统功能语言学的信息理论,以"英汉双语平行语料库"为基础,对英汉语中原因连接成分的信息功能,从实例分析和数据统计的角度进行了实证研究,旨在定性说明这些成分所具有的、引导已知信息和非已知(新)信息的系统特征。我们的尝试从概率分布的角度证明了我们的假设,并通过实例演示揭示了英汉语互译时的对应关系。可见,原因连接成分在语篇过程中具有双重作用:衔接连贯和信息导入,是一种典型的话语标记成分。上述研究对进一步明确认识英汉语的有关现象、了解它们的写作和互译参照依据,无疑具有指导意义。

附录：

表7-1：英汉语中主要原因连接成分引导已知信息和新信息之检验（G：已知；U：不确定；N：新）

例	a			b			c			d			对比值 X^2
	G	U	N	G	U	N	G	U	N	G	U	N	
(1)	16	0	1	12	0	5	1	2	14	1	1	15	
X^2		133.48			42.11			108.67			135.68		5.99
(2)	16	1	0	12	1	4	4	1	13	3	2	12	
X^2		133.48			67.15			67.15			62.99		5.99
(3)	11	2	4	10	3	4	4	1	12	2	2	13	
X^2		46.39			29.76			67.15			83.76		5.99
(4)	9	3	5	14	1	2	4	1	12	4	4	9	
X^2		19.38			108.67			67.15			17.32		5.99 ·
(5)	17	0	0	4	0	13							
X^2		133.36			58.73								5.99
(6)	15	1	1	14	0	3	3	0	14	1	0	16	
X^2		135.68			79.48			79.48			133.48		5.99
(7)	14	0	3	2	2	13							
X^2		79.48			83.76								5.99
(8)	11	1	5	0	1	16							
X^2		52.61			133.48								5.99

（续表）

例	a			b			c			d		对比值 X²
	G	U	N	G	U	N	G	U	N	U	N	
(9)	17	0	0	3	1	13						
X²		133.36			85.83							5.99
(10)	13	2	2	2	2	13						
X²		83.76			83.76							5.99
(11)	3	2	12	1	0	16						
X²		62.99			133.48							5.99
(12)	13	2	2	2	0	15						
X²		83.76			104.42							5.99
(13)	16	0	1	0	0	17						
X²		133.48			133.36							5.99
(14)	17	0	0	6	1	10						
X²		133.36			42.24							5.99
(15)	17	0	0	17	0	0						
X²		133.36			133.36							5.99
(16)	17	0	0	17	0	0						
X²		133.36			133.36							5.99

（拟合度检验标准值 X² = 0.05）

表 7 - 2：各原因连接成分的信息功能特征之检验

相关成分	语类	所引导之信息价值 已知信息 %	新信息 %	总	计	总百分比 已知 vs. 新	拟合度 检验值 X^2	对比概率率 0.05
because	文学	100/40.98	144/59.02	244	649	25.27 vs. 74.73	1.63 |23.39 **23.39**	3.84
	非文学	64/15.8	341/84.2	405			**12.13**	
for	文学	147/41.18	210/58.82	357	426	40.85 vs. 59.15	1.56 |2.36	3.84
	非文学	27/39.13	42/60.87	69			1.67	
since	文学	46/75.41	15/24.59	61	115	68.7 vs. 31.3	**12.91** |2.47	3.84
	非文学	33/61.11	21/38.89	54			**6.99**	
as	文学	28/57.14	21/42.86	49	152	50 vs. 50	1.02 |0.23	3.84
	非文学	48/46.6	55/53.4	103			0	
now that	两类	18/81.82	4/18.18	22	22	81.82 vs. 18.18	**20.25**	3.84
because of	文学	16/51.61	15/48.39	31	133	45.95 vs. 54.05	0.05 |2.59	3.84
	非文学	39/38.61	62/61.39	101			0.33	
thanks to	两类	8/42.11	11/57.89	19	19	42.11 vs. 57.89	1.25	3.84
owing to	两类	3/25	9/75	12	12	25 vs. 75	**12.5**	3.84
due to	两类	18/38.3	29/61.7	47	47	38.3 vs. 61.7	2.74	3.84
on account of	两类	5/45.46	6/54.54	11	11	45.46 vs. 54.54	0.41	3.84

（续表）

相关成分	语类	所引导之信息价值		总 计		总百分比 已知 vs. 新	拟合度 检验值 X^2	对比概率 0.05
		已知信息 %	新信息 %					
as a result of	两类	17/62.96	10/37.04	27	27	62.96 *vs.* 37.04	3.36	3.84
by reason of	两类	0/0	3/100	3	3	0 *vs.* 100	**50**	3.84
因为	文学	177/47.84	193/52.16	370	496	43.75 *vs.* 56.25	0.09 |**6.66**	3.84
	非文学	40/31.75	86/68.25	126			0.78	
由于	两类	24/48.98	25/51/02	49	49	48.98 *vs.* 51.02	0.02	3.84
既然	文学	55/100	0/0	55	65	100 *vs.* 0	**50/50** |**50**	3.84
	非文学	10/100	0/0	10			**50**	
鉴于	两类	7/100	0/0	7	7	100 *vs.* 0	**50**	3.84

（注：1. 当相关成分在文学语类与非文学语类中出现的几率很低时，统计结果并为一值；2. 拟合度检验之标准值为 $X^2 = 0.05$，因此，X^2 大于 3.84 时具有显著差异（粗体数字）；3. "拟合度检验值"一栏，各语类及总的 X^2 值分别计算列出。）

第八章

语篇元功能维度的功能
文体学研究

Functional Stylistics in the Textual Respect: Some Message Organization Patterns for Literary Discourse Analysis[①]

8.1 Introduction

Functional Stylistics, which focuses on Style in the sense of "forms of wording to which value has been attached" "when used in contradistinction to 'meanings'" (Halliday 2008: 124), has so far concerned itself mainly (i) with the Ideational and Interpersonal Grammars of Systemic Functional Linguistics (SFL) since its start (Halliday 1971, 1977, 1982b, 1988; Fowler 1981; Burton 1982; Nash 1982; Kennedy 1982; Traugott 1982; Toolan 1986, 1988; O'Toole 1988; Durey 1988; Hasan 1985c, 1988, 2007; Haynes 1989; Blake 1990; Macleod 1992; Ryder 1999; Ji & Shen 2004; Shen 2007; Subramaniam 2008; Butt & Lukin 2009; to name just a

---

① 本章原载于 *Linguistics and the Human Sciences*, 2014, 10(3): 263 - 294.

few); (ii) also with Context and Register (Genre) (e.g., Turner 1973: Chapters 5 and 6; Fairclough 1988; Kress 1988; Clark 1992; Hastert & Weber 1992; Simpson & Montgomery 1995; Miller & Turci 2007 *passim*); and (iii) even with the whole semiotic system of human interaction, of which language or Lexicogrammar is the central part (Hasan 1985; Threadgold 1988). Comparatively, however, much less has been said about the issues relating to the Textual Grammar.

There do have some explorations in this last area. Hasan (e.g., 1967, 1985: Chapter 2; 2007: 24−27) has been working on this since 1960s and fully developed some general principles. Halliday (see, e.g., 1994: 64−67) has studied the ways of thematic organization for general text analysis (see also Halliday 1988a). Francis and Kramer-Dahl (1992) have noticed the "typical choice of theme" for method of development (including nominalized and "abstract" themes) and the thematic organization for discourse structure. Agorni (2007: 205−206) discusses a similar issue from the perspective of translation. Goatly (2008: 59−96) analyzes the marked theme distributions in a poetic text.[1] Green (1992) discusses the Given−New value of deixis in poem. Short (1996: 266−268) sketches an application of given-new function to literary discourse analysis; he mentions in particular the technique of "'in medias res' (Latin for 'into the middle of things')" for treating new as given at beginning of literary texts. Furthermore, there are numerous practices over the decades that have studied the functions of Cohesion (e.g., Halliday 1964a, 1964b; Chapman 1973; Leech & Short 1981; Ebrlich 1990; Wright & Hope 1996: 176−179).

Nevertheless, there is still much room for further explorations, regarding, in particular, the notions of Thematization and Information; in fact, no systematic account of some widely-adopted patterns in literary discourses has so far been taken for observing their stylistic effects. This

---

[1] Incidentally, Enkvist (1973), following the Prague tradition of "thematic progression" (e.g., Daneš 1970a, 1970b), studied statistically for theme/rheme iterations and progressions, a way that bears similarity to the SFL approach even though that concept of theme is information value oriented.

chapter aims at that goal, with the help of some other concepts in SFL, e.g., Projection, and some key concepts in Narratology, such as Perspective, as Hasan does (1985: Chapter 3). Now let me specify these terms to be used.

Thematization treats the clause as having "the character of a message" organized by "giving it the status of a communicative event"; the organization contains two functions: Theme and Rheme. The theme is "one element in a particular structural configuration which, taken as a whole, organizes the clause as a message"; it is the "starting-point ..., the ground from which the clause is taking off"; the rheme is what specifies the relevant theme and the two make up a unit of message (Halliday 1994: 37 - 38).

Information is concerned with the "newsworthiness" aspect of language: "Information is presented by the speaker as recoverable (Given) or not recoverable (New) to the listener. What is treated as recoverable may be so because it has been mentioned before; but that is not the only possibility. It may be something that is in the situation, like *I* and *you*; or in the air, so to speak; or something that is not around at all but that the speaker wants to present as Given for rhetorical purposes. The meaning is: this is not news. Likewise, what is treated as non-recoverable may be something that has not been mentioned; but it may be something unexpected, whether previously mentioned or not. The meaning is: attend to this; this is news." (Halliday 1994: 298)

As for the "close semantic relationship" between thematization and information, Halliday elaborates as follows: "Other things being equal, a speaker will choose the theme from within what is Given and locate the focus, the climax of the New, somewhere within the Rheme". "But although they are related, Given + New and Theme + Rheme are not the same thing. The theme is what I, the speaker, choose to take as my point of departure. The Given is what you, the listener, already know about or have accessible to you. Theme + Rheme is speaker-oriented, while Given + New is listener-oriented ..."; but both are "speaker-selected" (Halliday 1994: 299 - 300).

At the discourse level, thematization along message replacement in text proceeds repetitively in a "diminuendo" way, whereas information flows in "crescendo", the two of which may share the same pieces of messages but distribute alternatively in position: one gains its prominence at the beginning and one towards the end (see Halliday 1994: 337). There are hence two "prominences" in a unit of message: the theme is a prominence of **Noteworthiness**, that is, what the speaker or author takes as "the point of departure" for orienting the listeners or readers to attend the aboutness meaning with "noteworthiness", while the New is the prominence of **Importance** in the sense of "newsworthiness" to the reader, or what the addressee is supposed to expect in message consumption. Therefore, message configuration and displacement at the discourse level appears in a successive "culmination": "At any point of the discourse process, there will have been built up a rich verbal and non-verbal environment for whatever is to follow; the speaker's choices are made against the background of what has been said and what has happened before. The environment will often create local conditions which override the globally unmarked pattern of Theme within Given, New within Rheme." (Halliday 1994: 299 - 300)

Meanwhile, some key notions in Narratology will be adopted, too, including Narratology itself, Narration, Focalization and their respective subordinate notions.

Narratology "studies the nature, form, and functioning of narrative ... and tries to characterize NARRATIVE COMPETENCE" (Prince 1989: 65; emphasis original).

Narration is concerned with "a discourse representing one or more events" (Prince 1989: 57). Narration is related to Narrator and Narratee. Narrator is the "one who narrates, as inscribed in the text": some narrator is also character of a story (Prince 1989: 65), as *Marlow* in *Lord Jim*; and some not, as *Marlow* in *The Heart of Darkness*. Narratee is the one "who is narrated to, as inscribed in the text" (Prince 1989: 57), as both *Jane* and *Peter* in the above mentioned examples.

Focalization is the "PERSPECTIVE in terms of which the narrated situations and events are presented; the perceptual or conceptual position in terms of which they are rendered (Genette)" (Prince 1989: 31), as in, e. g., *along the road walked an old man* and *an old man walked along the road*, in which the focalizations or perspectives are *the road* and *an old man* respectively. Associated with focalization are Focalizer and Focalized. Focalizer refers to the "subject of FOCALIZATION", or "the holder of POINT OF VIEW", or "the focal point governing the focalization" while Focalized is hence the "object" of focalization (Prince 1989: 32). For the present purpose, perspective or focalization usually works at a higher layer to guide all laid out in text, a point to be particularized below.

Thematization in the present respect is responsible for embodying narrative perspective or focalization and pins the latter down at the lexicogrammatical level. Information is the goal of perspective or focalization orientation: to convey to readers the supposed known and unrecoverable. It is apparent that information has no immediate relation with focalization, but usually functions to present the communicative value of narrative discourse.

Narratology is both functionally compatible and complementary to SFL. Its functional nature lies in the Narrative Communicative Model, first put forward by Chatman (1978: 151): real author → narrator → narratee → implied reader → real reader, which enriches and specifies the middle part between (real) author and (real) reader, along with such important narratological concepts as perspective (focalization), focalizer and focalized, and narrator and narratee. It is therefore more practical than the traditional communication model of verbal interaction. Meanwhile, thematization and information in SFL are both speaker- and listener-conscious, an intersubjective observation most useful for literary text analysis. Therefore, their harmonious marriage provides a better vantage point than the mere attention on one of them.

In the main part of this chapter below, the discussion will focus on analyzing two texts, one short narrative entitled *Gehenna* and one flash fiction named *The Illustrated Woman*, along with supplementary passages cited from other sources.①

8.2 Thematization: (implied) author-oriented "noteworthiness" displacements and beyond

With what has been introduced about regarding the concept of theme, I should now specify the descriptive model. Theme in SFL is specified into three "foregrounded patterns" of "prominence" along text organization: local, hyper and macro. Local theme is concerned with the message represented by the clause; hyper-theme with "an introductory sentence or group of sentences which is established to predict a particular pattern of interaction among strings, chains and theme selection in following sentences"; and macro-theme with "an sentence or group of sentences ... which predicts a set of hyper-Themes" (Martin 1992: 437), all being associated with the "subject-matter" of a text. Apart from those three "immediate" theses, there may be "underlying theme" or "deeper preoccupation" or "deeper meaning", as Halliday calls it, that motivates "the choice of subject-matter" at work (Hasan 1967; Halliday 1971; *cf.* Butt 1988).

DEEPER	→	IMMEDIATE
Underlying Theme	↘	Macro-Theme
	↘	Hyper-Theme
	↘	Local Theme

Figure 8 - 1: Types of theme and their relations in literary text

---

① For convenience, readers are referred to the text *Gehenna* at http://www.fictionwise. com/ebooks/b132/Gehenna/Barry-N-Malzberg/?, and *The Illustrated Woman* at www.vestalreview.net/theillustratedwoman.htm.

In addition, the concept of Projection in SFL is required for observing thematic status (see also Hasan 1985c: Chapter 3). Projection stands for one **logic-semantic** relationship between two clauses that it "in the environment of clause complexes sets up one clause as the representation of the linguistic content of another either as **idea**s in a mental clause of sensing or **locution**s in a verbal clause of saying" (cited from Matthiessen et al. 2010: 165; emphasis original; see Halliday 1994: Chapter 7). That is, since thematization is concerned not only with simple clause, but also with clause complex, the discussion will involve both. For example, in *John said/ thought about something interesting*, *John* is the theme of the clausal message; but in the clause complex, such as *John said/thought that something interesting would happen soon*, the main, projecting clause *John said/thought* is the theme of the whole message expressed by the clause complex and the rest is the rheme, within which there are local theme and rheme in turn. Therefore, hierarchy in thematic status arises: those in the projecting clauses command those in the projected, even though the projecting themes are occasionally omitted in narrative texts, a technique frequently utilized for achieving aesthetic value.

It should also be noted beforehand that there is a big difference between classical and modern narrative texts. Classical narrative texts occasionally have explicit macro-theme, locating somewhere (i) at the beginning, such as the first sentence(s) in *A Tale of Two Cities*, *Pride and Prejudice* or *Anna Karenina*, or (ii) some other places in text, as "*[a] man can be destroyed but not defeated*" that appears in three-fourth the length in *The Old Man and The Sea*. (But of course that is not always true, as, e.g., the cases in *Gulliver's Travels*, *Oliver Twist*, *Jane Eyre*, *Vanity Fair*, or *Martin Eden*.) Typical modern narrative texts seldom proceed likewise, as exemplified, for instance, even with the novels written by Thomas Hardy who stands at the stage of transition from the classical to the modern in the history of the English literature. Therefore, the underlying theme of a literary discourse may be overtly expressed as one macro-theme of that text, or implicitly conceived along the macro-, hyper- and local themes. In what follows, I start from the middle line in Figure 1: the relationship between "underlying theme" and "hyper-themes" because this is a complicated matter; and then that between "underlying theme" and "macro-" and "local" themes.

8.2.1 *From "hyper-theme" to "underlying theme"*

This subsection works for revealing how "deeper preoccupation" is led up by immediate hyper-themes of a case text, the latter being a science fiction entitled *Gehenna* (1971) by a contemporary American writer named Barry N. Malzberg.

The story unfolds in sequence with four different external narrators in the third person who tell four stories from their respective unique perspectives; each part develops by focalizing on one main character: *Edward*, *Julie*, *Vincent* (*Julie*'s former boyfriend) and *Ann* (daughter of *Edward* and *Julie*); all the four parts see no explicit formal connection in between and the only clues one can associate is the names of the characters and the partially related events, "partial" because the events presented by each narrator different to some extent from one another. At the beginning of each of the previous three parts, the character started from a place that bears a like name (*at 42nd Street*) to take a train that also bears a like name (*the IRT downtown local*), maybe at different times, to go to party that still bears the same name at the centre of New York City (*Greenwich Village*). There, conflict began with the meeting of *Edward*, *Julie* and a mandolin player (introduced in the second part as one named *Vincent* whom *Julie* had turned to when she was lonely). *Edward* won the love of *Julie* from the musician, then cohabited with her and soon married her. The couple lived together for three years and had a daughter *Ann*. It is a family of happiness. But the story proceeds with successive unreasonable suicide of one adult from another's perspective. Finally, *Ann* grows up into *a young woman* with no single skill for making a living and takes *the train* and *is going to a party in the Greenwich Village*. The whole story ends there.

The four immediate leading themes of this narrative discourse, in particular that of the **topical** themes that accumulate to be the highest of all in frequency, are prominently laid out by virtue of projection and focalization strategies. That is, the themes that concern the same signified character with the highest percentage of all in each part suggest the main hyper-theme of that specific section, and hence contribute their own to the organization of the whole text to point to something more important than what each individual part of the text can imply. In what follows, I will first sort out the leading thematic concern (hyper-theme) in each part and then account for the underlying theme.

The first part has a total of 68 topical thematic features[1], of which those concerned with *Edward* amount to 25 times, *Julie* 24, *Vincent* 3 and others 16. I cite the first two paragraphs of the text for readers to have an immediate understanding of the way the story is narrated (# for paragraph designation).

(1) Edward got on the IRT downtown local at 42nd Street for Greenwich Village. The train stopped at 33rd Street, 27th Street, 17th Street and Christopher Circle. As it turned out he met his wife at this party. # It was a standard, Greenwich Village all-of-us-are-damned gathering. She was sitting in a corner of the room, her feet bare, listening to a man with sad mustaches play a mandolin. Edward went over to say hello to her. She looked at him with vague disinterest and huddled closer to the mandolin player, who turned out — on further inspection — to be her date for the night. But Edward was persistent — his parents had always told him that his fearfulness was his chief detracting characteristic — and later that night he got her address.

---

[1] This expression is used for telling apart the thematic characteristics that are compounded into one linguistic element, such as the plural form *they* which contains two thematic features when the referred are two different entities (e.g. one for *Edward* and one for *Julie* in the ensuing example to be analyzed).

The topical themes in this passage include: *Edward*, *the train*, *it*, *he*, *it*, *she*, *her feet*, *Edward*, *she*, *(the mandolin player) who*, *Edward*, *his parents*, *his fearfulness* and *he*. There are two strings of thematic progression among them, each formed with more than one element of the same referent: (i) *Edward* → *he* → *Edward* → *Edward* → *his* (*parents*) → *his* (*fearfulness*) → *he*; and (ii) *she* → *her* (*feet*) → *she* (those within braces do not count as the same referential themes owing to their respective, heterogeneous referents). The third adult *Vincent* does not appear in name, but in professional role *the mandolin player*, which is thematized as a relative pronoun *who* in the message expressed by an embedded clause. The other themes do not share like referents and are disparate in signification. It is hence apparent that the passage in (1) is organized around *Edward* as he is the most frequently talked about.

In fact, the whole first part of the text is thematically organized likewise around *Edward* when two factors are taken into account simultaneously: (i) projection and other related logico-semantic relations and (ii) narratological perspective/focalization. To be specific, the elements around *Julie* occur 24 times, a number being almost the same as those around *Edward*. It hence seems that *Julie* should be the leading theme too along *Edward*; but most of them are down-layered in grammatical status regarding those two criteria. The messages in the second and fourth sentences of the second paragraph in (1), for example, are concerned with perspective or focalization: *Julie*'s behaviours were narrated from *Edward*'s perspective; that is, *Edward saw* where *Julie* was sitting and what she was doing. Meanwhile, those about (*the mandolin player*) *who* and the background messages between the dashes relating to *his parents*' comment on him for his coward character are associated with the respective co-texts: the former is embedded for elaborating who that player was while the latter is adversative addition of extension, a logico-semantic relation that adds one adversative thesis to another (Halliday 1994: 230).

Also, consider the other cases concerning *Julie* in this first part, all occurring in three passages.

（2）Two days later he showed up with a shopping cart filled with gourmet food and asked her if **she** would help him eat it. **She** shrugged and introduced him to her cats.

（3）Three years later Edward opened the door and found **Julie** playing with their year-old daughter, shaking a rattle and putting it deep into the baby's mouth. **The scene** was a pleasing one and he felt quite contented until **she** looked up at him and he saw that **she** was crying. #He put down his briefcase and asked her **what** was wrong. **She** told him that **their life** had been an utter waste. **Everything <u>she</u>** wanted **she** had not gotten — **everything** that **she** had gotten **she** did not want. **She** was surrounded by things, **she** told him, **she** had prepared herself as a child to despise. And **the worst of it** was that all of it was her own fault. **She** talked of divorce but only by inference.

（4）And so he did — all of it and they were very happy for a while if gravely in debt — until he came home from the circus one night with his daughter and found that **Julie**, feet bare, had drowned herself in the bathtub.

Here all the secondarily layered themes are bold-faced. The first *she* in （2）is hypotactically projected by the first-layer theme *he … asked her*, and the projected message as a whole is in fact the verbiage of what Edward *asked*. The next scene expressed by the sentence that follows in （2）is what was perspectivized by the male character. All the bold-faced themes in （3）may be treated as focalized from Edward's perspective too. The same goes to the case in （4）.

Therefore, the whole first part of the text is thematically organized around *Edward* as the main concern; and the stylistic effect of the narration lies in constant resorting to that definite character *Edward* as the leading theme to maintain the reader's attention.

Next, we turn to the second part of the story. The total thematic features in this part are 107, of which those concerning *Julie* are 44 times, *Edward* 32, *Vincent* 9, *Ann* 2 and others 20. As for the themes around *Edward*, 17 are projected, a phenomenon that, to a large extent, reduces his thematic status to a subsidiary one.

(5) It was a standard Greenwich Village we-are-finding-ourselves party and **he** came in late, dressed all wrong, **his** hands stretching his pockets out of shape. **He** was already very drunk.

(6) But when her **husband-to-be** came over and spoke to her — **his** name was Edward as it turned out -... **He** wanted her telephone number.

(7) Three days later, while she was still in bed, **he** came with flowers and candy and told her that **he** could not forget her ... **Edward** was gone when Vincent came later that evening ...

(8) After that she saw nothing of either Vincent or Edward for a week. Then **Edward** came with a suitcase. **He** said **he** had moved out of his parents' home and had come to marry her.

(9) Edward said that they would have to find a real home now — he was very proud — but she said that **the** old life could keep up, at least until Ann was ready for school.

(10) But Edward, for no reason, began to get more and more depressed and one morning when she awoke to find his bed empty, she went into the bathroom to find **him** slumped over the bathtub, **his** wrists open, [**his**] blood all over the floor, a faint, [**his**] fishlike look of appeal in his stunned and disbelieving eyes.

The themes related to *Julie* in this part are absolute in distribution number and *Julie* is hence the noteworthy point of departure while *Edward* is subordinate, at least from the angle of the external perspective per se in this part.

The third part chiefly applies the focalization to *Vincent*, who, as the main thematic message, repeats 32 times in linguistic forms, while *Julie* 21 times, *Edward* 9 and others 13. Here *Vincent* is the leading salience of all; but the narration in this part differs to some extent from that of the previous two parts. There are of course similarities, such as the embedding focalization on *Julie* by *Vincent* in some places. For example,

(11) Halfway to the street he *told* her that **she** had betrayed them.

(12) ... when he *saw* that **she** was looking at another man in the corner of the room ...

Nevertheless, the presentation for most of the time gives one the impression that *Julie* remains herself aloof from *Vincent* and that she has the power to decide what to do while staying with *Vincent*. For example,

(13) **She** was sad that night, sad with a misery **he** could not touch, much less comprehend.

(14) [succeeding citation (11)] **She** did not answer, later murmured that **she** could not help herself, much less another person — but **she** would make this night the best of all, the nights that **she** had ever given him.

Vincent was helpless, as described in citations (15 - 16) below, and just went on currying favour with her (see the second part of (16): *he helped her with her coat*):

(15) **The man** was looking back at her and in that moment **Vincent** knew that **he** was quite doomed, that **he and Julie** were quite finished.

(16) When he came back they sprang apart like assassins. **There** was nothing to do, of course, but to leave the party and **he** helped her with her coat, put his mandolin over his shoulder and led her down the stairs.

The only thing *Vincent* could do is to fight in dignity with *Edward*: He *knocked the man to the door and smashed him there to the floor*, a justification behavior done to *Edward* to make a balance.

Remember that *Vincent* in the first part only appears 3 times and no name of his is directly mentioned; in this third part the items concerning *Edward* appear 9 times, an apparent unbalance: *Julie* had approached *Vincent* for loving *his mandolin* and *found her whole soul in his music* rather than *Vincent* the person at a time when she was down in life; but she offered her telephone number to *Edward* for the first time they met. She drew herself closer to *Vincent* at the first sight of *Edward*, which could only suggests that *Edward* had something that disturbed her and *Vincent* was but someone she had known earlier and as an momentary refuge. In other words, her reaction was a designation that *Edward* meant something to her, but *Vincent* did not. In fact, there is message at the beginning of the third part that does suggest her relation with *Vincent*:

> (17) … and **it** was a strange thing *that **the two of them** went separately since the 42nd Street stop was the nearest to both of their apartments.* But **she** believed in *maintaining her privacy in small, damning ways.*

The text therefore implies that *Vincent* is a character that plays a role to help *Edward* and *Julie* carry out their life performances.

The last part focalizes on *Ann*, which as theme appears 11 times; others occur 9 times but no two of them share a like signified; there is no mention any more of her parents or *Vincent* because they have gone away from this world, as the previous parts of the text have narrated. That is, the noteworthy message of the whole fourth part is *Ann*, who seems to have failed in learning anything to make a living but now would start her fresh adult life in that particular place where her parents met for the first time. Hence it gives way to one's imagination: *Ann* is following the steps of their parents and will most probably lead a life as her parents did.

To sum up, *Edward* has the highest prominence in the first part, which is, reasonably, down-graded in the second and third parts. *Julie* and *Vincent*, which are secondary in the first part, attain the most salient status in the second and third parts respectively. *Ann*, who in the second part is secondary as she is just mentioned for designating the state of her parents' life, receives the most attention in the last part, where the other previously prominent messages all withdraw. Therefore, each of the four main parts of the story presents its due perspective that brings in the focalized messages arranged as they are. What follows is the summary of the occurrence number of each character throughout the text:

Edward: 66 times

Julie: 89 times

Vincent: 44 times

Ann: 11 times

These numbers themselves suggest the statuses of the characters in the discourse. To be specific, the themes that stand for *Julie* occur 89 times in all, which means that this is the most important character of all; in fact, she is, as she is associated with all the other three protagonists. The themes around Edward come the second after *Julie*, as he wins Julie's love from Vincent, who, occurring only 44 times, is a minor role functioning to serve Edward and Julie's love performance. The number of themes concerning Ann is the lowest, but it does not imply that this role is not important; in fact, the arrangement of this role is to suggest a fate that may resemble to her seniors, even though the text ends earlier than that to become reality.

Incidentally, compare the temporal circumstantial themes in the first two parts, which are also stylistically suggestive. They are listed below, apart from the messages implied by the two *until*'s in citations (3 - 4).

(18) ... and **later that night** he got her address

(19) **Two days later** he showed up with a shopping cart filled with gourmet food and asked her

(20) **Three weeks later** they slept with one another for the first time

(21) ... and **the week after** that the mandolin player and he had a fight,

(22) ... at **the end of which** (the two men had a fight) the mandolin player wished them well and left her flat forever.

(23) ... and **during the month** he married her in Elktown.

(24) **Three years later** Edward opened the door and found Julie playing with their year-old daughter, shaking a rattle and putting it deep into the baby's mouth.

The part does not have a spatial theme but has so many temporal points of departure, a phenomenon that reads like a mere flow of time and events through which the protagonists lived a life of emptiness: nothing meaningful was gained in the constant experiencing of their life states and behaviours.

The second part is also characterized with rich temporal circumstantial themes, such as *when*, *while*, *three days later*, *when*, *now*, *then*, *after that*, *then*, *one evening*, *a week later*, *for a long time*, *just before*, *then*, *eventually*, *one night* and *one morning*. In addition, there is one spatial theme:

> (25) But a week later they were married in Yonkers and went to a resort upstate, **where** they were happy for a few days.

However, different from those rapid displacements introduced in the first part, such circumstantial themes here provide one with the impression of temporary peace and stability in the period after *Julie*'s marriage with *Edward*, in particular during the time they were fostering their daughter *Ann*, as in the examples cited below.

> (26) ... she gave him her address instead **while** Vincent was off changing his clothes.
>
> (27) Edward was gone **when** Vincent came later that evening ...
>
> (28) ... she told him that she had been lusting after the sea all her life — **now** she at least had found a pond.
>
> (29) **For a long time** her days were simple — they were, as a matter of fact, exactly like the days she had known just before she met Edward ...

Also, it is in such a peaceful condition that, *one morning*, *Julie* found *Edward* killed himself, a sudden incident beyond any of her expectation, as is so narrated. In fact, the slow rhythm in presenting *Edward*'s suicide scene suggestively reveals the stunned psychology of the housewife. Compare such a mental state with that when the narration is carried out from the perspective of *Edward*, as, e.g., represented in the citations (2-3) above, where *Julie* is told as one who seems only to know pleasure and lack an active or contented attitude towards their family life.

Finally, there is a similar clause pattern at the beginning of each part, expressing a similar event, a pattern that sounds monotonous to point to something beyond.

(30) Edward got on the IRT downtown local at 42nd Street for Greenwich Village. The train stopped at 33rd Street, 27th Street, 17th Street and Christopher Circle.

(31) Julie got on the IRT downtown local at 42nd Street for Greenwich Village. The train stopped at 32nd Street, 24th Street, 13th Street and the Statue of Christ.

(32) Vincent got on the IRT downtown local at 42nd Street for Greenwich Village. The train stopped at 37th Street, 31st Street, 19th Street and Christ Towers.

(33) The train stops at 34th Street, 28th Street and 14th Street. Now she is going to a party in Greenwich Village.

Each of the first three parts begins with the same clause construction, and the only variation is the replacement of the name of the main character *per se*, a stylistic marker implying that all the characters were doomed to have a like end; in fact, all of them committed suicide. The last is about *Ann*, where the tense changes from the simple past to the current simple present and even "future in present", indicating something unknown; but to a large extent she will have a similar destiny of the three adults. Furthermore, the street numbers rapidly flash back with each character seem to respond to their meaningless lives: life is nothing else but a series of stops. Such expressions look much like topic sentences in classical works, but the general theme hinted is implicit for the reader to co-work out.

Such a thematic organization is a typical postmodern technique attempting to construct a world without order, dull, inactive, meaningless and condemned, like the place of *Gehenna*. It is manifested also in the rather baffling descriptions of the fortune of the three adults from each other's perspective: from *Edward*'s angle on *Julie*, she *drowned herself in the bathtub*; but from *Julie*'s aspect on *Edward*, he died in the bathroom, with lots of blood coming out from his cut wrist; yet for *Julie*, *Vincent* committed suicide; and from an omniscient focalization on *Vincent*, he jumped off from the roof of a house. Moreover, there are messages in other places of the text that disagree with one another as well owing to different narration perspectives too. For example, when *Edward* is focalized, he is said to give up *mathematics ... and became an accountant*; but when the perspective is switched to *Julie* by another covert narrator, the narration says that *Edward dropped out of astronomy and became an industrial research assistant — or something like that.* When the focalization is on *Julie*, there is a sentence saying that *Ann* was born with *a music capacity*, which is confirmed with her interest in taking *flute lessons* laid out in the last part, a hint that her father should be *Vincent*, which agrees well with what the first part says that *Ann* was born in the second year of *Julie* and *Edward*'s marriage. So on and so forth.

Therefore, the immediate leading themes in the four parts are all framed against a general "underlying" theme that is associated with the postmodern world, as implied with the title of the text *Gehenna*, a world that people are lost and hence condemned for, as it might be, lacking belief or faith or a meaningful goal of life. In fact, all the behaviours and performances and final results of the characters are oriented to that general theme.

But here comes a puzzle: how can the connection between the "surface" and "underlying" themes be possibly established? It can only be worked out by readers since the text does not explicitly say it. Therefore, stylistics, as all other literature studies as well, should take into account (implied) author, text and (real) readers all at the same time, and one-sided observation is apparently insufficient in theory.

8.2.2 From " macro-" and " local themes" to " underlying theme"

Let us see a short text in which the underlying theme and the macro-themes disagree. The text is entitled *The Illustrated Woman* by Pedro Ponce and cited below as (34), with all the topical themes bold-faced and the sequential numbers of the sentences added at the beginning of them.

(34) **This** was during better times. 2 **She** called with her itinerary, reciting airline and gate numbers, **her voice** edged with hunger. 3 **I** vacuumed, scrubbel, and launched, shopped for two at the grocery store. #4 **I** waited at the gate, bouquet in hand. 5 **Next to me, a man** was listening to the radio. 6 **The volume on his headphones** was so loud, *I could hear* Liz Phair comparing a lover to the explosion of a dying star. #7 **She** surprised me from behind and pressed her lips to my ear. 8 **We** collected her bags and left the terminal. 9 **I** splurged for a cab. 10 **While the driver cursed between lane changes,** *I could feel* the rush of the chassis through her clenched thighs. #11 **We** were barely through the door when **she** led me to the bedroom. 12 **We** fell together, a tangle of hair and tongues. 13 **The front of her jeans** gave way to my fingers. 14 **She** lifted her hips and slid them down. 15 **An unfamiliar mark** appeared just above her hip bone. # 16 **What** is that? *I asked.* # 17 **She** smiled and gathered the hem of her sweater up with both hands.18 **It**'s Chinese, *she said.* 19 **Do you** like it? #20 **I** leaned closer. 21 **It** was a symbol I recognized from bumper stickers and New Age bookstores. 22 **Two tailless fish — one black, one white** — curled next to each other to form a circle. # 23 **I** thought you hated needles. #24 **I** hate getting shots, *she said.* 25 **I**'ve always wanted a tattoo. # 26 **She** was drawn to its simplicity, centuries of wisdom inscribed on her skin. 27 **Two sides** in opposition yet necessary to make a whole, discrete yet inseparable. #28 **It** made me think of you, she said. 29 Besides, **I** didn't like any of the other designs. 30 **Can you** imagine me with a sunflower on my ass? #31 **What** about my name? *I said.* #32 **She** wrestled me to the mattress, laughing. 33 Silly, *she said.* #34

第八章 语篇元功能维度的功能文体学研究

第三部分 应用研究

Later, **I** couldn't sleep. 35 **I** got out of bed and sat by the window, watching her. 36 **Her legs** kicked free of the sheets. 37 With every breath, **the shapes inked on her skin** rose and fell, two halves and the indelible border between.

The leading thematic elements along the text are *I* the narrator (also a character of the story) and *she*, the narratee, with occasionally other themes coming in between. The whole text is narrated from *my* perspective. The thematic features associated with the narrator *I* amount to 17 times (including *they*); and those with *her* 20 times, including 37 *with every breath*, but not 13 *the front of her jeans*, 15 *an unfamiliar mark* or 37 *the shapes inked on her skin*; and the rest 14 times. The reading of the text gives one the impression that the immediate concern of the text focuses on the two protagonists, concurring with the occurrences of the thematic prominences. However, the 27th and 37th sentences, along the series of story events told throughout, suggest something metaphorical and profound in meaning. In other words, the two sentences not only describe two scenes from the narrator's perspective; they also co-work to symbolize something underlying, namely, the interactive relation of a loved couple that may witness rhythmic emotive movement of constant ups and downs or close and remote terms, a dynamic, changing state as shown with the white and black fish figures in the Chinese YIN-YANG symbol. This should be the ideology of the flash fiction, and hence the underlying theme of the discourse. It is therefore apparent that the leading, immediate two sets of themes around the two characters just work to help bring about that deeper meaning for readers to think about couple relationship in philosophical term.

Note that the case just analyzed is common in modern fictions, even in short stories. Note also that the themes in a text that repeat and hence last as the longest throughout should also be the hyper- and macro-themes even though they may not be the underlying theme.

Against that general cotextual background, local themes may be varied along text progression. That is, there may be constantly changing in signified, as may be illustrated with a passage in Part Two of *To The Nighthouse by Virginia Woolf* (*themes boldfaced*).

(35) **So with the lamps all** put out, **the moon** sunk, and **a thin rain** drumming on the roof a downpouring of immense darkness began. **Nothing**, it seemed, could survive the flood, the profusion of darkness **which**, creeping in at keyholes and crevices, stole round window blinds, came into bedrooms, swallowed up here a jug and basin, there a bowl of red and yellow dahlias, there the sharp edges and firm bulk of a chest of drawers. **Not only** was furniture confounded; **there** was scarcely anything left of body or mind **by which** *one could say*, "**This** is he" or "**This** is she." **Sometimes a hand** was raised as if to clutch something or ward off something, or **somebody** groaned, or **somebody** laughed aloud as if sharing a joke with nothingness.

The themes vary in a wide range: from a cohesive *so*, to circumstantial *with the lamps all*, *by which* and *sometimes*, and to participants *the moon*, *a thin rain*, *nothing*, *the profusion of darkness which*, *one*, *one could say*, *this*, *this*, *a hand* and *somebody*.

There are two marked organizations in (35): "*This is he*" or "*This is she*", which are nominal groups. Meanwhile, Attribute participants of Relational Process in Transitivity (see Halliday, 1994: 119) may also be markedly placed as themes, as in (36), cited from *Villette* by Charlotte Brontë.

(36) Closer acquaintance, while it developed both faults and eccentricities, opened, at the same time, a view of a character I could respect. **Stern and even morose** as she sometimes was, I could wait on her and sit beside her with that calm which always blesses us when we are sensible that our manners, contact, please and soothes the persons we serve.

Themes tend to be participants; but in some local areas they may not be participants at all. For example, in the following passage cited from the

第八章 语篇元功能维度的功能文体学研究

second chapter of *Christmas Carole* by Charles Dickens（bold-face added），
the adverbs（particles）and the lexical verbs work together as themes.

(37) **In came** a fiddler with a music-book, and went up to the lofty
desk, and made an orchestra of it, and tuned like fifty stomach-
aches. **In came** Mrs. Fezziwig, one vast substantial smile. **In came**
the three Miss Fezziwigs, beaming and lovable. **In came** the six
young followers whose hearts they broke. **In came** all the young
men and women employed in the business. **In came** the
housemaid, with her cousin, the baker. **In came** the cook, with
her brother's particular friend, the milkman. **In came** the boy from
over the way, who was suspected of not having board enough
from his master; trying to hide himself behind the girl from next
door but one, who was proved to have had her ears pulled by her
mistress. **In they all came**, one after another; some shyly, some
boldly, some gracefully, some awkwardly, some pushing, some
pulling; **in they all came**, anyhow and every how. **Away they** all
went, twenty couples at once; hands half round and **back** again
the other way; **down** the middle and **up** again; **round and round**
in various stages of affectionate grouping; old top couple always
turning up in the wrong place; new top couple starting off again,
as soon as they got there; all top couples at last, and not a bottom
one to help them.

The perspective is set up omnisciently: there were people who came in
constantly; then away they all went; then came back again; and went down
the middle; came up again; and walked round and round. The whole passage
renders a lively, animated atmosphere, created with the process elements
（with particles）that receive the highest salience. It is apparent that such an
organization is not common in literary or any generic texts at all.

The case below stands in contrast to (37) in that it is a static presentation
of a scene, laid out with a radiation perspective from certain point of view.

(38) **On a chair** lay a razor, besmeared with blood. **On the hearth**

were two or three long and thick tresses of gray human hair, also dabbled with blood, and seeming to have been pulled out by the roots. **Upon the floor** were found four Napoleons ... (Edgar Allan Poe: *The Murders in the Rue Morgue*)

Such circumstantial themes may be one repetitive entity, which serves to up-grade the strength of fact presentation, as *one hundred years later* in Martin Luther King's public speech *I Have A Dream*. Of course, parallelism like this always has such a graduation function, whatever the repetitive expressions may be, as, also in there, the successive clause *I have a dream* does accumulatively in the latter part of the text.

To sum up, the thematic notion in the SFL sense is induced from particular linguistic phenomena, but it has a high stylistic appliability. The salient items may satisfactorily reveal the focalization to adjust narrative strategy and perspective status, and hence set up the focal attention of narrative discourse. Therefore, thematization and focalization or perspective have their due compatibility and consistency at work. But there are differences too: not all focalization in texts are related to macro-themes; in fact, some locate in the rhematic area, an issue which I am going to discuss in the next section where information flow is concerned.

8.3 Information: (implied) reader-oriented "importance" displacements

This aspect of message organization has two particularities for stylistic effect in narrative discourse: (i) "marked" ways of Given – New organization and (ii) the wave-like Given – New movement (in particular News) that exerts impact upon readers. The latter type has been entirely overlooked so far.

8.3.1 Types of "marked" information organization in literary texts

Here "markedness" is said in comparison to the unmarked, typical sense. There are five usual patterns one may come across in literary texts, all of which have appeared in those examples discussed in the above section.

The first of these is to present New as Given, as illustrated with some typical cases in classical English novels (see Short 1996: 166 - 168; Section 1 above). For this point, I would analyze briefly some applications of such technique used in *Gehenna*. For example, the thematic element *Edward* in the first clause of the text is assumed to be known to readers, even though it is New because it appears for the first time: it is something "not recoverable" as there is no previous co-text. However, it is narrated so for readers to be ready to accept it as referring to someone who seems already "there", in a place readers were aware of before and are only brought into their consciousness at the moment of reference. It is therefore what the author "wants to present as Given for rhetorical purposes", such as, for example, to rouse readers' curiosity and align them with the narrator so that they can very quickly co-work to see what is going to happen to this character or what and who he is in the fictional world. This has become a widely used strategy in adult fiction or in poetry. And only fairy tales tend to have a preparation leading over to upcoming news such as *Once upon a time, there was X* or *Long, long ago*, conventionalized patterns for introducing New messages.

This is also the case with *Julie* the female character. *Julie* first comes into readers' sight in the deictic form *she*: ***She*** *was sitting in a corner of the room*. The first paragraph has already laid out a nominal entity *his wife* (*As it turned out he met **his wife** at this party*), but readers need some efforts to set up the referential connection. That is, the pronoun appears unexpected to some degree; it at least needs time for the reader to relate the two elements as standing for the same person. The referential link therefore can give rise to sudden association that suggests some news value. Such a Given-like entity is a pseudo one, not a practical Given.

It is interesting to note that readers have no access to who *his wife* or this *she* is indeed. Yet the third paragraph suddenly brings in an entity named *Julie*, an unusual way of information layout in daily conversation but occasionally taken in narratives:

> (39) Three weeks later they slept with one another for the first time and the week after that the mandolin player and he had a fight, at the end of which the mandolin player wished them well and left her flat forever. Edward and **Julie** were engaged only a few days after that and during the month he married her in Elktown.

The identification of *Julie* with *[s]he* is realized by appealing to *his wife* in the sentence of the first paragraph; in fact, *Edward* is a conventionalized ordinary male name and *Julie* a common female symbol, and the message from *engaged* and *married* (see the last sentence in (39)) provides supporting or supplementary information for the relational concept (*his*) *wife* previously led up into the text. Of course, the deictic *[s] he* in the fifth sentence and the ensuing *they*, the nominal *the mandolin player* and the anaphora *he* (could only be *Edward* here) also play a role. The association makes *Julie* in the due context what Chafe (1994) calls accessible information, even though this item still has some newsworthiness; and that is the reason why *Prince* would term it Unused (see below).

Note also that the name *Julie* appears three times in the first part of the fiction; and in all other cases it is *she*. That gives one the impression of familiarity and intimacy. In fact, *Edward* and *Julie* were potential and future husband and wife, and it was natural and inevitable for them to meet in particular time and space: *she* seemed to be there too, in a certain place of this world waiting for him. Therefore, *she* was not strange to *him*, or at least the text experiences a narration for the reader to understand them empathically that way.

In the first part that witnesses *Edward* as the main focalized, the name *Vincent is never mentioned. The latter is indirectly referred to for three times: twice in* (39) as *the mandolin player*. It is referred to once as the first introduction in the fifth sentence: *a man with sad mustaches play a mandolin*. Therefore, *Vincent* is a failure in the eye of *Edward*, who holds an air of success towards this rival in love. In other words, *Vincent* appears as *a mandolin player*, which can only suggest that he is but a label that has no substantial content or does not deserve *Edward*'s attention to know who he is.

The second of the noticeable uses of Given and New order in narrative discourse is that Given is presented as New, the opposite case of the previous type. For example, when the perspective of narration in the third part of *Gehenna* is adjusted to *Vincent*, the text progresses by introducing *Edward* as New, even though it has been presented many times before:

> (40) He only wanted to meet *the man* **named Edward** (who might become his closest friend too), but *the man* did not want any part of him at all and there was a very bad scene — a scene that ended only when Vincent knocked *the man* to the door and smashed *him* there to the floor.

It hence expresses a sense of distance in the eyes of the focalized character *Vincent*, a sense of hostility towards one who took away his woman. This is also exemplified in another place of the text: when *Edward* and *Julie* had their eye contact for the first time, it gave *Vincent* a psychological impact and hence drove him to frustration:

> (41) ... when he saw that she was looking at another man in the corner of the room — a man of a different sort from the rest of them, since he was the only one who was not already drunk. The man was looking back at her and in that moment Vincent knew that he was quite doomed, that he and **Julie** were quite finished.

The passage is cited from the third part where the focalization is on *Vincent*; and the name *Julie* appears only once. There is also a sense of distance and strangeness as the straightforward naming suggests; yet this is not hatred towards her, but helplessness with himself.

(42) She was there with *a boy named Vincent* who meant little to her but who played the mandolin beautifully and sang her love songs. If the songs were derivative and the motions a trifle forced — well, it was a bad period for both of them and she took what comfort she could. But *when her husband-to-be came over and spoke to her — his name was Edward as it turned out* — she could see beyond his embarrassment and her misery that a certain period of her life and of the mandolin-player's was over.

Pay attention to the italicized parts: the former is described with a sense of objectivity as New information, *i. e.*, as the end focus of a clausal message. The detachment is confirmed with the apposition *who meant little to her*. But for the latter, what appears first is *her husband*, followed by the introduction *his name was Edward as it turned out*, which reads with intimacy: what is important is not his name but his status; in fact intimate couples do not usually address each other by name.

The third type is the afterthought technique, namely, to place the projecting main clause after the projected message, as *I asked* and *she said* in (1). In such a way of organization the order of the Participant and Process may be reversed, as in *said she*. (43) is cited from *The Mayor of Casterbridge* by Thomas Hardy.

(43) "I wish somebody would," said **she** firmly. "Her present owner is not at all to her liking!"

"Nor you to mine," said **he**.

But this may also be applied to nominal rather than pronominal cases. The following example is taken from *The Fox* by D. H. Lawrence.

(44) "Whatever have you been doing all this time?" *she asked fretfully*. "I thought you were never coming in. And it's ages since you stopped sawing. What were you doing out there?"

"Well," **said Henry**, "we had to stop that hole in the barn to keep the rats out."

"Why, I could see you standing there in the shed. I could see your shirt-sleeves," **challenged Banford**.

The fouth pattern is condensation of newsworthiness, namely, the thematic ellipsis technique introduced in the former section that is meant to reduce message redundancy and increase the degree of news values. The omitted is recoverable information in the given context at work. Such omitted messages are usually projecting, main clauses that command subordinate messages, which in turn have their own Given and New. Since too much Given will reduce literariness, the commanding themes are strategically left out for readers to fill up the gap, and the efforts usually do not take much time.

The last type has been witnessed with the use of the character names in *Gehenna*: *Edward*, *Julie*, *Vincent* and *Ann*. In fact, they are very common ones in the English speaking world; and their personal pronouns with newsworthiness are widely used, suggesting that those who are introduced into the text may be you or I or someone else we daily meet; one who has no particular personality, a methodology that has already been employed in Kafka's *Metamorphosis*. This is also demonstrated with the narrative method adopted in the flash fiction *The Illustrated Woman*: Who are the male and female characters in the story? Not important. What is noticeable is something ideologically motivated through the narration of fictive events.

At this point, let us consider the case of conflation of thematic status with information value, a phenomenon that occurs in nominal group. Read the following extract taken from Charlotte Brontë's *Villette* (Chapter VIII about *Madame Beck*).

(45) When attired, **Madame Beck** appeared a personage of a figure rather short and stout, yet still graceful in its own peculiar way; that is, with the grace resulting from proportion of parts. *Her complexion* was fresh and sanguine, not too rubicund; *her* *eyes*, blue and serene; *her dark silk dress* fitted her as a French sempstress alone can make a dress fit; **she** looked well, though a little

bourgeoise; as bourgeoise, indeed, **she** was. I know not what of harmony pervaded her whole person; and yet **her** *face* offered contrast, too: *its features* were by no means such as are usually seen in conjunction with a complexion of such blended freshness and repose: *their outline* was stern: **her** *forehead* was high but narrow; *it* expressed capacity and some benevolence, but no expanse; nor did **her** *peaceful yet watchful eye* ever know the fire which is kindled in the heart or the softness which flows thence. **Her** *mouth* was hard: *it* could be a little grim; **her** *lips* were thin. For sensibility and genius, with all their tenderness and temerity, I felt somehow that Madame would be the right sort of Minos in petticoats.

The leading theme in this passage is *Madame Beck*, around which there are three layers of hierarchy in thematic progression. The first is *Madame Beck*, the hyper-theme, which is developed into such subsequent anaphoric items as *[h]er (complexion)*, *her (eyes)*, *her (dark silk dress)*, *she*, *she*, *her (face)*, *her (forehead)*, *her (peaceful yet watchful eyes)*, *[h] er (mouth)* and *her (lips)*. The second comes from those that are put in the parentheses in the citations, including *(its) features (its = (her) forehead)*, *it (= her forehead)* and *it (= (her) mouth)* as well. The third is that advanced from one theme along the second layer: *(their) outline (their = her features)*. All the thematic features along the first layer are Given in the context, including *Madam Beck* because the latter item appeared for the first time in the previous chapter (Chapter VII Villette). The second layer themes have some news values according to Chafe (1976: 41) as they are not mentioned before. Accordingly, the third layer theme should have a similar information status as those along the second layer since it appears in a similar context in given-new displacement. The instance cited here displays three points. First, there does exist an overlapping area between theme and New. Second, thematic structure and information structure do exhibit their respective functional statues, not only for linguistic categorization as Halliday has advocated against the Prague School practice, but also for stylistic effect.

Third, thematic progression and information flow are harmoniously interwoven into a string of message advancement. But it is also obvious that all those thematic entities should be Given in the Hallidayan information sense as they are "recoverable".

To sum up, the aforementioned five are common strategies of Given – New organization to achieve literary stylistic effects. Such "marked" arrangements can attract readers, and hence enhance their attention degree and increase the readability of literary discourse.

8.3.2 *Given-new culminative pattern and its impact upon readers*

As for information, the classifications by Prince (1981: 237; *cf.* Brown & Yule 1983: 183 – 184) based on Halliday (1967 – 1968) will be adopted to specify Given and New more detailed while excluding, if any, their possible theoretical incompatibility.

(a) Situationally Evoked: ***Lucky me*** *just stepped in something.*

(b) Textually Evoked: *Susie went to visit her grandmother and **the sweet lady** was making Peking Duck.*

(c) Containing Inferrable: Have you heard *the incredible claim that the devil speaks English backwards?*

(d) Noncontaining Inferrable: *I went to the post office and **the stupid clerk** couldn't find a stamp.*

(e) Unused: ***Rotten Rizzo*** *can't have a third term.*

(f) Brand-new Anchored: ***A rich guy I know*** *bought a Cadillac.*

Brand-new Unchanchored: *I bought **a beautiful dress**.*

Generally, an information unit is structured with the lowest communicative value locating at the former part of the unit and the highest at the end, a way to meet reading requirement: the former aims to serve the basis while the latter to realize its importance of communication.

Schematically, New information in discourse recedes successively into Given that in turn provides contextual background for upcoming news; and the consumed messages dealt with before may occasionally come back to interact with the newly met, and such recovered information may appear as semi-Given or semi-New. For example, at the beginning of the previous three parts and the last of the fourth part of *Gehenna*, the actions of taking the train to go to the party at the New York downtown are all New. Indeed, the first use of the way of introduction is brand-new, but the ensuing three times' uses may be Inferrable owing to like sentence constructions as "they need less neural energy to follow" (Halliday 2008: 121).

I take *The Illustrated Woman* (see (34) above) as the example to make a detailed analysis. The text proceeds with one single perspective, *i.e.*, that of the narrator *I*, and the focalized shuffles back and forth between *I* and the narratee *she*, but lays more weight upon the later. The successively coming New messages become less important and hence give way to other New entities. Note the narrator and the narratee, both as Given, constitute two Given chains along the text, which are responsible for what comes next; and the New chains at stake are hence built up along these two Given chains.

The table in the Appendix is the result of the detailed analysis of the flash fiction, in which the relevant elements are marked with italics, and the sentential orders designated with "[ ]". The result shows that the Given and New items are almost equal in number, suggesting that, even in literary works that generally demand economic principle, the Given has a good percentage to guarantee introducing New units into discourse to avoid obscurity in meaning. And New items work to advance the story and maintain reading attention. Just as Martin remarks: "the News tell the story" (Martin 1992: 452). In fact, they are what a text, a literary text here, is assumed to have for readers; and that is the reason why they occupy almost one half of all. The text reads brief in expression, short in information unit layout and rapid in narration speed, an aesthetic effect of what the information organization has brought about. Meanwhile, the story is simple in plot but profound in significance; in fact it is what the implied author's ideology that

第三部分 应用研究

gives us readers the force.

Figure 8 - 2 is a visual representation of the "wave-like" flow of information throughout the text (S-Ekd: situationally evoked; T-Ekd: textually evoked; Infl: inferrable; Uud: unused; BdN: brand new).

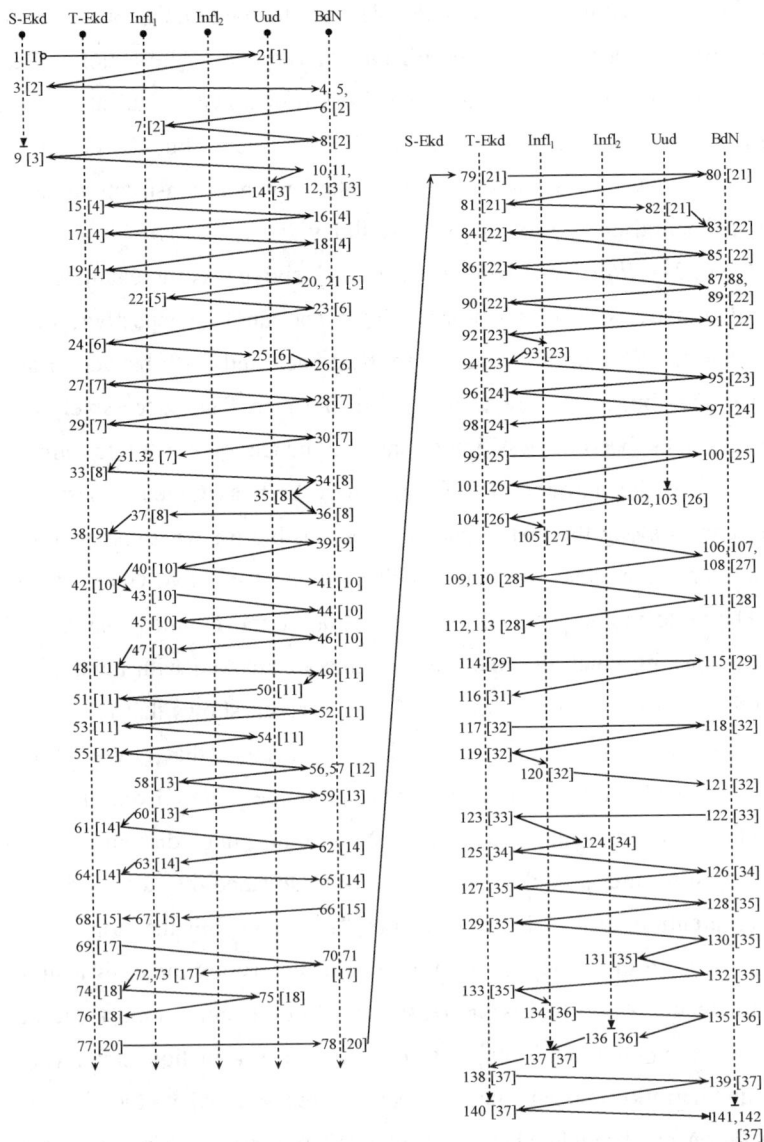

Figure 8 - 2: Sequential culminative movement of replacive Given and New

The schematic diagram shows in a straightforward manner how information items of different values alternate replacively through the text. The alternations are dynamic, rhythmic and generally balanced between Given and New. They are reader-oriented but the implied author selected. In particular, the speaker's selection arranges the Given and New messages for the reader to respond in correspondence, and hence brings him into a world different from what he is actually in. That is the virtue and merit of a narrative text. In one word, the presentation is one for describing the successive replacing process; and it is also one that visually describes the reader's response in a similar way, a process of assumed aesthetic appreciation.

To sum up, it is the (implied) author who sets up the value weight for reading expectation: the Given information has the lowest communicative value and the weight is therefore the lowest. The New information has high communicative importance, among which the Focus fulfills the culminative point of the whole stretch of new. Meanwhile, New information in reading passes away one after another and becomes Given and hence forms the background and context for ensuing news. Discourse proceeds likewise repeatedly and the reading therefore experiences successive aesthetic appeal. Finally, theme and Given should be realized with the same lexico-grammatical elements, even in literary texts.

8.4　Conclusion

Halliday (2008: 125) has found that "[1] iterary stylistics is much concerned with value, because it is trying to understand why a particular literary text is (or, perhaps, is not) highly valued in the writer's culture".

This chapter illustrated the point by exemplification. It aimed at sorting out a set of general foregrounding patterns for literary stylistic analysis by virtue of the Textual Grammar in SFL, in particular the process of thematization and information in narrative discourse. Thematization reveals perspectivization in terms of salience for guiding reading concern and hence particularizes the focalization strategies of narration. Information specifies what has been focalized for the importance of communication. Both categories are text-oriented. That is, their communicative goals come from a holistic vantage point at the discourse level, rather than individual message unit expressed by the clause. The alternations of the respective salience and importance in textual message progression achieve their due textuality, successive dynamicality and prominences. The foregrounding effects are attained by the interaction between local themes, general leading themes either being hyper- or macro-natured and the underlying theme, all being related to the subject-matter under discussion. In one word, thematization sets up an observation perspective and information specifies what should be interesting to readers, the two co-working for aesthetic effects in literary discourse. In that process, the principle of intersubjectivity is apparently observed while considering the nature of information as listener-oriented.

Of course, the patterns sorted out in this chapter are but some common ones, most of which have been ignored by the stylistics circle; further explorations await to reveal more linguistic facts for literary stylistic value.

Appendix:

Table 8 − 1: Information values sorted out from *The Illustrated Woman*

(X: sequential order of the information items occurring along the text and their due contexts; Y: occurrence order along X; Z: information item and its location in the relevant clause indexed with the clause order)

type	X	Y	Z
(a) SI Given (3 items)	1	1	*This* was during better times [1]
	2	3	*She* called with her itinerary ... [2]
	3	9	*I* vacuumed, scrubbed, and launched ... [3]

type	X	Y	Z
	4	15	*I* waited at the gate [4]
	5	17	I waited at *the gate* [4]
	6	24	*I could hear* Liz Phair [6]
	7	27	*She* surprised me from behind [7]
	8	29	She surprised *me* from behind [7]
	9	33	*We* collected her bags [8]
	10	38	*I* splurged for a cab [9]
	11	42	*I could feel* the rush of the chassis [10]
	12	48	*We* were barely through the door [11]
	13	51	When *she* led me to the bedroom [11]
	14	53	When she led *me* to the bedroom [11]
	15	55	*We* fell together [12]
(b) TI Given	16	61	*She* lifted her hips and slid them down [14]
(46 items)	17	64	She lifted her hips and slid *them* down [14]
	18	68	What is that? *I asked* [16]
	19	69	*She* smiled [17]
	20	74	*It*'s Chinese [18]
	21	76	It's Chinese, *she said* [18]
	22	77	*I* leaned closer [20]
	23	79	*It* was a symbol [21]
	24	81	*I* recognized from bumper stickers and New Age bookstores [21]
	25	84	*one* black, one white [22]
	26	86	one black, *one* white [22]
	27	90	curled next to *each other* to form a circle [22]
	28	92	*I* thought you hated needles [23]
	29	94	I thought *you* hated needles [23]

(continued)

type	X	Y	Z
(b) TI Given (46 items)	30	96	*I hate* getting shots, she said [24]
	31	98	I hate getting shots, *she said* [24]
	32	99	*I*'ve always wanted a tattoo [25]
	33	101	*She was drawn to* its simplicity [26]
	34	104	centuries of wisdom *inscribed on her skin* [26]
	35	109	*It* made me think of you, she said [28]
	36	110	It made *me* think of you, she said [28]
	37	112	It made me think of *you*, she said [28]
	38	113	It made me think of you, *she said* [28]
	39	114	*I* didn't like any of the other designs [29]
	40	116	What about my name? *I said* [31]
	41	117	*She* wrestled me to the mattress, laughing [32]
	42	119	She wrestled *me* to the mattress, laughing [32]
	43	123	Silly, *she said* [33]
	44	125	Later, *I* couldn't sleep [34]
	45	127	*I* got out of bed and sat by the window [35]
	46	129	I got out of *bed* and sat by the window [35]
	47	133	watching *her* [35]
	48	138	*the shapes inked on her skin* rose and fell [37]
	49	140	*two halves* and the indelible border between [37]
(c) Ct In (21 items)	50	7	*her voice* edged with hunger [2]
	51	19	bouquet in *hand* [4]
	52	22	*The volume on his headphones* was so loud [6]
	53	31	and pressed *her lips* to my ear [7]
	54	32	and pressed her lips to *my ear* [7]
	55	37	and left *the terminal* [8]

type	X	Y	Z
(c) Ct In (21 items)	56	40	While *the driver* cursed between lane changes [10]
	57	43	I *could feel* the rush of the chassis [10]
	58	45	I could feel the rush of *the chassis* [10]
	59	47	through *her* clenched *thighs* [10]
	60	58	*The front of her jeans* gave way to my fingers [13]
	61	60	The front of her jeans gave way to *my fingers* [13]
	62	63	She lifted *her hips* and slid them down [14]
	63	67	An unfamiliar mark appeared just above *her hip bone* [15]
	64	72	gathered *the hem of her sweater* up with both hands [17]
	65	73	with *both hands* [17]
	66	93	I *thought* you hated needles [23]
	67	105	*Two sides* in opposition [27]
	68	120	She wrestled me to *the mattress*, laughing [32]
	69	134	*Her legs* kicked free of the sheets [36]
	70	137	*With every breath* [37]
(d) UnCt In (4 items)	71	124	*Later*, I couldn't sleep [34]
	72	131	I got out of bed and sat by *the window* [35]
	73	136	Her legs kicked free of *the sheets* [36]
	74	141	two halves and *the* indelible *border between* [37]
(e) Used (10 items)	75	2	This was *during better times* [1]
	76	14	at *the grocery store* [3]
	77	25	I could hear *Liz Phair* [6]

第八章 语篇元功能维度的功能文体学研究

第三部分 应用研究

(continued)

type	X	Y	Z
(e) Used (10 items)	78	35	We collected *her bags* [8]
	79	50	We were barely through *the door* [11]
	80	54	when she led me to *the bedroom* [11]
	81	75	It's *Chinese*, she said [18]
	82	82	I *recognized from bumper stickers and New Age bookstores* [21]
	83	102	She was drawn to *its simplicity* [26]
	84	103	*centuries of wisdom* inscribed on her skin [26]
(f) Brand-new (58 items)	85	4	She *called* with her itinerary [2]
	86	5	She called with *her itinerary* [2]
	87	6	reciting airline and gate numbers [2]
	88	8	her voice *edged with hunger* [2]
	89	10	I *vacuumed*, scrubbed, and launched [3]
	90	11	I vacuumed, *scrubbed*, and launched [3]
	91	12	I vacuumed, scrubbed, and *launched* [3]
	92	13	*shopped for two* [3]
	93	16	I *waited* at the gate [4]
	94	18	*bouquet* in hand [4]
	95	20	(*Next to me*) *a man* was listening to the radio [5]
	96	21	a man was *listening to the radio* [5]
	97	23	The volume on his headphones was *so loud* [6]
	98	26	Liz Phair *comparing a lover to the explosion of a dying star* [6]
	99	28	She *surprised* me *from behind* [7]
	100	30	and *pressed* her lips *to* my ear [7]
	101	34	We *collected* her bags [8]

type	X	Y	Z
	102	36	and *left* the terminal [8]
	103	39	I *splurged for a cab* [9]
	104	41	the driver *cursed between lane changes* [10]
	105	44	I could feel *the rush* of the chassis [10]
	106	46	through her *clenched* thighs [10]
	107	49	We *were barely through* the door [11]
	108	52	when she *led* me *to* the bedroom [11]
	109	56	We *fell together* [12]
	110	57	*a tangle of hair and tongues* [12]
	111	59	The front of her jeans *gave way to* my fingers [13]
	112	62	She *lifted* her hips and slid them down [14]
	113	65	She lifted her hips and *slid* them *down* [14]
(f) Brand-new (58 items)	114	66	*An unfamiliar mark appeared just above* her hip bone [15]
	115	70	She *smiled* [17]
	116	71	*gathered ... up...* [17]
	117	78	I *leaned closer* [20]
	118	80	It was *a symbol* [21]
	119	83	*Two tailless fish* [22]
	120	85	one *black*, one white [22]
	121	87	one black, one *white* [22]
	122	88	*curled* next to each other to form a circle [22]
	123	89	curled *next to* each other to form a circle [22]
	124	91	curled next to each other to *form a circle* [22]
	125	95	I thought you *hated needles* [23]
	126	97	I hate *getting shots*, she said [24]

第八章 语篇元功能维度的功能文体学研究

第三部分 应用研究

(continued)

type	X	Y	Z
	127	100	I've *always wanted a tattoo* [25]
	128	106	Two sides *in opposition* [27]
	129	107	*yet necessary to make a whole* [27]
	130	108	*discrete yet inseparable* [27]
	131	111	It *made* me *think of* you, she said [28]
	132	115	I *didn't like any of the other designs* [29]
	133	118	She *wrestled* me *to* the mattress, laughing [32]
(f) Brand-new (58 items)	134	121	She wrestled me to the mattress, *laughing* [32]
	135	122	*Silly*, she said [33]
	136	126	Later, I *couldn't sleep* [34]
	137	128	I *got out of* bed and sat by the window [35]
	138	130	I got out of bed and *sat* by the window [35]
	139	132	*watching* her [35]
	140	135	Her legs *kicked free of* the sheets [36]
	141	139	the shapes inked on her skin *rose and fell* [37]
	142	142	two halves and the *indelible* border between [37]

视角逆行、评价隐喻与
情感—伦理诉求
《你还在我身旁》的评价文体效应与解读模型[①]

9.1 引言

最近微信里广泛地转发着一首题为《你还在我身旁》(简称《身旁》)的小诗,是香港中文大学《独立时代》杂志 2014 年"愿付雁书长思君——微情书大赛征文"一等奖获奖作品(下面是原作,各行之前用拉丁字母标上了序号,便于后文指代使用)。

    a. 瀑布的水逆流而上,

    b. 蒲公英种子从远处飘回,聚成伞的模样,

    c. 太阳从西边升起,落向东方。

    d. 子弹退回枪膛,

    e. 运动员回到起跑线上,

① 本章原载《外语学刊》2016 年第 1 期,第 41—48 页。

f. 我交回录取通知书，忘了十年寒窗。

g. 厨房里飘来饭菜的香，
h. 你把我的卷子签好名字，
i. 关掉电视，帮我把书包背上。

j. 你还在我身旁。

类似作品有特定读者群，也受表达空间制约，估计难于进入主流文学视野；但就莘莘学子而言，它确有独特的情感和伦理价值。

本章以此例为立足点，系统阐述一种综合性的文学文本解读模式。这既有演示一种解读路径的初衷，更有一名教育工作者的职责意识①。所谓"综合"，即一种既涉及作品、更有读者和作者介入的文本分析方法，入口是系统功能语言学视野里的前景化成分，目标是经验世界中的意识形态和价值观念。"评价"指作者寓于文学文本中的主体性与主体间性立场，以隐含读者意识［介入范畴］和叙事强弱口吻［级差等级］为调节手段，抒发情感［情感范畴：意愿、愉悦、满意、安全］，评判行为［判断范畴：是否常态、是否有能力、可靠、诚实、真诚、恰当］，品评事物［鉴赏范畴：是否冲击或吸引读者；构成是否均衡与复杂；是否有价值］。这在语言学中叫做评价范畴（Appraisal Category），属于系统功能语言学的一个人际意义次类（Martin & White 2005）；将它系统用于文学文本分析则是文体学性质的（彭宣维 2015b），为功能文体学的一个分支（如 Halliday 1971；Birch & O'Toole 1988；张德禄 1998）。

这里涉及三个策略性范畴，在从系统选择到实例化体现过程中发挥调节性策略作用。首先是"视角"，为谋篇策略。但在现有系统功能语言学的语篇语法模型中告缺，跟主位化（Thematisation）关系密切，却不属于主位化或信息化甚至衔接范畴；事实上，这是支配相关语篇语义选项进入词汇语法结构关系的一种策略机制，在叙事学中叫做视角化

———————
① 最近网络上流传着"百家讲台"某位名人"旗帜鲜明"的帖子：在教育中"我反对励志"，主张"快乐"成长。看来，这位自称"教书匠"的先生可能真的只有"教书匠"的认识水平：人的成长过程可能全然快乐？中国教育存在的问题是励志主张带来的吗？教育讲求方式方法就必须以牺牲励志原则为代价？这种因噎废食、低级迎合的问题意识，实在让人匪夷所思。

（Perspectivisation），即所述情景和事件的陈述角度（Prince 1989：31，71）。其实，作为一个学科的叙事学，它关注的基本议题具有突出的基础性，对语言学理论具有启示和补益作用。鉴于叙事学的出发点是语言交际，跟系统功能语言学在学理上兼容，因此，这里拟采用这一术语，但须做一点范畴化归口处理：根据系统功能语言学的扩展模式（Halliday 1995），视角化是从系统到实例的过程中采用的一种选择策略，旨在调节相关词汇语法的结构化配置方式。其次是语境性对比：褒扬的同时意味着贬抑，给予意味着接受，提问意味着陈述，敬人则意味着抑己，这是人际性话语策略。最后是投射，是概念性话语策略：说话人或作者的任何言语行为都是他/她思想的投射。（彭宣维 2015b）视角化在《身旁》一文中起了重要作用。

"评价隐喻"属于语法隐喻的一个次类，指采用带标记的评价意义确立方式。就评价意义的三大子范畴看，行文如果主要是通过纯粹经验意义来确立态度立场的，就属于态度隐喻；文本隐含了说话人或作者强烈的感情态度、行文却缺乏级差强弱成分的，近似于低调陈述（Understatement），属于级差隐喻；说话人或作者的立场本该鲜明典型，实际叙述却平实沉稳、立场不够明确的，则为介入隐喻。这些叙事方式与具有明确评价特征的铭刻性（Inscribed）词汇语法手段相对，在马丁等人的理论描述中叫做引发性（Invoked）评价意义：通过其他词汇语法手段临时引发的评价立场。

本章将阐述两个要点：《身旁》所用叙事策略以及相应文体措辞与美学意义层次；具体行文则细分为三个小节进行：（一）视角逆行：超常规叙事带来的解读张力，附带涉及语境性对比和投射叙事策略；（二）评价隐喻：态度立场的间接体现途径；（三）评价内容的可视化描述。最后我们从总体上概述评价文体分析的主导思想。

9.2 视角逆行：超常规叙事带来的解读张力

这里涉及语篇性视角、人际性对比和概念性投射三类话语策略，不过相比较而言,视角设计的修辞效果最为突出;其他两类对这里的文本解读虽然也很重要,但不是重点,所以放到之后讨论。

从内容构成看,《身旁》有四个小节,前、后二节相对独立,却是一个整体,衔接纽带是时空因素。直言之,这里的叙事策略采用了一种不同于常规的聚焦方式:它不是人们常见的倒叙,更不是顺时叙事,后二者均以叙述者时空为立足点呈现叙事者视野里的事件:一者回顾过去,一者着眼于当下或走向未来;而这里采用的是一种时空逆行叙事或视角逆行方法:以叙事者所在的当时作为立足点,叙事者自己沿着事件和时间轨迹逆行,从而回到先前经历过的时空中去。而整个过程又体现出明确的前后时空对比关系。这是一种谋篇策略,也叫管道隐喻(Conduit Metaphor):人们把时空看作一种流程,可以沿"路"返回,从而回到从前,整个过程将叙事者经历过的事件连缀成一个整体。这种视角化方式可以让常规日常事件,以反常规的叙述途径,创造一种超常规的感知体验,即与社会人在个体发生历程中获得的常规经验相悖,以便实现隐喻性的评价效果(见下一小节)。

文本最后两个小节似乎失去了时空进一步逆行的解读契机;不过,我们仍然可以做逆向理解。先让我们从顺时方向看,最后一句陈述自己被父母守候,说明叙事者还小,这自然应该是在入学之前;然后是叙述者上幼儿园大班或小学,因为自己还背不上书包的年龄,必定很小;再往后是我去上学了或者晚上看着电视入睡,之后父母把我打开的电视关上;最后是整个小学中学阶段:放学回家,我带回考试试卷让家长签字,知道父母已经做好了饭菜在等我。现在把上面的顺序倒过来,就是行文的逆行叙事。据此,整个行文叙事便都在视角逆行的范围之内。

把常规社会经验按反常规方式加以重组,这就是众所周知的时空倒流假设。当然,这里没有直接提及时空,而是直观陈述具体事件及其相关事物。它们构成一幅接一幅的经验动态画面,这一现象我们在影视作品的倒向放映时见过。但影视作品并没有起始参照点;而我们在这里接触到的是文字媒介,是语义措辞。它们总是提醒读者:我们始终立足当下,以此时此地为出发点,随事件回溯带动时空逆行,从而让读者进入一种非常规时空体验领域,给解读制造一种对比张力。人们会因此被吸引,并产生理性诘问:何以可能?

这是一种关于"现在"的观念:过去的经验和经历,一旦为记忆所捕捉,必定为当前调用,不管是听与说,还是阅读写作。从生命的成长历程看,尽管行文当下与孩提时光前后相隔十年二十年,但自己经历的一切,均由记忆加工一并呈现到当下,从而提供一个"整体语境"(the context of the whole),这就是大脑记忆的作用(Halliday 2008:183,189;彭宣维 2015b)。韩礼德明确指出:"系统有赖于记忆:有赖于每一个说话人铭刻在大脑中的内容,尤其是共享记忆,从而确保一定数量的、切实可行的不同说话人——大脑具有足够的共享基础,连续而无断裂。"(同上,第15页;另见 Hjelmslev 1943/1961:1)这一跟记忆联通有关的语言事实和社会经验事实,可为事件的逆行叙事提供社会心理基础,为可理解性解读做前提,从而成就"作者—文本—读者"一体化解读机制,因为是作者和前人的外在行为与内在思想共同创造了特定社团的文化与历史。而具有不同社会经历的个体会有不同的编码和解码倾向,从而确立不同的解读立场,甚至相互对立(伽德默尔 1960/2010)。这些一同呈现到当下的相关经验和经历,构成文本解读的外部语境(Hasan 1995)。至于有悖常理的事件回溯问题,这是文学文本允许的:在叙事世界里,一切反常识的知识均可接受,因为它的目的不在于所述事件和情节本身,而是以此指向"经验和生命的真实质地",是"人类对生活和生命的认识、想象和选择"(李敬泽 2009:59)。事实上,由记忆支配的思维活动可以对自身经验进行随意重组,构成一种心理实在(彭宣维 2015b)。所以,这种能够引起读者好奇心的叙述方式,不会因为超越常理的经验世界而迫使读者终止阅读。

这种叙事视角是一种底层操作,支配行文"表层"的措辞配置,从而在前景化"层面"呈现出相关行文走向。底层操作是在语义特征的结构化过程中选择涉及的。不过,是什么促成了这样的选择而非别的选择?这是作者在关注潜在读者可能的社会经历与体验范围时所制定的行文决策。

现在我们转向人际性的语境性对比策略。叙述者陈述的是代表性中国父母对成长中的儿女的关爱行为。因为习以为常,所以儿女们总是一种心安理得的接受心理,一般很少念及这一份恩情。不仅如此,还可能出现理所当然的极端情况,如一味"啃老"。下面这个片段也引自微信,是一位母亲写给儿子的告白信的开头部分:

> 儿子,今天你又装作若无其事地暗示妈妈,说市中心的房价又在飙升,如果再不行动,或许以后你和女友连一间栖息的小屋都没有。我淡淡地看你一眼,终于没有像你希望的那样,说出"妈妈给你们买"这样的话

来。而你,也在尴尬的沉默里,随即气嘟嘟地放下碗筷,甩门出去⋯⋯你已经 25 岁了,有一份稳定的工作,有一个需要呵护的女友,还有两位日益老去、需要你照顾的父母,难道这些还不足以让你成熟、让你彻底地离开父母的羽翼、放下啃老的惰性、独自去承担一个成人应该承担的责任吗? 记得从很小的时候,你就习惯有事找妈妈。你总是说:"妈妈,我的衣服脏了,你帮我洗洗。""妈妈,明天我们去郊游,你帮我收拾好要带的行李。""妈妈,女友想吃老醋茄子,记得下班后给她做。"⋯⋯

也许叙事者本人也有过类似经历,而一旦完全明白"你"不再"在我身旁"时,前后对比可能让人幡然醒悟。这里的叙述间接地将当前社会中的相关人文诉求关联起来,形成一种反差,从而达到扬此抑彼的用语效果。这里有语境因素的促成作用:倘若缺乏当前这种后现代文化语境,把类似叙述改用文言文前推到明清时代,那将是另一番情形。此外,这种对照让我们看到了行文背后可能存在的两种情感因素:一是后悔、内疚,属于情感中的消极满意范畴;另一个是对亲人的思念,当为情感中的积极意愿意义;而它们还会提醒读者回归亲情,学会感恩,主张一种更深层次的可靠性社会评判伦理。

最后,我们来看此文中采用的投射策略。投射,本来指行文中的言说者直接或间接引出的言辞或思想(Halliday 1994:250-273):言辞性投射如上引文中加引号的部分;思想性投射如开篇"暗示妈妈说"后面的内容——虽然这里用了一个"说"字,其实是"儿子"暗示母亲的心理意向,毕竟没有说出来,仍然是思想投射。当然,思想投射通常是一种全知叙事,因为任何人也无法直接进入别人的思维领域去探个究竟。在《身旁》中,叙事者作为行文中的一种角色、以第一人称叙事的方式向叙述对象"你"表达自己的体验和情感,这也是一种投射,一种概念性表征策略。在这里,我们可以把整个文本看作双重投射:言辞和思想,只是缺乏明确的"我说"和"我看见"或"我感觉到"之类的元话语成分。这里有明确的隐含作者介入:他或她将自己的相关心理活动通过文字叙述的方式呈现出来。①

---

① 试比较下面这种直抒胸臆的行文方式:"苦日子过完了/妈妈却老了/好日子开始了/妈妈却走了/这就是我苦命的妈妈/妈妈健在时/我远游了/我回来时/妈妈却远走了/这就是你不孝的儿子。"同一个题材,相近的内容,不同的表述方式(http://weibo.com/p/1001593782614140996948? from = page_100505_profile&wvr = 6&mod=wenzhangmod)。

总之,文化共同体在促成群体心理时,也为个体造就了分享社会经验的阅读基础,从而成为语义内容跟语境关联的依据。当然,这可能是整个大的社会文化背景,也可能是临时面临的具体情境语境,但前者蕴涵在后者之中,成为支配言语行为的潜在因素。这里有一个潜在的认识论立场,即记忆为我们提供的当前语境。

9.3 评价隐喻:态度立场的间接体现途径

上面从整体上分析了叙事策略尤其是视角效果带来的评价效应;这里拟对上述效果与相关语言成分做出具体关联,并在最后对全文的评价特征成分,无论是隐喻性的还是一致式的,给予总结。

我们先看态度隐喻,这在《身旁》中是通过及物性过程(Process of Transitivity)来间接确立的(Halliday 1994)。《身旁》的基调并非直接的情感与伦理诉求,而是以直观陈述的方式展示叙事者的经历,从而达到引发读者相应情感的目的。

全文的及物性过程成分一共 15 个。其中,物质过程成分 11 个:逆流、飘回、聚(成)、升起、落向、退回、回到、交回、飘来、关掉、背上,占总数的 73.33%。心理过程 1 个:忘了十年寒窗,占总数的 6.67%,但它跟整个行文的情感主旨无关,只是说明时空逆行而阻断所有求学的甘苦经历、踯躅于儿时感知的局部心理体验。另有两个关系过程句:(蒲公英聚)成伞的模样、你还在我身旁,占 13.33%。行为过程 1 个:签(名字),占 6.67%。注意,"聚成"是一个复合成分,包含两个及物性特征,"聚"为物质过程特征,"成"为关系过程特征。而以物质过程为主导的文本,追求的自然就是意象效果和直观体验(另见申丹 2009)。

在这 15 个特征中,前面 4 行涉及的 6 个成分,即逆流、飘回、聚成、升起、落向、退回,均指向事物,引发鉴赏性态度意义,即反应中的冲击类(Impact of reaction):所述现象是否抓住了我?后 5 行的及物性过程小句确立判断意义:隐含作者不再关注事物,而是被叙述者的可靠性行为

（Tenacity）；这些特征成分一共 8 个：运动员回到起跑线上；我交回录取通知书；忘了十年寒窗；你做好了饭菜等我吃；为我从学校拿回的考试试卷签上名字；在我上学前或者看着电视入睡后帮我关掉了电视；你总是陪着我，所以我"现在"的感觉是"你还在我身旁"。其中，"忘了"和"寒窗"是两个非常态性的判断成分（Normality）：记忆力好坏在这里不是能力问题，"寒窗"也指不寻常的求学经历；"签名"是一个关于行为的可靠特征，而"签"后的"好"是对"签名"结果的圆满性描述，应将"好"表达的平衡构成特征单列；第三行后一句中的"聚成"，跟"签好"一样，也是一个动补结构，但应作整体成分看待："聚"和"成"一起体现完满平衡性。第三节第一句"厨房里飘来饭菜的香"，似乎应该从字面上作物质过程分析，即引发性反应特征；但它间接陈述的是母亲做好饭菜等"我"回家的常态，揭示的是一种潜在的行为特征，宜作可靠性判断成分看。

　　注意后面的 5 个可靠性成分，都是跟"你"有关的行为，它们构成一个积极的可靠性特征集。即是说，叙述对象"你"始终是我的依靠，无微不至，无处不在。这里虽无明确的判断成分，但特定经历伴随着特定的情感取向，从而促成相关解释。理由很简单：人类的身体构造大致相当，会在同一社会和文化历史背景下经历大致相当的家庭、学校和传媒教育，从而积累有差别的共享经验领域；据此，即便是这样的间接陈述，读者同样可能获得叙述者希望达到的效果：中国父母的可依赖性。

　　语音也有直接表达评价意义的作用。一方面，押韵模式可以体现"构成"意义（Composition），从而给人均衡性。类似特征成分全文一共 9 个：（逆流而）上、（模）样、（东）方、（枪）膛、（起跑线）上、（寒）窗、（饭菜的）香、（背）上、（身）旁。它们能营造一种协和、均衡与平稳之感，所以体现的是构成范畴中的平衡义，即音韵效果的和谐一体性。另一方面，这些不断累增的语音效果还有级差调节作用：从第二个押韵的韵脚开始到结束，每个韵脚的出现便会增加一个品质强化特征，这样的特征成分应该是 8 个。相关行文也可以看作一种隐喻式，一种超出常规的标记性前景化体现成分。

　　或许有人会认为这种押韵方式有些像歌词。其实，从发生学的意义上说，诗和歌本来就是一体的，如《诗经》和《坎特伯雷故事集》以及所有人类文明早些时候产出的文学文本，莫不如此。虽然当代诗歌早已不再主张这种规整的修辞组织技巧，但后现代毕竟是一个多元时代。在重申这种回归亲情的主张时,采用押韵格式来配伍,十分合拍:年轻人写给年轻人读,无需世故口吻。事实上,我们应该为他们在步入社会之前留下这样一片成长天地,毕竟这是人类的"精神原点"和"生命原点"。

此外,《身旁》的介入和级差方式也带有语法隐喻性质。从介入角度看,整个行文是一种独白式的倾诉:一种收缩性主体间性叙述方式:直观陈述自己所"见"所"闻"所"感",既没有对话,也没有留给读者认可与否的机会;叙述者为"我",叙述对象是"你",很直接。这种主体间性方式可以看作一种断言性收缩介入(Pronounce):毋庸置疑的排他性口吻。从级差角度看,文中有 3 个量化语力成分:"远(处)"(空间)、"十年"和"还(在)"(时间);而叙述过程显得平实沉稳,虽然暗含的情感催人泪下,但既没有明确的"想念"与"追悔"之类的字眼,也缺乏锐化(Sharpening)甚至柔化(Softening)等明确的强度成分来凸显叙述者的强烈意愿。经验可以补足作者这一创作动机留下的空位,从而在显性事件陈述与隐性思亲意愿之间形成一种动态平衡,在一定程度上回避直接情感诉求带来的直白感。

这里,我们对语法隐喻手段促成的评价特征成分给予小结。隐喻性成分本身是语义性质的,它们在及物性关系结构中与其他相关成分一起构成组合性措辞。这些成分间接体现的是评价语义特征,彼此关联则构成有关评价意义的措辞关系(见图 9－1)。

代表性及物性成分及其指向的态度特征:

逆流 飘回 升起 落向 退回 回到 交回 忘了 寒窗 飘来 签字 关掉 背上 在

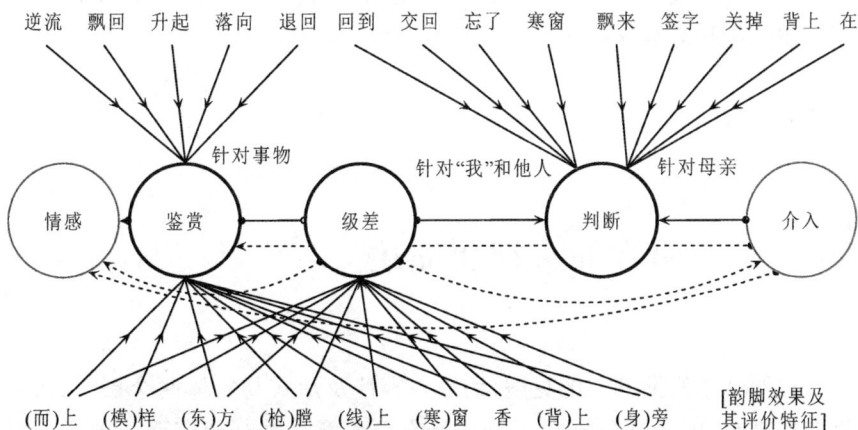

针对事物　　针对"我"和他人　　针对母亲

情感　鉴赏　级差　判断　介入

(而)上　(模)样　(东)方　(枪)膛　(线)上　(寒)窗　香　(背)上　(身)旁

[韵脚效果及其评价特征]

图 9－1:文本中出现的隐喻性评价特征成分

上面讨论的主要是隐喻性评价成分;现在我们对全文的所有评价成分给予归纳总结,包括尚未提及的非隐喻性成分。这样的成分全文一共53个。

一、由及物性过程成分引发的积极冲击性反应成分5个:逆流、飘回、升起、落向、退回;

二、由及物性过程成分引发的积极可靠性判断成分5个:飘来、签(好)名字、关掉、背上、在(母亲);非常态成分4个:回到、交回、忘了、寒窗(前三者是引发性的);

三、由韵脚带来的协和平衡效果特征9个(构成性):(逆流而)上、(模)样、(东)方、(枪)膛、(起跑线)上、(寒)窗、(饭菜的)香、(背)上、(身)旁;

四、铭刻性鉴赏成分3个:香[积极品质性反应];聚成、(签)好(名字)[积极完满平衡];

五、引发性积极估值鉴赏成分2个:录取通知书、饭菜;

六、由全文14个小句的肯定命题确立的断言性收缩特征14个;

七、明确的跨度级差成分3个:远处(空间)、十年(时间)、还(时间);韵脚组织的协和匀称特征8个。

需要特别说明的是,这里列出的只是一些关键性词语;事实上,相关评价特征是在整体语句甚至语境中才会产生的,这些只是索引符号而已。

至此,我们通过文字叙述的方式陈述了我们对样本的理解;我们还需要考虑由这些前景化成分构成的在线组织特点。

9.4 评价内容的可视化描述

按照叶尔姆斯列夫的见解,话语内容涉及形式与实体两个层次;按照笔者的理解,前者是《身旁》一文中所有评价意义特征组织而成的评价措辞,后者是它们整合而成的整体评价意义单位。为此,我们先来梳理上面总结的特征成分在行文中的序列化依据。

首先,文本话语是一个过程,是时间序列或相关语言成分次第加工出现的生成过程,是由解读加工可能涉及的评价体验确立的先后顺序。这是话语组织的一个核心要素。

由过程成分引发的态度特征是在加工完成每一个命题之后才可能获得的。这样,从整体上看,每一个诗行结束时至少涉及三个特征:引发性态度特征、由韵脚押韵效果表达的匀称特征以及断言性收缩介入特征;一行若有两个命题,则同时确立两个断言特征,每个命题结束时即累增一个特征成分,无需等到整个诗行结束,因为到那时又会增加一个新的介入特征。阅读每个诗行的过程中遇到的铭刻性鉴赏成分,则随即进行累积;第一行结束时无所谓韵律效果,要等到第二行结束时"样"回应第一行结束时的"上",甚至第三行结束时的"方"才会让第一行末的"上"带上均衡特征,因此,在结束对"样"的加工后才会出现"上"的韵律应和效应,所以"上"应在"样"后面。断言顺序放在韵脚特征之后,因为只有在处理完所有其他特征之后才会获得相应的介入体验。沿此,我们对上述53个特征成分做如下解读排序(罗马字母顺序为诗行行号,上标为所在诗行的命题序号,○代表韵律的级差增值特征;后文在进行可视化描述时逐一使用):

1 逆流、2a、3 远处、4 飘回、5b^1、6 聚成、7(模)样、8(而)上、9○、10b^2、11 升起、12c^1、13 落向、14(东)方、15○、16c^2、17 退回、18(枪)膛、19○、20d、21 回到、22(起跑线)上、23○、24e、25 录取通知书、26 交回、27f^1、28 十年、29 寒窗、30 忘了、31(寒)窗、32○、33f^2、34 饭菜、35 香(反应)、36 香(韵脚)、37○、38 飘来、39g、40 签(名字)、41(签)好(名字)、42h、43 关掉、44i^1、45 帮……背上、46(背)上、47○、48i^2、49 还、50 在、51(身)旁、52○、53j。

有了上面的准备,我们就可以对这些成分在建构文本过程中涉及的"表层"措辞平面给予直观描述,这是可视化描述的第一步,即由上述前景化特征成分组织而成的网状关系(texture),它们在系统功能语言学中属于词汇语法的范围(Hasan 1978:229)。为此,我们把从《身旁》中梳理出来的所有评价特征成分,按照它们出现的次第顺序以及分别所属的范畴类别,用图9-2的方式描述出来。

判断	鉴赏	介入	级差

1 逆流　2 a　3 远处
4 飘回　5 b¹
6 聚成
7 (模)样
8 (而)上　9 ○
11 升起　10 b²
13 落向　12 c¹
14 (东)方　15 ○
17 退回　16 c²
18 (枪)膛　19 ○
20 d
21 回到　22 (起跑线)上　23 ○
24 e
26 交回　25 录取通知书
27 f¹　28 十年
29 寒窗
30 忘了　31 (寒)窗　32 ○
34 饭菜　33 f²
35 香(反应)
36 香(韵脚)
37 飘来　38 ○
39 g
40 签(名)　41 (签)好(名)　42 h
43 关掉　44 i¹
45 帮……背上　46 (背)上　47 ○
48 i²　49 还
50 在　51 (身)旁　52 ○
53 j

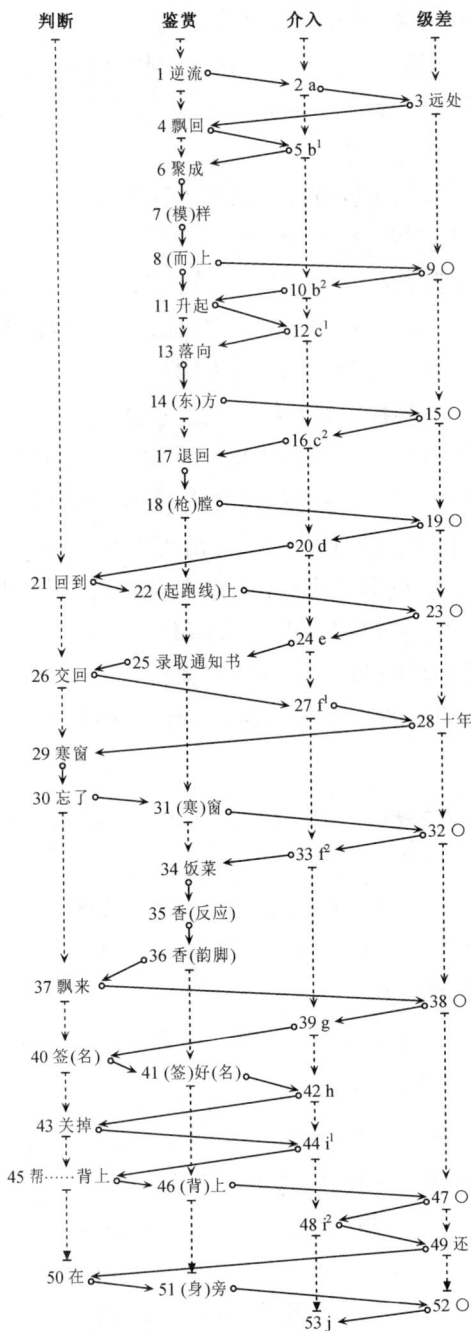

图 9－2:《身旁》措辞平面模型

从发展走向看,这是一种波动模型:评价叙述次第呈现于不同范畴特征之间,往复穿梭,逐步推进,从而编织成一张评价措辞网,构成评价的词汇语法层面。这是一个由在线特点确定的两维平面模型。注意,全文鉴赏性特征成分一共 19 个,占总数(53)的 36%,符合行文铺陈直观意象的阅读感知。

不过,这样一种描述还不足以说明整个文本涉及的所有评价意义,尤其是深层评价主旨的成形方式。而前文第 2 节讨论的一些内容也没有在该图中体现出来。我们还需要做进一步思考。这就是下面要讨论的内容。

我们发现,在上述平面模型之外,还有一个居于底层的伴随性评价意义单位的生成过程。直言之,伴随着图 9-2 的形成,各范畴领域的量也随之累增。其中,判断特征在总体评价成分中占 8/53 即 15.09%;鉴赏占 20/53 即 37.74%;介入占 14/53 即 26.42%;级差占 11/53 即 20.75%。我们可以直观描写这些成分在分布数量上的总体效果(图 9-3)。

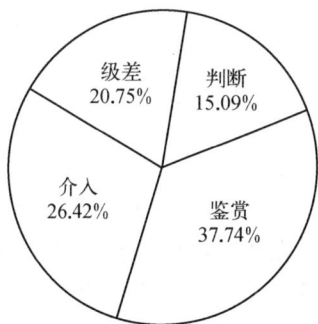

图 9-3: 各类主要范畴随文本过程的累增结果

根据这个最终结果,我们反过来设想一下:这其中的每一个范畴都是从第一个成分开始逐渐累增的。如果把这些范畴的累增过程加入图 9-3中,那么圆面背后就应该是一个不断变大的圆锥模型。可见,图 9-2 只是一种依据文本表层延伸的形式描写;图 9-3 倒是考虑到了态度、介入和级差之间的并行关系,但毕竟是静态的。我们需要把这两个方面结合起来。于是得到图 9-4(a)。

对比图 9-2 和图 9-4(a)。图 9-2 只是二维平面,只关注相关特征次第出现的序列及其在不同范畴之间的交替关联特点,没有考虑态度、介入和级差的并行合取关系,即它们之间是同时进入待选状态的。但图 9-4(a)揭示了态度立场受介入和级差调节的思想。具体而言,《身旁》平实沉稳(级差)而不容忍其他声音(介入)的叙事策略,体现的是叙事者"我"的情感表征方式:寻常周遭(瀑布长流、蒲公英播种、太阳运行)触动了"我"的亲情记忆。总之,级差和介入是为态度意义的确立做策略调节之用的,它们之间不是序列关系。

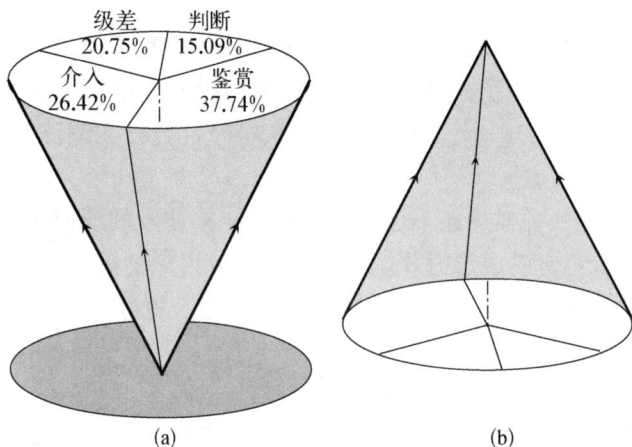

图 9－4：相关语义范畴的累增(a)与整合(b)

　　还有一个与图 9－4(a)累增方向相反的缩减或整合过程。这就是文本在整体评价主旨引导下、通过相应词汇语法手段体现的整个文本的评价意义单位。换言之,我们还需要从整合上看文本话语的组织方式。在《身旁》中,隐含作者采用的是传统修辞策略。第一节是对周围自然事件的重组,看似天马行空,却是一种起兴方式。第二节将叙述对象转向"人",而且有远近之别:先是物"子弹",然后是人"运动员",最后回到叙述者自己身上,从全局看这是承接第一段时光逆行的进一步叙述,更是过渡到行文主旨的中间环节。第三节是转,转向亲人,根据常识应该是母亲,从而进入主体叙述对象,包括"你"为"我"从生活到学习的日常操劳。最后一节是合,以简洁的一行识解体验——你并没有离开我,从而走向叙事者的评价主旨。换言之,也许当事人还没有在生活中熬到"子欲养"的阶段,但从叙述内容看,"亲不待"已成现实①。根据常理,这里便出现了由"你还在我身旁"的思念[态度:积极意愿情感]引发的"你已经不在我身旁"的追悔与遗憾心理[态度:消极满意情感],从而对同伴做出伦理上的告诫[亲情无价,且行且珍惜]。

　　这是一种与图 9－4(a)相对的创作与解读过程:既是在具体意象之

————————

① 皋鱼对孔子说:"吾失之三矣:少而学,游诸侯,以后吾亲,失之一也;高尚吾志,闲吾事君,失之二也;与友厚而小绝之,失之三也。树欲静而风不止,子欲养而亲不待也。往而不可追者,年也;去而不可见者,亲也。"(《韩诗外传》卷九)。

外孕育的一种主旨,也是从纷繁的意象铺陈中梳理的叙事意图。但创作与解读过程正好相对:创作是从抽象到具体、从少到多;解读则从多到少、从具体到抽象。这个过程可用图9-4(b)的反向圆锥模型来描述。此外,如果将图9-4(a)和9-4(b)对接成一个整体,我们就有图9-5的模型,即由两个圆锥体合成的纺锤型话语意义单位(a是分析性演示;b是合成外观)。阅读过程往往"得鱼而忘筌",措辞如何并不在关注范围内,即便随文记住一些引人注意的词句,也是支离破碎的,于是有图9-5(c)。所以,从纯粹意义生成的过程看,我们获得的应该是9-5(c)那样的构造。

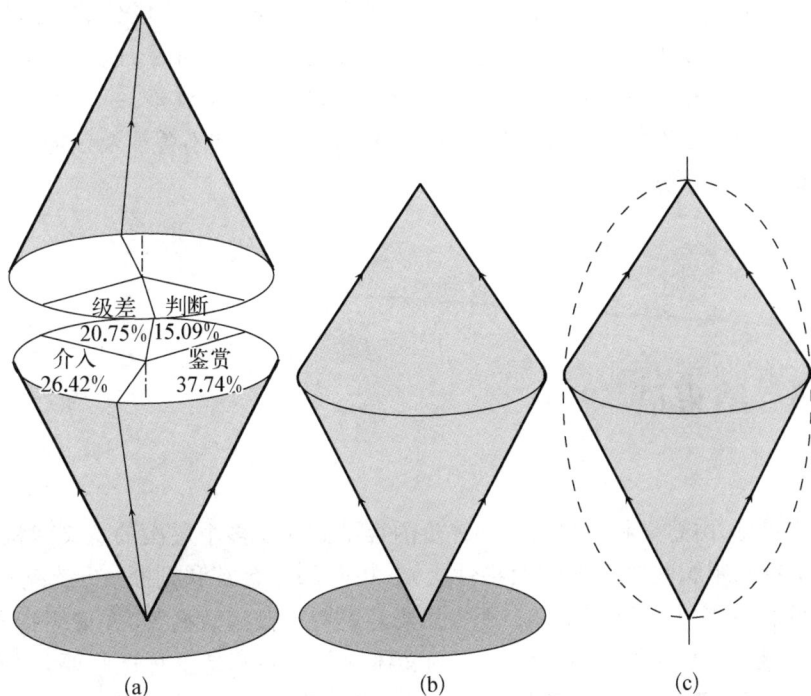

图9-5:文本的措辞与意义组织示意图

前文在做问题分析时同时涉及相关评价因素的社交基础,它们是生成整体评价意义单位的必要条件,故在图9-5(c)的外围加上了一个虚线椭圆,以示一种相互依存特点:评价主旨引导并构建文本的评价意义,而评价意义的建构过程同时意味着创立相应的评价语境:——上下两端的竖向短线表示整体评价意义单位的非封闭性。

再次回顾整个文本。其中存在一个三段论式的行文组织特点:假如时光可以倒流,那么我就可以回到从前去,跟母亲待在一起;现在"我"用视角逆行的方式"看到了"世事回溯,所以"我"实实在在地感觉到了母亲在"我"身旁的"现实"。这种"自欺欺人"的叙事策略并非实在的自然与社会过程,但也不是为了欺骗读者,而是为了提升一种由情感引发的理性,一种社会评判(Social Sanction)诉求:感念亲情、且行且珍惜吧。这是《身旁》一文积极思念意愿与消极追悔满意指向的终极伦理价值。这是一个由整个网状铺陈平面同时走向纺锤型意义组织的动态生成过程,在模型中用上面的尖端代表。

可见,一个文本的潜在评价主旨并非完全由表层评价成分类别来确定:《身旁》以可靠性判断为明确评价取向,但全文只有 4 个成分,而且还是引发性的;其他类别的评价成分,包括鉴赏、介入和级差,一并为此服务。而更深层次的情感和伦理诉求(意愿和可靠性)却不曾涉及任何一个前景化评价成分。

9.5　结束语

可见,由意义和措辞构成的评价内容平面涉及多个层次的意义建构:(1)视角组织间接表征的及物性类别,指向(2)鉴赏和判断——态势性与可靠性,它们一同带来(3)积极思念意愿与消极满意痛苦,并最终指向(4)感念亲情的伦理主张。先前的文体学研究并不是没有这些要素,但缺乏一种机制和模型来做明确的分层处理。我们的工作有望使相关研究走向具体和深入。

这里,我们换一个角度来总结本章涉及的基本主导思想:文学,包括创作实践与批评审美,是以评价为特点、手段和目的的互动性艺术话语行为。首先,《身旁》关注的是某种评价主旨、意愿情感和伦理诉求,从而为整个行文赋予突出的立场特点。其次,相关题材极其普通,但叙述过程去凡求新,以视角逆行的方式、用具体意象引发性地凸显情感和判断诉求;同时,鉴于文本延伸空间受限,隐含作者在设计上惜墨如金,小心翼翼地围绕评价主旨给予组织表述。最后，这是一个从"铭刻性及物性过程"到"引发性鉴赏和判断"、到"思念与追悔情感"、再到"且行且珍惜的伦理诉求"逐层深入的体现过程：文本围绕这一目的展开，并以间接体现的途径点明评价主旨，从而实施以评价为目的的话语策略。作者以对话诉说的方式追求一种互动效应；以字斟句酌的话语修辞构建一个相对独立的时空世界，以此彰显一种精巧的艺术性。可见，文学性就是评价性。

行文中梳理归纳的纺锤型意义组织模式，不只适用于《身旁》，所有文学文本的意识形态和价值观念的形成，均可由此表达；而从整个社会符号系统的角度看，以文学为契机的一切人学甚至一切人类行为，包括日常生活的与道德修为的，传统理性的与现代后现代解构的，均以评价意义建构与价值凝聚为终极目的，从而实现思想与行为的增值效应，不管是有规划的还是潜意识的，只是表述和组织方式不同罢了。据此，真正的文学实践自有其潜在的生命价值。

第十章

学科英语研究
——我国高层次英语教育的问题分析与基本对策述要[①]

10.1 问题的提出

数年前,笔者认识了一位就职于某知名文化企业的年轻朋友。由于他需要确证下面这个句子的意思,当时又受条件限制,他便求助于在场的各位英语同行。

(1) In bridging river valleys, the early engineers built many notable masonry viaducts of numerous arches. (早期的工程师们逢河搭桥,建造了许多著名的带有无数拱形结构的砖石高架桥。)

他是国内某知名高校英语文学方向的硕士毕业生,少有机会接触这一类话语,理解困难情有可原。不过,这倒让我联想到自己的教学体会与有关耳闻,也引发了我的某种想法。鉴于(1)是我教授的一门语言学课程中的例子,我特地拿给一位即将毕业的英语教学方向的硕士生,她说自己能猜个大概,但 *masonry*［水泥砖石结构］、*viaduct*［高架桥］和 *arch*［拱形结构］是生词。她这么说,我倒怀疑了:理解谓语动词 built 后面的部

① 本章原载于《外语教学》2019 年第 2 期,第 1—7 页。这里有改动。

分果真只是生词问题？再看例(2－3)：

(2) A symmetric matrix whose quadratic form $x^T Ax$ takes on both positive and negative values is called *indefinite*.(如果一个对称矩阵的二次型 $x^T Ax$ 既可以取正值也可以取负值,这个对称矩阵则是非确定的。)

(3) Median prostate-specific antigen nadir level in the eight patients with biopsy-proven local recurrence after initial low-dose rate brachytherapy was 0.75 ng/ml.(在最初的低剂量率近距离放射疗法之后,八个经活检证明的局部复发病人,他们的前列腺特异性抗原中值最低点水平是每毫升 0.75 纳克。)

如果有人认为我们难以理解(2—3)的根本原因在于专业术语,那就仍然没有脱离传统教学把词汇放到中心位置的误识,毕竟词汇突显而语法隐晦(Halliday 1989)。但如果我们面对下面这样一个没有生词的句子和这一类语篇而无所适从,又该如何解释?

(4) The argument to the contrary is basically an appeal to the lack of synonymy in mental language.

专业词汇学习相对容易(Halliday 1989),但专业词汇的形成本身也是语法化的一部分:它们需要语法手段对相应经验进行范畴化与概念化(Halliday 1993b)。此类英语变体的真正难点在于:它们通过专业话语的理性、客观、非人际化词汇语法手段构筑藩篱,将非同行读者排斥于外;读者只有通过专门学习与潜心研究才能有效接近(Halliday 1989)。

一般的硕士毕业生连(1)都无法顺利理解,而即便是博士毕业生尤其是不做学科英语研究的学生,又有多少人能理解(2—4)? 虽然我国高校的英语教师队伍庞大,但能够顺利写出(1)这个水平的人不会太多,能理解(2—4)的更是少数。已经走上工作岗位的姑且不论,目前我国高校的在校学生 3 000 多万,他们需要把这一类英语变体作为学习对象,达到进行基本的专业和职业交流的目的(如 Huckin & Olsen 1991),可绝大部分英语教师如何能胜任相关工作?

客观地说,改革开放以来,我国的外语教育教学事业在短短 30 来年时间里取得了巨大成就;就英语教育而言,所培养的学生,无论是语音语调还是读写能力,远远超出周边大多数国家和地区(胡壮麟 2002a;何其莘等 2008)。但随着改革开放规模的逐步扩大和我国经济文化国际化转型的飞速发展,我们培养的高层次外语人才,已经远远无法满足国家经济建设尤其是"一带一路"倡议发展的迫切需要,(2—4)向我们提出的严峻挑战能在很大程度上说明问题(另见束定芳 2013)。社会各界纷纷向高校外语教育工作者提出了前所未有的质疑、挑战和要求(且见戴炜栋 2001),也就不足为怪了。

就大学外语而言,蔡基刚(2005)总结了五个方面的要素:(一)高校外语教学定位的"基础性"——"把听说能力培养从原教学大纲的第二层次地位转变到一个突出的位置上";(二)基础性教学的超长过程造成的"费时低效性";(三)采用多媒体网络教学模式解决扩招带来的师资紧缺问题的优势、可能的局限以及对传统课堂教学模式的长处的肯定;(四)大学英语四、六级考试的是与非;(五)双语教学的有效性和政治立场问题。针对上述第二点,他后来又指出了基础性教学的方向性错误以及"学术英语"教学的根本出路(蔡基刚 2010a;王守仁、姚成贺 2013;文秋芳 2014)。

同时,作为外国语言文学学科的"外语专业"情况好一些,但问题同样突出。胡壮麟(2002a)就此做过历史性反思。我们也意识到,刚入学的研究生,其专业学习大都几乎从零开始,而此时文史哲学科的学生已经具备了相当程度的专业知识和创新能力;问题的严重性在于,学生经过四年的听说读写技能训练,不但没能充分发展思辨能力,反而在相关方面大大退化了(王星、彭宣维 2007;另见黄源深 1998,2010;王守仁 2001;戴炜栋 2001;何其莘等 2008;有关深入研究可见文秋芳、周燕 2006;孙有中 2011;文秋芳 2008,2012,2014;文秋芳等 2014;文秋芳、孙昊 2015 等)。

这一尴尬现状敦促我们再一次思考一个根本性的问题:如何为国人提供一套有效的英语(外语)教改方案?

10.2 问题分析

我们认为,上述困境源于两个导向性问题:我国英语教育的英语语言文学定位及其基础性。英语语言文学定位与我国当代外语教育的传统与认识有关(束定芳 2013)。综观我国高等教育自 1949 年以来的发展史,尤其是改革开放 30 多年来的基本格局变化,外语人才培养原则上是以语言文学为主导的,突出听说读写以及相关语种所在的语言文学的文化与互译技能等;只是在 2004 年以来的大纲内容调整与修订中(教育部 2004,2007),大学外语因实践的推动才涉及"双语教学"的思想(另见李翠香 2008;张修海等 2011)。事实上,自 20 世纪 80 年代末以来的相当长一段时间内,国内各类大学无论是新增的外语系或改建的外语(文)学院,无论是硕士点还是博士点,学科建设的基本格局均侧重于语言文学;近十来年逐渐加强了外国语言学与应用语言学学科的建设,但也只有理工科院校意识到加强专业外语教育的必要性,可他们普遍缺乏资源,几乎束手无策。这个模式就是:外语语言文学→教师→学生→教师(专业外语)。而问题的关键在于,相关教师都是从外语语言文学环境下培养出来的,面对语言文学以外的其他专业的外语教学时,其相关知识储备与能力水平可谓捉襟见肘。面对市场需要,我们的外语教师何以能在短短的二十多年时间内迅速转变知识结构体系、顺利适应大学外语的教学需求? 近年来,一批学者一直在提倡并尝试外语加学科专业学习的"复合型人才"培养模式,有一定收效,但并不理想。

上述指导思想的直接结果就是强调课程设置的"基础性"。所谓基础性,就英语而言,指"日常英语"或"共核英语",是英语本族语者在家庭及日常交往中自然学会的。就外国语言文学专业而言,很多高校除了听说读写等基本技能课程之外,根本没有全面开设语言学、文学和文化等专业课程;即便到了高年级阶段,学生仍然要面对一大堆延伸了的读写视听说课程(另见胡壮麟 2002b),从而使高等学校的外语教学成了高中外语教学的延伸,大学的外语专业教学便被人们戏称为高四、高五、高六、高七。大多数学校的学生普遍厌学,教师普遍厌教。在这种情况下,近年来我国南方的一些大学,如中山大学、汕头大学等,率先在读写技能发展尤其是和专业知识相结合的读写训练方面有所突破。但全国的整体状况并不理想,这至少在研究生招生人数逐年递减、生源质量每况愈下等方面有所体现。但外语教师面临的上述问题,很少有人做理性探究,深挖根由。我们浏览了上千篇长长短短有关教改的文章,既有发表在外语类核心期刊上的,也有跟外语毫不相关的学术与娱乐性杂志上的。文章内容涉及专门用途外语教学(以学术英语教学为多)、大学外语教学目标的"基础性"和"工具性"、专业知识教学从"双语化"向外语单语的过渡策略、结合外语和各专业方向的"复合化"、解决师资紧缺问题而诉诸计算机辅助教学的"技术化",以及外国语言文学教育的"人文性"、"创造性"、"生态化"、"科学素养"、"文化认同"等主题。这些论述基本上是围绕基础性展开的,大都浅尝辄止,感想体会居多,谈不上系统性。

基础性外语教学无疑具有重要性,但我们的教师缺乏足够的专业语言训练,内容的整体性被肢解,系统性被极大地压缩简化,高层次和高水平教育问题尤为严重。由于对语言学成果缺乏应有的把握,我国不少教材都是拍脑子编出来的,编写教材的师生大都没有相关知识储备与应有素养;大家在这种情况下谈教改,视野与水平自然受限。

人类的专业知识领域远非日常体验所能涵盖。就英语发展而言,它经历了名词的分类扩展(expanding)、基于词类转换的语义范畴超越(transcategorizing)、说理过程涉及的内容压缩(compacting)以便适应基于逻辑理据的信息流动、对范畴超越与内容压缩结果的提炼(distilling)从而创造出对抽象事物的专门分类、最后使用特定句子类型重构经验并建构科学理论(Halliday 1998a)。这是一个从日常英语到学科英语的概括化(generalization)、抽象化(abstraction)与隐喻化(metaphorization)的过程(Halliday 1998b)。专业化的英语就是在这三个层次上逐步推进的,是进入任何学科的必由之路,是英、美、澳、加等英语为母语的国家高中阶段需要初步解决的问题(见 Halliday 1998a:xxvii;O'Halloran 2000;Veel 1998;Martin 2002;Fang & Schleppegrell 2008;Christie 2012),相当于《欧洲语言共同参照框架》确定的共同语言能力量表的"中高级"(B2;Conseil de L'Europe)或我国高中毕业生的汉语水平。

可是,国内英语专业的不少学生在硕士甚至博士毕业时,还没有达到(2—4)这个层次的读写能力,能够进入非英语专业领域进行英语教学研究的更是凤毛麟角,由此培养出来的教师何以能胜任相关语言问题的教学? 因此也就只能是有意回避与忽略了。

10.3 解决方案

要解决外语学科的困境,尤其是高层次人才的培养问题,专门用途外语教学的确是一个切实有效的方案(见蔡基刚 2011,2012a & b,2014;王守仁 2016),至少大方向是正确的,因为只要涉及专业知识和学术领域,无论哪一个学科,只要用外语表征相关知识体系,都属于专门用途外语的范围。这就是系统功能语言学说的语域概念(Register;俗称语类 Genre 或篇类 Text Type;Halliday et al. 1964;Halliday 1978a;对比 Martin 1984,1992,2012a;Artemeva & Freedeman 2015),已经在澳大利亚和美国的中学教学实践中获得成功应用(*Australian Curriculum*;Rose & Martin 2012;de Oliveira & Iddings 2014)。

但这么些年来我们在国内的尝试效果为什么并不理想? 有人认为,这是"受教师英语能力或专业知识的制约以及受基础英语打压和双语课程挤压,专业英语教学效率低下,乃至 ESP 发展逐渐边缘化"等造成的(蔡基刚 2010b)。我们认为,当中还有别的原因,因为英语教师仅仅知道专门用途英语教学的一般原理还远不足以应对专业英语的教育问题:我们需要从当代语言学理论的高度来寻找出路(另见蔡基刚 2012a & b)。韩礼德早就强调过作为"深层原则"的语言学理论对于教好英语的重要性(Halliday 1967;也见 Halliday 2007a)。Strevens(1988)则明确指出:做专门用途英语研究的前提之一是对英语的全面描写;虽然这一主张有其不足,如单纯的描写会缺乏解释,但后来相应的语类语境和语用研究甚至语料库方法的介入,则给予了相应补足(Swales 1990;Bhatia 1993)。对于我国的 EFL 教育来说,这一思路应该也是有效的:只有先明确教什么,才便于确定怎么教。

迄今,学界在学科英语研究中已经取得了一些成果,如物理(如 Halliday 1988b)、地理(Martin et al. 1989;Martin 2002)、数学(Adler 2001;Gerofsky 2004;Pimm 1987;O'Halloran 2000;Anderson et al. 2002;Schleppegrell 2007;Moschkovich 2010)、化学(Sriniwass 2010)、历史(Martin 1993;Martin et al. 1993;Fuller 1998;Coffin 2006;顾乡 2008;

Schleppegrell et al. 2008）、工业与工程（Rose 1998；Esteras & Fabre 2007；Ibbotson 2009）、农学与自然生态（Goatly 2004；Rata et al. 2012）、经济（Dudley-Evans & Henderson 1990；Samuels 1990；Bondi 1999；MacKenzie 2006；Camiciottoli 2007；Farrall & Lindsley 2008；Alejo 2010；Tribe 2015）、法学（Brown & Rice 2007；Lee et al. 2007；Coulthard & Johnson 2013；Coulthard et al. 2016；Kibbee 2016）、医学（Francis & Kraner-Dahl 2004；Lu & Corbett 2012）、文学（Cranny-Francis 1998；Halliday 2002；Hillier 2004；Miller & Turci 2007；Webster 2015；Hasan *forthcoming*）、心理学（Matthiessen 1998）、人文社科（Berkenkotter & Nuckin 1995；Wignell 1998；Stubbs 2004）、教育（Christie 1998；Halliday 2005b；Barry 2007；杨信彰 2007）、管理（Mckeown & Wright 2011）、广告和媒体（黄国文 2001；White 2004）等等。但其中不少探讨还只是初步的，包括剑桥大学出版社推出的系列丛书。它们的着力点不均衡，更不系统，缺乏有效的语言学范畴指导；国外的成果多一些，也更为深入；国内的整体情况差强人意，与我们这个英语使用大国的国情不符。

为此，我们拟从概括性的学科门类的角度入手，来确定学科英语的研究范围。我们以我国教育部颁发的 12 个学科门类为出发点，从议题和大致表达特点的角度，确立 13 个总体研究领域：哲学英语、经济学英语、法学英语、管理学英语、理学英语、工学英语、军事学英语、教育学英语、农学英语、历史学英语、文学艺术英语、医学英语，以及语言学、心理学、社会学和人类学英语。最后四个学科合并一类，因为它们的研究思路和方法相近甚至相当：从归纳和演绎相互参照的角度处理观察对象。

这些都是我们说的学科英语（Disciplinary English）的主要领域：用来组织不同领域的经验知识所采用的英语变体，为高校英语教育的基本内容（见 Halliday 1998a；Christie & Maton 2011；Kurdali 2014），属于专门用途英语（ESP；如 Halliday et al. 1964；Hutchinson & Waters 1987；Benesch 2001；Flowerdew & Peacock 2001）。它与行业/职业英语（Professional English）的所指对象相近，但侧重点有别：学科英语作为一个术语，特指以学科群（subject group）为代表的学校教育专业涉及的英语变体，如上述 13 个学科大类涉及的英语变体；而行业/职业英语侧重于不同职业领域的专门用途英语，包括法庭（Gunnarsson et al. 1997；Benesch 2001）、课堂（Yang 2010）、商场销售方面的职业培训（后者如 Halliday 1994：368）、桥牌(Benson & Greaves 1992)和带有学术特点的英语变体(如 Gunnarsson et al. 1997)等。不过,其中那些包括职业培训和桥牌在内的英语变体一旦作为知识体系写进教科书,也是学科英语的内容之一。在此,行业/职业英语与专门用途英语所指是一致的。

学科英语是一组变体,从高度专业化的表述到普及读物(且见 Martin & Veel 1998;Fuller 1998;Cranny-Francis 1998)。有些学科英语,如理论物理学、医学、生物学,其英语表达的专业性很强;有些学科,如经典哲学英语,其抽象化程度很高;而课堂话语等学科的英语就相对容易(如 Christie & Derewianka 2008;Yang 2010)。它们在复杂性与难度上形成一个连续体。其中,高度专业化的英语就是科学英语(Scientific English;Halliday 2004),也称学术英语(Academic English;也见 Hyland 2004,2006,2009,2012;Hyland & Shaw 2016)。这是本项目的重点和难点,是"引导"学生逐步与口语表达方式脱离、学会使用学科话语的理性依据(Halliday 1978b),因为"学习第二语言或者外语是一个再社会化过程,在学习过程中创造一个新的社会现实,在新的文化环境中表达和创造新的意义"(转引自张德禄 2007)。

不同学科门类及其包含的各个学科有自身的特点。正如海兰德(Hyland 2004)所说:哲学语言做"论辩",工程英语做"汇报",生物语言做"描述"。这就要求学科英语研究进行学科门类之间及其内部特点的深入对比:先研制 13 个学科领域的语料库,做比较描述,给予总体归纳与相应解释,继而系统梳理具有不同难易程度的语言项目。

10.4 科学英语的 7 个基本特点

但作为整体的学科英语同时存在一些共同要素,这里拟就主要的共同特点做一概述。虽然高层次外语教育还包括高层次的听力和口语、体现在科学英语语篇中的社会文化、情感等因素(见 Bernstein 1971,1990;于晖 2003;Leaver & Shekhtman 2002 等),但以下归纳足以从一个方面体

第十章 学科英语研究

第三部分 应用研究

现本研究的基本思路：这既是有关共性的研究内容，也是研究方法。

韩礼德（Halliday 1989）曾对科学英语进行过系统研究，归纳出 7 个基本的语法要素。本小节拟对这些要素做扼要介绍，并根据本章议题适当补充相关内容。其他相关阐述散见于《韩礼德文集》第 5 卷和第 9 卷（Halliday 2004，2007b）有关章节（另见 Hasan 2011；Martin 2012b 等）。

（一）连锁定义。下面这个语段涉及一组概念，相互诠释：A circle is a plane curve with the special property that every point on it is at the same distance from a particular point called the *centre*. This distance is called the *radius* of the circle. This *diameter* of the circle is twice the radius. The length of the circle is called its *circumference*. 其中，circle［圆］的定义有赖于 centre［圆心］与 radius［半径］，两者的距离设定 diameter［直径］，共同确立 circumference［圆周］。换言之，一个术语的理解同时涉及对另外四个术语的理解，它们通过解释性措辞发生关联，形成一个概念群。由此识解的学科知识便进入相应话语中，因为"语言是表达人类经历和建构人类经历的唯一因素"。这是一种理论操作，一种隐喻化过程：它把经验重新加工成为符号术语，以便构拟符号世界，与物理世界平行。其实，人们认定的"科学"理论是一种经过设计或半设计的语义系统，核心成分是语法隐喻或虚拟事物的语言分类；此类表述一旦用日常语言解构，相关理论便不复存在。因为不同学科自有一套表达方式，学科发展促成了相应表述特点的突显，学科与语言是一体的。（Halliday 1988b，1998c）可见，把语言或外语学习同专业学习对立起来的"培养复合型外语人才"的提法，只是一种分析性思维。

（二）专门分类。例如，在介绍 climate（气候）这个概念时，可采用两个维度的分类方式做描述：一是类别，包括 *tropical*、*sub-tropical*、*temperate*、*cold* 和 *dry*，而 *cold* 又可分为 *boreal*、*polar* 与 *highland* 等；二是不同气候的构成因素，如 *solar radiation*、*temperature*、*pressure systems* 与 *atmosphere moisture*。这些分类带有很强的专业性，但它们是通过特定语篇语法全方位体现的。

（三）特殊表达。这一点可通过（2—4）代表的语类来说明。（2）是数学：*symmetric matrix*、*quadratic form*、$x^T Ax$、*positive value*、*negative value*、*indefinite*；（3）是医学工程：*prostate-specific antigen*、*nadir*、*biopsy-proven local recurrence*、*low-dose rate brachytherapy*、0.75 ng/ml；（4）是人文社科：

argument、*to the contrary*、*basically*、*appeal to*、*synonymy*、*mental language*。各组词语与特定专业有关。

同样,如果缺乏应有的语法手段,它们便难于组织成为专业性话语,所以这同样不能仅作词汇现象看待。换言之,不同学科的英语教学发展到今天,几乎均已梳理出全套的专业术语及其英汉对照表(如 Glendinning & Howard 2007);但相关语类差异才是我们关注的重点,因为语类涉及整体语篇特征及其彼此之间的异同。系统功能语言学者在这方面做过大量工作,如对小说、历史、医学语类的全面对比与描写分析(可见 Christie & Martin 1997;Ravelli & Ellis 2005;Martin & Rose 2008;Slade et al. 2008;Sriniwass 2010;Matthiessen 2013 等)。此外,从高度专业化的特殊表达到半专业、特殊的非专业用语,也存在一个等级问题(见本节末)。

(四)词汇密度。下面各例中加下划线的成分是实词,后面方括号内的数字代表相应句子的实词数:(a)But we never did anything very much in science at our school [2];(b)My father used to tell me about a singer in his village [4];(c)A parallelogram[平行四边形]is a four-sided figure with its opposite sides parallel [6];(d)The atomic nucleus absorbs and emits energy in quanta, or discrete units [8]。实词数与句子总词数的比就是相应句子的词汇密度。这一点跟连锁定义、特殊表达以及语法隐喻(后文)关系紧密,共同构筑科学英语的学术性。

(五)句法模糊性。在下面三例中,(a)Increased responsiveness may be reflected in feeding behaviour、(b)Lung cancer death rates are clearly associated with increased smoking、(c)Higher productivity means more supporting services,各句前一项(如 increased responsiveness)与后一项(feeding behaviour)之间是起因还是证据关系?这种关系由谁引出谁?如果缺乏上下文,学习者会无所适从。这就要求读者对类似话语推进的基本内容始终保持清醒认识。

(六)语义非连续性。在 Strong anti-pollution laws over the last twenty years have resulted in cleaner factories, cleaner countryside and an increase in the number of light-coloured pepper moth 中存在两个过程(由 have 分开),它们通过一个逻辑连接词 result 连接:"*a* 发生了, 所以 *x* 发生了",并通过"事件 *a* 导致了事件 *x* 的发生"(*strong anti-pollution laws ...* 导致了 *cleaner factories ...*)这样的隐喻化途径来表征。我们可以把这个部分改

写为：Over the last twenty years，［the government have passed］strong laws to stop［people］polluting；so the factories［have become］cleaner …，其语义的连贯性就清楚了。此类英语变体是学习和使用的难点之一。

（七）语法隐喻。对语法隐喻的教学是学校语言教育的基本职责，因为它们系统地出现在不同学科的语言表征中。例如，下面这个句子：*the cast*［参与者/名词］*acted*［过程/动词］*brilliantly*［环境/副词］*so*［过程之间的关系/连词］*the audience*［参与者/名词］*applauded*［过程/动词］*for a long time*［环境/介词短语］，相应的学术话语可以是：*the cast's brilliant acting*［名词/参与者］*drew*［动词/过程］*lengthy applause*［名词/参与者］*from the audience*［介词短语/环境］。表述方式与（2—3）一致：以级转移和名词化途径，将多个小句内容压缩到一个小句中。这里是两个小句体现的因果关系压缩到一个物质小句中；（2—4）中的名词化成分 *indefinite*，*factorization*，*recurrence*，*argument*，*synonymy* 也是用级转移手段构拟的语法隐喻。

从复杂度看，从高度学术化的表述到日常话语，中间会有不同抽象度和词项密度（Halliday 2004），如（5）（引自 Halliday 1998b）。这个等级梯度正是学校语言教育由浅入深的工作内容。

(5) a. Osmolarity［渗透性］increases, so putrescine［腐胺］is rapidly excreted［排出］.

b. Because osmolarity increases, putrescine is rapidly excreted.

c. That osmolarity increases means that putrescine is rapidly excreted.

d. Osmolarity increasing leads to putrescine being rapidly excreted.

e. Increasing of osmolarity causes rapid excreting of putrescine.

f. Increase of osmolarity causes rapid excretion of putrescine.

g. Increase of osmolarity causes rapid excretions of putrescine.

句子级阶上的语法隐喻还有一类：由两个及物性过程并合而成。认知语言学称为跨域映射（见 Halliday 1994：340‑367；阐述见彭宣维 2016；对比 Lakoff & Johnson 1980/2003；Lakoff 1987）。（6）是从《罗密欧与朱丽叶》前面部分随意摘录的。

(6) a. For beauty, starv'd with her severity, /Cuts beauty off from all posterity

b. Let two more summers wither in their pride / Ere we may think her ripe to be a bride.

c. Earth hath swallowed all my hopes but she; / She is the hopeful lady of my earth.

d. You are a lover; borrow Cupid's wings / And soar with them above a common bound. / Rom. I am too sore empierced with his shaft / To soar with his light feathers; and so bound / I cannot bound a pitch above dull woe. / Under love's heavy burden do I sink … Is love a tender thing? It is too rough, // Too rude, too boist'ous, and it pricks like thorn.

e. Alas, poor Romeo, he is already dead: stabb'd with a white wench's black eye; run through the ear with a love-song; the very pin of his heart cleft with the blind bow-boy's butt-shaft.

　　从前三句看,相关语法隐喻只是句子级阶现象;后两段引文表明,语法隐喻是语篇现象。这在经典文学语篇中常见。特定语篇类型决定了语法隐喻的使用方式和频次;类似《罗密欧与朱丽叶》的文学语类则侧重于不同语域或次语域之间的跨类接合。(2—3)对于英语语言文学学习者来说是主攻方向;但文学是一个综合语类,尤其是经典英语文学,可能涉及(1—4)的所有行文方式,虽然会适当降低(2—3)的表述方式以增强可读性。又如,

(7) I am satisfied, and will trouble you no more when these few lines are dismissed. The engagement which you were eager to form a fortnight ago is no longer compatible with your views, and I rejoice to find that the prudent advice of your parents has not been given in vain. Your restoration to peace will, I doubt not, speedily follow this act of filial obedience, and I flatter myself with the hope of surviving my share in this disappointment. (Jane Austen: *Lady Susan*)

　　总之,语法隐喻是通过特定语类及其相应的语法结构,如关系小句等静态语法手段,协同表征的(后文)。人们通常说的词汇隐喻,如上述跨域映射现象,也是语法隐喻,但映射说是从语义角度界定的,语法隐喻侧重

第十章　学科英语研究

于语言层面的形成机制。

我们需要在此引入另一项研究成果。有人在学术语篇的专业词汇之外梳理了关于次专业、半专业或特殊的非专业词汇,也称框架词或学术词汇,包括原话语成分(*argue*, *examine*, *survey*, *recommendation*)、描述性话语(*analyze*, *examine*, *survey*, *implementation*)、主题成分(*current*, *present*, *recent*, *ability*, *impossibility*, *change*, *development*, *process*, *structure*, *quality*, *expansion*, *increase*, *decline*, *reduction*, *arising*, *affecting*, *contribute*)等。与不同学科的典型专业词相比,这些成分的学术性相对偏低。此外,专业词汇的专业性存在一个程度的问题,包括:(一)某一特定专业领域的词汇:*jactitation*, *per curiam*, *cloture*(法学)、*morpheme*, *happax legomena*, *lemma*(语言)、*anode*, *impedannce*, *galvanometer*, *dielectric*(电子)、*wysiwyg*, *rom*, *pixel*, *modem*(计算);(二)专业与非专业通用,但意义有别:*cite*(*to appear*), *caution*(*v.*)(法学)、*sense*, *reference*, *type*, *token*(语言)、*induced*, *flux*, *terminal*, *earth*(电子)、*execute*, *scroll*, *paste*(计算);(三)专业与非专业通用,但主要用法还是跟特定专业领域有关:*accused*(*n.*), *offer*, *reconstruction*(*of a crime*)(法学)、*range*, *frequency*(语言)、*coil*, *energy*, *positive*, *gate*, *resistance*(电子)、*memory*, *drag*, *window*(计算);(四)更多地出现在某一特定领域:*judge*, *mortgage*, *trespass*(法学)、*word*, *meaning*(语言)、*drain*, *filament*, *load*, *plate*(电子)、*print*, *programme*, *icon*(计算)(见 Coxhead & Nation 2001)。

总体来看,科学英语的语法结构大都简单;但经过语法化手段加工的词语会十分复杂,如词组和短语结构,特别是名词化成分,往往十分抽象(Halliday 2004)。这是高层次英语教学的核心内容。

10.5 跟语法隐喻有关的其他相关特点

这里介绍三点:内容表述的平稳性、意义抽象性以及 EFL 学习者的思维方式差异。

　　科学语篇表征的学科内容给人一种**平稳感**,诸如确定性、恒定性与静态性(Halliday, 1999)。在这里,关系过程的结构,*x* be（at）/have *a*,是正式语篇的一个特点,其静态性可以使正式性程度高的语篇,尤其是学术语篇,在内容表述上增加厚重感,与口语性强的叙事语篇的不确定性、变异性和流动性相对,因为叙事语篇的目的是快速推进事件和情节发展,产生阅读吸引力。但在学术语篇中,大量信息被压缩到简单的句子结构中,级转移现象大幅度增量(Halliday 2004)。例如,(2)中由 *whose* 引导的嵌入从句就是一个从句级阶向下转移成名词组 *a symmetric matrix* 的后置修饰成分,相当于一个词的作用。同时,该类语篇含有较长甚至超长的名词词组或短语,如(2)中的 *a symmetric matrix*、*whose quadratic form* $x^T Ax$ 和 *both positive and negative values*,(3)中的 *median prostate-specific antigen nadir level*、*the eight patients with biopsy-proven local recurrence* 和 *initial low-dose rate brachytherapy*,以及(4)中的 *the argument to the contrary* 和 *the lack of synonymy in mental language*,这是平稳性的一个标志,可以让读者就每一信息片段花费更多的加工时间进行识别和构建意义,从而与物质、行为和言语过程带来的快速移动效应对立(另见 Halliday 2004:121,129)。这种经验性语法隐喻,既是教授对象,也是高层次外语水平的修养标志。所以,科学语言已经变成了一种关于读写能力的教育内容,是构建和维系超常复杂的意识形态大厦的工具,语法则通过演化使这种话语变成现实,成为重构科学经验的途径(Halliday 1993b;另见 Ravelli & Ellis 2005)。

　　语法隐喻的一个可能结果是意义表达的**抽象性**(abstractness),这一点在人文社科话语中尤为突出,与科技语篇的技术性和理性有别(technicality 和 rationality;Halliday 2008:97;Martin 1993;Wignell 1998;Christie 2002)。我们仍以(4)为例。*Argument* 本来就相对抽象:*an exchange of diverging or opposite views, typically a heated or angry one*(争论;辩论),所以学界有 *argument is war* 的分析。但其后置修饰成分 *to the contrary* 虽然有方向上的明确性,但跟 *argument* 搭配则变得更为抽象,因为争辩的相反方向会让不熟悉类似表达方式的读者无所适从。接下去的 *appeal to* 是一个本来就更为抽象的成分(*try to persuade someone to do something by calling on* [*a particular principle or quality*]),在日常汉语中

缺乏相近的对等项。即便它在当代社会已为中学水平的读者所掌握,也难以让普通读者获得清晰的认识。而 *appeal to* 之后是一个没有具体所指内容的事物 *lack*,且 *synonymy* 在一般语文词典里不作为词条列入,虽然 *synonym* 可以帮助理解,但抽象化了的 *synonymy* 会让人茫然。此外, *mental language* 中缺乏 *synonymy* 当为何意? 如果例(4)用一致式来体现,其大意便是: *In order to argue that [this] is not so [he] simply points out that there are no synonyms in mental language.* 其实,像(4)这种表述的抽象性在哲学尤其是现当代思想界产出的语篇中常见;在政府报告、法律文本(如合同条款)中俯拾即是。这正是语言权势的体现方式:确立一种远离日常意象的表征程式,避免让局外人分享有关信息内容。如果外语教师本人无法理解,就不会把相关语类的语篇作为教材使用。如此,学生便缺失了学习并建构类似话语体系的环节。

跟语法隐喻相关的另一类现象是其背后的**思维方式**。语法隐喻对词汇语法有两个可能的结果:构成要素之间的层次性,与此伴生的是逻辑性。以(4)为例,其语法结构很简单:载体+过程+属性。其中,载体 *the argument to the contrary* 的中心(Head)是 *argument*,前面有修饰成分 *the*,后接由介词 *to* 引导的修饰成分,核心成分是 *argument*。这种多层次的逻辑关系由整个名词词组的语法功能统合,在关系过程中作载体参与者。属性部分的结构相当,中心语是 *an appeal*,后跟修饰语;修饰语的中心是 *lack*,后面还有一个介词短语在级转移后作 *synonymy* 的修饰语。如果接受定式成分(Finite)就是整个小句的中心语这一观点,那么这种最大括弧切分法带来的多层次性,最终指向的是过程成分中的定式语,从而形成一个金字塔模型。其实,其他过程类别也可做类似分析。这种方法在布龙菲尔德那里诞生,在形式语言学中广泛使用,在系统功能语言学中经由功能性获得类范畴的地位(class; Halliday 1961),跟级阶和语境发生关联,让我们认识到语法类别范畴(包括词类)的功能价值。如果缺乏功能性的统合作用,这种层析性则无法说明任何问题。我们说(4)涉及思维问题,而(2—3)同样涉及思维问题:不熟悉的学科内容是由经验知识的差异带来的;学科语言教育的任务之一就是通过语言模式了解和熟悉这些结构和组织化了的经验知识。

以层次性为着眼点,可以发现英汉语在组织上的诸多**差异**根源,这就给学习英语等欧洲语言的中国学生带来了思维方式上的障碍。例如,英汉语在语篇组织上有一个突出差别,那就是汉语的汇聚型结构关系与英语的汇聚型+发散型结构模式,以及由此带来的层次差别。如 *And as we walk we must make the pledge that we shall always march ahead*,对比:当我们行动时,我们必须保证勇往直前。在这里,英语的第二级层次有前后两个,即前后从句;但汉语的第二层次只有前面一个。事实上,英语可将从属性成分(包括词组、短语、小句甚至复句)放在一个小句或复句的前、中、后任何位置,方式有从句、品质语、嵌入句、插入语等,促成因素是语篇的衔接与连贯;典型汉语则只有从属成分+统领成分这一模式。这就是汉语的相对平面性与英语的相对多层次关系(彭宣维 2000)。不过,层次性差异还有不少,如汉语中存在无法判断是省略还是隐性被动的大量实例:车开走了、苹果吃了等;英语在类似地方有明确的语法关系标识。其实,句级阶的层次性差异是由英汉两种语言的组织类型差异带来的:汉语以主题方式组织语篇推进方式,出现平面化的流水句,如无从判断主语的非完整句、层次结构的相对单一性、连接关系的弱化、时态特征的缺乏等;英语除了主题组织,必须兼顾语句的完整性,从而表现出高度的明晰性与逻辑关系。明确认识类似差异,也是高层次英语教育的必要途径。

至此,我们概述了学科英语的一些基本共同点,这些内容足以从共性方面表明学科英语研究的基本思路及其教改的内容方向。当然,正如前文所说,梳理出不同语域的差异也是本项目的重点之一;不过,上述共性也是洞开相关差异的有效途径。

10.6　小结

从目标看,无论是专业英语还是英语专业,英语学习过程的目的都是要熟悉并逐步学会建构相关学科的知识结构与相应话语体系,最终进行熟练读写。这一点尤应成为语言学方向高层次学习者探究的基本对象。这是一项庞大的智力工程,应当成为今后我国一段时间内英语教学的重点攻坚对象,以便系统确定英语教改内容,包括英语教育的整体理念与政策制定、目的与目标的全程构拟、教学大纲的重新规划与具体设计、系列教材的研制与开发等。因此,这应该成为国家层面的任务,给予整体规划,分步实施,逐级督导;缺乏其中任何一个环节都将成为高层次职业话语发展的障碍。因此,相关研究不能削弱,高层次人才的培养,无论是数量还是质量,都亟待加强。

参考文献

Adamson, Sylvia. Literary language. In Roger Lass (ed.), *The Cambridge History of the English Language (Volume III)*. Cambridge: Cambridge University Press, 1999; Beijing: Peking University Press, 2002, pp.539 – 653.

Adler, Jill. *Teaching Mathematics in Multilingual Classrooms*. Dordrecht & Norwell: Kluwer Academic, 2001.

Agorni, Mirella. Translation teaching and methodology: a linguistic analysis of a literary text. In Donna Miller R. & Monica Turci (eds.), *Language and Verbal Art Revisited* 2007, pp.197 – 211.

Aktas, Rahime N. & Viviana Cortes. Shell nouns as cohesive devices in published and ESL student writing. *Journal of English for Academic Purposes* 2008, 1(7): 3 – 14.

Alejo, Rafael. 2010. Where does the money go? An analysis of the container metaphor in economics: the market and the economy. *Journal of Pragmatics* 2010, 42: 1137 – 1150.

Anderson, Myrdene, Adalira Sáenz-Ludlow, Shea Zellwegr & Victor V. Cifarelli (eds.) *Educational Perspectives on Mathematics as Semiosis: From Thinking to Interpreting to Knowing*. Ottawa: Legas, 2002.

Aristotle 原著, 秦典华(译), "解释篇". 苗力田(主编),《亚里士多德全集》(第一卷), 北京: 中国人民大学出版社, 1997 年, 47—80 页。

Artemeva, Natasha & Aviva Freedeman. *Genre Studies around the Globe: Beyond the*

Three Traditions. Bloomington, IN: Trafford Publishing, 2015.

Australian Curriculum. Http: //www.australiancurriculum.edu.au/? dnsi=1.

Baddeley, Alan D. *Working Memory*. Oxford: Clarendon, 1986.

Baddeley, Alan D. Memory. In Robert A. Wilson & Frank C. Keil (eds.), *The MIT Encyclopedia of the Cognitive Sciences*. Cambridge, Mass.: MIT. Shanghai: Shanghai Foreign Language and Education Press, 1999/2000, pp.514 – 517.

Baddeley, Alan D. & Graham J. Hitch. Working memory. In Gordon H. Bower (ed.), *The Psychology of Learning and Motivation: Advances in Research and Theory (Volume 8)*. New York: Academic, 1974, pp.47 – 89.

Barry, Anita K. *Linguistic Perspectives on Language and Education*. Westport, CT: Pearson, 2007.

Bateman, John A. & Cécile L. Paris. Constraining the deployment of lexicogrammatical resources during text generation: towards a computational instantiation of register theory. In Eija Ventola (ed.), *Functional and Systemic Linguistics: Approaches and Uses*. Berlin & New York: Mouton, 1991, pp.81 – 106.

Benesch, Sarah. *Critical English for Academic Purposes: Theory, Politics, and Practice*. Mahwah, NJ & London: Lawrence Erlbaum Associates, 2001.

Benson, John D. & Williams S. Greaves. The notion of technicality in register: a case study from the language of bridge. In Martin Davies & Louise Ravelli (eds.), *Advances in Systemic Linguistics: Recent Theory and Practice*. London & New York: Pinter, 1992, pp.205 – 220.

Berkenkotter, Carol & Thomas N. Nuckin. *Genre Knowledge in Disciplinary Communication: Cognitive/Culture/Power*. Hillsdale, NJ: Lawrence Erlbaum Associates, 1995.

Bernstein, Basil. *Class, Codes and Control: Volume I: Theoretical Studies towards a Sociology of Language*. London & New York: Routledge, 1971.

Bernstein, Basil. *Class, Codes and Control: Volume IV: The Structuring of Pedagogic Discourse*. London & New York: Routledge, 1990.

Bhatia, Vijay K. *Analyzing Genre: Language Use of Professional Settings*. London: Longman, 1993.

Biber, Douglas, Stig Johansson, Geoffrey Leech, Susan Conrad & Edward Finegan. *Longman Grammar of Spoken and Written English*. London: Longman, 1999.

Birch, David & Michael O'Toole (eds.). *Functions of Style*. London & New York:

Pinter, 1988.

Birner, Betty J. & Gregory Ward. *Information Status and Noncanonical Word Order in English.* Amsterdam: John Benjamins, 1998.

Blake, Norman F. *An Introduction to the Language of Literature.* London: Macmillan, 1990.

Bloomfield, Leonald. *Language.* London: Allen & Unwin, 1933/1955.

Bloor, Thomas & Meriel Bloor. *The Functional Analysis of English: A Hallidayan Approach.* London: Arnold, 1995.

Bolinger, Dwight. *Meaning and Form.* London & New York: Longman, 1977.

Bondi, Marina. *English across Genres: Language Variation in the Discourse of Economics.* Modena: Il Fiorino, 1999.

Bowcher, Wendy L. Structure and multimodal texts. In Janina Wildfeuer (ed.), *Building Bridges for Multimodal Research: International Perspectives on Theories and Practices of Multimodal Analysis.* Frankfurt: Peter Lang, 2016, pp.167 - 192.

Brazil, David. *A Grammar of Speech.* Oxford: Oxford University Press, 1995.

Brown, Roger & Albert Gilman. The pronoun of power and solidarity. In Thomas A. Sebeok (ed.), *Style in Language.* Cambridge, Mass.: MIT, 1960, pp.253 - 276.

Brown, Gillian & George Yule. *Discourse Analysis.* Cambridge: Cambridge University Press, 1983.

Brown, Gillian D. & Sally Rice. *Professional English in Use: Law.* Cambridge: Cambridge University Press, 2007.

Burton, Deirdre. Through glass darkly: through dark glasses — on stylistics and political commitment via a study of a passage from Sylvia Plath's *The Bell Jar.* In Ronald Carter (ed.), 1982, pp.195 - 214.

Bussmann, Hadumod. 1996. *Routledge Dictionary of Language and Linguistics.* London: Routledge.

Butler, Christopher S. *Structure and Function.* Amsterdam: John Benjamins, 2003.

Butt, David. Randomness, order and the latent patterning of text. In David Birch & Michael O'Toole (eds.), *Functions of Style.* London: Pinter, 1988, pp.74 - 97.

Butt, David, Rhondda Fahey, Susan Feez, Sue Spinks & Collin Yallop. *Using Functional Grammar: An Explorer's Guide* (2nd edition). Macquarie University: National Centre for English Teaching & Research, 2000.

Butt, David & Annabelle Lukin. Stylistic analysis: construing aesthetic organization. In Michael A. K. Halliday & Jonathan J. Webster (eds.), *Continuum Companion to*

参考文献

Systemic Functional Linguistics. London: Continuum, 2009, pp.190 – 215.

Butt, David, Alison Moore, Caroline Henderson-Brook, Joan Haliburn & Russell Meares. Dissociation, relatedness, and 'cohesive harmony': a linguistics measure of degree of 'fragmentation'. *Linguistics and the Human Sciences* 2007, 3(3): 263 – 293.

Caldwell, Candice. *Lexical Vagueness in Student Writing. Are Shell Nouns the Problem?* Saarbrücken: VDM Verlag, 2009.

Camiciottoli, Belinda C. *The Language of Business Studies Lectures: A Corpus-Assisted Analysis*. Amsterdam/Philadelphia: John Benjamins, 2007.

Carter, Ronald (ed.). *Language and Literature: An Introductory Reader in Stylistics*. London: George Allen & Unwin, 1982.

Chafe, Wallance L. Givenness, contrastiveness, definiteness, subject, topics, and point of view. In Charles Li (ed.), *Subject and Topic*. New York: Academic, 1976, pp.25 – 55.

Chafe, Wallance L. *Discourse, Consciousness, and Time: The Flow and Displacement of Conscious Experience in Speaking and Writing*. Chicago & London: University of Chicago Press, 1994.

Chapman, Raymond. *Linguistics and Literature: An Introduction to Literary Stylistics*. London: Edward Arnold, 1973.

Chatman, Seymour. *Story and Discourse: Narrative Structure in Fiction and Film*. Ithaca: Aornell University Press, 1978.

Christie, Francis & James R. Martin (eds.). *Genre and Institutions: Social Processes in the Workplace and School*. London & New York: Continuum, 1997.

Christie, Francis. Science and apprenticeship: the pedagogic discourse. In Martin, James R. & Robert Veel (eds.), *Reading Science: Critical and Functional Perspectives on the Discourses of Science*, 1998, pp.152 – 177.

Christie, Francis. The development of abstraction in Adolescence in subject English. In Mary J. Schleppegrell & María C. Colombi (eds.), *Developing Advanced Literacy in First and Second Language: Meaning with Power*. Mahwah, NJ & London: Lawrence Erlbaum Associates, 2002, pp.45 – 66.

Christie, Francis & Beverly Derewianka. *School Discourse: Learning to Write across the Years of Schooling*. London: Continuum, 2008.

Christie, Francis & Karl Maton. *Disciplinarity: Functional Linguistics and Sociological Perspectives*. London: Continuum/Bloomsbury, 2011.

Christie, Francis. *Language Education throughout the School Years: A Functional Perspective*. Malden, MA & Oxford: Wiley-Blackwell, 2012.

Clark, Kate. The linguistics of blame: representation of women in *The Sun*'s reporting of crimes of sexual violence. In Michael Toolan (ed.), *Language, Text and Context: Essays in Stylistics*. London & New York: Routledge, 1992, pp.208-226.

Clark, Herbert H. & Susan E. Haviland. Comprehension and the given-new contract. In Roy O. Freedle (ed.), *Discourse Production and Comprehension*. Hillsdale NJ: Erlbaum, 1977, pp.1-40.

Cloran, Carmel. *Rhetorical Units and Decontextualisation: An Enquiry into Some Relations of Context, Meaning and Grammar. Monographs in Systemic Linguistics*, 6. School of English Studies, Nottingham University, 1994.

Cloran, Carmel. Defining and relating text segments. In Ruqaiya Hasan & Peter Fries (eds.), *On Subject and Theme: A Discourse Functional Perspective*. Amsterdam: John Benjamins, 1995, pp.361-403.

Cloran, Camel. Rhetorical unit analysis and Bakhtin's chronotype. *Functions of Language* 2010, 17(1): 29-70.

Cloran, Carmel, Virginia Stuart-Smith & Lynne Young. Models of discourse. In Ruqaiya Hasan, Christian M. I. M. Matthiessen & Jonathan J. Webster (eds.), *Continuing Discourse on Language: A Functional Perspective, Volume 2*. London: Equinox, 2007, pp.647-670.

Coffin, Caroline. *Historical Discourse: The Language of Time, Cause and Evaluation*. London: Continuum, 2006.

Coffin, Caroline, Ann Hewings & Kieran O'Halloran (eds.). *Applying English Grammar: Functional and Corpus Approaches*. London: Hodder Arnold, 2004.

Conseil de L'Europe. *Common European Framework of Reference for Languages: Learning, Teaching and Assessment*. Strasbourg: Language Policy Unit. www.coe. int/lang-CEFR.刘骏、傅荣主译,《欧洲语言共同参照框架:学习、教学与评估》, 北京: 外语教学与研究出版社,2008 年。

Coote, Maria-Elisabeth, János S. Petöfi & Emel Sözer. *Text and Discourse Connectedness: Proceedings of the Conference on Connexity and Coherence, Urbino, July 16-21, 1984*. Amsterdam/Philadelphia: John Benjamins, 1989.

Corbett, Greville G. *Number*. Cambridge: Cambridge University Press, 2000.

Coulthard, Malcolm & Alison Johnson (eds.). *The Routledge Handbook of Forensic Linguistics*. London & New York: Routledge, 2013.

参考文献

Coulthard, Malcolm, Alison Johnson & David Wright. *An Introduction to Forensic Linguistics: Language in Evidence* (2nd edn.). London & New York: Routledge, 2016.

Coxhead, Averil & Paul Nation. The specialised vocabulary of English for academic purposes. In John Flowerdew & Matthew Peacock (eds.), *Research Perspectives on English for Academic Purposes*, 2001, pp.239 - 267.

Cranny-Francis, Anne. The 'science' of science fiction: a sociocultural analysis. In James R. Martin & Robert Veel (eds.), 1998, pp.63 - 80.

Cross, Marilyn. Choice in lexis: computer generation of lexis as most delicate grammar. *Language Science* 1992, 14(4): 579 - 605.

Cross, Marilyn. Collocation in computer modeling of lexis as most delicate grammar. In Mohsen Ghadessy (ed.), *Register Analysis: Theory and Practice*. London: Pinter, 1993, pp.196 - 220.

Cruse, David A. The lexicon. In Mark Aronoff & Janie Rees-Miller (eds.), *The Handbook of Linguistics*. London: Blackwell, 2001, pp.238 - 264.

Crystal, David. *The Cambridge Encyclopedia of Language*. Cambridge: Cambridge University Press, 1997.

Daneš, František. Zure linguistichen Analyse der Textstruktur. *Folia Linguistica* IV, 1970a, 72 - 78.

Daneš, František. One instance of Prague school methodology: functional analysis of utterance and text. In Paul L. Garvin (ed.), *Method and Theory in Linguistics*. The Hague: Mouton de Gruyter, 1970b, pp.132 - 141.

Daneš, František. Functional sentence perspective and the organization of the text. In František Daneš (ed.) *Papers on Functional Sentence Perspective*. Prague: Mouton, 1974, pp.106 - 128.

de Beaugrande, Robert & Wolfgang U. Dressler. *Introduction to Text Linguistics*. London: Longman, 1981.

de Oliveira, Luciana C. & Joshua Iddings. *Genre Pedagogy across the Curriculum: Theory and Application in U.S. Classrooms and Contexts*. London: Equinox, 2014.

de Saussure, Ferdinand. *Course in General Linguistics*. Tr. Roy Harris. Chicago: Open Court, 1998.

Dik, Simon C. *The Theory of Functional Grammar: Parts 1 & 2* (2nd edn.). Berlin & New York: Mouton, 1997.

Dudley-Evans, Tony & Willie Henderson (eds.). *The Language of Economics: The*

Analysis of Economics Discourse. London: MEP/British Council, 1990.

Durey, Jill. Middlemarch: the role of the functional triad in the portrayal of hero and heroine. In David Birch & Michael O'Tool (eds.), 1988, pp.234 – 248.

Ebrlich, Susan. *Point of View: A Linguistic Analysis of Literary Style*. London & New York: Routledge, 1990.

Eggins, Susanne. *An Introduction to Systemic Functional Linguistics* (1st & 2nd edn.). London: Continuum, 1994/2004.

Enkvist, Nils E. "Theme dynamics" and style: an experiment. *Studia Anglica Posnaniensia* 1973, 5(1 – 2): 127 – 135.

Enkvist, Nils E. Text and discourse linguistics, rhetoric and stylistics. In Teun A. van Dijk (ed.) *Discourse and Literature: New Approaches to the Analysis of Literary Genres*. Amsterdam: John Benjamins, 1985, pp.11 – 38.

Ericsson, K. Anders & Walter Kintsch. Long-term working memory. *Psychological Review* 1995 (2): 211 – 245.

Esteras, Santiago R. & Elena M. Fabre. *Professional English in Use: Information Communications Technology*. Cambridge: Cambridge University Press, 2007.

Fairclough, Norman. Register, power and socio-semantic change. In David Birth & Michael O'Toole (eds.), *Functions of Style*. London & New York: Pinters, 1988, pp.111 – 125.

Fairclough, Norman. *Language and Power*. London: Longman, 2001.

Fang, Zhihui & Mary J. Schleppegrell. *Reading in Secondary Content Areas: A Language-Based Pedagogy*. Ann Arbor: University of Michigan Press, 2008.

Farrall, Cate & Marianne Lindsley. *Professional English in Use: Marketing*. Cambridge: Cambridge University Press, 2008.

Fawcett, Robin. *Cognitive Linguistics and Social Interaction*. Herstellung: Groos, 1980.

Fawcett, Robin. The semantics of clause and verb for relational processes in English. In Michael A. K. Halliday & Robin Fawcett (eds.), *New Developments in Systemic Linguistics, vol. 1: Theory and Description*. London & NY: Pinter, 1987, pp.130 – 183.

Fawcett, Robin. On the subject of the Subject in English: two positions on its meaning (and on how to test for it). *Functions of Language* 1999, 6(2): 247 – 273.

Fawcett, Robin. *A Theory of Syntax for Systemic Functional Linguistics*. Amsterdam: John Benjamins, 2000.

参考文献

参考文献

Fawcett, Robin. *The Functional Semantics Handbook: Analyzing English at the Level of Meaning*. London: Equinox, forthcoming.

Firbas, Jan. On defining the theme in Functional Sentence Perspective. In Josef Vachek (ed.), *Travaux Linguistiques de Prague 1: L'école de Prague d'Aujourd'hui*. Prague: Academic Tchicoslovaque des Sciences, 1964, pp.267 – 280.

Firth, John R. The technique of semantics. In Frank R. Palmer (ed.), *Papers in Linguistics 1934 – 1951*. Oxford: Oxford University Press, 1957, 7 – 33.

Firth, John R. A synopsis of linguistic theory. *Studies in Linguistic Analysis* (Special Volume of the Philological Society). London: Blackwell, 1957, pp.1 – 32. In Frank R. Palmer (ed.), *Selected Papers of J. R. Firth 1952 – 59*. London: Longman, 1968, pp.168 – 205.

Fish, Stanley E. *Is There a Text in this Class?: The Authority of Interpretative Communities*. Cambridge, Mass.: Harvard University Press, 1980.

Fish, Stanley E. What is stylistics and why are they saying such terrible things about it? In Seymour Chatman (ed.), *Approaches to Poetics*. Columbia University Press, 1973; reprinted in Donald C. Freeman (ed.), *Essays in Modern Stylistics*. London & New York: Methuen, 1981, pp.53 – 82.

Flowerdew, John & Matthew Peacock (eds.). *Research Perspectives on English for Academic Purposes*. Cambridge: Cambridge University Press, 2001.

Fontaine, Lise, Tom Bartlett & Gerard O'Grady (eds.). *Systemic Functional Linguistics: Exploring Choice*. Cambridge: Cambridge University Press, 2013.

Forey, Gail & Geoff Thompson (eds.). *Text Type and Texture*. London: Equinox, 2008.

Fowler, Roger. *Literature as Social Discourse: The Practice of Linguistic Criticism*. London: Batsford Academic & Educational, 1981.

Francis, Gill & Anjneliese Kraner-Dahl. Grammar in the construction of medical care histories. In Caroline Coffin, Ann Hewings & Kieran O'Halloran (eds.), 2004, pp.172 – 190.

Fries, Peter. On the status of theme in English: argument from discourse. *Forum Linguisticum* 1981, 6: 1 – 38.

Fries, Peter H. Themes, methods of development, and texts. In Ruqaiya Hasan & Peter Fries (eds.), 1995a, pp.317 – 359.

Fries, Peter H. Patterns of information in initial position in English. In Peter Fries & Michael Gregory (eds.), *Discourse in Society: Systemic Functional Perspectives*,

Meaning and Choice in Language: Studies for Michael Halliday. Norwood, New Jersey: Ablex, 1995b, pp.47 – 66.

Fries, Peter. The flow of information in a written English text. In Peter Fries, Michael Cummings, David Lockwood & William Spruiell (eds.), *Relations and Functions Within and Around Language.* London & New York: Continuum, 2002, pp.117 – 155.

Fuller, Gillian. Cultivating science: negotiating discourse in the popular texts of Stephen Jay Gould. In James R. Martin & Robert Veel (eds.), *Reading Science: Critical and Functional Perspectives on Discourses of Science*, 1998, pp.35 – 62.

Gaitet, Pacale. *Political Stylistics: Popular Language as Literary Artifact.* London & New York: Routledge, 1992.

Gardiner, Michael. *The Dialogics of Critique: M. M. Bakhtin and the Theory of Ideology.* London & New York: Routledge, 1992.

Gerofsky, Susan. *A Man Left Albuquerque Heading East: Word Problems as Genre in Mathematics Education.* Frankfurt: Peter Lang, 2004.

Ghadessay, Mohsen (ed.). *Thematic Development in English Text.* London & New York: Pinter, 1995.

Giora, Rachel. Segmentation and segment cohesion: on the thematic organization of the text. *Text* 1983, 3(2): 155 – 181.

Glendinning, Eric & Ron Howard. *Professional English in Use: Medicine.* Cambridge: Cambridge University Press, 2007.

Goatly, Andrew. *The Language of Metaphors.* London: Routledge, 1997.

Goatly, Andrew. Nature and grammar. In Caroline Coffin, Ann Hewings & Kieran O'Halloran (eds.), 2004, pp.198 – 215.

Goatly, Andrew. *Explorations in Stylistics.* London: Equinox, 2008.

Goldberg, Adele E. *Constructions: A Construction Grammar Approach to Argument Structure.* Chicago: University of Chicago Press, 1995.

Green, Keith. Deixis and the poetic persona. *Language and Literature* 1992, 2: 121 – 134.

Gregory, Michael & Sussanne Carroll. *Language and Situation: Language Varieties and Their Social Contexts.* London, Henley & Boston: Routledge & Kegan Paul, 1978.

Gunnarsson, Britt-Louise, Per Linell & Bengt Nordberg (eds.). *The Construction of Professional Discourse.* London & New York: Longman, 1997.

参考文献

参考文献

Hajicova, Eva. Topic/Focus and related research. In Philip A. Luelsdorff (ed.), *The Prague School of Structural and Functional Linguistics*. Amsterdam: John Benjamins, 1994, pp.245 – 275.

Halliday, Michael A. K. Grammatical categories in modern Chinese. *Transactions of the Philological Society*, 1956, pp.177 – 224.

Halliday, Michael A. K. Categories of the theory of grammar. *Word* 1961, 17(3): 241 – 292.

Halliday, Michael A. K. The linguistic study of literary texts. In Horace G. Lunt (ed.), *Proceedings of the Ninth International Congress of Linguists*. Cambridge, MA, 1962. The Hague: Mouton, 1964a, pp.302 – 307.

Halliday, Michael A. K. Descriptive linguistics in literary studies. In Alan Duthie (ed.), *English Studies Today: Third Series*. Edinburgh: Edinburgh University Press, 1964b, pp.23 – 39.

Halliday, Michael A. K. Grammar, society and the noun. Speech given at University College London, 24 November, 1966a.

Halliday, Michael A. K. The concept of rank: a reply. *Journal of Linguistics* 1966b, 2(1): 110 – 118.

Halliday, Michael A. K. English system networks. Unpublished paper as a course material used at Indiana University in 1964; in Gunther R. Kress (ed.), 1976, pp.101 – 158.

Halliday, Michael A. K. Lexis as a linguistic level. In Charles E. Bazell, John C. Catford, Michael A. K. Halliday & Robert H. Robins (eds.), *In Memory of J. R. Firth*. London: Longman, 1966c, pp.148 – 162.

Halliday, Michael A. K. Some notes on 'deep' grammar. *Journal of Linguistics* 1966d, 2(1): 57 – 67.

Halliday, Michael A. K. Linguistics and the teaching of English. In James N. Britton (ed.), *Talking and Writing: A Handbook for English Teachers*. London: Methuen, 1967, pp.80 – 90.

Halliday, Michael A. K. Notes on transitivity and theme in English. *Journal of Linguistics* 1967, (3): 37 – 81; (4): 199 – 244; 1968, (4): 179 – 215.

Halliday, Michael A. K. Types of processes. In Gunther R. Kress (ed.), *Halliday: System and Function in Language: Selected Papers*. Oxford: Oxford University Press, 1969/1976, pp.159 – 173.

Halliday, Michael A. K. Language structures and language function. In John Lyons

(eds.), *New Horizons in Linguistics*. Harmondsworth: Penguin, 1970, pp.140 – 165.

Halliday, Michael A. K. The form of functional grammar. In Gunther R. Kress (ed.), *Halliday: System and Function in Language. Selected Papers*. Oxford: Oxford University Press, 1970/1976, pp.7 – 25.

Halliday, Michael A. K. Linguistic function and literary style: an inquiry into the language of William Golding. In Seymour Chatman (ed.), *The Inheritors. Literary Style: A Symposium*. London & New York: Oxford University Press, 1971, pp.330 – 368.

Halliday, Michael A. K. *Explorations in the Functions of Language*. London: Edward Arnold, 1973.

Halliday, Michael A. K. *Halliday: System and Function in Language*. Ed. Gunther R. Kress. Oxford: Oxford University Press

Halliday, Michael A. K. Text as Semantic Choice in Social Contexts. In Teun A. van Dijk & Jenos S. Petofi (eds.), *Grammar and Description*. Berlin: Walter de Gruyter, 1977, pp.176 – 226.

Halliday, Michael A. K. *Language as Social Semiotic: The Social Interpretation of Language and Meaning*. London: Edward Arnold, 1978a.

Halliday, Michael A. K. Is learning a second language like learning a first language all over again? In D. E. Ingrain & T. J. Quinn (eds.), *Language Learning in Australian Society: Proceedings of the 1976 Congress of the Applied Linguistics Association of Australia*. Melbourne: Australian International Press & Publications Pty, 1978b, pp.3 – 19.

Halliday, Michael A. K. Systems of the English clause: a trial grammar for the PENMAN text generation project. Information Sciences Institute, University of Southern California, 1980.

Halliday, Michael A. K. Text semantics and clause grammar: some patterns of realization. In James E. Copeland & Philip W. Davis (eds.), *The Seventh LACUS Forum*. Columbia, SC: Hornbeam Press, 1981, pp.31 – 59.

Halliday, Michael A. K. How is a text like a clause? In Stu Allen (ed.), *Text Processing: Text Analysis and Generation, Text Typology and Attribution* (Proceedings of Nobel Symposium 51). Stockholm: Almqvist & Wiksell International, 1982a, pp.209 – 247.

Halliday, Michael A. K. The de-automatization of grammar: from Priestley's *An*

参考文献

Inspector Calls. In John M. Anderson (ed.), *Language Form and Linguistic Variation: Papers Dedicated to Angus McIntosh*. Amsterdam: John Benjamins, 1982b, pp.129 – 159.

Halliday, Michael A. K. *An Introduction to Functional Grammar* (1st edn.). London: Edward Arnold, 1985.

Halliday, Michael A. K. Poetry as scientific discourse: the nuclear sections of Tennyson's ' *In Memoriam* '. In David Birch & Michael O'Tool (eds.), 1988a, 31 – 44.

Halliday, Michael A. K. On the language of physical science. In Mohsen Ghadessy (ed.), *Registers of Written English: Situational Factors and Linguistic Features*. London & New York: Pinter, 1988b, pp.162 – 178.

Halliday, Michael A. K. Language and socialization: home and school. In Linda Gerot. Jane Oldenburg & Theo van Leeuwen (eds.), *Language and Socialization, Home and School: Proceedings from the Working Conference on Language in Education*. Macquarie University, 17 – 21 November 1986; Macquarie University, 1988c, pp.1 – 14.

Halliday, Michael A. K. Some grammatical problems in scientific English. *Australian Review of Applied Linguistics* 1989, 6: 13 – 37.

Halliday, Michael A. K. New ways of meaning: the challenge to applied linguistics. *Journal of Applied Linguistics* 1990, 6: 7 – 36.

Halliday, Michael A. K. The history of a sentence. *Boogna: La Cultura Italiana e le Letterature Straniere Moderne* 1992a (30): 29 – 45.

Halliday, Michael A. K. Language as system and language as instance: the corpus as a theoretical construct. *Directions in Corpus Linguistics: Proceedings of Nobel Symposium 82*. Ed. Jan Svartvik. Berlin: Mouton de Gruyter, 1992b, pp.61 – 78.

Halliday, Michael A. K. Quantitative studies and probabilities in grammar. In Michael Hoey (ed.), *Data, Description and Discourse: Papers on the English Language in Honour of John M. Sinclair on His Sixtieth Birthday*. London: Harper Collins, 1993a, pp.1 – 25.

Halliday, Michael A. K. General orientation to *Writing Science: Literacy and Discursive Power*. In Michael A. K. Halliday & James R. Martin (ed.), *Writing Science: Literacy and Discursive Power*. London & Washington D.C.: The Falmer Press, 1993b, pp.2 – 24.

Halliday, Michael A. K. *An Introduction to Functional Grammar* (2nd edn.).

London: Edward Arnold, 1994. 彭宣维等译,功能语法导论(第二版),北京:外语教学与研究出版社,2010 年。

Halliday, Michael A. K. Computing meanings: some reflections on past experience and present prospects. *Journal of Japan Society for Fuzzy Theory and Systems* 1995a (5): 23 – 42.

Halliday, Michael A. K. Language and the reshaping of human experience. In Bessie Dendrinos (ed.), *Proceedings of the Fourth International Symposium on Critical Discourse Analysis*. Athens: University of Athens Press, 1995b, pp.19 – 32.

Halliday, Michael A. K. Linguistics as metaphor. In Anne-Marie Simon-Vandenbergen, Kristin Davidse & Dirk Noel (eds.), *Reconnecting Language: Morphology and Syntax in Functional Perspectives*. Amsterdam: John Benjamins, 1997, pp.3 – 27.

Halliday, Michael A. K. Things and relations: regrammaticizing experience as technical knowledge. In James R. Martin & Robert Veel (eds.), *Reading Science: Critical and Functional Perspectives on Discourses of Science*, 1998a, pp.185 – 235.

Halliday, Michael A. K. Language and knowledge: the "unpacking" of text. In Desmond Allison, Lionel W. B. Zhiming & Sunita A. Abraham (eds.), *Text in Education and Society*. Singapore: Singapore University Press & World Scientific, 1998b, pp.157 – 178.

Halliday, Michael A. K. The grammatical construction of scientific knowledge: the framing of the English clause. In Rema R. Favretti, Giorgio Sandi & Roberto Scazzieri (eds.), *Incommensurability and Translation: Kuhnian Perspectives on Scientific Communication and Theory Change*. Cheltenham: Edward Elgar, 1999, pp.85 – 116.

Halliday, Michael A. K. Is the grammar neutral? Is the grammarian neutral? In Jessica de Villiers & Robert J. Stainton (eds.), *Communication in Linguistics, Volume 1: Papers in Honour of Michael Gregory*. Toronto: Editions du Gref, 2001, pp.179 – 204.

Halliday, Michael A. K. *Linguistic Studies of Text and Discourse, Volume 2 in the Collected Works of M. A. K. Halliday.* Ed. Jonathan J. Webster. London: Continuum, 2002.

Halliday, Michael A. K. Toward a sociological semantics. In Jonathan J. Webster (ed.), *On Language and Linguistics.* London: Continuum, 2003a, pp.238 – 239.

Halliday, Michael A. K. *On Language and Linguistics, Volume 3 in the Collected*

Works of M. A. K. Halliday. Ed. Jonathan J. Webster. London: Continuum, 2003b.

Halliday, Michael A. K. *The Language of Science, Volume 5 in the Collected Works of M. A. K. Halliday.* Ed. Jonathan R. Webster. London: Continuum, 2004.

Halliday, Michael A. K. *Computational and Quantitative Studies, Volume 6 in the Collected Works of M. A. K. Halliday.* Ed. Jonathan R. Webster. London: Continuum, 2005a.

Halliday, Michael A. K. *Studies in English Language, Volume 7 in the Collected Works of M. A. K. Halliday.* Ed. Jonathan J. Webster. London: Continuum, 2005b.

Halliday, Michael A. K. The notion of "context" in language education. In Jonathan J. Webster (ed.), *Language and Education, Volume 9 in the Collected Works of M. A. K. Halliday.* London: Continuum, 2007a, pp.269 - 290.

Halliday, Michael A. K. *Language and Education, Volume 9 in the Collected Works of M. A. K. Halliday.* Ed. Jonathan J. Webster. London: Continuum, 2007b.

Halliday, Michael A. K. *The Complementarities of Language.* Beijing: The Commercial Press, 2008.

Halliday, Michael A. K. *Halliday in the 21st Century.* Ed. Jonathan R. Webster. London: Bloomsbury, 2013.

Halliday, Michael A. K., Angus McIntosh & Peter Strevens. *The Linguistic Sciences and Language Teaching.* London: Longmans, 1964.

Halliday, Michael A. K. & Christian M. I. M. Matthiessen. *Construing Experience Through Meaning: A Language-Based Approach to Cognition.* London: Continuum, 1999.

Halliday, Michael A. K. & Christian M. I. M. Matthiessen. *An Introduction to Functional Grammar* (3rd edn.). London: Edward Arnold, 2004.

Halliday, Michael A. K. & Christian M. I. M. Matthiessen. *Halliday's Introduction to Functional Grammar* (4th edn.). London: Routledge, 2014.

Halliday, Michael A. K. & Ruqaiya Hasan. *Cohesion in English.* London: Longman, 1976.

Halliday, Michael A. K. & Jonathan J. Webster. *Text Linguistics: The How and Why of Meaning.* London: Equinox, 2014.

Hancock, Braig. *Meaning-Centered Grammar: An Introductory Text.* London: Equinox, 2005.

Hasan, Ruqaiya. Linguistics and the study of literary texts. *Edudes de Linguistique Appliquee* 1967, (5): 106 - 115.

Hasan, Ruqaiya. Text in the systemic-functional model. In Wolfgang U. Dressler (ed.), *Current Trends in Textlinguistics.* Berlin & New York: Walter de Gruyter, 1978, pp.228 - 246.

Hasan, Ruqaiya. On the notion of text. In János S. Petöfi (ed.), *Text vs. Sentence: Basic Questions of Textlinguistics.* Hamburg: Helmet Buske, 1979, pp.369 - 390.

Hasan, Ruqaiya. Coherence and cohesive harmony. In James Food (ed.), *Understanding Reading Comprehension.* Delaware: International Reading Association, 1984, pp.181 - 219.

Hasan, Ruqaiya. The structure of a text. In Michael A. K. Halliday & Ruqaiya Hasan (ed.), *Language, Context, and Text: Aspects of Language in a Social-Semiotic Perspective.* Geelong, Vic.: Deakin University Press, 1985a, pp.52 - 69.

Hasan, Ruqaiya. The texture of a text. In Michael A. K. Halliday & Ruqaiya Hasan (ed.), *Language, Context, and Text: Aspects of Language in a Social-Semiotic Perspective.* Geelong, Vic.: Deakin University Press, 1985b, pp.70 - 96.

Hasan, Ruqaiya. *Linguistics, Language and Verbal Art.* Melbourne: Deakin University, 1985c.

Hasan, Ruqaiya. The grammarian's dream: lexis as most delicate grammar. In Michael A. K. Halliday & Robin Fawcett (eds.), *New Developments in Systemic Linguistics: Theory and Application.* London: Pinter, 1987, pp.183 - 211.

Hasan, Ruqaiya. The analysis of one poem: theoretical issues in practice. In David Birch & Michael O'Toole (eds.), *Functions of Style,* 1988, pp.45 - 73.

Hasan, Ruqaiya. Contexts for meaning. *Language, Communication and Social Meaning.* In James E. Alatis (ed.), *Georgetown University Round Table on Languages and Linguistics.* Washington: Georgetown University Press, 1993, pp.79 - 103.

Hasan, Ruqaiya. Situation and the definition of genre. In Allen D. Grimshaw (eds.), *What's Going on Here? Complementary Studies of Professional Talk.* Norwood, NJ: Ablex, 1994, pp.127 - 167.

Hasan, Ruqaiya. The conception of context in text. In Peter H. Fries & Michael Gregory (eds.), *Discourse in Society: Systemic Functional Perspective: Meaning and Choice in Language: Studies for Michael Halliday.* Norwood, NJ: Ablex, 1995: 183 - 283.

Hasan, Ruqaiya. Speaking with reference to context. In Mohsen Ghadessy (ed.), *Text and Context in Functional Linguistics.* Amsterdam: John Benjamins, 1999, pp.219 - 328.

Hasan, Ruqaiya. The uses of talk. In Srikant Sarangi & Malcolm Coulthard (eds.), *Discourse and Social Life*. London: Longman, 2000, pp.28 - 47.

Hasan, Ruqaiya. Understanding talk: directions from Bernstein's sociology. *International Journal of Social Research Methodology: Theory and Practice* 2001, 4(1): 5 - 9.

Hasan, Ruqaiya. Private pleasure, public discourse: reflections on engaging with literature. In Donna Miller R. & Monica Turci (eds.), *Language and Verbal Art Revisited*, 2007, pp.13 - 40.

Hasan, Ruqaiya. *Language and Education: Learning and Teaching in Society*. London: Equinox, 2011.

Hasan, Ruqaiya. *Context in the System and Process of Language: Volume 4 in the Collected Works of Ruqaiya Hasan*. Ed. Jonathan J. Webster. London: Equinox, 2016.

Hasan, Ruqaiya. *Verbal Art: A Social Semiotic Perspective, Volume 7 in the Collected Works of Ruqaiya Hasan*. Ed. Jonathan J. Webster. London: Equinox, *forthcoming*.

Hasan Ruqaiya & Peter Fries (eds.). *On Subject and Theme: A Discourse Functional Perspective*. Amsterdam: John Benjamins, 1995.

Hastert, Marie P. & Jean J. Weber. Power and mutuality in Middlemarch. In Michael Toolan (ed.), *Language, Text and Context: Essays in Stylistics*. London & New York: Routledge, 1992, pp.163 - 178.

Haynes, John. *Introducing Stylistics*. London, Boston, Sydney, Wellington: Unwin Hyman, 1989.

Hengeveld, Kees & J. Lachlan Mackenzie. *Functional Discourse Grammar: A Typologically-Based Theory of Language Structure*. Oxford: Oxford University Press, 2008.

Hill, Archibald A. *Introduction to Linguistic Structures*. New York: Harcourt, Brace & Company, 1958.

Hillier, Hilary. Researching the grammar of a 'literary' text. In Caroline Coffin, Ann Hewings & Kieran O'Halloran (eds.), 2004, pp.117 - 133.

Hjelmslev, Louis. *Prolegomena to a Theory of Language*. Tr. Francis J. Whitfield. Madison: University of Wisconsin Press, 1943/1961.

Hockett, Charles F. *A Course in Modern Linguistics*. New York: Macmillan, 1958.

Hoey, Michael. *On the Surface of Discourse*. London: Allen & Unwin, 1983.

Hoey, Michael. *Patterns of Lexis in Text*. Oxford: Oxford University Press, 1991a.

Hoey, Michael. Another perspective on coherence and cohesive harmony. In Eija Ventola (ed.), *Functional and Systemic Linguistics: Approaches and Uses*. Berlin & New York: Mouton de Gruyter, 1991b, pp.385 – 414.

Hoey, Michael. *Textual Interaction: An Introduction to Written Discourse Analysis*. London: Routledge, 2001.

Hoey, Michael. *Lexical priming: A New Theory of Words and Language*. London: Routledge, 2005.

Hoey, Michael. *Text, Discourse and Corpora: Theory and Analysis*. London: Continuum, 2007.

Huckin, Thomas N. & Leslie A. Olsen. *Technical Writing and Professional Communication: For Nonnative Speakers of English* (2nd edn.). New York & London: McGraw-Hill, 1991.

Hunston, Susan. *Corpus Approach to Evaluation*. London: Routledge, 2013.

Hunston, Susan & Gill Francis. *Pattern Grammar: A Corpus-Driven Approach to the Lexical Grammar of English*. Amsterdam: John Benjamins, 2000.

Hunston, Susan & Geoff Thompson. *Evaluation in Text*. Oxford: Oxford University Press, 2000.

Hutchinson, Tom & Alan Waters. *English for Specific Purposes*. Cambridge: Cambridge University Press, 1987.

Hyland, Ken. *Disciplinary Discourses: Social Interactions in Academic Writing*. Michigan: University of Michigan Press, 2004.

Hyland, Ken. *English for Academic Purposes: An Advanced Resource Book*. London & New York: Routledge, 2006.

Hyland, Ken. *Academic Discourse: English in a Global Context*. London: Continuum, 2009.

Hyland, Ken. *Disciplinary Identities: Individuality and Community in Academic Discourse*. Cambridge: Cambridge University Press, 2012.

Hyland, Ken. & Philip Shaw. *The Routledge Handbook of English for Academic Purposes*. London: Routledge, 2016.

Ibbotson, Mark. *Professional English in Use: Engineering with Answers: Technical English for Professionals*. Cambridge: Cambridge University Press, 2009.

Jespersen, Otto. *The Philosophy of Grammar*. London: Allen & Unwin, 1924.

Jespersen, Otto. *A Modern English Grammar* (volumes I – VII). Copenhagen: Ejnar

Munksgaard, 1940 – 1949.

Ji, Yinglin & Dan Shen. Transitivity and mental transformation in Shella Watson's *The Double Hook. Language and Literature* 2004, (4): 335 – 348.

Johnson, Mark. *The Bodies in the Mind: The Bodily Basis of Meaning, Imagination, and Reason.* Chicago & London: University of Chicago Press, 1987.

Joos, Martin. *The Five Clocks: A Linguistic Excursion into the Five Styles of English Usage,* with introduction by Albert H. Marckwardt. New York: Harcourt, Brace & World, Inc., 1967.

Kennedy, C. Systemic grammar and its use in literary analysis. In Ronald Carter (ed.), *Language and Literature: An Introductory Reader in Stylistics.* London: George Allen & Unwin, 1982, pp.83 – 99.

Kibbee, Douglas A. *Language and the Law: Linguistic Inequality in America.* Cambridge: Cambridge University Press, 2016.

Kies, Daniel. Marked theme with and without pronominal reinforcement: their meaning and distribution in discourse. In Erich H. Steiner & Robert Veltman (eds.), *Pragmatics, Discourse and Text: Some Systemically Inspired Approaches.* London: Pinter, 1988, pp.47 – 97.

Kintsch, Walter, Vimla L. Patel & Anders K. Ericsson. The role of long-term working memory in text comprehension. *Psychologia* 1999 (4): 186 – 198.

Kress, Gunther R. Textual matters: the social effectiveness of style. In David Birch & Michael O'Tool (eds.), 1988, 127 – 141.

Kurdali, Bader. *Across-Disciplinary Variations: A Systemic Functional Perspective.* Saarbrucken: Lap lambert Academic, 2014.

Labov, William & Joshua Waletsky. Narrative analysis: Oral versions of personal experience. *Journal of Narrative and Life History* 1967, 7: 3 – 38.

Lakoff, George & Mark Johnson. *Metaphors We Live By.* Chicago: University of Chicago, 1980/2003.

Lakoff, George. *Women, Fire and Dangerous Things: What Categories Reveal About the Mind.* Chicago: University of Chicago Press, 1987.

Lakoff, George & Mark Johnson. *Philosophy in the Flesh: the Embodied Mind and Its Challenge to Western Thought.* New York: Basic Books, 1999.

Lamb, Sidney M. *Outline of Stratificational Grammar.* Washington, D. C.: Georgetown University Press, 1966.

Lamb, Sidney M. *Pathways of the Brain.* Amsterdam: John Benjamins, 1999.

Lamberts, Koen & David R. Shanks (eds.). *Knowledge, Concepts and Categories.* Cambridge, Mass.: The MIT Press, 1997.

Lambrecht, Koen. *Information Structure and Sentence Form: Topic, Focus, and the Mental Representations of Discourse Referents.* Cambridge: Cambridge University Press, 1994.

Langacker, Ronald W. *Foundations of Cognitive Grammar, Volume I: Theoretical Prerequisites.* Stanford: Stanford University Press, 1987.

Langacker, Ronald W. *Foundations of Cognitive Grammar, Volume II: Descriptive Application.* Stanford: Stanford University Press, 1991.

Langacker, Ronald W. *Cognitive Grammar: A Basic Introduction.* Oxford: Oxford University Press, 2008.

Leaver, Betty L. & Boris Shekhtman. *Developing Professional-Level Language Proficiency.* Cambridge: Cambridge University Press, 2002.

Lee, Debra S., Charles Hall & Susan Barone. *American Legal English: Using Language in Legal Contexts* (2nd edn.). Cambridge: Cambridge University Press, 2007.

Leech, Geoffrey N. *Principles of Pragmatics.* London: Longman, 1983.

Leech, Geoffrey N. & Mick Short. *Style in Fiction: A Linguistic Introduction to English Fictional Prose.* London & New York: Longman, 1981.

Lemke, Jay L. *The Topology of Genre.* Unpublished manuscript, 1987.

Levelt, Willem J. M. *Speaking: From Intention to Articulation.* Cambridge, Mass.: The MIT Press, 1989.

Longacre, Robert E. The paragraph as a grammatical unit. In Talmy Givón. (ed.), *Syntax and Semantics, Volume 12: Discourse and Syntax.* New York: Academic Press, 1979, pp.115 – 133.

Longacre, Robet E. *The Grammar of Discourse* (2nd edn.). New York: Springer Verlag, 2007.

Lu, Peih-ying & John Corbett. *English in Medical Education: An Intercultural Approach to Teaching Language and Values.* Bristol: Multilingual Matters, 2012.

Lukin, Annabelle. What do texts do? The context-construing work of news. In Geoff Thompson (ed.), Special Issue of *Text and Talk* 2013, (4 – 5): 523 – 552.

Lukin, Annabelle. Language and society, context and text: the contributions of Ruqaiya Hasan. *Society in Language, Language in Society: Essays in Honour of Ruqaiya Hasan.* Eds. Wendy L. Bowcher & Jennifer Yameng Liang. London:

Palgrave Macmillan, 2016, pp.143 - 165.

MacKenzie, Ian. *Professional English in Use: Finance*. Cambridge: Cambridge University Press, 2006.

Macleod, Norman. Lexicogrammar and the reader: three examples from Dickens. In Michael Toolan (ed.), *Language, Text and Context: Essays in Stylistics*. London & New York: Routledge, 1992, pp.138 - 157.

Martin, James R. How many speech acts? *University of East Anglia Papers in Linguistics* 1981, (14 - 15): 52 - 77.

Martin, James R. Language, register and genre. In Francis Christie (ed.), *Children Writing: Reader*. Geelong, Vic.: Denkin University Press, 1984, pp.21 - 30.

Martin, Jimes R. *English Text: System and Structure*. Amsterdam/Philadelphia: John Benjamins, 1992.

Martin, James R. Technicality and abstraction: language for the creation of specialized texts. In Michael A. K. Halliday & James R. Martin (ed.), *Writing Science: Literacy and Discourse Power*. London & Washington D.C.: The Falmer Press, 1993, pp.223 - 241.

Martin, James R. Text and clause: fractal resonance. *Text* 1995, 15(1): 5 - 42.

Martin, James R. Types of structure: deconstructing notions of constituency in clause and text. In Eduard H. Hovy & Donia H. Scott (eds.), *Computational and Conversational Discourse: Burning Issues: An Interdisciplinary Account*. Heidelberg, New York, Dordrecht & London: Springer-Verlag, 1996, pp.39 - 66.

Martin, James R. From little things big things grow: ecogenesis in school geography. In Richard Coe, Lorelei Lingard & Tatiana Teslenko (eds.), *The Rhetoric and Ideology of Genre: Strategies for Stability and Change*. New York: Hampton Press, 2002, pp.243 - 271.

Martin, James R. Genre, ideology and intertextuality: a systemic functional perspective. *Linguistics and Human Sciences* 2006, (2): 275 - 298.

Martin, James R. *Genre Studies, Volume 3 in the Collected Works of J. R. Martin*. Ed. Wang Zhenhua. Shanghai: Shanghai Jiaotong University Press, 2012a.

Martin, James R. *Language in Education, Volume 7 in the Collected Works of J. R. Martin*. Ed. Wang Zhenhua. Shanghai: Shanghai Jiaotong University Press, 2012b.

Martin, James R. (ed.). *Interviews with M. A. K. Halliday: Language Turned Back on Himself*. London: Bloomsbury, 2013.

Martin, James R., Peter Wignell & Suzanne Eggins. The discourse of geography:

ordering and explaining the experiential world. *Linguistics and Education* 1989, 1(4): 359 – 392.

Martin, James R., Suzanne Eggins & Peter Wignell. The discourse of history: distancing and recoverable past. In M. Ghadessy (ed.), *Register Analysis: Theory and Practice*. London & New York: Pinter, 1993, pp.95 – 109.

Martin, James R., Christian M. I. M. Matthiessen & Clare Painter. *Working with Functional Grammar*. London: Edward Arnold, 1997.

Martin, James R. & Peter White. *The Language of Evaluation: Appraisal in English*. Hampshire & New York: Macmillan, 2005.

Martin, James R. & David Rose. *Working with Discourse: Meaning beyond the Clause* (2nd edition). London: Bloomsbury, 2007.

Martin, James R. & David Rose. *Learning to Write, Reading to Learn: Genre, Knowledge and Pedagogy in the Sydney School*. London: Equinox, 2008.

Martin, James R. & Robert Veel (eds.). *Reading Science: Critical and Functional Perspectives on Discourse of Science*. London & New York: Routledge, 1998.

Mathesius, Vilém. Functional linguistics. Tr. Libuse Duskova. In Josef Vachek & Libuse Duskova (eds.), *Praguiana: Some Basic and Less Known Aspects of the Prague Linguistic School*. Amsterdam: John Benjamins, 1929/1983: 121 – 142.

Mathesius, Vilém. On the so-called Actual Division of Sentence. 张惠芹、武爱华、于淑杰译,朱威华校,王福祥、白春仁编,《话语语言学论文集》,北京: 外语教学与研究出版社,1939/1989 年,10—17 页。

Mathesius, Vilém. *A Functional Analysis of Present Day English on A General Linguistic Basis*. Ed. Josef Vachek. Tr. Libuse Duskova. The Hague, Paris: Mouton, 1975.

Matthews, Peter H. *Morphology* (2nd edn.). Cambridge: Cambridge University Press, 1991.

Matthiessen, Christian M. I. M. Lexico(grammatical) choice in text generation. In Cecile Paris, Wiliam Swartout & William C. Mann (eds.), *Natural Language Generation in Artificial Intelligence and Computational Linguistics*. Kluwer, Boston: Dordrecht, 1991, pp.249 – 292.

Matthiessen, Christian M. I. M. Construing processes of consciousness: from the commonsense model to the uncommonsense model of cognitive science. In James R. Martin & Robert Veel (eds.), 1998, pp.327 – 356.

Matthiessen, Christian M. I. M. The system of TRANSITIVITY: an exploratory study of text-based profiles. *Functions of Language* 1999, 6(1): 1 – 51.

Matthiessen, Christian M. I. M. Lexicogrammar in systemic functional linguistics: descriptive and theoretical developments in the 'IFG' tradition since 1970s. In Ruqaiya Hasan, Christian M. I. M. Matthiessen & Jonathan J. Webster. (eds.), *Continuing Discourse on Language: A Functional Perspective*, vol. 2. London: Equinox, 2007, pp.765 – 858.

Matthiessen, Christian M. I. M. Appliable discourse analysis. In Yan Fang & Jonathan J. Webster (eds.), *Developing Systemic Functional Linguistics: Theory and Application*. London: Equinox, 2013, pp.138 – 208.

Matthiessen, Christian M. I. M. Applying systemic functional linguistics in healthcare contexts. *Text & Talk* 2013, 33(4 – 5): 437 – 466.

Matthiessen, Christian M. I. M., Kazuhiro Teruya & Marvin Lam. *Key Terms in Systemic Functional Linguistics*. London: Continuum, 2010.

Mcgregor, William. The concept of rank in systemic linguistics. In Eija Ventola (ed.), *Functional and Systemic Linguistics: Approaches and Uses*. Berlin & New York: Mouton de Gruyter, 1991, pp.121 – 138.

Mckeown, Authur & Ros Wright. *Professional English in Use: Management*. Cambridge: Cambridge University Press, 2011.

Mead, George H. *The Philosophy of the Present*. New York: Prometheus Books, 1932/2002.

Miller, Donna R. & Monica Turci (eds.). *Language and Verbal Art Revisited: Linguistic Approaches to the Study of Literature*. London: Equinox, 2007.

Miller, Jim. *Semantics and Syntax: Parallels and Connection*. Cambridge: Cambridge University Press, 1985.

Mitchell, Terence F. The language of buying and selling in Cyrenaica: a situational statement. *Hesperis* 1957, 26: 31 – 72.

Moschkovich, Judit (ed.). *Research on Language and Mathematics Education: Multiple Perspectives, Challenges, and New Directions*. Charlotte, NC: Information Age Publishing, 2010.

Nash, Walter. On a passage from Lawrence's 'Odour of Chrysanthemums'. In Ronald Carter (ed.), *Language and Literature: an Introductory Reader in Stylistics*. Allen & Unwin, 1982, pp.101 – 120.

Nesbitt, Christopher & Guenter A. Plum. Probabilities in a systemic grammar: the clause complex in English. In Robin Fawcett & David Young (eds.), *New*

Developments in Systemic Linguistics. London: Pinter, 1988, pp.6 – 38.

O'Grady, Grady, Tom Bartlett & Lise Fontaine (eds.). *Choice in Language: Applications in Text Analysis.* London: Equinox, 2013.

O'Halloran, Kay L. Classroom discourse in mathematics: a multisemiotic analysis. *Linguistics and Education* 2000, 10(3): 359 – 388.

O'Toole, Michael. Henry Reed, and what follows the 'naming of parts'. In David Birch & Michael O'Tool (eds.), 1988, pp.12 – 30.

Pace-Sigge, Michael. *Lexical Priming in English Usage.* Houndmills, Basingstoke Hampshire & New York: Palgrave Macmillan, 2013.

Pearsall, Judy. *The New Oxford Dictionary of English.* Oxford: Clarendon, 1998.

Pearson. David. Imagery and the visuo-spatial sketchpad. In Jackie Andrade (ed.), *Working Memory in Perspective.* Hove: Psychology Press, 2001, pp.33 – 59.

Peng, Xuanwei (彭宣维). *A Comprehensive Comparison between English and Chinese* (英汉语篇综合对比). Shanghai: Shanghai Foreign Language Education Press, 2000.

Peng, Xuanwei (彭宣维). The Pro-form System in Chinese: a systemic functional account of rank status, scope of typicality and semantic classification (代词的语篇语法属性、范围及其语义功能分类). *Language Teaching and Research* 2005, (1): 56 – 65.

Peng, Xuanwei (彭宣维). *An Introduction to Language and Linguistics: Chinese Systemic Functional Grammar* (语言与语言学概论: 汉语系统功能语法). Beijing: Peking University Press, 2011.

Peng, Xuanwei (彭宣维). Halliday in China: legacies and advances from LUO, WANG and beyond. In Jonathan R. Webster (ed.), *Continuum Companion to M. A. K. Halliday.* London: Bloomsbury, 2015a, pp.62 – 71.

Peng, Xuanwei (彭宣维). *Appraisal Stylistics* (评价文体学). Beijing: Peking University Press, 2015b.

Pike, Kenneth L. & Evelyn G. Pike. *Text and Tagmeme.* Norwood, NJ: Ablex, 1983.

Pimm, David. *Speaking Mathematically: Communication in Mathematics Classrooms.* London: Routledge and Kegan Paul, 1987.

Poyton, Cate M. *Address and the Semiotics of Social Relations: A Systemic-Functional Account of Address Forms and Practices in Australian English.* Ph.D. Dissertation, Department of Linguistics, University of Sydney, 1990.

Prince, Ellen F. Toward a taxonomy of given/new information. In Peter Cole (ed.),

Radical Pragmatics. New York: Academic Press, 1981, pp.223 – 255.

Prince, Gerald. *Dictionary of Narratology*. Lincoln & London: University of Nebraska Press, 1989.

Quirk, Randolph, Sidney Greenbaum, Geoffrey Leech & Jan Svartvik. *A Comprehensive Grammar of the English Language*. London: Longman, 1985.

Rashidi, Linda S. Toward an understanding of the notion of Theme: an example from Dari. In Martin Davies & Louise Ravelli (eds.), *Advances in Systemic Linguistics: Recent Theory and Practice*. London & New York: Pinter, 1992, pp.189 – 204.

Robins, Robert H. *A Short History of Linguistics* (4th edition). London & New York: Longman, 1997.

Rata, Georgeta, Florin Sala & Ionel Samfira. *Agricultural English*. Cambridge: Cambridge Scholar Publishing, 2012.

Ravelli, Louise J. & Robert A. Ellis (eds.). *Analysing Academic Writing: Contextual Frameworks*. London & New York: Continuum, 2005.

Ricoeur, Paul. *Time and Narrative (Volume 1)*. Tr. Kathleen McLaughlin & David Pellauer. Chicago: University of Chicago Press, 1983.

Romaine, Susanne. *The Cambridge History of the English Language, Volume IV, 1776 – 1997*. Cambridge: Cambridge University Press, 1998.

Rose, David. Science discourse and industrial hierarchy. In James R. Martin & Robert Veel (eds.), 1998, pp.236 – 265.

Rose, David & James R. Martin. *Learning to Writing, Reading to Learn: Genre, Knowledge and Pedagogy in the Sydney School*. London: Equinox, 2012.

Rothkegel, Annely. *Text Knowledge and Object Knowledge*. London & New York: Pinter, 1993.

Ryder, Mary E. Smoke and mirrors: event patterns in the discourse structure of a Roman novel. *Journal of Pragmatics* 1999, (8): 1067 – 1080.

Samuels, Warren J. (ed.). *Economics as Discourse: An Analysis of the Language of Economists*. Boston: Kluwer, 1990.

Schleppegrell, Mary J. The linguistic challenges of mathematics teaching and learning. *Reading and Writing Quarterly* 2007, 23: 139 – 159.

Schegloff, Imanuel. *Sequence Organisation in Interaction: A Primer in Conversation Analysis*. Cambridge: Cambridge University Press, 2007.

Schleppegrell, Mary J., Stacey Greer & Ssarah Taylor. Literacy in history: language and meaning. *Australian Journal of Language and Literacy* 2008, 31 (2):

174 – 187.

Schmid, Hans-Jörg. *English Abstract Nouns as Conceptual Shells: From Corpus to Cognition*. Berlin: Mouton de Gruyter, 2000.

Sgall, Petr, Eva Hajicova & Jarmila Panevova. *The Meaning of the Sentence in Its Semantic and Pragmatic Aspects*. Ed. Jacob L. Mey. Dordrecht, Boston, Lancaster, Tokyo: Reidel, 1986.

Shen, Dan. Internal contrast and double decoding: transitivity in Hughes's 'On the Road'. *JLS: Journal of Literary Semantics* 2007, 36: 53 – 70.

Shibatani, Masayoshi. Voice. In Ronal E. Asher (ed.), *The Encyclopedia of Language and Linguistics* (Volume 9). Oxford, New York: Seoul & Tokyo: Pergamon, 1994.

Shibatani, Masayoshi (ed.). *The Grammar of Causation and Interpersonal Manipulation*. Amsterdam: Benjamins, 2001.

Short, Mick. *Exploring the Language of Poems, Plays and Prose*. London: Longman, 1996.

Simpson, Paul & Martin Montgomery. Language, literature and film: the stylistics of Bernard MacLaverty's *Cal*. In Peter Verdonk & Jean J. Weber (eds.), *Twentieth Century Fiction: From Text to Context*. London: Routledge, 1995, pp.138 – 164.

Slade, Diana, Hermine Scheeres, Marie Manidis, Rick Iedema, Rpger Dunston, Jane Stein-Parbury, Christian M. I. M. Matthiessen, M. Herke & J. McGregor. Emergency communication: the discursive challenges facing emergency clinicians and patients in hospital emergency departments. *Discourse & Communication* 2008, 2(3): 271 – 298.

Sperber, Dan & Wilson Deirdre. *Relevance: Communication and Cognition* (2nd edn.). Oxford/Cambridge: Blackwell.

Sriniwass, Sridevi. *Knowledge Construction in the Genre of Chemistry Textbooks: A Systemic Functional Perspective* (Parts 1 & 2). Saarbrucken: VDM Verlag Dr. Müller, 2010.

Stoddard, Sally. *Text and Texture: Patterns of Cohesion*. Norwood, NJ: Ablex. 1991.

Strevens, Peter. ESP after twenty year: a re-appraisal. In Makhan Tickoo (ed.), *ESP: State of the Art*. Singapore: SEAMEO Regional Language Centre, 1988, pp.1 – 13.

Stubbs, Michael. Human and inhuman geography. In Caroline Coffin, Ann Hewings & Kieran O'Halloran (eds.), 2004, pp.247 – 274.

参考文献

Subramaniam, Ganakumaran. *Ideological Stylistics and Fictional Discourse*. Newcastle upon Tyne: Cambridge Scholars Publishing, 2008.

Sun, Li. (孙骊). English subject-verb concord: an overview,《外语教学与研究》, 1979 年第 1 期,13—20 页。

Swales, John. *Genre Analysis: English in Academic and Research Settings*. Cambridge: Cambridge University Press, 1990.

Taglicht, Josef. *Message and Emphasis: On Focus and Scope in English*. London: Longman, 1984.

Talmy, Leonard. *Toward a Cognitive Semantics (Volume a & b)*. Cambridge, Mass.: The MIT Press, 2001.

Thompson, Geoff. *Introducing Functional Grammar* (1st edn.). London: Edward Arnold, 1996.

Thompson, Geoff. *Introducing Functional Grammar* (2nd edn.). London: Taylor & Francis, 2004.

Thompson, Geoff. *Introducing Functional Grammar* (3rd edn.). London: Routledge, 2013.

Threadgold, Terry. Stories of race and gender: an unbounded discourse. In David Birch & Michael O'Toole (eds.), 1988, pp.169–204.

Toolan, Michael. Poem, reader, response: making sense with *Skunk Hour*. In Colin E. Nicholson & Ranjit Chaterjee (eds.), *Tropic Crucible: Self and Theory in Language and Literature*. Singapore: Singapore University Press, 1986, pp.84–97.

Toolan, Michael. Compromising positions: systemic linguistics and the locally managed semiotics of dialogue. In D. Birch & Michael O'Toole (eds.), 1988, pp.249–260.

Traugott, Elizabeth C. From propositional to textual and expressive meanings: some semantic-pragmatic aspects of grammaticalization. In Winfred P. Lehmann & Yakov Malkiel (eds.), *Perspectives on Historical Linguistics*. Amsterdam: John Benjamins, 1982, pp.245–271.

Traugott, Elizabeth C. Syntax. In Richard M. Hogg (ed.), *The Cambridge History of the English Language* (Volume I). Cambridge: CUP; Beijing: Peking University Press, 2002, pp.168–289.

Tribe, Keith. *The Economy of the Word: Language, History and Economics*. Oxford: Oxford University Press, 2015.

Tsui, Amy B. M. *English Conversation*. Oxford: Oxford University Press, 1994.

Tucker, Gordon. *The Lexicogrammar of Adjectives: A Systemic Functional Approach to Lexis*. London: Cassell, 1997.

Tucker, Gordon. Between lexis and grammar: towards a systemic functional approach to phraseology. In Ruqaiya Hasan, Christian M. I. M. Matthiessen & Jonathan J. Webster (eds.), *Continuing Discourse on Language: A Functional Perspective, Volume 2*. London: Equinox, 2007, pp.953 - 977.

Turner, George W. *Stylistics*. London: Penguin Books, 1973.

van Dijk, Teun. *Macro-Structures*. Hillsdale, NJ: Erlbaum. 1979.

Veel, R. The greening of school science: ecogenesis in secondary classroom. In James R. Martin & Robert Veel (eds.), *Reading Science*, 1998, pp.114 - 151.

Ward, Geoff. A critique of the working memory model. In Jackie Andrade (ed.), *Working Memory in Perspective*. Hove: Psychology Press, 2001, pp.219 - 239.

Webster, Jonathan J.(卫真道). *Text Linguistics*(篇章语言学). Tr. Jiujiu Xu (徐赳赳译). Beijing: China Press of Social Sciences, 2002.

Webster, Jonathan J. *Understanding Verbal Art: A Functional Linguistics Approach*. Heidelberg: Springer, 2015.

Wegener, Rebekah. *Parameters of Context: From Theory to Model and Application*. Unpublished Ph. D. dissertation, Department of Linguistics, Macquarie University, 2011.

Weil, Henri. *The Order of Words in the Ancient Languages Compared with That of the Modern Languages*, new edition with an introduction by A. Scaglione. Amsterdam: John Benjamins, 1844/1978.

White, Peter. Subjectivity, evaluation and point of view in media discourse. In Caroline Coffin, Ann Hewings & Kieran O'Halloran (eds.), 2004, pp.229 - 246.

Wignell, Peter. Technicality and abstraction in social science. In James R. Martin & Robert Veel (eds.), 1998, pp.297 - 326.

Williams, Geoff & Len Unsworth. Big books or big basals?: The significance of text form in constructing contexts for early literacy development through shared reading. *Australian Journal of Reading* 1990, 13: 100 - 111.

Wright, Laura & Jonathan Hope. *Stylistics: A Practical Coursebook*. London & New York: Routledge, 1996.

Yang, Xueyan (杨雪燕). *Modelling Text as Process: A Dynamic Approach to EFL Classroom Discourse*. London: Continuum, 2010.

Zerubavel, Eviatar. *Social Mindscapes: An Invitation to Cognitive Sociology*.

Cambridge, Mass.：Harvard University Press，1997.

Zerubavel, Eviatar. *Time Maps: Collective Memory and the Social Shape of the Past.* Chicago：University of Chicago Press，2004.

Zhou, Xiaokang（周晓康）. *Material and Relational Transitivity in Mandarin Chinese.* Ph.D. Dissertation. Melbourne：University of Melbourne，1997.

蔡基刚,大学英语教学若干问题思考,《外语教学与研究》2005 年第 2 期,83—91 页。

蔡基刚,关于我国大学英语教学重新定位的思考,《外语教学与研究》2010a 年第 4 期,68—70 页。

蔡基刚,廖雷朝,学术英语还是专业英语——我国大学 ESP 教学重新定位思考,《外语教学》2010b 年第 6 期,47—50 页。

蔡基刚,CBI 理论框架下的分科英语教学,《外语教学》2011 年第 5 期,39—42 页。

蔡基刚,大学英语教学转型时期的我国英语专业课程设置改革,《中国外语》2012a 年第 1 期,12—17 页。

蔡基刚,全球化背景下我国大学英语教学目标定位再研究,《外语与外语教学》2012b 年第 3 期,8—11 页。

蔡基刚,从通用英语到学术英语——回归大学英语教学本位,《外语与外语教学》2014 年第 1 期,12—17 页。

陈脑冲,论"主语",《外语教学与研究》1993 年第 4 期,1—9 页。

程雨民,《英语语体学》(修订版),上海：上海外语教育出版社,2004 年。

戴炜栋,外语教学的"费时低效"现象——思考与对策,《外语与外语教学》2001 年第 7 期,1,32 页。

伽德默尔著,洪汉鼎译,《真理与方法》,北京：商务印书馆,2007 年。

古德曼著,姬志闯译,《构造世界的多种方式》,上海：上海译文出版社,2008 年。

顾乡,《试论近代历史语篇的语言变化——系统功能语言学视角》,博士学位论文,上海：复旦大学,2008 年。

海德格尔著,陈嘉映、王庆节合译,熊伟校,陈嘉映修订,《存在与时间》,北京：商务印书馆,2006 年。

何其莘、黄源深、秦秀白、陈建平,近三十年来我国高校英语专业教学回顾与展望,《外语教学与研究》2008 年第 6 期,427—432 页。

胡辉华,马克思的意识形态概念,《暨南学报》2001 年第 6 期,18—25 页。

胡壮麟,英汉疑问语气系统的多层次和多功能解释,《外国语》1994 年第 1 期,1—7 页。任绍曾主编《语言·系统·结构》,杭州：杭州大学出版社,1995 年,1—13 页。

胡壮麟,《语篇的衔接与连贯》,上海:上海外语教育出版社,1994 年。

胡壮麟,中国英语教学中的"低效"问题,《国外外语教学》2002a 年第 4 期,3—7 页。

胡壮麟,对中国英语教育的若干思考,《外语研究》2002b 年第 3 期,2—5 页。

胡壮麟、朱永生、张德禄,《系统功能语法概论》,长沙:湖南教育出版社,1989 年。

胡壮麟、朱永生、张德禄、李战子,《系统功能语言学概论》,北京:北京大学出版社,2005 年。

黄国文,《语篇分析的理论与实践——广告语篇研究》,上海:上海外语教育出版社,2001 年。

黄国文,生态语言学的兴起与发展,《中国外语》2016 年第 1 期,1,9—12 页。

黄源深,思辨缺席,《外语与外语教学》1998 年第 7 期,2,18 页。

黄源深,英语专业课程必须彻底改革——再谈"思辨缺席",《外语界》2010 年第 1 期,11—16 页。

教育部,《大学英语课程教学要求》,上海:上海外语教育出版社,2004 年。

教育部,《大学英语课程教学要求》,2007。http://www.chinanews.com/edu/kong/news/2007/09-26/1036804.shtml.

李翠香,ESP 教学改革思考与探索,《新课程》2008 年第 10 期,27—29 页。

李敬泽,《为文学申辩》,北京:作家出版社,2009 年。

刘海涛,《依存语法的理论与实践》,北京:科学出版社,2009 年。

米勒著,申丹译,亨利·詹姆斯与"视角",或为何詹姆斯喜欢吉普,载费伦(James Phelan)与拉比诺维兹(Peter J. Rabinowitz)主编,申丹等译,《当代叙事理论指南》,北京:北京大学出版社,2007 年,第 122—136 页。

彭宣维,英汉语在语篇组织上的差异,《外语教学与研究》2000 年第 5 期,329—334 页。

彭宣维,《英汉语篇综合对比》,上海:上海外语教育出版社,2000 年。

彭宣维,韩礼德"主位"的形式特征及其相应的语义范畴"主题",《语言学研究》,北京:高等教育出版社,2002 年第 1 期,21—28 页。

彭宣维,《语言过程与维度》,北京:清华大学出版社,2002 年。

彭宣维,从语场到概念意义——经验知识词义化过程的认知描述,载杨忠、张绍杰(主编),《语篇·功能·认知》(第七届全国系统功能语法研讨会文集),长春:吉林人民出版社,2003a 年,81—103 页。

彭宣维,以社会·认知为基础的"过程-维度"语言模式概说,《外语教学与研究》2004 年第 3 期,171—179 页。

彭宣维,*An Introduction to Functional Grammar* 的"集大成"地位,《中国外语》2009

年第 1 期,105—110 页。

彭宣维,《语言与语言学概论——汉语系统功能语法》,北京:北京大学出版社,2011 年。

彭宣维,过程语言学——语言的四个维度及其认知加工模型,《北京师范大学学报》(社科版)2013 年第 4 期,33—48 页。

彭宣维,《评价文体学》,北京:北京大学出版社,2015b 年。

彭宣维,《韩礼德文集》主编导引,北京:北京大学出版社,2015c 年。

彭宣维,韩礼德与中国传统学术——系统功能语言学的范式设计溯源,《中国人民大学学报》(社科版)2016 年第 5 期,130—138 页。

彭宣维,词汇语法级阶视角下的经验语法隐喻新解,《语言学研究》2016 年第 2 期,59—76 页。

彭宣维、何中清、杨晓军,汉英对应评价意义语料库,《外语电化教学》2012 年第 5 期,3—10 页。

彭宣维、刘玉洁、张冉冉、陈玉娟、谈仙芳、王玉英、杨晓军,《汉英评价意义分析手册——评价语料库的语料处理原则与研制方案》,北京:北京大学出版社,2015 年。

钱军,《结构功能主义:布拉格学派》,长春:吉林教育出版社,1998 年。

申丹,休斯《在路上》的及物性系统与深层意义,载申丹著《叙事、文本、潜文本——重读英美经典短篇小说》,北京:北京大学出版社,2009 年。

束定芳,关于我国外语教育规划与布局的思考,《外语教学与研究》2013 年第 3 期,108—117 页。

孙有中,突出思辨能力培养,将英语专业教学改革引向深入,《中国外语》2011 年第 3 期,49—58 页。

王力,中国语法理论,上海:商务印书馆,1947 年。

王守仁,关于英语教育的思考,《光明日报》2001 年 10 月 18 日。

王守仁,谈中国英语教育的转型,《外国语》2016 年第 5 期,2—4 页。

王守仁、姚成贺,关于学术英语教学的几点思考,《中国外语》2013 年第 5 期,4—10 页。

王星、彭宣维,关于调整英语专业本科课程设置的构想——从硕士研究生对本科教学的评价反观本科教改,《中国外语》2007 年第 6 期,9—14 页。

文秋芳,论外语专业研究生高层次思维能力的培养,《学位与研究生教育》2008 年第 10 期,29—34 页。

文秋芳,《中国外语类大学生思辨能力现状研究》,北京:外语教学与研究出版社,2012 年。

文秋芳、周燕,评述外语专业学生思维能力的发展,《外语学刊》2006 年第 5 期,76—80 页。

文秋芳,大学英语教学中通用英语与专用英语之争:问题与对策,《外语与外语教学》2014 年第 1 期,1—8 页。

文秋芳、张伶俐、孙旻,外语专业学生的思辨能力逊色于其他专业学生吗?《现代外语》2014 年第 6 期,794—804 页。

文秋芳、孙旻,评述高校外语教学中思辨力培养存在的问题,《外语教学理论与实践》2015 年第 3 期,6—12 页。

杨宁,语义和句法依存结构,载邵敬敏(编)《九十年代的语法思考》,北京:北京语言学院出版社,1994 年,100—112 页。

杨信彰,系统功能语言学与教育语篇分析,《四川外语学院学报》2007 年第 6 期,17—20 页。

于晖,《语篇题材分析:学术论文摘要的符号学意义》,开封:河南大学出版社,2003 年。

张德禄,《功能文体学》,济南:山东教育出版社,1998 年。

张德禄,《语言与教育》导读,《韩礼德文集第 9 卷》,北京:北京大学出版社,2007 年,ix—xxx 页。

张修海、刘宏伟、苏广才,从基础英语及专业英语教学到专业课程,《中国现代教育装备》2011 年第 13 期,77—78,87 页。